C000090525

Henry Vaughan's
Silex Scintillans

Henry Vaughan's
Silex Scintillans

Scripture Uses

PHILIP WEST

OXFORD
UNIVERSITY PRESS

This book has been printed digitally and produced in a standard specification
in order to ensure its continuing availability

OXFORD
UNIVERSITY PRESS

Great Clarendon Street, Oxford OX2 6DP

Oxford University Press is a department of the University of Oxford.
It furthers the University's objective of excellence in research, scholarship,
and education by publishing world-wide in

Oxford New York

Auckland Bangkok Buenos Aires Cape Town Chennai
Dar es Salaam Delhi Hong Kong Istanbul Karachi Kolkata
Kuala Lumpur Madrid Melbourne Mexico City Mumbai Nairobi
São Paulo Shanghai Taipei Tokyo Toronto

Oxford is a registered trade mark of Oxford University Press
in the UK and in certain other countries

Published in the United States
by Oxford University Press Inc., New York

© Philip West 2001

The moral rights of the author have been asserted
Database right Oxford University Press (maker)

Reprinted 2004

All rights reserved. No part of this publication may be reproduced,
stored in a retrieval system, or transmitted, in any form or by any means,
without the prior permission in writing of Oxford University Press,
or as expressly permitted by law, or under terms agreed with the appropriate
reprographics rights organization. Enquiries concerning reproduction
outside the scope of the above should be sent to the Rights Department,
Oxford University Press, at the address above

You must not circulate this book in any other binding or cover
And you must impose this same condition on any acquirer

ISBN 0-19-818756-4

Cover illustration : Jacob's dream (Genesis 28) from the Bishops' Bible , 1568.
Reproduced by kind permission of the Master and Fellows of Trinity College , Cambridge.

Antony Rowe Ltd., Eastbourne

For JEREMY MAULE

Bis ternos, *illo me Conducente, per* annos
  Profeci, & geminam *Contulit unus opem,*
Ars & amor, mens *atque* manus *certare solebant,*
  Nec lassata Illi mensue, manusue *fuit.*

Preface

This book began life as a doctoral thesis researched and written in Cambridge between 1994 and 1997. I would like to express my gratitude to the British Academy, which supported me with a research grant during that period, and to the several libraries and institutions which made it possible to live and work in extraordinarily helpful and stimulating conditions. In particular I am grateful to the fellows and staff of Selwyn College and Trinity College, to Cambridge University Library's superb Rare Books Room, to the ever helpful staff of the Cambridge English Faculty Library, and to the British Library and Dr Williams's Library. Further thanks must go to the many friends and colleagues in the Cambridge English Faculty, particularly the Renaissance Graduate Seminar and Renaissance Research Group, who have offered intellectual and professional advice over the past two years.

I am also immensely indebted to John Kerrigan and Robert Wilcher, my thesis examiners, for their useful criticisms of the original work and their advice both at the viva and since. This book and I have further benefited from conversations with James Cannon, Nicholas Cranfield, Ariel Hessayon, Jessica Martin, Mary Morrissey, David Smith, and Elliot Vernon. Jonathan Post read several chapters of the book at various stages of completion and offered kind advice and encouragement. The thoughts of my anonymous readers for Oxford University Press were extremely welcome when it came to revising the original typescript; Sophie Goldsworthy has been a supportive editor, and I would also like to thank my copy-editor, Edwin Pritchard, and the production controller, Frances Whistler. Finally, thanks to Wil Sanders for introducing me to the seventeenth century, to Jean Chothia for nudging me towards graduate study, and to Stephen Logan for being a truly careful and inspiring teacher.

My greatest debt in writing this book is difficult to measure and impossible to repay. Jeremy Maule supervised my work from 1993 to 1997—not quite the twice three years that Henry Vaughan studied with his teacher, Matthew Herbert, but Jeremy did have a way of cramming a lot in. His death in November 1998 left Cambridge struggling to comprehend a truly vast and unforeseen loss. Jeremy's immense learning and firm advice, poured out along with invariably strong coffee or strung across a hundred palaeographical postcards, is present in all that is good about this book. Any errors that remain after Jeremy's tireless reading and the sound advice of my friends and colleagues, must indeed be mine to own.

Finally I would like to thank those whose love and friendship have helped this book on its way: thanks, then, to my family, to the saints of the Radegund, to the kind people of Newnham Village, to the Dubliners, and to the good sports of Trinity College.

P.G.W.
Trinity College, Cambridge

Contents

Abbreviations and references

Vaughan's works are cited throughout from *The Works of Henry Vaughan*, ed. L. C. Martin, 2nd revised edn. (Oxford, 1957), which is abbreviated as *V*. Regular reference is also made to the annotations of *Henry Vaughan: The Complete Poems*, ed. Alan Rudrum, 2nd revised edn. (Harmondsworth, 1983), which is abbreviated as *R*. Quotations are given in original spelling and punctuation, with u/v and i/j conformed to modern practice, with the exception of the bible, which is given from the Authorized Version in modern spelling unless stated.

Silex Scintillans is a cumulative work: unsold sheets of the first edition of 1650 were bound up with newly printed sheets in 1655 to make a two-part book. All references in the text and notes to *Silex Scintillans* are to this two-part book, whilst *Silex Scintillans* (1650) refers to the first edition and *Silex* Part 1 and *Silex* Part 2 refer to each part of the 1655 book respectively.

BCP *The First and Second Prayer Books of King Edward VI* (1910), with an Introduction by Bishop E. C. S. Gibson

DNB *The Dictionary of National Biography*, ed. Leslie Stephens and Sidney Lee, 63 vols. (1885–1900)

Life F. E. Hutchinson, *Henry Vaughan: A Life and Interpretation*, corr. repr. (Oxford, 1971)

OED *The Oxford English Dictionary*, 2nd edn., prepared by J. A. Simpson and E. S. C. Weiner, 17 vols. (Oxford, 1989)

R *Henry Vaughan: The Complete Poems*, ed. Alan Rudrum, 2nd rev. edn. (Harmondsworth, 1983)

STC *A Short-Title Catalogue of Books Printed in England, Scotland and Ireland and of English Books Printed Abroad 1475–1640*, first compiled by A. W. Pollard and G. R. Redgrave, 2nd edn. revised and enlarged, begun by W. A. Jackson and F. S. Ferguson, completed by Katharine F. Pantzer, 3 vols. (1976–91)

TLS *Times Literary Supplement*

TV *The Works of Thomas Vaughan*, ed. Alan Rudrum with the assistance of
      Jennifer Drake-Brockman (Oxford, 1984)

V   *The Works of Henry Vaughan*, ed. L. C. Martin, 2nd rev. edn. (Oxford,
      1957)

Wing *A Short-Title Catalogue of Books Printed in England, Scotland, Ireland,
        Wales and British North America and of English Books Printed in Other
        Countries 1641–1700*, compiled by Donald Wing, 2nd edn. revised and
        enlarged by the Index Committee of the Modern Language Association
        of America, 3 vols.: i (New York, 1972; newly revised and enlarged 1994);
        ii (1982); iii (1988)

CHAPTER ONE

Introduction: scripture uses

In the half-century since Molly Mahood's revaluation of Vaughan in *Poetry and Humanism*, readers, critics and scholars have increasingly affirmed her judgement that 'probably there is no poet of the period whose work reveals a more intimate knowledge of the Bible'. 'Vaughan, I feel,' she wrote, 'had a deeper and finer knowledge of them [the scriptures] than even Bunyan attained.'[1] Considerable light was rayed into the project of demonstrating the depth and fineness of that knowledge by Alan Rudrum's edition of the complete poems for Penguin, which appeared a quarter of a century later (1976; revised in 1983). Rudrum's notes did Vaughan and his readers the great service of identifying many of the poems' hundreds of scripture borrowings, a task L. C. Martin had thought unnecessary in both editions of his standard text of Vaughan's *Works* (1914, revised 1957).[2] Armed with the new edition, readers turned increasingly to scripture as a key to the strange riches of Vaughan's plangent lines. The best of these critical works, particularly the readings found in the work of Jonathan Post, Geoffrey Hill and Stevie Davies, continue to affirm that the most fruitful criticism of Vaughan begins and ends by consulting the bible.[3]

[1] M. M. Mahood, 'Vaughan: The Symphony of Nature', 252–95 (255) in her *Poetry and Humanism* (1950).

[2] Martin wrote: 'It also seemed unnecessary to give chapter and verse for all Vaughan's citations and reminiscences of the Bible' (*V*, p. iv); see also his original edition of *The Works of Henry Vaughan*, 2 vols. (Oxford, 1914), i. p. iv; and for Rudrum's comments, *R*, 18. Recognition of the nature and function of Vaughan's biblical allusiveness was greatly advanced by two helpful articles written before Rudrum's edition was published: Leland H. Chambers, 'Henry Vaughan's Allusive Technique: Biblical Allusions in "The Night"', *Modern Language Quarterly*, 27 (1966), 371–87 and Eluned Brown, 'Henry Vaughan's Biblical Landscape', *Essays and Studies*, NS 30 (1977), 50–60.

[3] Jonathan Post, *Henry Vaughan: The Unfolding Vision* (Princeton, 1982), ch. 7; Geoffrey Hill, 'A Pharisee to Pharisees: Reflections on Vaughan's "The Night"', *English*, 38 (1989), 97–113; Stevie Davies, *Henry Vaughan*, Borderline Series (Bridgend, 1995), 21–3, 113–19. Attention to scripture is also the strength of accounts of Vaughan in Barbara K. Lewalski's seminal *Protestant Poetics and the Seventeenth-Century Religious Lyric* (Princeton, 1979),

Scriptural readings of Vaughan caught the wave of renewed historiographical interest in seventeenth-century religion produced by such sizeable drops in the ocean as Christopher Hill's *The World Turned Upside-Down* (1972) and Keith Thomas's *Religion and the Decline of Magic* (1971).[4] The enormous influence of these works has kept theology, prophecy and popular religion firmly in the main stream of early modern historiography ever since. Initially, the historiographical sea-change offered little to readers of Vaughan, since the emphasis of most historians was firmly on the insurgent and the new: Milton's revolutionary bible was Christopher Hill's preferred text, Puritans (the most visible scripture users of the period) his chosen people.[5] It took some time for the focus to broaden and take in Royalists and Anglicans. Eleven years were to follow Hill's excellent account of Antichrist in revolutionary literature before Jonathan Post's equally penetrating chapter on Vaughan's apocalyptic 'late and dusky age'.[6]

A glance at the most recent surveys of mid-century literature by Michael Wilding, Thomas Corns and Nigel Smith shows that a 1970s preference for what is radical and revolutionary still prevails. Royalist literature is allowed into the frame only in its more overtly political forms, with the result that Vaughan's Christian writing is badly neglected. Corns considers Lovelace, Herrick, Cowley and the *Eikon Basilike*, but omits Vaughan completely from his account of 'English Political Literature 1640–60'; Wilding, though he offers a revisionary account of Browne's *Religio Medici* as a combatively reactionary text, can find no place for Vaughan in his picture of 'Literature in the English Revolution'. Although Nigel Smith affords greater place to biblical literature, his treatments of Vaughan are either contrastive, or too brief; and James Loxley's *Royalism and Poetry in the English Civil Wars* (1997) touches only Vaughan's explicit war poems: the elegies for deceased Royalist soldiers in *Olor Iscanus* and 'The King Disguis'd'.[7]

317–51, and John Wall's splendidly detailed *Transformations of the Word: Spenser, Herbert, Vaughan* (Athens, Ga., 1988), ch. 4.

[4] Christopher Hill, *The World Turned Upside-Down: Radical Ideas During the English Revolution* (1972); Keith Thomas, *Religion and the Decline of Magic: Studies in Popular Beliefs in Sixteenth- and Seventeenth-Century England* (1971).

[5] See particularly his *Milton and the English Revolution* (1977) and the reflections of *The Experience of Defeat: Milton and Some Contemporaries* (1984).

[6] Christopher Hill, *Antichrist in Seventeenth-Century England* (1971); Post, *Henry Vaughan*, ch. 7.

[7] Michael Wilding, *Dragon's Teeth: Literature in the English Revolution* (Oxford, 1987);

Vaughan's omission from such 'general' surveys must now be deemed all the more striking given recent widenings of the historiographical canvas by historical and literary studies such as Lois Potter's account of *Secret Rites and Secret Writing* and John Morrill's revisionist argument for a covert, 'Survivalist' perpetuation of Anglicanism in literature and worship of the 1650s. By their recovery of the deliberately coded and unobtrusive means by which Interregnum Royalists and Anglicans expressed their loyalties, Potter, Morrill and others have prepared the way for others to relate Vaughan's Christian writing to the sorts of Interregnum political writing dwelt on by existing surveys.[8] And yet despite such welcome broadening of the field of Civil War writing, there has yet to be a decisive study of Vaughan's deep, biblically coded lamentations.

That coding has presented its own difficulties, of course. Rudrum's editing labours made it clear that to understand the plaints of Vaughan's *Silex Scintillans* (1650, 1655) and *The Mount of Olives* (1652), one must also understand Vaughan's bible; to replace his works in their right contexts now demanded the sort of precise and continuous attention to the biblical aspects of his work hitherto afforded to Milton, Winstanley or Bunyan; or, indeed, to John Donne or George Herbert.[9] For while scripture has been placed very rightly as a major influence on the work of such writers, Vaughan's scripturalism has yet to be considered in the full context of the poet's early manhood: particularly, that is, in the light of the scripture-using culture of the 1650s in all its many forms and occasions, whether Parliamentary fast sermons, popular books of practical divinity, or radical prophecies of the Second Coming of Christ. Treatments are

Thomas Corns, *Uncloistered Virtue: English Political Literature 1640–1660* (Oxford, 1992); Nigel Smith, *Literature and Revolution in England, 1640–1660* (New Haven, Conn., 1994), 267–73; James Loxley, *Royalism and Poetry in the English Civil Wars: The Drawn Sword*, Early Modern Literature in History (Basingstoke, 1997), 144–7, 170–2, 193, 209.

[8] Lois Potter, *Secret Rites and Secret Writing: Royalist Literature 1640–1660* (Cambridge, 1989), esp. 45, 99, 133, 136, 141, 187; John Morrill, 'The Church in England, 1642–49', in John Morrill (ed.), *Reactions to the English Civil War, 1642–9* (New York, 1982), 89–114. Derek Hirst has begun to consider the implications of this readjustment with reference to a broad range of Royalist writers in 'The Politics of Literature in the English Republic', *Seventeenth Century*, 5 (1990), 133–55.

[9] Chana Bloch, *Spelling the Word: George Herbert and the Bible* (Berkeley, Calif., 1985); Barbara Kiefer Lewalski, 'Typological Symbolism and the "Progress of the Soul" in Seventeenth-Century Literature', 239–60 in Gary A. Stringer (ed.), *New Essays on Donne* (Salzburg, 1977); Heather Asals, 'David's Successors: Forms of Joy and Art', *Proceedings of the PMR Conference: Annual Publication of the International Patristic, Medieval and Renaissance Conference*, 2 (1977), 23–37.

often either properly aware of scripture but tightly limited in scope—
Jonathan Post's work on Vaughan's Apocalypse is one example, or the brilliant glancing phrases of Geoffrey Hill's encounter with 'The Night'; or
else, like Helen Wilcox's suggestive article about the self-questioning of
mid-century religious lyric (including Vaughan's), criticism remains inat-
tentive to scripture, as though Mahood, Rudrum and their successors had
never made their mark.[10]

To overcome existing critical limitations, this study attends to the presence of scripture in Vaughan's poetry both historically (by reading in
works of theology, biblical commentary and other scriptural literature of
the period), and most of all *scripturally*: with a bible open and active at all
times. This meant, initially, a much more complete recovery of scriptural
words and allusions within *Silex Scintillans* than even Alan Rudrum's edition was able to offer. On the basis of these annotations, the chapters
below explore in precise scriptural and contextual detail the different
ways in which Vaughan, like other seventeenth-century Protestant
Britons, had learnt to manipulate scripture to read the shape of his life
and to compose the shape of its return to God. The ways Vaughan
adopted and adapted, and those he invented, are the *uses* of my title. Of
course, those *uses* are also, most ingenuously, the pieces of scripture in
Silex Scintillans, Vaughan's borrowed scriptural words, phrases and extracts.[11] But it is another sense of *use* which brings *Silex Scintillans* into a
new, sharper focus: Vaughan's *habitual* uses, his *customary* ways with
scripture, his *practice* of scriptural poetry.

To shift the angle of critical attention toward *uses* it is vital to consider
the poems of *Silex Scintillans* in the context of Vaughan's other scripture-
using works, especially his devotional manual *The Mount of Olives; or,
Solitary Devotions* (1652), but also *Flores Solitudinis: Certaine Rare and
Elegant Pieces* (1654) which includes Vaughan's great hagiographical exercise, *The Life of Holy Paulinus*. On occasion it also involves comparing
Vaughan's scriptural approaches to a topic with his earlier secular (often
satirical) treatments in *Poems, with the Tenth Satyre of Juvenal Englished*
(1646) and *Olor Iscanus* (published 1651; written c.1646–48) and comparing his later translations *Hermetical Physick* (1655) and *The Chymists Key*
(1657). It is to insist that Vaughan did not 'use' scripture to write the

---

[10]   Helen Wilcox, 'Exploring the Language of Devotion in the English Revolution',
75–88 in Thomas Healy and Jonathan Sawday (eds.), *Literature and the English Civil War*
(Cambridge, 1990).
[11]   *OED*, use, *sb.*, I, 1a.

poetry and prose these volumes contain. He turned to its power to release him from a 'world of thrall' and to ask God to 'turn his sad captivity' in his time of greatest need.[12] This is the note struck at the very end of the two-part *Silex Scintillans* when, in 'L'Envoy', Vaughan petitions God to turn the 'sad captivity' of his children, a request which remembers Psalm 126: 'When the Lord turned again the captivity of Zion, we were like them that dream . . . Turn again our captivity, O Lord, as the streams in the south' (Psalm 126: 1, 4). For Vaughan, who was sure that the world would not see God again until the Last Judgement,[13] the present turning of his captivity was overwhelmingly a matter of turning the pages of scripture. Until the end of all things (which Vaughan expected to be soon[14]), these two turnings were effectively one and the same: the promise contained in God's Word was enough.

Any critical reorientation must overcome certain difficulties. What I have no wish to overcome, though the interests of space and clarity perhaps lead me to overlook, are some of the other critical approaches to Vaughan that have brought his work so successfully to twentieth-century readers. In particular, I have in mind the long tradition of attention to Vaughan's alchemical and hermetic imagery, an exegetical line stretching from the compact scholarship of Elizabeth Holmes's *Henry Vaughan and the Hermetic Philosophy* (1933) to Frank Kermode's influential account of 'The Private Imagery of Henry Vaughan' (1950) and Alan Rudrum's essays on Vaughan's 'The Book' (1961) and 'The Night' (1969).[15] The authors of these articles would, no doubt, acknowledge their debt to T. E. Waite's 1919 edition of Thomas Vaughan's alchemical tracts, a work finally

---

[12] 'L'Envoy', l. 62; 'They are all gone into the world of light!', l. 35.

[13] Discussed in Chapter 5, 'These new lights'.

[14] Discussed in Chapter 6, 'Vaughan's expectancies'.

[15] Elizabeth Holmes, *Henry Vaughan and the Hermetic Philosophy* (Oxford, 1932); Wilson O. Clough, 'Henry Vaughan and the Hermetic Philosophy', *Publications of the Modern Language Association of America*, 48 (1933), 1108–30; Frank Kermode, 'The Private Imagery of Henry Vaughan', *Review of English Studies*, ns 1 (1950), 206–25; L. C. Martin, 'Henry Vaughan and Hermes Trismegistus', *Review of English Studies*, 18 (1942), 301–7; Alan Rudrum, 'Henry Vaughan's "The Book": A Hermetic Poem', *Journal of the Australasian Universities Language and Literature Association*, 16 (1961), 161–6; Rudrum, 'Vaughan's "The Night": Some Hermetic Notes', *Modern Language Review*, 64 (1969), 11–19; Rudrum, 'The Influence of Alchemy in the Poems of Henry Vaughan', *Philological Quarterly*, 49 (1970), 469–80. See also Stanton J. Linden, 'Alchemy and Eschatology in Seventeenth-Century Poetry', *Ambix*, 31 (1984), 102–11; Linden, 'Walter Charleton and Henry Vaughan's "Cock-Crowing"', *Notes and Queries*, 234 (1989), 38–9; David Crane, 'The Poetry of Alchemy and the Alchemy of Poetry in the Work of Thomas and Henry Vaughan', *Scintilla*, 1 (1997), 115–22.

superseded by Alan Rudrum's edition in 1984.[16] Not for nothing is Vaughan widely known as an alchemical and a hermetic poet, and I would not dispute the various permutations of this thesis. There was, for Vaughan, no essential conflict between the alchemical and scriptural interests of his writing. Christ, after all, shall 'sit as a refiner' at the Last Judgement, an image from the book of Malachi very dear to Vaughan's reading of the Apocalypse as well as to his alchemical and hermetic interests. The reader coming to Vaughan from an interest in alchemical or scientific writing will find plenty of interest, I hope, in Vaughan's scriptural debates about the when and where of the Apocalypse and its spiritual refining.[17]

One modern tradition which it has been necessary to understand and to overcome is ignorance of the bible. Recognizing a scripture when one sees it can be a demanding and frustrating task, as well as a rewarding and enlightening one. For just as Coleridge (that astute observer of the seventeenth century) worried that nineteenth-century readers could not admire Herbert's *The Temple* because they were simply not interested in the struggles of a Christian life,[18] so one might now reflect that without reading the bible on a daily basis and meditating on its stories and lessons, one cannot read *Silex Scintillans* as did Vaughan and his contemporaries. Even Christopher Hill, an experienced and accomplished scripture reader, has ruefully noted that literature of the mid-seventeenth century 'is crammed with allusions to the Old and New Testaments, many of which we now miss'.[19] Hill's remark makes the point that present-day poetry readers are by no means also bible readers; and yet, as Vaughan's recent critics acknowledge, the texts that *Silex Scintillans* most requires its readers to have at their fingertips are the bible, *The Temple*, and the English and Latin poets. Given this discouragement, it might seem that Vaughan's scripture-using culture, the period of 'the short-lived sovereignty of scripture in England'[20] as Patrick Collinson has dubbed it, is too

---

[16] *The Works of Thomas Vaughan*, ed. T. E. Waite, 2 vols. (1919); *TV*.

[17] Vaughan's uses of Mal. 3: 1–3 are explored in Chapter 6.

[18] Notebook entry of Feb. 1826 (in *Samuel Taylor Coleridge*, ed. H. J. Jackson, Oxford Authors Series (Oxford, 1985), 556). Some of Coleridge's other insights into seventeenth-century literature and letters are collected in *Coleridge on the Seventeenth Century*, ed. Roberta Florence Brinkley (New York, 1968).

[19] Christopher Hill, *The English Bible and the Seventeenth-Century Revolution* (1993), 31.

[20] Patrick Collinson, 'The Sense of Sacred Writ: Radical Politics and the Short-Lived Sovereignty of Scripture in England', *TLS*, 9 Apr. 1993, 3–4 [review of Hill, *The English Bible*].

divorced from present tastes and concerns to make its critical recovery a fruitful task.

And yet readers of the great biblical poetry of *Silex Scintillans*—be it 'The Night', 'The Retreate', or 'And do they so?'—soon realize that reading the bible does quicken appreciation of Vaughan's poems, however imperfect any recovery of 1650s reading habits must be. One may take heart, also, by reflecting that Vaughan himself did not imagine only 1650s readings of scripture. When he thought of the Christian church, it was as a transhistorical body of believers as well as an historical institution. The preface to *The Mount of Olives* (1652) comforts its readers with the thought—which glances at the cloud of witnesses passage in Hebrews chapter 11 and John's vision of the company of Saints in Revelation—that 'thou art [not] alone upon this Hill, there is an innumerable company both before and behinde thee'.[21] But for all these enforcements, Vaughan had also to concede that his writing was difficult: 'The Authors Preface' to *Silex* (1655) admits mysteriously to certain '*passages*, whose *history* or *reason* may seem something *remote*; but were they brought *nearer*, and plainly exposed to your view, (though that (perhaps) might quiet your *curiosity*) yet would it not conduce much to your greater *advantage*' (*V*, 392). Vaughan's motives for revealing this remoteness are themselves obscure, yet his words may be a reassurance to any reader and to my hopes of bringing the scriptural back into appreciation of Vaughan's poetry. If it is no longer possible to appreciate *Silex Scintillans* without a conscious effort or the help of editorial notes, so be it: one may reflect that a 'full' understanding was never Vaughan's intention.

WELCOME DEAR BOOK

The bible was the only book Vaughan loved more than George Herbert's *The Temple*, and the only book to have permeated *Silex Scintillans* more thoroughly. Gerald Hammond has rightly observed that Vaughan treats Herbert's verse in a way quite different from his use of the other good book: whereas the biblical echoes in *Silex Scintillans* are 'precise and purposeful' (a judgement with which this book wholeheartedly agrees), 'Herbert's lines, images and words often have no relevance to the Vaughan poem they find themselves in . . . Vaughan merely used Herbert's poetry as a store-house of ideas and images, paying little obvious attention to

[21] 'TO THE Peaceful, humble, and pious READER', 141; Heb. 12: 1; Rev. 6: 9–10.

their original application'.[22] Qualifying this general thesis, Hammond then goes on to detail poems where influence is more than decorative, including some where Vaughan has chosen a mode or form on the basis of Herbert's example.

When Vaughan offers a sonnet in tribute to the 'H. Scriptures' in *Silex Scintillans* (1650), he is clearly recalling Herbert's 'To the H. Scriptures', the double sonnet which makes a similar tribute in *The Temple*.

H. Scriptures

> Welcome dear book, souls Joy, and food! The feast
>   Of Spirits, Heav'n extracted lyes in thee;
>   Thou art lifes Charter, The Doves spotless neast
> Where souls are hatch'd unto Eternitie.
>
> In thee the hidden stone, the *Manna* lies,
>   Thou art the great *Elixir*, rare, and Choice;
>   The Key that opens to all Mysteries,
> The *Word* in Characters, God in the *Voice.*
>
> O that I had deep Cut in my hard heart
>   Each line in thee! Then would I plead in groans
>   Of my Lords penning, and by sweetest Art
> Return upon himself the *Law*, and *Stones.*
>   Read here, my faults are thine. This Book, and I
>   Will tell thee so; *Sweet Saviour thou didst dye!*

'H. Scriptures' stands out among the poems of *Silex Scintillans* as one of few texts to offer a *welcome*, a greeting Vaughan reserves for his greatest spiritual supports and stays. 'White Sunday' (in *Silex* Part 2) begins by greeting the day which reassures Vaughan's faith in the power of the Holy Spirit: 'Wellcome white day!'; 'Affliction [II]', published in *Thalia Rediviva* (1678) similarly greets the strong medicine Vaughan came to love: 'O come, and welcom! Come, refine' (l. 1). There are no other such welcomes in Vaughan's whole body of writing. Neither does *Silex Scintillans* lavish the term 'dear' on anything less than the divine. Vaughan husbands it for

---

[22] Gerald Hammond, ' "Poor dust should still lie low": George Herbert and Henry Vaughan', *English*, 35 (1986), 1–22 (1). Herbert's influence on Vaughan is discussed by E. C. Pettet, *Of Paradise and Light: A Study of Vaughan's 'Silex Scintillans'* (Cambridge, 1960), ch. 3; Thomas O. Calhoun, *Henry Vaughan: The Achievement of 'Silex Scintillans'* (Newark, NJ, 1981), 67–72; Post, *Henry Vaughan*, chs. 4–5; Robert Wilcher, ' "The Present Times Are Not/To Snudge In": Henry Vaughan, *The Temple*, and the Pressure of History', 185–94 in Helen Wilcox and Richard Todd (eds.), *George Herbert: Sacred and Profane* (Amsterdam, 1995).

the beginning of 'Jesus Weeping [II]', which asks 'My dear, Almighty Lord! why dost thou weep?', charging the small word of affection with a powerful intimacy, something of which resides in one striking secular use, Vaughan's translation of Ovid's 'To his Wife at *Rome*, when he was sick', which begins, with a surprising intimacy of Vaughan's own making— '*Dearest!*'

The Silurist's love for scripture breaks forth again in the new collection of poems added to *Silex Scintillans* in 1655. Published in that volume, 'The day of Judgement' likens misreading to a brutal forcing of 'pure lines',[23] and when Vaughan returned to address the bible in *Silex Scintillans'* penultimate poem, it was with a 'sacred parody' of profane love poetry (suggesting that the earlier sonnet, 'H. Scriptures', might also be read as a parodic love sonnet).[24] 'To the Holy Bible' addresses scripture as though it were a lover from whom Vaughan must shortly be separated by death:

> O book! lifes guide! how shall we part,
> And thou so long seiz'd of my heart!
> Take this last kiss, and let me weep
> True thanks to thee, before I sleep.
>
> ('To the Holy Bible', ll. 1–4)

Life's guide. The love and thanks bestowed here are a token return (Vaughan cannot repay the debt in full) for the incalculable usefulness of the bible which operates between the lines of *Silex Scintillans*; scriptural '*Effects*', as Vaughan calls them later in 'To the Holy Bible' (l. 35). This emphasis on *use* pervades even 'H. Scriptures' and 'To the Holy Bible', the two rare occasions in which Vaughan sees scripture as his object, rather than seeing by its light. What the praises of 'H. Scriptures' reveal first and foremost is not the bible's essence or nature, but rather its uses to Vaughan. The sonnet's octet piles up noun phrases which, though they refer ostensibly to what scripture *is*, also strongly suggest what scripture *does* or can *have done* to it: Vaughan can consume scriptural nourishment, be reprieved by the Word, rest on it, and ultimately, he hopes, be cured and transformed by it.

---

[23] 'The Day of Judgement', ll. 35–8.

[24] For a discussion of sacred parody see Rosemary Freeman, 'Parody as a Literary Form: George Herbert and Wilfred Owen', *Essays in Criticism*, 13 (1963), 307–22; Christina Malcolmson, 'George Herbert and Coterie Verse', *George Herbert Journal*, 18 (1994), 159–84; Anthony Martin, 'George Herbert and Sacred "Parodie"', *Studies in Philology*, 93 (1996), 443–70.

The greatest scripture use of all, for Vaughan as for most Christians of his day, was for salvation.[25] When he writes about the crucifixion, the poet can only let gratitude and love dazzle, between wonder and incomprehension, as he contemplates Christ's washing away of sins with the blood that 'I feel as Wine, | But thy faire branches felt as bloud'.[26] But when scripture is his subject, Vaughan prefers to linger on the processes whereby Christians are made holy, never forgetting that the Redemption is what makes salvation possible. 'To the Holy Bible' welcomes the bible so joyously because, like the church festival of White Sunday (Whitsun) and the continuing trial of affliction, scripture *refines* his soul. 'Affliction [II]' welcomes refinement—'O come, and welcom! Come, refine' (l. 1)—and 'White Sunday' opens in greeting and ends with desires for refinement, addressing the Holy Spirit: 'O come! refine us with thy fire! | Refine us! we are at a loss' (ll. 61–2). Afflictive and Spiritual refinement both conduce to holiness and so bring the Christian to salvation. It is a measure of Vaughan's equal faith in the power of scripture, therefore, that 'To the Holy Bible' expresses gratitude to scripture in similarly *refining* terms:

> And oft left open [thou, the bible] would'st convey
> A sudden and most searching ray
> Into my soul, with whose quick touch
> Refining still, I strugled much.
> By this milde art of love at length
> Thou overcam'st my sinful strength,
> And having brought me home, didst there
> Shew me that pearl I sought elsewhere.
>
> (ll. 19–26)

Unlike the merchant man of Christ's parable, who, when he had found the kingdom of heaven, that 'pearl of great price', sold all he had to buy it, the young Vaughan could not see the jewel he already possessed.[27] The bible was his pearl, his key to heaven; he did not even need to seek it out. Having brought the Prodigal home, the precious book began to refine

---

[25] Some of those who dissented from this view are attacked, for example, by Thomas Edwards, *Gangraena*, 2nd edn. (1646); Ephraim Pagitt, *Heresiography*, 2nd edn. (1645); *A True Picture of Our Present Reformation; or, The Christians Prospective, To Take a Short View of the New Lights That Have Brake Forth Since Bishops Went Downe* (1648), sigs. A2ʳ–A2ᵛ.

[26] 'The Passion', ll. 17–18, reversing the order of George Herbert's 'The Agonie': 'Love is that liquour sweet and most divine, | Which my God feels as bloud; but I, as wine' (ll. 17–18).

[27] Matt. 13: 45–46.

him, just as God's 'milde art of love' refined him through affliction and the reassurance of White Sunday. Each refining agent is sent from God: His only Son, to redeem man; the Spirit of White Sunday, to empower Christ's Apostles; affliction, to bring true 'Physick' (as Vaughan saw it) to the soul; and the bible, as a guide in all of these things.[28]

Though salvation is the glorious end of scripture, 'H. Scriptures' delights in the diverse means by which scripture brings man home. These means reveal the manifold *uses* to which Vaughan put scripture, and from which his poems emerge. The first is as food. The poem knows that 'Man shall not live by bread alone, but by every word that proceedeth out of the mouth of God' (Matthew 4: 4) and can offer the lesson back as praise for the teacher which is also the food: 'Welcome dear book, souls Joy, and food! The feast l Of Spirits, Heav'n extracted lyes in thee' ('H. Scriptures', ll. 1–2). Feasting the spirit, the bible fuels intellectual life as food does the bodily. 'The Agreement', in *Silex* Part 2, sees other books as 'chaff' next to the bible's nourishing grain (l. 26); and in 'The World [II]', published in *Thalia Rediviva*, scripture is the food of Christian pilgrims on life's way. Metaphors of spiritual food dominate Vaughan's many poetic digressions on the bible. 'The World [II]' continues with a vow to eat the Word only as God meant it to be consumed 'As thou hast dress'd it: not as *Witt* l And *deprav'd tastes* have poyson'd it' (ll. 84–5). Disgust at the disputes of scriptural commentary and argumentation pervades Vaughan's writing. His bible is simple until man's fallen understanding makes it hard; anyone can consume scripture 'properly', unsauced by interpretation, if they pray rightly: is it not after all '*Manna*' from God ('H. Scriptures', l. 5)?

For Vaughan, the bible was all sufficient for salvation; all readers, as long as they had the Holy Spirit as their guide, could understand and interpret it correctly. In this view, which Vaughan shared with all but the most radical of seventeenth-century Puritans, apparent contradictions in scripture and disagreements over its meaning, were the product of bad reading, not a problem with the Word itself. Vaughan scorns those who disfigure the *Doves spotless neast* with hermeneutical graffiti:

> The *truth*, which once was plainly taught,
> With *thorns* and *briars* now is fraught.
> Some part is with bold *Fables* spotted,
> Some by strange *Comments* wildly blotted:
>
> ('The Bee', ll. 63–6)

---

[28] 'Affliction [I]', l. 1.

The Word written is, for Vaughan, as spotless as Christ 'who through the eternal Spirit offered himself without spot, [to] purge your conscience from dead works to serve the living God' (Hebrews 9: 14).[29] Only the wild *Fables* and *Comments* which roll carelessly off the printing presses and the tongues of the ignorant cover the Word with blemishes. *Comments* is a straightforward reference to learned commentaries, some of which Vaughan must surely have consulted, although this side of his reading proves extremely difficult to reconstruct.[30] *Fables* is the stronger term here, and almost certainly refers to the new emphasis on allegorical reading among Antinomians, who read biblical events as accounts of internal, spiritual processes. Vaughan may also intend some allusion to the political allegories of the Welsh Puritan Saints responsible for evangelizing during the early 1650s. Morgan Llwyd, the foremost literary talent among Vaughan's Puritan enemies, wrote a famous allegory called *Llyfr y Tri Aderyn* (*The Book of the Three Birds*) (1653) in which the Episcopal church is represented by a raven, Cromwell by an eagle, and the Independent churches by a dove. As Nigel Smith has noted, Llwyd's raven sees the dove's highly allegorical speech as 'threats of dream'. Vaughan's *bold Fables* is unashamed to share such a view.[31]

The scriptures' plainness was upheld in the increasingly rational and sceptical era of the Restoration by Bishops Tillotson, South and Barrow, who argued that reason could approach scripture truths.[32] Vaughan, though, seems to have conceived of a bible whose truth was explicable only in terms of itself. He felt (rather than argued about) how its truths emerged—with Herbert he could wish 'Oh that I knew how all thy lights

---

[29] See also 1 Peter 1: 19.

[30] A few of Vaughan's *devotional* sources have been established (none are commentaries): Graeme J. Watson, 'Two New Sources for Henry Vaughan's *The Mount of Olives*', *Notes and Queries*, 230 (1985), 168–70; Hilary M. Day, 'Bayly's *The Practice of Piety*: A New Source for Henry Vaughan's *The Mount of Olives*', *Notes & Queries*, 233 (1988), 163–5. Vaughan's surviving autograph books, all medical works, are listed in Edwin Wolf II, 'Some Books of Early English Provenance in the Library Company of Philadelphia', *Book Collector*, 9 (1960), 275–84; Margaret Munsterberg, 'The Swan of Usk, More Books', *Boston Public Library Bulletin*, 18, no. 7 (1943), 341; and Peter Beal, *Index of English Literary Manuscripts*, vol. ii, part 2 (1993), 542–3.

[31] Nigel Smith, *Perfection Proclaimed: Language and Literature in English Radical Religion, 1640–1660* (Oxford, 1989), 223–5; cf. 107–8. Smith is citing the English translation of *Llyfr y Tri Aderyn* made by L. J. Parry in *Transactions of the New Eisteddfod of Wales* (Liverpool, 1898), 192–275. Morgan Llwyd and the Welsh Saints are discussed at length in Chapters 5 and 6, below.

[32] See Gerard Reedy, *The Bible and Reason: Anglicans and Scripture in Late Seventeenth-Century England* (Philadelphia, 1985), ch. 1.

combine' without thinking it possible that he could ('To the H. Scriptures' [II], l. 1)—and he viewed rival interpretations, particularly those of the Puritan revolution, as spiritually disastrous. Of course this meant that Vaughan could be every bit as partisan in his readings as his Puritan opponents were in theirs, and every bit as convinced by what he read. It is really not surprising that, as one critic has suggested, Vaughan 'insists on a distinction between his own polished allusions to Scripture and the vulgar appropriations' of the Puritan scripture users of the 1650s. His enemies, after all, made similar claims: interpretative supremacy was one of the most important engines and stays of the revolution.[33]

Puritan scripture using draws persistent criticism from the pages of *Silex Scintillans* and *The Mount of Olives*, particularly in passages that reflect on prophecy and the Apocalypse. Having identified a biblical verse as one often appropriated (and so, in his view, misread) by Puritans, Vaughan ranges widely across the bible, gathering around that verse other scriptures which mark each other from far off as correct guides to interpretation (that is, ones which support Vaughan's understanding). 'Ascension-day', for instance, brings together prophecies from Malachi, Luke's gospel, Revelation and Acts to support its anti-radical visions; 'The Men of War' darts backwards and forwards between the gospels, epistles and Revelation, conspicuously allowing texts on Christian patience from Jesus's life and ministry to colour others concerned with prophesying the apocalyptic victories of the Army of the Lamb. (The lesson is that the New Model Army is not to be mistaken for the heavenly one.) This method of urging one scripture to explain another is no different at heart to those of other religious disputants of the mid-century, though I hope to suggest that the intensity and range of allusion in Vaughan's writing is extraordinary, even for the 1650s. Its compactness and beauty must have provided sympathetic readers with a powerful expression of their identity as the defeated of God, just as Milton's *Samson Agonistes* and *Paradise Regained* offered Nonconformists a way to understand the Lord's obscure dealings with his chosen ones in a time of trouble.

If Vaughan shared the prejudice that beneath interpretative turbulence lay still, certain scriptural truths (to which he, a true and competent reader, was privy), his image of the Word 'dress'd' nevertheless admits that scripture is a kind of mediation, a version of the truth. The bible, too,

---

[33] Matthew Prineas, 'The Dream of the Book and the Poetry of Failure in Henry Vaughan's *Silex Scintillans*', *English Literary Renaissance*, 29 (1996), 333–55 (334).

distinguishes *degrees* of revelation: the author of Hebrews speaks of the child who needs to be fed milk, and 'them that are of full age', for whom strong meats are fit (Hebrews 5: 12–13). God dressed the Word for man's consumption because human minds cannot stomach a full revelation, cannot look at God face to face, but only 'through a glass darkly' (1 Corinthians 13: 12). A similar sense of partial revelation lies in the opening lines of 'H. Scriptures', which address the bible as 'The feast | Of spirits, Heav'n extracted lyes in thee' (ll. 1–2). *Extracted* cleverly has one foot in the world of book-learning, so that the bible is seen to be a part of the divine comedy, an extract, not the whole story; and another in the world of medicine to which Vaughan was soon to turn for a profession, so that the bible is an extract, a 'preparation containing the active principle of a substance in a concentrated form', heaven on a spoon, 'medicine for the wounded'.[34] Doses of concentrated heaven can bring man to grace, but they are still the Word dressed, not the Word Himself.

The opening stanza of 'H. Scriptures' develops the papery suggestions of *extracted*, telling the bible 'Thou art lifes Charter, The Doves spotless neast | Where souls are hatch'd unto Eternitie' (ll. 3–4). After the fourteenth century, 'charter' (from Latin *cartula*, a small piece of paper) was so often used to mean a royal pardon that 'to have one's charter' eventually became synonymous with receiving a royal pardon or act of grace. Moreover, the modern sense of a contract (as Vaughan surely knew) developed during the sixteenth century, and at the same time began to exert a far stronger grip on Christian minds when they thought about God's pardoning of man in covenantal terms. So in 'H. Scriptures' the bible is man's charter, his royal pardon, a message of life from the highest legislature and supernatural sovereign.[35] As well as feeding Christian pilgrims, revealing an extract of the divine 'story'[36] and supplying heavenly cordial, scripture also witnesses the agreement between man and God. When the second stanza of 'H. Scriptures' calls scripture 'The Doves spotless neast | Where souls are hatch'd unto Eternitie' (ll. 3–4), Vaughan is brilliantly sustaining

---

[34] *OED*, extract, *sb.*, 4, 2a; T. C., *A Glasse for the Times, by Which According to the Scriptures, You May Clearly Behold the True Minister of Christ, How Farre Differing from False Teachers* (1648), sig. B1ʳ.

[35] *OED*, charter, *sb.*, 1, 1b, 2; cf. 'The Agreement' for other images of covenant and chartered assurance (esp. ll. 2, 13–14, 52).

[36] Vaughan makes great use of the word 'story' to mean 'life's story' (the story written in God's book of life) in *Silex Scintillans*. See particularly 'The Waterfall', l. 15; 'The Feast', l. 60; 'The Dwelling-place', l. 4; 'The Timber', l. 42; 'The Check', l. 2; 'Content', l. 18; 'The Proffer', l. 35; 'Repentance', l. 31; 'Son-dayes', l. 22.

the paper conceit begun in lines 1 and 2: a nest is made from *leaves*, like the leaves of the bible or a charter; and by nestling among the bible's leaves, mankind is warmed by the Holy Spirit and so hatched. Hatched chicks (called *fledglings* in contemporary usage) have wings but cannot fly until their down turns to feather. Souls are not so slow. They 'need not time', as Menalcas tells Damon in Vaughan's '*DAPHNIS*. An Elegiac *Eclogue*', 'the early forward things | Are always fledg'd, and gladly use their Wings'.[37] 'H. Scriptures" image of the Dove's nest further invigorates what is already an arresting image of the soul's ascent in Donne's Second Anniversarie: 'Thinke thy shell broke, thinke thy Soule hatch'd but now'.[38] In 'H. Scriptures', Vaughan makes the image new (as Carew had, in a different way[39]) through a typical act of literal thinking: he puts the bird back into the hatching conceit, and imagines a form for the nest, the bible, 'the Doves spotless neast | Where souls are hatch'd unto Eternitie'.

Silex Scintillans feels the Spirit's presence in the bible as a warmth and as a breath. Clinging gratefully to its charter of life, 'The Agreement' praises scripture as 'the present healing leaves | Blown from the tree of life to us' (ll. 19–20), and this same breath of God is more plainly identified with the Holy Spirit by 'Religion', the fifth of *Silex* (1650):

> My God, when I walke in those groves,
> And leaves thy spirit doth still fan,
> I see in each shade that there growes
> An Angell talking with a man.
>
> (ll. 1–4)

This fanning Spirit was also thought to have *inspired* Moses, the prophets and the other scribes who set down the books of scripture: hence the Spirit was the ultimate 'author' of the bible. This notion was especially important to Protestants, of course, and central to the principle of *sola scriptura*. For Calvin, the biblical writers were 'the secretaries of the Holy Ghost, *authentici amanuenses, notaires authentiques*'; John Donne, too, sermonized on the authorial style of the Spirit, teaching that 'The Holy Ghost is an eloquent Author, a vehement, and an abundant Author'.[40]

---

[37] '*DAPHNIS*. An Elegiac *Eclogue*', in *Thalia Rediviva* (1678), ll. 31–2.

[38] 'Of the Progresse of the Soule', The Second Anniversarie, l. 184 (*Poems of John Donne*, ed. Herbert J. C. Grierson, 2 vols. (Oxford, 1912)).

[39] In his epitaph for Maria Wentworth, whose 'soul grew so fast within | It broke the outward shell of sin, | And so was hatched a cherubin' (ll. 4–6, in *Poems 1640, Together with Poems from the Wyburd Manuscript* (Menston, 1969).

[40] *The Cambridge History of the Bible*, iii: *The West from the Reformation to the Present*

The idea of Spiritual authorship strongly influenced Vaughan's conception of his own moral responsibilities as a writer. 'The Authors Preface' to *Silex* (1655) warns that putting pen to paper is a dangerous act, since 'he that writes *idle books*, makes for himself another *body*, in which he always *lives*, and *sins* (after *death*) as *fast* and as *foul*, as ever he did in his *life*' (*V*, 390). The idea of sinning in one's literary, as well as bodily, works returns in '*On Sir* Thomas Bodley's *Library*' (from *Thalia Rediviva*). While Milton's *Areopagitica* speaks of books as the 'pretious life-blood of a master spirit, imbalm'd and treasur'd up to a life beyond life', Vaughan's poem avers that they 'are not dead, but full of *Blood* again, | I mean the *Sense*, and ev'ry *Line* a *Vein*' (ll. 5–6).[41] The couplet's wit works twice over: a *vein* is a streak of ore, rich for mining by its avid readers; but it is also the tenor of a piece of writing, a course of thought, along which blood can flow.[42] That an author's blood flows into his writing is an idea that recurs with greater force later on in the poem, where the underlying conceit— that blood is a kind of ink—is used with a magnificent metamorphic directness: 'Afflictions turn our *Blood* to *Ink*, and we | Commence when *Writing*, our *Eternity*' (ll. 21–2). Vaughan takes this conceit far beyond the merely witty through the simple verb *turn*; that monosyllable bravely acknowledges that true afflictions have drained him, like it or not, of his blood. There is no choice in the word *turn*, no ease: blood *turns* as milk turns, sours. In afflictive times, life is translated from the circulations of the bodily veins to the circulations of pen and press: life's blood is spent for their ink.

The Spirit's continued presence within the scriptures it dictated, fanning the bible's leaves with its wings to bring Christians to the truths contained thereon and to guide their understanding of them, was an important idea not only for Vaughan but for all Protestant scripture users, especially Puritans. In the mid-seventeenth century, however, some openly subordinated the authority of scripture to their supposed direct

---

Day, ed. S. L. Greenslade (Cambridge, 1963), 12; P. G. Stanwood and Heather Ross Asals (eds.), *John Donne and the Theology of Language* (Columbia, Mo., 1988), 29–35 (33), citing *The Sermons of John Donne*, ed. George R. Potter and Evelyn M. Simpson, 10 vols. (Berkeley and Los Angeles, 1953–62), v. 280–8.

[41] It is impossible to date this poem. L. C. Martin 'points out that this poem is unlikely to date from Vaughan's residence in Oxford' (*R*, 658), but Vaughan's biographer F. E. Hutchinson is not so sure (*Life*, 31); John Milton, *Areopagitica* (1644), in *Complete Prose Works of John Milton*, ed. Don M. Wolfe and others, 8 vols. (New Haven, 1953–82), ii. 493, ed. Ernest Sirluck (New Haven, 1959).

[42] *OED*, vein, II, 7; III. fig. 9a, b; see also sense 12.

inspiration by the Holy Spirit.[43] 'H. Scriptures' responds implicitly to such anti-scriptural religion with the idea that the Spirit's original inspiring and her present breathing onto the leaves of Vaughan's bible are continuous: the Dove built the nest, now she comes to sit and brood. This point is reinforced if one notes that Vaughan firmly believed that having once descended to crown the Apostles with holy fire, the Spirit would not be manifested again directly in the world until the last day. 'The Jews' (in *Silex* Part 2) teaches that 'the bright *Dove*' will return only when 'the fair year | Of [the] deliverer comes' (ll. 8, 1–2) and not before: in the meantime, she breathes in scripture.

Vaughan locates within scripture the mysterious properties and powers that more radical Christian of the mid-century believed were now embodied in their own prophecies and revelations:

> Thou art the great *Elixir*, rare, and Choice,
> The Key that opens to all Mysteries
> The *Word* in Characters, God in the *Voice*.
>
> ('H. Scriptures', ll. 6–8)

The scriptures are the λόγος of John's gospel, God's original simultaneous act of naming and creating, and they have some of His qualities: they are the manna, and the hidden stone which will be given to the regenerate Saints (Revelation 2: 17), the philosopher's stone or elixir which can cure all ills, a book version of God, divinity spoken, 'Gods bright minde exprest in print' as Vaughan later wrote in 'The Agreement' (l. 24). That 'exprest', however, inevitably bespeaks some secondary process, and acknowledges that the scriptures are not God Himself. For Vaughan, the greatest translation of biblical translations (and translators) was Christ, the Word made flesh, and there can be no second translation of equal height. It is Christ, not the bible, that he addresses in 'The Incarnation, and Passion':

> To put on Clouds instead of light,
> And cloath the morning-starre with dust,
> Was a translation of such height
> As, but in thee, was ne'r exprest.
>
> (ll. 5–8)

---

[43] Discussed by Smith, *Perfection Proclaimed*, 268–76; John R. Knott, Jr, *The Sword of the Spirit: Puritan Responses to the Bible* (Chicago, 1980), 13–41. The Spirit's threat to the Word is discussed in Chapter 5, below.

The bible is not yet God, but it is God's mind in print, a refining influence on the soul, food for the faithful, a chapter of God's story, and a witness to the promises on which faith rests.

SCRIPTURE USERS

The qualities Vaughan attributes to the bible have one thing in common: they all suggest the various *uses* to which he put the holy book. For Vaughan was born into a scripture-using culture. The penultimate poem in *Silex Scintillans*, 'To the Holy Bible' looks back across thirty years to Vaughan's infancy and remembers that the bible was 'the first [book] put in my hand'—as a christening present, perhaps.[44] Like most seventeenth-century children, the young Henry was taught to read with the bible:

> Thou wert the first put in my hand,
> When yet I could not understand,
> And daily didst my yong eyes lead
> To letters, till I learnt to read.

('To the Holy Bible', ll. 5–8)

A common way of teaching young children to read was by encouraging them to recognize the large capital *letters* at the beginning of each chapter of the bible; then when they had been led to *letters*, they were taken on to the words.[45] 'To the Holy Bible' is remembering the bookish foundation of its author's faith. One name for the alphabet at this time was 'Christ-cross-row', after the figure of a cross prefixed to the alphabet in horn-books. The term came to mean the first elements or rudiments of any subject, its ABC; for Vaughan, learning to read his ABC was the first, un-witting step towards learning to know his God, scripture and reading an integral part of religion and holiness.[46]

Octavo or duodecimo bibles could be bought for around 2s. in the seventeenth century, and had been fairly cheaply available for half a cen-

---

[44] Baptism gifts are considered by David Cressy, *Birth, Marriage & Death: Ritual, Religion, and the Life-Cycle in Tudor and Stuart England* (Oxford, 1997), 157.

[45] Geraint H. Jenkins, *Literature, Religion and Society in Wales, 1660–1730*, Studies in Welsh History 2 (Cardiff, 1978), 63–6 (64); *The Life and Opinions of Robert Roberts, A Wandering Scholar*, ed. J. H. Davies (1923), 13.

[46] *OED*, Christ-cross-row, or criss-cross-row 1, 2b *fig*; abecedary, *sb.* 1, 2. Both practice and metaphor are well developed by John Scattergood in a fine essay on *Pierce the Ploughmans Crede*, 77–104 in Margaret Aston and Colin Richmond (eds.), *Lollardy and the Gentry in the Late Middle Ages* (Stroud, 1997).

tury before Vaughan's youthful fingers turned the pages of 'my first cheap book' in the late 1620s.[47] The vernacular bible was a given for Vaughan, a fact of life as well as life's charter. Moreover, it was having perhaps its most dramatic effect on the British way of life during his early manhood: the revolutionary decades are perhaps the most intensely *scriptural* period in British history, the one time when the vernacular bible was in the mouth of every Briton.[48] At this time as never before, most educated Britons (and many uneducated ones[49]) could lay claim to the title *scripture users*, readers of God's word who could cite it as a divine authority on topics from deportment to good housekeeping, and for whom scripture was the central arena of social, political and religious debate.

Vaughan's 'first cheap book' was probably the Authorized Version, and probably in the original English translation of 1611. Elizabeth had commissioned the first Welsh bible for publication in 1566, and after various delays the translation of William Morgan, later bishop of Llandaff and St Asaph, eventually appeared in 1588.[50] Morgan's work was conformed to the Authorized Version in 1620, a year before Vaughan's birth, thus producing what was to be the standard Welsh bible for almost two centuries and making Vaughan one of the first Welshmen to grow up able to read a Church of England bible in his native tongue.[51] This coincidence of translation lives on in Vaughan's writing, where an overwhelming majority of Vaughan's biblical citations are from the Authorized Version. The only major exception to this rule are the Psalms, which he often liked to cite in the more lyrical Coverdale translation (1535) included in the Book of Common Prayer. But however strong Vaughan's attachment

[47] 'To the Holy Bible', l. 16; Hill, *The English Bible*, 9; W. M. Clyde, *The Struggle for Freedom of the Press* (Oxford, 1934), 225, 281–2.

[48] Britishness itself was a newly emerging concept. For recent thought on the subject of nationhood, see Brendan Bradshaw and John Morrill (eds.), *The British Problem, c.1534–1707: State Formation on the Atlantic Archipelago*, Problems in Focus Series (Basingstoke, 1996); Steven G. Ellis, *Tudor Frontiers and Noble Power: The Making of the British State* (Oxford, 1995).

[49] For a discussion of seventeenth-century levels of literacy, see David Cressy, *Literacy and the Social Order* (Cambridge, 1980), chs. 1–2; Peter Laslett, *The World We Have Lost*, 2nd edn. (1971), 207–12; Lawrence Stone, 'The Educational Revolution in England 1560–1640', *Past and Present*, 42 (1969), 69–139. The sub-debate on scriptural literacy is best entered through the work of Tessa Watt (see her *Cheap Print and Popular Piety 1560–1640*, Cambridge Studies in Early Modern History (Cambridge, 1991), 138, 220, 227, 328–31) and the recent discussion by Margaret Spufford, 'The Importance of Religion in the Sixteenth and Seventeenth Centuries', in Margaret Spufford (ed.), *The World of Rural Dissenters, 1520–1725* (Cambridge, 1995), 1–102, esp. 4–5, 44–9.

[50] This bible is *STC* 2347.   [51] *Cambridge History of the Bible*, iii. 170–2.

to the Authorized Version, he did not shut his eyes to other transformations of the Word, consulting the Roman Vulgate and the Junius-Tremellius Protestant Latin bible, too.[52] The Genevan bible and Beza's Latin New Testament were also on Vaughan's bookshelf; the latter suggested to him the small but powerful detail (the idea that the creatures could look up to God) which forms the nub of 'And do they so?', one of the poet's most individual creations.[53]

Of the most important uses to which Vaughan put these many versions of the Word, five are considered in this study. Each chapter below turns on a different way in which Vaughan was using scripture in the years following his conversion experience (around 1648), the Royalist defeat, and Parliament's closure of the established church. Each use, in turn, looks to one of the five different groups of biblical book commonly identified by sixteenth-century Protestants.[54] The *historical* books (Genesis to Nehemiah) are the focus of Chapter 2, which unveils the ways in which the story of Jacob provided Vaughan with a powerful typological image of God's chosen people (and their king) in exile. Chapter 3 has most to do with the *prophetical* (Isaiah to Malachi) and *poetical* (Job, the Psalms, Ecclesiastes, the Song of Solomon); it explores how Vaughan conceived of the enlarged *Silex Scintillans* as an offering of thanks modelled on the song of King Hezekiah of Judah, who, like Vaughan, had been ill 'nigh unto death'. God's miraculous intervention to prolong Hezekiah's life gave the recovered Vaughan a new intimation of Providence, and inspired him to continue with scriptural poetry despite growing fears that artistic praise might easily become tainted by man's inherent (and ever growing) corruption. Poetry, then, is itself a *scripture use*, a custom inspired by scripture, authorized by scriptural stories like Hezekiah's, as well as consisting, in part, of scripture's words.

Chapter 4 explores Vaughan's practical use of the life of Christ in the four gospels to fashion a rule for holy living in the absence of the established church. It dwells on the nature of routine, habit, order, *use*, and sees scriptural injunctions to order, obedience and regularity beneath Vaughan's unusual admiration of the creatures. And in reminding present-day poetry readers that the bible founded and funded Vaughan's

---

[52] Vaughan's reputation as a Latinist is considered by Philip Macon Cheek, 'The Latin Element in Henry Vaughan', *Studies in Philology*, 44 (1947), 69–88; see *R*, 543 for Vaughan's quotation from Tremellius in 'The Brittish Church'.

[53] Discussed, with supporting scholarship from Alan Rudrum, in Chapter 4, 'Disorder'd man'.

[54] Divisions of scripture are detailed by Lewalski, *Protestant Poetics*, 32.

every hour, Chapter 4 suggests that critical attention to Vaughan's scriptural poetry must look beyond the scripture-texts on the page to their
larger roles in the poet's life and times. Chapters 5 and 6 concentrate on
prophecies of the Apocalypse, mostly drawn from Revelation. Reading
that book (and the gospels and the epistles of Paul, Peter and John),
Vaughan found evidence that his enemies, Parliament's radical preachers
responsible for gathering Independent churches in Wales, were the false
prophets and truce-breakers predicted by Christ and the apostles
(Chapter 5); Vaughan's unveiling of their culpable misunderstanding of
scripture for self-ends, and his attack on the millenarian belief supported
by that misuse, are the subject of the last chapter.

This scheme does not intend to show that Vaughan drew equally on all
parts of the bible—no seventeenth-century writers did, or wanted to—
but it does emphasize the equal importance of Old and New Testaments
in Vaughan's work, something seldom appreciated by his critics, who have
tended to associate him most closely with Genesis, the Song of Songs, and
Revelation. It also highlights Vaughan's 'interscripturality', the tendency
of *Silex Scintillans* to advance one scripture to interpret another, or to set
scriptures ringing in harmony by sounding them together. Chapters 4, 5
and 6 listen for the strong verbal interchange between the gospels, epistles
and Revelation in Vaughan's work, and suggest that Vaughan took great
pleasure and comfort from the scripture harmonies he discovered. For example, the close study of Vaughan's co-opted phrase 'new lights' in Chapter 5 closely considers the apocalyptic warnings of Peter and Paul's
epistles, but locates their sources in Christ's prophecies in the gospels.
And Chapter 4 notes Vaughan's use of Christ's night-time vigil and
prayers on Mount Olivet as an example of Christian duty; but also sees
that Vaughan discusses those vigils in a vocabulary drawn largely from the
epistles.

The keynote of all Vaughan's uses is affliction. 'To Mr M. L. *upon his
reduction of the* Psalms *into Method*'[55] makes a description of the Psalmist
ring with an autobiographical and afflictive note when it praises the way
the Psalmist David's hasty *Medley* (a collection of songs of all sorts, put together, as it were, *en route*: a quodlibet)[56] has now been rectified:

---

[55] This poem from *Thalia Rediviva* has so far eluded all editorial effort to localize it (*R*,
652).
[56] *OED*, medley, A. *sb.* 2. A combination, mixture; 6. A musical composition consisting of parts or subjects of a diversified or incongruous character; 7. As the title of a
literary miscellany; *OED* quodlibet, 2. A fanciful combination of several airs; a fantasia, a
medley.

SIR,
You have oblig'd the *Patriarch*. And tis known
He is your Debtor now, though for his own.
What he wrote, is a *Medley*. We can see
Confusion trespass on his Piety.
Misfortunes did not only Strike at him;
They charged further, and oppress'd his pen.
For he wrote as his *Crosses* came, and went
By no safe *Rule*, but by his *Punishment*.
His *quill* mov'd by the *Rod*; his witts and he
Did know no *Method*, but their *Misery*.

(ll. 1–10)

The bible is Vaughan's best method; Cromwell his best occasion. If the Silurist's place in the literature of the mid-seventeenth century is to be properly established, it must be on the back of critical commentary (and, indeed, editing) that reveals his scriptural genius without crushing it beneath a weight of contextual and scriptural annotation. All the same, Vaughan's readers will always have to overcome a sense of distance from the bible if they are to re-engage with his poetry's figurative imagination. Yet the effort is extraodinarily worthwhile. No other poet of the 1650s represents so fully the intersection of scripture and tradition resulting from the various accommodations of the Church of England. Whilst other writers—Clarendon not least among them—later reflected, with the bible never far from their thoughts, on the nightmares of the Grand Rebellion, Henry Vaughan was the best able to express the pain and sorrow of those years as they happened and to see them through such a dark and dazzling scriptural veil. Among the poets, only Vaughan's spirituality was at once captured and released by the afflictions of Cromwellian England. It is the aim and scope of this book to let that double motion into the light.

CHAPTER TWO

Patriarchs and pilgrims

In the late 1620s, alarmed by the 'perilous' view that monarchs derived their power from a popular mandate, the Kentishman and friend of George Herbert, Sir Robert Filmer, composed a treatise arguing instead that royal power was absolute—given directly by God, and placing the monarch above earthly laws—and moreover patriarchal, like a father's power over his family.[1] Not published until 1680, when it played a part in the Tory propaganda campaign against Whig exclusionists, Filmer's *Patriarcha* circulated widely among gentry readers during the years of Charles I's personal rule, 1629–40, and may have been read at court, too, since Robert's brother Edward was a member of the royal household.[2]

Though Locke's stinging rebuttal of Filmer's views in the *Two Treatises of Government* was not itself printed until 1690, the assumptions on which *Patriarcha* rested were under almost continual attack in the sixty years following its composition. Filmer's response to theories of popular mandate was based on scriptural proofs (as he saw it) that royal power had been invested by God in Adam and had passed down from father to son ever since. As he summarizes his arguments:

This Lordship which Adam by creation had over the whole world, and by right descending from him the patriarchs did enjoy, was as large and ample as the

---

[1] Sir Robert Filmer, *Patriarcha and Other Writings*, ed. Johann P. Sommerville (Cambridge, 1991), 3. The political thought of Filmer and his contemporaries is explored in Gordon J. Schochet, *Patriarchalism and Political Thought* (Oxford, 1975); Sommerville, 'From Suarez to Filmer: A Reappraisal', *Historical Journal*, 25 (1982), 525–40; Sommerville, *Politics and Ideology in England, 1603–1640* (1986), 27–34.

[2] On the date of *Patriarcha*, see Sommerville's Introduction to *Patriarcha and Other Writings*, pp. xxxii–xxxiv. Filmer's connections with Herbert, and his brother Edward's place in the royal household, are discussed by Sommerville, p. x, who also notes that Ben Jonson wrote a poem to Edward Filmer in 1629. On Filmer's circle, see Peter Laslett, 'Sir Robert Filmer: The Man Versus the Whig Myth', in *William and Mary Quarterly*, 5 (1948), 523–46, Laslett, 'The Gentry of Kent in 1640', *Cambridge Historical Journal*, 9 (1948), 148–64 and Laslett's introduction to *'Patriarcha' and Other Political Works of Sir Robert Filmer* (Oxford, 1949).

absolutest dominion of any monarch which hath been since the creation . . . Not only until the Flood, but after it, this patriarchal power did continue—as the very name of patriarch doth in part prove.[3]

As this passage shows, Filmer's political theory rested on the universally accepted view that the bible was absolutely and literally true. *Patriarcha* ranges through the books of the bible, but is drawn most to the Old Testament, and within it to the book of Genesis, whose account of mankind's origins had become increasingly important in sixteenth-century theological and political writing.[4] Particularly crucial to Filmer were God's decrees of man's dominion over the world, which *Patriarcha* cites in number to support the conclusion that although royal lines might suffer disruption through death, marriage and war, the rightful king always holds an absolute power by virtue of his lineage. Furthermore the Fifth Commandment, 'Honour thy father and mother', should be understood to relate to monarchs as well as to natural parents, making resistance to patriarchs and patriarchalism an act of rebellion against God's Word.

'This patriarchal power did continue, as the very name of patriarch doth in part prove'. The English *patriarch* springs from Tertullian's Latin translation of the Greek πατριάρχης, the term used in Hebrews and Acts (and only in those books) to refer to the pre-Christian heroes of faith: antediluvian patriarchs like Abel, Enoch and Noah, and also their descendants Abraham, Isaac, Jacob, Joseph, Moses, Gideon, Samson, David and so forth.[5] In the primitive church of the first five centuries, *patriarch* became an honorific designation for bishops, and was later applied to chief dignitaries of other churches and the fathers and founders of orders, institutions and traditions.[6] In their capacity as Defenders of the Faith since Henry VIII, the Tudor and Stuart monarchs had a good claim to the title of *patriarch* of the national church and hence of the nation. At the end of the seventeenth century, Dryden could make the connection between monarchy and fatherhood almost in passing: 'The monarch oak, the patriarch of the trees' (*Palamon and Arcite*).[7] Fifty years earlier, Henry

---

[3] *Patriarcha and Other Writings*, 3, 7.

[4] Arnold Williams, *The Common Expositor: An Account of the Commentaries on Genesis 1527–1633* (Chapel Hill, NC, 1948), chs. I, II. Among other bible texts, patriarchalist political theorists often cited Prov. 8: 15 and Ps. 82: 6.

[5] Acts 7: 8, 9; Heb. 7: 4.   [6] *OED*, patriarch, *sb.* 1, 3a, 4, 5b.

[7] *John Dryden*, ed. Keith Walker, Oxford Authors Series (Oxford, 1987), 632. *Palamon and Arcite* was published in Dryden's *Fables Ancient and Modern* (1700).

Vaughan, too, was thinking patriarchally when he saw the execution of Charles I as an almost Oedipal monstrosity: 'The sons the father kil, | The Children Chase the mother' ('The Constellation', ll. 37–8). The 'mother' is of course the Church of England, abused (as Vaughan saw it) by her own dissenting and rebellious offspring, the subject-children of the patriarch Charles.

The power of Britain's beheaded king passed, patriarchally speaking, to his son Charles, who was crowned king of Scotland on 1 January 1651. During the nine remaining years of Charles's exile from the throne of England and Wales, Henry Vaughan made repeated reference in his poetry and prose to all of the Old Testament patriarchs, father-king ancestors of the banished monarch now forced, like Abraham, to travel abroad with the chosen people, or like Jacob, to escape a murderous brother.[8] Though they do not themselves describe a patriarchal system of government or propose a political theory, Vaughan's writings nevertheless deploy patriarchal figures in a far more politically nuanced fashion than his modern readers have realized.[9] His writing offers, in its reworkings from Genesis, an understanding of the state of Britain which to his contemporary audience would have seemed indubitably that of a Royalist and adherent to the established (and proscribed) Church of England. Through the figures of Ishmael, Moses, Abraham and particularly Jacob, Vaughan articulated his deepest hopes and fears for the Anglican church, for its patriarch Charles II, and, their professed faithful subject, for himself.

The patriarch Jacob is prominent in the very first poem in *Silex Scintillans* (1650), 'Regeneration', where the holiness of churches—a strongly Anglican idea in an age when Puritans increasingly disdained ecclesiastical buildings—is figured through Jacob's desert bed, Bethel ('The house of God'). In *The Mount of Olives* (1652) and *Silex* (1655), Vaughan draws on the Protestant view that Jacob is a type of the invisible church of the elect, forced to flee into the desert to escape Esau's murderous revenge;

---

[8] Most frequently mentioned in *Silex Scintillans* are Moses, Jacob and Ishmael (all discussed below), then Abraham and Solomon (for Abraham see 'Jesus Weeping', l. 6, 'Religion', l. 13, 'The Rain-bow', l. 5, *The Mount of Olives* 146, 147, 148; for Solomon 'The Shepheards', l. 23, 'Man', l. 14, *The Mount of Olives*, 152).

[9] Brief but helpful comments on Jacob are made by Eluned Brown, 'Henry Vaughan's Biblical Landscape', 56–8. Barbara Lewalski, 'Typology and Poetry: A Consideration of Herbert, Vaughan and Marvell', in *Illustrious Evidence: Approaches to English Literature of the Early Seventeenth Century*, ed. Earl Miner (Berkeley and Los Angeles, 1975), 41–69, draws attention to the three main patriarchal presences in *Silex* and lists some of their appearances.

and in several prayers and admonitions for travelling Christians, Vaughan affirms that in the 1650s, the fleeing elect are suffering Anglicans, forced out of God's church (and in the case of some, from His nation) by reprobate rebels. The same typological association is made in 'Jacobs Pillow and Pillar', a poem from the later *Silex* which sets out a cataclysmic vision of Vaughan's times as those in which corruption of religion had finally become so widespread that God has retreated to barren, rocky places: the desert landscape of the Old Testament and Vaughan's own stony heart, the *silex* of his title. This heart, Vaughan's chosen emblem of repentance and regeneration, also links him with Jacob, whose travels in Genesis involve him with a series of sacred and sacrificial stones (rather than the sacred trees and groves with which Abraham is most associated, for instance).[10] This chapter concludes by suggesting that Jacob's stony desert altars held specifically Royalist associations for Vaughan and for others loyal to the Stuarts, and wonders whether the Silurist made a further identification with Jacob through the meaning of his own surname *Vaughan*.

Though Jacob is the most important, he is not the most ubiquitous patriarch in the two-part *Silex Scintillans*. That place must be granted to Moses, whose presence is born out of the sheer number of momentous events with which he is associated: the Egyptian bondage (which Vaughan treats in 'The Relapse', 'The Mutinie' and 'Corruption'), the striking of the rock at Horeb (referred to in 'Authoris (de se) Emblema', 'The Passion'), the giving of the manna ('Rules and Lessons', 'The Feast', 'The Holy Communion', 'The Morning-watch', 'H. Scriptures') and the Law-giving ('The Law, and the Gospel', 'Mans fall, and Recovery'). Yet Vaughan does not figure himself, his monarch, or his church through Moses, even though Exodus was a popular source of images of pilgrimage for seventeenth-century Christians. Neither is Vaughan much interested in the story of Ishmael, the exiled son of Abraham and Hagar. God's care for the boy, who will father 'a great nation' (Genesis 21: 18), was seen by many Protestants as an image of themselves, the gentiles 'who were to become heirs to the promise'.[11] To Vaughan, however, it figured God's

---

[10] Rudolf Frieling, *Old Testament Studies: Essays: Trees Wells, and Stones in the Lives of the Patriarchs: From Sabbath to Sunday*, trans. Margaret and Rudolf Koehler (1963; Edinburgh, 1987), 105–36.

[11] Lewalski, 'Typology and Poetry', 57; Vaughan's treatment of Ishmael's story is discussed by Ross Garner, *Henry Vaughan: Experience and the Tradition* (Chicago, 1959), 21–2.

constant watching over those whom the world exiles, and so might have been brought to bear on the plight of Anglicans and Royalists in the 1650s.[12] But Vaughan was to use Ishmael more generally in his poetry as a way of discussing Providence. His blacker moods were plagued by the fear that God might stop watching over him: 'Well fare those blessed days of old | When thou didst hear the *weeping lad!*' he wrote in 'Begging [II]' (ll. 11–12), a poem published in *Flores Solitudinis* (1654) and again in the second volume of *Silex Scintillans* (1655).

Though Vaughan's writing is permeated by patriarchs, only three out of 140 poems in the finished *Silex Scintillans* mention them in their titles. These are 'Jacobs Pillow and Pillar', '*Isaacs* Marriage' and 'Abels Blood'. Superficially, then, patriarchs are less important to Vaughan than, say, to Francis Quarles, who wrote dozens of meditations on them, including several on Jacob and one about 'Jacob's Pillow'.[13] But statistics do not reveal the originality or the passion of Vaughan's uses of the patriarchal stories. Unlike *The Temple*, which draws relatively little direct poetic inspiration from the patriarchs or the Old Testament,[14] Vaughan's writing is indelibly marked by his meditations on Genesis, and especially on Jacob. However, *The Temple* may have inspired Vaughan to apply the patriarchs' stories to his own life in a different way. Ending his unsigned eulogy of Herbert, 'The Printers to the Reader', Nicholas Ferrar remembered how his friend 'used to conclude all things that might seem to tend any way to his own honour' with a seven-word motto taken from Genesis: '*Lesse then the least of Gods mercies*'.[15] This pious disclaimer, afterwards

---

[12] For a discussion of wilderness narrative, a genre whose seventeenth-century revival was sparked by the Pilgrim Fathers, see Perry Miller, *Errand into the Wilderness* (1956; New York, 1964), ch. 1; Peter N. Carroll, *Puritanism and the Wilderness: The Intellectual Significance of the New England Frontier 1629–1700* (New York, 1969), 10–13, 16–25; Roderick Nash, *Wilderness and the American Mind,* 3rd edn. (New Haven, 1982), 1–7, 13–42.

[13] *Francis Quarles: The Complete Works in Prose and Verse,* ed. Alexander B. Grosart, 3 vols. (1880–1; repr. Hildesheim, 1971): 'Jacob's Purchase', 'On Esau', 'On the Absence of a Blessing', 'On Jacob's Pillow', 'On Jacob', 'On Esau and Jacob', 'On Jacob' (Bk. I, nos. 58, 59, 60, 65; III, 35, 41; IV, 18). For other meditations on Jacob's story see: Joseph Beaumont, *Psyche: or, Loves Mysterie* (1648), stzs. 56–164; Rowland Watkyns, 'A Friend', in *Flamma sine Fumo; or, Poems without Fictions* [1662], ed. P. C. Davies (Cardiff, 1968); Milton, *Paradise Lost,* III. 498–515; Dryden, 'To my Honour'd Kinsmen, John Driden', ll. 40–3, 'To Sir Godfrey Kneller', ll. 89–96.

[14] The important exceptions for Vaughan are Herbert's 'Aaron', 'Decay' and 'The Bunch of Grapes' (discussed below in 'With Jacob').

[15] Genesis 32: 10; *The Works of George Herbert,* ed. F. E. Hutchinson (Oxford, 1941), 4–5 (all quotations of Herbert's works are from this edition and will be cited in the text);

adopted by Ferrar's community at Little Gidding, recalls Paul's belief that he was 'less than the least of all saints' (Ephesians 3: 8). But Paul, too, is thinking of a scriptural passage, the prayer for deliverance offered by Jacob at Mahanaim: 'I am not worthy [or 'am less than all'] the least of all the mercies, and of the truth, which thou hast shewed unto thy servant'.[16] Herbert's motto, adopted from Jacob, is remembered several times among the scriptural embroidery of eighteen prayers and meditations that makes up Vaughan's devotional manual, *The Mount of Olives* (1652). Its rules for preparing for the Eucharist include Jacob's words both in the prayer 'Immediately before the receiving [of communion]' and again in the 'Prayer for the grace of repentance, together with a Confession of sins';[17] earlier, five allusions to Jacob punctuate Vaughan's politically loaded advice on what to do and say when leaving home.[18] *The Mount of Olives* was written alongside or just after the first volume of *Silex Scintillans*, a work with which it shares its particular interest in 'the most earthly of the patriarchs'.[19] Jacob is the first biblical figure to appear in *Silex* (1650) when, in the fourth stanza of 'Regeneration', Vaughan's pilgrim-narrator reposes on '*Jacobs* bed'; and the patriarch quickly returns in 'Religion', '*Isaacs* Marriage' and 'The Search', as well as later in 'The Pilgrimage'.[20]

C. A. Hunter, 'Old Testament Sainthood', *Notes and Queries*, 209 (1964), 86–8. Vaughan refers to Herbert's 'holy life and verse' in 'The Authors Preface' to *Silex* (1655), 391.

[16] Nicholas Ferrar, 'The Printers to the Reader' (*The Works of George Herbert*, 4–5; and on Ferrar's authorship, 476). C. A. Patrides notes that the motto was also adopted at Little Gidding and cites *The Ferrar Papers*, ed. B. Blackstone (Cambridge, 1938), 178 (*The English Poems of George Herbert* (1974), 31).

[17] V, 164, ll. 5–6; 159, ll. 37–8.

[18] V, 146, ll. 12–18; 146, ll. 35–8; 147, ll. 34–7; 152, ll. 26–7. The prayer 'Immediately before the receiving' extends Herbert's motto with the rest of Gen. 32: 10 before dovetailing skilfully into Gen. 48: 15: 'O Lord I am not worthy of the least of all the mercies, and of all the truth which thou hast shewed unto thy servant, I all my life long unto this very day' (V, 164, ll. 5–7).

[19] Frieling, *Old Testament Studies*, 129.

[20] Like *The Temple*, *Silex Scintillans* was not necessarily meant to be read through linearly—the presence of indexical tables, for instance, suggests that like books of devotion and practical divinity, they were partly designed to be consulted topically. But there are also undeniably short sequences of poems on related themes, including the opening sequence of *Silex* (1650) on the subject of death and regeneration or the Four Last Things which ends 'The Church' section of *The Temple*. On the ordering of poetic collections see Neil Fraistat (ed.), *Poems in Their Place: The Intertextuality and Order of Poetic Collections* (Chapel Hill, NC, 1986) and on poetry books as devotional manuals, T. A. Birrell, 'The Influence of Seventeenth-Century Publishers on the Presentation of English Literature', 163–73 in Mary-Jo Arn and Hanneke Wirtjes, with Hans Jansen (eds.), *Historical & Editorial Studies in Medieval & Early Modern English* (Groningen, 1985), esp. 163–6.

His words glimmer in other poems, too. The first line of 'Mans fall, and Recovery', for instance, remembers Jacob's acknowledgement of his blessings, which he says have 'prevailed above the blessings of my progenitors unto the utmost bound of the everlasting hills', as Vaughan starts to contemplate how the blessings of the new covenant have now prevailed even over those of the old: 'Farewell, you Everlasting hills!'[21]

While most Reformed ministers, theologians and scriptural interpreters concentrated on Jacob's winning of his birthright and Esau's loss of inheritance, more unorthodox Renaissance thinkers were drawn to what is now perhaps the most famous image of Jacob's story: 'a ladder set up on the earth, and the top of it reached to heaven: and behold, the angels of God ascending and descending on it' (Genesis 28: 12). Jacob's ladder held a key place in the hermetical philosophy that Henry shared, in part, with his twin brother Thomas, whose alchemical treatises bore the pseudonym 'Eugenius Philalethes'. Published in 1650, Thomas's *Magia Adamica* expressed the belief, widespread among hermeticists, that Jacob's ladder was 'the greatest *Mysterie* in the *Cabala*', while Jacob himself was a magician whose '*Propagation* of his *speckled Flocks* [in Genesis 30–1] . . . is an effect so purely *Magicall* that our most obstinat *Adversaries* dare not Question it'.[22] Whereas alchemists supposed the existence of a philosopher's stone and sought to produce it, hermeticists believed that they could possess secret knowledge of the universe, and sought a unified vision of the mechanics whereby heaven and earth were linked. This ultimate vision would be revealed to the initiate in a mystical trance, the sleep which is '*Death*, namely that *Death* which the *Cabalist* calls *Mors Osculi*, or the *Death* of the *Kiss*, of which I must not speake one syllable'.[23] Jacob's vision of the ladder fuelled such fantasies. Samuel Pordgage's hermetical epic *Mundorum Explicatio* (1663)—which was published by the same Lodowick Lloyd who sold Vaughan's second edition of *Silex Scintillans*—places itself firmly in this interpretative tradition:

[21] 'Regeneration', l. 28; 'Religion', l. 9; '*Isaacs* Marriage' (marginal note); 'The Search', ll. 22, 32; Genesis 49: 26.

[22] *TV*, 180, 171 (from *Magia Adamica* (1650)); C. A. Patrides, 'Renaissance Interpretations of Jacob's Ladder', *Theologische Zeitschrift*, 18 (1962), 411–18; cf. Calvin, *A Commentary of John Calvine, upon the First Booke of Moses called Genesis*, trans. Thomas Tymme (1578), 597; Henry Ainsworth, *Annotations upon the First Book of Moses, Called Genesis* (1621), sig. X1ᵛ; John Trapp, *A Clavis to the Bible; or, A New Comment upon the Pentateuch* (1650), 226; John Diodati, *Pious Annotations upon the Holy Bible Expounding the Difficult Places Thereof Learnedly and Plainly*, 3rd edn. (1651), sig. E4ʳ; Augustine, *Lectures or Tractates on the Gospel According to Saint John*, trans. John Gibb, 2 vols. (Edinburgh, 1873), 111–12.

[23] Thomas Vaughan, *Magia Adamica* (*TV*, 181).

> Rap'd was I into a heav'nly *Lethargy*.
> This is the sleep of *Jacob*, this the Trance
> Of *Paul*, when he did to the Heav'ns advance:
> This is the state, in which the Soul's blest eye
> Sees God (beyond Thoughts) intellectually.[24]

Poems like 'Cock-crowing' and 'Resurrection & Immortality' leave little doubt that Henry, too, was well versed in occult knowledge; but others suggest that he came to question hermetical ambition. 'Vanity of Spirit', in particular, offers a convincing rejection of the hermetic philosopher's attempt

> to know
> Who gave the Clouds so brave a bow,
> Who bent the spheres, and circled in
> Corruption with this glorious Ring,
> What is his name, and how I might
> Descry some part of his great light.

(ll. 3–8)

Whether or not Vaughan humbled the sorts of hermetic desire that led his brother to live and die (in a laboratory accident) a radical and experimental chemist, the sorts of hermetical literature possessed and consulted by the Vaughan brothers in the late 1640s can only have led them again and again to the story of Jacob.[25]

JACOBS BED

Silex Scintillans (1650) begins with Jacob. He enters, somewhat mysteriously, in 'Regeneration', a poem whose allegories, emblems and soteriology have delighted and taxed its readers and given it one of the richest legacies of critical interpretation among Vaughan's poems.[26] But if some

---

[24] Samuel Pordage, *Mundorum Explicatio; Wherein are Couched the Mysteries of the External, Internal and Eternal Worlds* (1663), 197 (ll. 2892–6). On Lloyd's role in publishing Vaughan see the start of Chapter 3; his esoteric interests are placed in a professional and political context by D. F. McKenzie's unpublished Sandars Lectures, 'The London Book Trade in the Later Seventeenth Century' (Cambridge, 1976) [Cambridge University Library 850.b.188], ch. 1 and table of 'Names in Imprints of Radical Literature 1641–1660'.

[25] The range of Thomas Vaughan's eclectic reading is suggested by Alan Rudrum's annotations to *TV*, 597–753 and his death is noted by Charles Webster, *The Great Instauration: Science, Medicine and Reform 1626–1660* (1975), 147.

[26] Important readings of 'Regeneration' include those of Edmund Blunden, *On the*

of the poem's obscurities are quickly illuminated by notes on its scriptural and literary allusions, others prove harder to light up.[27] Why, in particular, should the journey to regeneration pass through *Jacobs Bed*?

3.
So sigh'd I upwards still, at last
'Twixt steps, and falls
I reach'd the pinacle, where plac'd
I found a paire of scales,
I tooke them up and layd
In th'one late paines,
The other smoake, and pleasures weigh'd
But prov'd the heavier graines;

4.
With that, some cryed, *Away*; straight I
Obey'd, and led
Full East, a faire, fresh field could spy
Some call'd it, *Jacobs Bed*;
A Virgin-soile, which no
Rude feet ere trod,
Where (since he stept there,) only go
Prophets, and friends of God.

5.
Here, I repos'd; but scarse well set,
A grove descryed
Of stately height, whose branches met
And mixt on every side.

(ll. 17–36)

Poems of Henry Vaughan (1927), 20–1; Garner, *Henry Vaughan*, 47–62; Pettet, *Of Paradise and Light*, 104–7; R. A. Durr, *On the Mystical Poetry of Henry Vaughan* (Cambridge, Mass., 1962), 82–9; Louis L. Martz, *The Paradise Within: Studies in Vaughan, Traherne, and Milton* (New Haven, 1964), 8–12; Post, *Henry Vaughan*, 82–94, 196–98; Wall, *Transformations of the Word*, 305–17.

[27] On Vaughan's relationship with the emblem book tradition see Michael Rothberg, 'An Emblematic Ideology: Images and Additions in Two Editions of Henry Vaughan's *Silex Scintillans*', *English Literary Renaissance*, 22 (1992), 80–94; Calhoun, *Henry Vaughan*, Appendix; Peter M. Daly, *Literature in the Light of the Emblem* (Toronto, 1979), ch. 3; Rosemary Freeman, *English Emblem Books* (1948), 150–1. The larger problems of obscurity in poetry are the subject of William Empson, 'Obscurity and Annotation', in *Argufying: Essays on Literature and Culture*, ed. John Haffenden (1988), 70–87, and John Press, *The Chequer'd Shade: Reflections on Obscurity in Poetry* (Oxford, 1958).

What and where is *Jacobs Bed*? The speaker seems to approach this place of curious repose in a dream.[28] Locations change, but movement between scenes is sudden, its narrative elliptical. The pilgrim-narrator is unsure of exactly when and how his climbing ends, though the poem delights in the betwixt-and-betweenness of the moment as it does other happy uncertainties and mysteries: ' 'Twixt steps, and falls I I reach'd the pinacle'. Between stanzas three and four voices, perhaps the verdict of the scales, intrude upon a hitherto solitary landscape, commanding Vaughan's pilgrim away from the hilltop scales and eastward toward *Jacobs Bed*. But is he led, passively, Full East (with its hint of being 'East-er'), or does he lead himself there? In grammar and in spiritual apprehension, the poem recognizes actions, not their causes; the ways of grace are remembered, not scrutinized, seen in their effects, not their causes.

Modern editors, recognizing that the clouds of time which form over Vaughan's lines are often dispersed by identifying the scriptural passage to which he is alluding, direct their reader to Genesis 28: 12, where Jacob is asleep in the desert near a city called Luz: 'And he dreamed, and behold a ladder set up on the earth, and the top of it reached to heaven: and behold the angels of God ascending and descending on it' (Genesis 28: 12).[29] This is certainly a bed of Jacob's. Yet why should a regeneration narrative encompass this one place out of the bible's numerous sites of spiritual awakening? The specificity of Vaughan's choice is the more noticeable since the first three stanzas of the poem traverse a landscape that is allegorical, not scriptural. It is this added scriptural dimension in 'Regeneration' that sets it apart most clearly from its best model, Herbert's 'The Pilgrimage':

> And so I came to Fancies medow strow'd
> >   With many a flower:
> > Fain would I here have made abode,
> > But I was quicken'd by my houre.
> So to Cares cops I came, and there got through
> >   With much ado.
>
> >   ('The Pilgrimage', ll. 7–12)

Here and throughout the poem, locations take their names from vices and virtues in the manner of Spenser or Bunyan, a method borrowed by

---

[28] On early modern dream narratives, see Manfred Weidhorn, *Dreams in Seventeenth-Century English Literature* (The Hague, 1970), ch. 2.

[29] R, 531; *George Herbert and Henry Vaughan*, ed. Louis Martz (Oxford, 1986), 485.

'Regeneration' as its speaker walks the '*Primros'd*' way of dalliance and climbs the hill of spiritual struggle. After these familiar stages, though, Vaughan's poem arrives at the entirely unfamiliar ground of *Jacobs Bed* and everything changes, for the reader as for the pilgrim.

'Regeneration' abandons allegorical for physical landscape at the moment the pilgrim arrives at *Jacobs Bed*. As always in Vaughan, the physical and natural world are revered primarily because they manifest divinity or holiness,[30] in this case God's appearance to Jacob in a desert place called Luz, some 1,700 years before Christ's birth:[31]

And Jacob went out from Beersheba, and went toward Haran. And he lighted upon a certain place, and tarried there all night, because the sun was set; and he took of the stones of that place, and put them for his pillows, and lay down in that place to sleep. And he dreamed, and behold a ladder set up on the earth, and the top of it reached to heaven: and behold the angels of God ascending and descending on it. (Genesis 28: 10–12)

One scholar of Vaughan has argued that *Jacobs Bed* is not the place where the patriarch dreams, but Peniel, where he wrestles with an angel.[32] However, the geography of 'Regeneration' is alluding obscurely to Luz in the phrase 'Full East': Jacob continues his travels 'into the land of the people of the east' just after he sleeps and dreams (Genesis 29: 1). Vaughan glossed this eastward itinerary in a marginal note to '*Isaacs* Marriage', the fourth poem of *Silex* (1650): '*a wel in the South Country where* Jacob *dwelt, between* Cadesh, *&* Bered; Heb[rew], *the well of him that liveth, and seeth me*' (*V*, 409). And in a prayer for 'When we go from home', in *The Mount of Olives*, Vaughan eagerly lists the parameters of Jacob's journey 'from *Beer-she-ba* unto *Padan-aran*' as he does Abraham's 'from *Ur* of the *Chaldees* into a land flowing with milk and honey' (*V*, 146–7). Vaughan

---

[30] Compare the mixed description of landscape in 'The Morning-watch', which combines natural observation and evocation of the morning with the morning of the Manna-giving in Exod. 16. 'Religion' puns on 'leaves' to identify the pages of the bible with Old Testament groves; and the landscape of 'Joy of my life!' recalls the jewelled streets of the New Jerusalem in Revelation; see Chris Fitter, 'Henry Vaughan's Landscapes of Military Occupation', *Essays in Criticism*, 42 (1992), 123–47.

[31] The authoritative chronology for Vaughan's period was James Ussher, *Annales Veteris Testamenti* (1650); see the discussion of Hugh Trevor-Roper, *Catholics, Anglicans and Puritans: Seventeenth-Century Essays* (1987), 159–61.

[32] In an uncharacteristic slip, Wall writes that 'This is an allusion to Genesis 28 where Jacob wrestles with God for a blessing and declares the place to be holy ground because of the encounter with God in a specific moment of historical time' (309). The ensuing argument, based on the uses of Gen. 28 in the Prayer Book, is therefore somewhat disabled (309–11).

probably gleaned his information from the maps of the Holy Land frequently included in annotated bibles, particularly the ever informative Genevan translation, which Vaughan clearly consulted on many occasions.[33]

The briefest consultation of Genesis 28 reveals that *Jacobs Bed* is also some kind of a church. The place where Jacob dreams was originally called Luz; but when he wakes the next morning, he is inspired to rename it *Bethel*, meaning the house of God:

Surely the Lord is in this place; and I knew it not. And he was afraid, and said, How dreadful is this place! this is none other but the house of God, and this is the gate of heaven. And Jacob rose up early in the morning and took the stone that he had put for his pillows, and set it up for an pillar, and poured oil upon the top of it. And he called the name of that place Beth-el: but the name of that city was called Luz at the first. (Genesis 28: 16–19)

In an important article, Claude Summers and Ted-Larry Pebworth have argued that *Jacobs Bed* is a 'church in nature', noting that 'Regeneration' describes it as a 'grove' of trees resembling Anglican architecture.[34] They identify the major context of 'Regeneration' as the programme of Puritan reformation which followed Parliament's victory in the first Civil War. In the late 1640s, efforts to eradicate established worship took shape in a series of Ordinances prohibiting Prayer Book worship and imposing a new *Directory for Public Worship*, 'an adaptation of Calvin's Genevan rite and the *Book of Common Order* used by Scottish Calvinists'.[35] In Wales, a group of young Independent preachers including Vavasor Powell and Morgan Llwyd was determined to sweep away the church discipline of

---

[33] See, for instance, the 'Map of the Holy Lands, Canaan, and the bordering countries', which details dozens of Old Testament sites, in *The Bible* [Genevan] (for Robert Barker, 1610), sigs. F1^r–[F2]^v. Of Vaughan's many citations from Geneva the most notable is Romans 18: 19, used as the end text for 'Mans fall, and Recovery' (R, 544).

[34] Claude J. Summers and Ted-Larry Pebworth, 'Vaughan's Temple in Nature and the Context of "Regeneration"', *Journal of English and Germanic Philology*, 74 (1975), 351–60; repr. in Alan Rudrum (ed.), *Essential Articles for the Study of Henry Vaughan* (Hamden, Conn., 1987), 215–25 (217); page numbers in ensuing notes refer to the reprinted text.

[35] Nigel Yates, *Buildings, Faith and Worship: The Liturgical Arrangement of Anglican Churches 1600–1900* (Oxford, 1991), 17; Morrill, 'The Church in England, 1642–9', in Morrill (ed.), *Reactions to the Civil War*, 89–114; Claire Cross, 'The Church in England, 1646–1660' in G. E. Aylmer (ed.), *The Interregnum*, rev. edn. (1974); *Acts and Ordinances*, ed. Firth and Rait, i. 600–7. Welsh Anglican responses to Parliament's efforts are discussed by Philip Jenkins, 'Welsh Anglicans and the Interregnum', *Journal of the Historical Society of the Church in Wales*, 27 (1990), 51–9.

Vaughan's youth—episcopal government and an increasingly ceremonious liturgy—on a tide of reformation.[36] Already struck by his brother William's death and the king's execution, Henry was sunk further into despair by the evangelizing of these 'Welsh Saints': 'when he was writing the poems of *Silex Scintillans*, Vaughan had no way of knowing that there would be a Restoration of the Church in 1660, nor did he have much opportunity to know that in various parts of England and Wales Anglicanism successfully defied its Parliamentarian enemies'.[37]

Noting that Parliament ejected many Royalist ministers and left their churches closed until a suitable replacement could be found, Summers and Pebworth read 'Regeneration' as Vaughan's revelation that God and His church can be found in nature when church buildings were barred up. They saw its 'grove . . . Of stately height' as a natural temple where the presence of the Holy Spirit blows mysteriously, and drew attention to the allusion (in the penultimate stanza of 'Regeneration') to Christ's revelation that 'the wind bloweth where it listeth, and thou heareth the sound thereof, but canst not tell whence it cometh, and whither it goeth: so is everyone that is born of the Spirit'.[38] Thus Vaughan's pilgrim (they argued) learns that God's Spirit is ubiquitous, omnipresent and omnipotent, not restricted to buildings of stone and wood which bear the name of church. Jacob re-enters the story here, because one of God's promises during the patriarch's desert vision is 'I will be with thee, and will keep thee in all places whither thou goest' (Genesis 28: 15). John Quarles versified this moment in his *Divine Meditations* (1679), though stressing God's sustenance and protection, rather than His ubiquity:

> Thus saith the *Lord*, that takes delight to dwel
> Amongst his *Saints*, that formed *Israel*,
> Created *Jacob*, let thy sorrows flee
> Out of thy brest, I have redeemed thee:
> 'Twas I that made thy clouded visage shine,
> And called thee by my Name, for thou art mine.
> I will be with thee, when thy feet shall wade
> Thorow the waters; I will be thy aid.[39]

---

[36] Geraint H. Jenkins, *Protestant Dissenters in Wales, 1639–1689*, The Past in Perspective Series (Cardiff, 1992); Geoffrey F. Nuttall, *The Welsh Saints, 1640–1660 (Walter Cradock, Vavasor Powell, Morgan Llwyd)* (Cardiff, 1957).
[37] Summers and Pebworth, 'Vaughan's Temple', 217. [38] John 3: 8 (cited by *R*).
[39] John Quarles, *Divine Meditations upon Several Subjects* (1679), 69.

Summers's and Pebworth's suggestion is that Vaughan brings together God's promise to Jacob with the omnipresence of the Holy Spirit: He will be with Vaughan wherever he chooses to worship him.

The 'temple in nature' article seems to have prompted the much-needed effort of critics like Jonathan Post, Graeme Watson, Alan Rudrum and Chris Fitter to replace Vaughan's writing in closer historical contexts.[40] But although they correctly identified *Jacobs Bed* as the house of God, Summers and Pebworth overlooked evidence in Vaughan's other works which casts doubt on their conclusion that Vaughan found Bethel in nature. For one thing, they failed to explain why Vaughan should discourse reverently on church buildings and the correct way to behave when entering them in *The Mount of Olives*, his devotional work published only a year after 'Regeneration'. More importantly, though their argument rests on an autobiographical reading of the poem, they forget that Vaughan's conversion occurred around 1647–8, before the series of church closures began, and not in 1650, when 'Regeneration' was published.[41] It is doubtful that Vaughan was denied all access to 'the earthly church', as Pebworth and Summers believed. Since the 1960s, historians of early modern England have been suggesting that those who wished to continue using the Prayer Book during the Commonwealth found ways of doing so. Like Clare Cross, G. J. Cuming notes that 'there was a certain amount of clandestine use', and more recently John Morrill and Judith Maltby have argued that many churches begrudged purchasing the *Directory for Public Worship*, slowing down its dissemination and making it hard for Parliament to enforce reform.[42] Though ejections of ministers

[40] Post, *Henry Vaughan, passim*; Graeme J. Watson, 'The Temple in "The Night": Henry Vaughan and the Collapse of the Established Church', *Modern Philology*, 84 (1986), 144–67; Alan Rudrum, 'Henry Vaughan, the Liberation of the Creatures, and Seventeenth-Century English Calvinism', *Seventeenth Century*, 4 (1989), 33–54; Fitter, 'Henry Vaughan's Landscapes'.

[41] On Vaughan's conversion see *Life*, ch. 8; Davies, *Henry Vaughan*, 78–104.

[42] G. J. Cuming, *A History of Anglican Liturgy* (1969), 146. John Evelyn knew which chapels would administer communion according to the Anglican form (Morrill, 'The Church in England', 144). Covert Anglican activity in Vaughan's Oxford is brought to light by R. A. Beddard in 'Restoration Oxford and the Remaking of the Protestant Establishment', in Nicholas Tyacke (ed.), *The History of Oxford*, iv: *Seventeenth-Century Oxford* (Oxford, 1997), 803–62 (esp. 804–8). Some Anglican clergymen wrote alternative liturgies resembling the Book of Common Prayer: Robert Sanderson, *A Liturgy in Times of Rebellion*, in *Fragmentary Illustrations of the History of the Book of Common Prayer*, ed. W. K. Jacobson (1874), 1–40 (and see Isaak Walton, *The Life of Dr. Sanderson*, in *The Works of Robert Sanderson, D.D.*, 6 vols. (Oxford, 1844), vi. 312); 'An Anglican Family Worship Service of the Interregnum: A Cancelled Early Text and a New Edition of Owen Felltham's "A

had been occurring in Breconshire since 1645, Thomas Vaughan managed to keep his living at Llansantffraed until 1650, making it quite possible that Henry attended some form of illicit Anglican service until then, and almost certain that he was able to enter a church when he wrote 'Regeneration'.[43] Although *Jacobs Bed* is certainly a church, there is certainly no substantial historical evidence that Vaughan meant it to be a temple in nature, or that 'Regeneration' is primarily a lesson in divine ubiquity.

Quite the opposite, in fact. Far from the irrelevance to which Summers and Pebworth reduce it, place is *especially* sacred to 'Regeneration', which tacitly acknowledges a vein of seventeenth-century Anglican ecclesiology according to which *Jacobs Bed* was a particular illustration of how and why churches are especially holy places. Vaughan's narrator-pilgrim's sensations of delight are created, or at least effected, by the properties of the curious bed into which he has come; as he enters, a *new spring* washes over his senses, lively and vital with spiritual excitement, recalling and overpowering the delusional *stage and show* of his youth. Springtime in Vaughan is always associated with rebirth, most importantly Christ's Ascension and the apocalyptic Ascension of the elect;[44] and here it gives the pilgrim the new birth of regeneration:

> I entred, and once in
> (Amaz'd to see't,)
> Found all was chang'd, and a new spring
> Did all my senses greet.
>
> (ll. 37–40)

Note *once in*. Seasonal change hits the pilgrim's senses with an immediate and appreciable effect emanating from the very place itself. The transformation is not simply known, but immediately felt along the senses (intellectual, as well as physical), casting a glow of physical well-being which begins to explain the 'repose' the pilgrim found on reaching *Jacobs Bed*.[45]

Form of Prayer"', ed. Ted-Larry Pebworth, *English Literary Renaissance*, 16 (1986), 206–33; Horton Davies, *Worship and Theology in England from Andrewes to Baxter and Fox, 1603–1690* (Princeton, 1975), 357; Judith Maltby, *Prayer Book and People in Elizabethan and Early Stuart England* (Cambridge, 1998); Cross, 'The Church in England, 1646–60', in Aylmer (ed.), *The Interregnum*.

[43] *TV*, 7.

[44] I discuss 'Ascension-day', the locus of springtime purity in Vaughan's writing, in Chapter 6, 'Smiles of the Day-star'.

[45] Ross Garner reads 'all my senses' as a purely 'spirituall allegory' (Garner, *Henry Vaughan*, 60); see 'A prayer when thou art going into bed', where the night-time is for

Bethel, then, is less a signification of *any* place than a *special* place, a house of God where He especially dwells among His people and where His transforming power is strongest, bringing a new spring to those who, like the pilgrim, have seen through the false seasons of the world.

Whilst seventeenth-century Puritans grew increasingly less and less content to worship in church buildings, virtually all Anglicans believed that churches were holy, generating much ecclesiological debate concerning how, why, and to what extent. In 1620s sermons dedicating and consecrating churches, Jeremiah Dyke and Joseph Hall argued moderately that the place where God's people gather together is holy through 'testification of presence', that is 'where two or three are gathered together in my name, there am I in the midst of them' as Christ promised (Matthew 18: 20).[46] Modelling their dedication liturgies on Lancelot Andrewes's 1620 order for consecrating St Mary's, Southampton, Laudians in the 1630s developed the stronger view that churches possessed an actual holiness.[47] Unlike God's 'essentiall, originall, and primitive' holiness, this sanctity was 'accidentall and derivative', given 'in relation to the holy use, whereto it is assigned'; nevertheless, churches demanded the respect and reverence Christians afforded true holiness. Foulke Robarts's *Gods Holy House and Service* (1639), from which these terms come, is perhaps the fullest exposition of Laudian sacrality, whose roots lie in Hooker's comments on the dedication of churches in *Of the Laws of Ecclesiastical Polity* book V.[48]

'repose and refreshing' (*The Mount of Olives*, 152, l. 29) and my discussion of *wits* in Chapter 3, 'Fire to me'.

[46] Joseph Hall, *A Sermon Preached at the Happily-Restored and Reedified Chappell of the Right Honorable the Earle of Exceter in His House of S. Johns* (1624), 2; Jeremiah Dyke, *A Sermon Dedicatory, Preached at the Consecration of the Chappell of Epping in Essex, October 28, 1622* (1623). I am grateful to James Cannon here. Chapter 1 of his Ph.D. thesis 'The Poetry and Polemic of English Church Worship, *c.*1617–1640' (Cambridge, 1998) contains a full discussion of the spectrum of Laudian beliefs on sacrality.

[47] See Lancelot Andrewes, *The Form of Consecration of a Church* (1659) [*Wing* A3126], reprinted in *The Minor Works of Lancelot Andrewes* (Oxford, 1846). Laud himself acknowledged a debt to Andrewes's liturgy (Paul A. Welsby, *Lancelot Andrewes 1555–1626* (1958), 131).

[48] Foulke Robarts, *Gods Holy House and Service, According to the Primitive and Most Christian Forme Thereof* (1639), esp. 1–12; Richard Hooker, *Of the Laws of Ecclesiastical Polity, Book V* (1597), vol. ii of *The Folger Library Edition of the Works of Richard Hooker*, gen. ed. W. Speed Hill, Medieval and Renaissance Texts and Studies, 6 vols. (Binghamton, NY, 1977–93): XII (The Dedication of Churches), XIV (The Sumptuousness of Churches), XVI (The Special Holiness of Churches), cf. P. Panter, *De Non Temerandis Ecclesiis, Whereof the Name and Sacrednesse of Churches (against Those, Who in Contempt Do Call Them Steeple-Houses) Proposed by Way of Conference* (1650).

Like the sermons of Dyke and Sampson Price, John Donne's sermon on *The Feast of Dedication Celebrated at Lincolnes Inne* (1623) instances acts of dedication and consecration from the Old Testament, including Jacob's pouring of oil onto the pillow-pillar stone at Bethel: 'even in *Nature*, there was a consecration of holy places; *Jacob* in his journey, before the *Law*, consecrated even that stone, which he set up, in intention to build *God* a House there.'[49] The same point is made in Walter Balcanquall's 1633 work *The Honour of Christian Churches*, by Robarts, and in the first of Robert Shelford's *Five Pious and Learned Discourses* (1635).[50] Joseph Hall's gloss on Genesis 28 in his *A Plaine and Familiar Explication of the Old and New Testament* (1633) sees Bethel as the first church to be both sanctified and dedicated in the Reformed Anglican sense, paraphrasing Jacob's words to God in the more ecclesial language of *sanctification* and *dedication*:

How full of awe and reverend respect is this place, which God hath thus sanctified by his presence, having so familiarly manifested himselfe to me here, as men doe in their dwelling houses to their friends; this is no other than a representation of Gods spirituall house, his Church, by which we enter the glory of heaven . . . The place where I set up this stone shalbe dedicated to the worship and service of my God, where I will build an altar to his name.[51]

Hall remained distanced from Laudian ecclesiology, but he does not hesitate to see Jacob's desert oblation as a sort of church dedication.[52] Robarts is careful to point out that Jacob 'powred his oyle, not upon the ground; but upon the toppe of the stone, which he had set up on end for that purpose': hence Jacob's pillar became the first altar and Jacob a minister in the first church.[53]

[49] John Donne, *The Feast of Dedication, Celebrated at Lincolnes Inne in a Sermon There upon Ascension Day 1623*, repr. in *The Sermons of John Donne*, iv. 364–79 (372); Dyke, *Sermon Dedicatory*, 3–5; Sampson Price, *The Beauty of Holiness* (1618).

[50] Walter Balcanquall, *The Honour of Christian Churches; and the Necessitie of Frequenting of Divine Service and Publike Prayers in Them* (1633), 5–6; Robarts, *Gods Holy House and Service*, 5; Robert Shelford, *Five Pious and Learned Discourses* (Cambridge, 1635), 2–3.

[51] Joseph Hall, *A Plaine and Familiar Explication of All the Hard Texts of the Whole Divine Scripture of the Old and New Testament* (1633), 32.

[52] Anthony Milton notes that Hall's and Dyke's consecration sermons place an overwhelming emphasis on the importance of the Word preached in order to avoid suggesting Roman Catholic sacrality (*Catholic and Reformed: Roman and Protestant Churches in English Protestant Thought, 1600–40*, Cambridge Studies in Early Modern British History (Cambridge, 1995), 70).

[53] Robarts, *Gods Holy House and Service*, 5. Discussing this anointing, Augustine is

In contrast to the various degrees of reverence Anglicans paid to churches, most Puritans felt an increasing disdain for the concept of holy space, an emotion no doubt stirred up further by Laud's controversial beautifying of churches in the 1630s.[54] Parliament's 1645 Ordinance putting the *Directory for Public Worship* into practice asserted flatly that 'no place is capable of any holiness under pretence of whatsoever Dedication or Consecration', appalling conformists and demanding a drastic re-ordering of church furnishing across the country.[55] In Wales, some parts of which did not eradicate Catholic practices until the end of the sixteenth century, this new disrespect for churches (and its stronger, iconoclastic expression in the defacing and removal of church ornaments) came as an appalling shock.[56] The palpable holiness which infuses the holy grove of Bethel in Vaughan's 'Regeneration' belongs to an Anglican tradition of revering churches which became highly unacceptable to Puritans at precisely the time Vaughan turned to God. So although Summers and Pebworth got their dates slightly wrong, they were correct to feel that 'Regeneration' is infused with an Anglican response to the troubles of the church; Ruth Preston Lehmann's conclusion that *Jacobs Bed* is not 'a grove that resembles a church, but a church interpreted as a grove' gets the poem round the right way.[57] The simple fact that the *new spring* of grace which enters Vaughan's pilgrim soul bursts from the power of God's house reveals a profoundly Anglican mode of thought and signals Vaughan's conformity in his first avowedly Christian work.

The holiness of churches, then, featured strongly in Vaughan's understanding of his conversion experience; he must have been deeply trauma-

quick to defend Jacob against charges of worshipping an image; he interprets the pillar as Christ, and notes that Jacob's oil is not idolatrous, because Christ's name is derived from *chrism* (Augustine, *The City of God against the Pagans*, Loeb Classical Library, 7 vols. (New Haven, 1965), V, Bk. 16, ch. 38, 179).

[54] On Laud and the beauty of holiness, see Nicholas Tyacke, *Anti-Calvinists: The Rise of English Arminianism, c.1590–1640* (Oxford, 1987), 55, 194; Milton, *Catholic and Reformed*, 78–82, 315–16; Peter Lake, 'The Laudian Style: Order, Uniformity and the Pursuit of the Beauty of Holiness in the 1630s', 161–85 in Kenneth Fincham (ed.), *The Early Stuart Church*, Problems in Focus Series (Basingstoke, 1993).

[55] *Acts and Ordinances*, ed. Firth and Rait, i. 607.

[56] Yates, *Buildings*, 23; Geraint Jenkins, *The Foundations of Modern Wales, 1642–1780* (Oxford, 1987), 43–55; Watson, 'The Temple in "The Night"', 145.

[57] Ruth Preston Lehmann, 'Characteristic Imagery in the Poetry of Henry Vaughan', Ph.D. thesis (Wisconsin, 1942), 91; quoted by Garner, *Henry Vaughan*, 59. On *groves*, see Leah S. Marcus, *The Politics of Mirth: Jonson, Herrick, Milton, Marvell, and the Defense of the Old Holiday Pastimes* (Chicago, 1986), ch. 7, esp. 218–33 and P. W. Thomas, 'The Poisoned Grove', *Scintilla*, 1 (1997), 27–44 for other author contexts.

tized by the pattern of church closures across Wales in the early 1650s. *The Mount of Olives* (1652) reflects the complex situation of Welsh churches during the Propagation years, quoting repeatedly from Lamentations in its prayers 'In time of persecution and heresie' and 'In troubles occasioned by our enemies' to express sorrow and longing for the 'courts of the Lord'.[58] In a passage which speaks loudly to 'Regeneration', Vaughan's 'Admonitions how to carry thy self in the church' lament that:

These reverend and sacred buildings (however now vilified and shut up) have ever been, and amongst true Christians still are the solemne and publike places of meeting for Divine Worship: There the *flocks feed at noon-day*, there the great *Shepherd* and *Bishop* of their souls is *in the midst of them*, and where he is, that *Ground is holy*. (*V*, 147)

Foregrounding scriptural texts in italics, Vaughan's prose deftly weaves its defence of the idea behind *Jacobs Bed*, the idea that *ground is* holy; the allusion is to Exodus, where God instructs Moses to take off his shoes 'for the place whereon thou standest is holy ground' (Exodus 3: 5). Vaughan's complaint that churches are *vilified and shut up* relates to Parliament's campaign to eject undesirable Welsh ministers, a swift programme of expulsions which left dozens of parishes without a pastor and many churches shut up or unused.[59] Where an approved incumbent could be found, services would be conducted according to the Presbyterian rite of the Westminster Assembly's *Directory for Public Worship*; Anglicans could attend, but the much reduced liturgy would hardly have satisfied their desire for fit ceremony. The etymology of *vilified* witnesses the ecclesiological conflict between those, like Vaughan, for whom churches were Bethels, holy houses of God, and those whose belief that churches were incapable of holiness under any pretence whatsoever made church space *vilis*: worthless.

WITH JACOB: THE ELECT AND THE INVISIBLE CHURCH

Bethel was more than a *symbol* of Anglican church buildings for the poet of 'Regeneration'; it was a *type* of all churches. Since St Paul, Christian writers had interpreted Old Testament figures and objects as typological prefigurations or foreshadowings of Christ: Moses, for instance, was a

[58]   *V*, 166–7 alludes heavily to Lam. 1: 5 (esp. in ll. 22–7); cf. Ps. 84.

[59]   Jenkins, *Foundations*, 56; Alexander Griffith, *Mercurius Cambro-Britannicus; or, News from Wales* (1652), 7–9.

type because he led the chosen people out of bondage as Christ led them
to heaven; the ladder of Jacob's vision was a type because it bodied forth
how man could climb to heaven, even if that could only truly happen
through the Redemption; and to Augustine, Jacob's anointed pillar was a
type of Christ because Christ comes from the Greek *chrism*, anointed,
and He was the anointed of God.[60] Through such typological patterns,
the Old Testament was effectively reframed as a *partial* revelation of the
whole truth revealed by Christ's great entry into history, accommodating
old scriptures to a new religion and preserving Judaism as a kind of im-
mature version of Christianity.[61]

Vaughan was influenced by the Protestant typology that developed
from what Aquinas (systematizing what others had long practised) called
the *tropological*, or moral sense of scripture. Rather than reading the Old
Testament for types of Christ, this new typology read scriptural persons,
objects and events as types of the spiritual lives of individual believers and
events of the present day. To take an example based on Jacob's story in
Genesis 28, when Augustine taught that Jacob's pillar was a type of Christ,
he was seeing Jesus as the great fulfilment (the *antitype*) of a shadowy Old
Testament type. In contrast, when Vaughan read the same passage (in
writing 'Regeneration', for instance), he took Christian churches as his
antitype, and saw Bethel—a place made sacred by God and dedicated by
a holy man and therefore a church in all but name—as their shadowy
forerunner.[62] This new emphasis within typology was widespread in
seventeenth-century England, and features heavily in Vaughan's work.

---

[60] *The City of God*, Bk. 16. Ch. 38, 179.

[61] For standard accounts of typological writing and interpretation, I rely on Erich
Auerbach, *Mimesis: The Representation of Reality in Western Literature*, trans. Willard Trask
(Princeton, 1953), 63–6, 170–6; G. W. H. Lampe and K. J. Woollcombe, *Essays on Typology*
(1957); Jean Daniélou, *From Shadows to Reality: Studies in the Biblical Typology of the Fathers*,
trans. Wulston Hibberd (Westminster, Mass., 1960). On its uses in seventeenth-century
literature, see Murray Roston, *Biblical Drama in England from the Middle Ages to the
Present Day* (Evanston, Ill., 1960), 51–5, 69–77; William G. Madsen, *From Shadowy Types
to Truth: Studies in Milton's Symbolism* (New Haven, 1968), 1–52; Barbara K. Lewalski,
'*Samson Agonistes* and the "Tragedy" of the Apocalypse', *Publications of the Modern Language Association of America*, 85 (1970), 1050–62; Victor Harris, 'Allegory to Analogy in the
Interpretation of the Scriptures during the Middle Ages and the Renaissance', *Philological
Quarterly*, 45 (1966), 1–23; Earl Miner, *Literary Uses of Typology from the Late Middle Ages to
the Present* (Princeton, 1977); Paul J. Korshin *Typology in England 1650–1820* (Princeton,
1982), 3–38 and 44–58 on the years 1640–70.

[62] Protestant typology is discussed by Lewalski, 'Typology and Poetry', 42; Richard
Strier, *Love Known: Theology and Experience in George Herbert's Poetry* (Chicago, 1983), 152.

'Rules and Lessons', for instance, uses moral typology to draw another lesson from Jacob's story:

> Serve God before the world; let him not go
> Until thou hast a blessing, then resigne
> The whole unto him; and remember who
> Prevail'd by *wrestling* ere the *Sun* did *shine*.
> Pour *Oyle* upon the *stones*, weep for thy sin,
> Then journey on, and have an eie to heav'n.

(ll. 19–24)

Jacob's wrestling is a type of the Protestant's spiritual struggle with God as he or she grapples valiantly with God for a blessing (and, as Vaughan interprets this passage in *The Mount of Olives*, rises early to do so).[63] This sort of reading prevails, in Vaughan's writing, over the kind of typological reading which would attend to Christ as the antitype of the angel who wrestles with Jacob and blesses him afterward for continuing to struggle (Genesis 32: 24).

The poetry of Herbert and Vaughan was so strongly affected by tropological typology that it is worth digressing briefly, before unveiling Vaughan's typologies of Jacob in *The Mount of Olives*, to note the course of its influence on the liturgy and devotion of Reformed religion. Perhaps the biggest boost to this new typology came from the marked Protestant emphasis on personal, unmediated intercourse with God, an emphasis which underlay Calvin's influential view of life as an antitypical recapitulation of the struggles of David recorded in the Psalms, that 'Anatomy of all the Parts of the Soul'.[64] The Psalms became an important centre of typological consideration of the spiritual life in the sixteenth and seventeenth centuries: their liturgical use offered Protestants a reassuring sense of communal spiritual experience as antitypes of David, whilst their private form stressed the Reformed Christian's unmediated communication with God. One of George Herbert's great achievements in *The Temple* (1633) was to use the Psalms, read typologically, as a pattern of Christian struggles, as well as a model of Christian verse.[65] He made less original use

---

[63] 'God the Son appeared to him, and wrestled with him in the likeness of a man' (Joseph Hall, *A Plaine and Familiar Explication*, 34); cf. Calvin, *A Commentary upon Genesis*, 672. On early rising as a Christian duty, see Chapter 4, 'Holy, hourly'.

[64] Quoted by Strier, *Love Known*, 152.

[65] On Herbert's use of typology see Bloch, *Spelling the Word*, 127–46 and for his use of the Psalms 16–18, 23–6 and esp. 231–305; Lewalski, *Protestant Poetics*, 246–7, 300–4; Louis

of the Old Testament than Vaughan was to, but could work a typology with some flair: in 'Frailtie', for instance, the tower of Babel becomes a type of the individual Christian's pride, 'a Babel . . . | Commodious to conquer heav'n and thee | Planted in me' (ll. 22–4).

Vaughan was fond enough of 'Frailtie' to rework its images of rebellion and dust in 'Distraction' and *The Mount of Olives*, but he was far more influenced by Herbert's other, more complex typological poems like 'Aaron', 'Sion' and 'The Bunch of Grapes', all of which search Old Testament stories for typological truths about the present.[66] Stanza 2 of 'The Bunch of Grapes' explains:

> For as the Jews of old by Gods command
>   Travell'd, and saw no town:
> So now each Christian hath his journeys spann'd:
>   Their storie pennes and sets us down.
>   A single deed is small renown.
> Gods works are wide, and let in future times;
> His ancient justice overflows our crimes.
>
>   (ll. 8–14)

Here, the lives of the ancient patriarchs are seen as grand types of present-day Christian experience, a pattern for understanding the individual's spiritual struggles and also—since 'a single deed is small renown'—their place in the greater *shared* history of the chosen people. Like Calvin, Herbert's poem shows an awareness that 'it tends greatly to lighten grief to consider that . . . we are just called to engage in the same conflicts with which David and the other Holy patriarchs were exercised'.[67] This typological assurance of 'The Bunch of Grapes'—that Moses, Aaron and the Exodus belong to the reader's past as they do to the writer's—confirms community between Christian and pre-Christian, type and antitype, and bonds the people of God through their shared experience of *types* of conflict.[68]

Martz, *The Poetry of Meditation: A Study of English Religious Literature of the Seventeenth Century*, rev. edn. (New Haven, 1962), 273–82; Noel Kinnaman, 'Notes on the Psalms in Herbert's *The Temple*', *George Herbert Journal*, 4 (1981), 10–29.

[66] Noted by R. Compare Vaughan's 'If therefore the dust of this world chance to prick thine eyes, suffer it not to blinde them' (141, ll. 6–7), 'Come, and releive | And tame, and keepe downe with thy light | Dust that would rise, and dimme my sight' ('Distraction', ll. 28–30); Bloch, *Spelling the Word*, 21.

[67] Quoted by Lewalski, 'Typology and Poetry', 48.

[68] Bloch, *Spelling the Word*, 128.

The sharing and bonding of a Christian community returns me to Jacob, and to Vaughan's devotional manual *The Mount of Olives* (1652), a work written to succour and strengthen afflicted Anglicans during the Interregnum. In it, Vaughan thinks typologically to figure the great continuous community of ancient and modern Christians, typical and antitypical yet one faithful band of elect souls, through the figure of *Jacob*. His preface to the 'Peaceful, humble, and pious reader'—evidently, it becomes clear, a reader dismayed by the events of the 1640s—counsels against despair, comforting each faithful soul with an image of the whole company of the faithful: 'Think not that thou art alone upon this Hill, there is an innumerable company both before and behinde thee' (*V*, 141). His share in the isolation of Interregnum Anglicans draws from Vaughan this comforting and scriptural vision of a vast, invisible company of the faithful, a scene which gestures toward St Paul's revelation of the cloud of Christian witnesses (Hebrews 12) and that vast company of elect souls groaning under the altar seen by John in Revelation (chapter 6). With prayers and warnings strongly marked by his rebellious conformity, Vaughan implicitly identifies the persecuted and afflicted Anglicans of the Interregnum with these souls, and counsels them to be *with Jacob*:

When thou art to go from home, remember that thou art to come forth into the *World*, and to Converse with an Enemy . . . Wouldst thou with *Jacob* passe over these *Waters* with thy staffe onely, and in thy return become two bands? *Gen*. 32. 10. ('Admonitions when we prepare for any farre Journey', *V*, 146)

Thou that didst go out with *Jacob* from *Beer-she-ba* unto *Padan-aran*, guiding him in the *waste plaines*, and watching over him on his *Pillow of stones*, be not now farre from me. [Genesis 28] ('When we go from home', *V*, 146)

Put off thy shoes then, thy worldly and carnall affections, and when thou beginnest to enter in [to church], say with *Jacob*, *How dreadful is this place! sure this is none other then the house of God, and this is the gate of heaven!* [Genesis 28: 17] ('Admonitions how to carry thy self in the Church', *V*, 147)

To be *with Jacob* is to belong to the elect and to the true church. Vaughan's advice depends upon two Reformed readings of Genesis: first, the typological reading of Jacob and Esau as types of election and reprobation, a view strengthened in the sixteenth century by Calvin's thirteen sermons on the matter; the second, to which I will return shortly, is the identification of Jacob with the invisible church of the elect.[69] The story of Jacob

---

[69] Calvin, *Thirteene Sermons, Entreating of the Free Election of God in Jacob, and of*

and Esau is told by chapters 25–49 of Genesis, a book which Jews and Christians alike took to be the first of five written by Moses chronicling the history of the world from the Creation to his death. Though Moses was the first to set it down, many believed that all the patriarchs before him—Abel, Enoch, Noah, Abraham, Jacob and so on—had been made aware of this history by divine revelation.[70] In Genesis 27, Esau becomes angry and murderous when Jacob tricks their father Isaac into giving him the blessing due to the older brother. Rebekah, the boys' mother, is told by God to send Jacob away: 'Behold, thy brother Esau, as touching thee, doth comfort himself, purposing to kill thee. Now therefore, my son, obey my voice; and arise, flee thee to Laban my brother to Haran; And tarry with him a few days, until thy brother's fury turn away' (Genesis 27: 42–4). It is during this flight that Jacob dreams at Bethel and is told that he shall father a great race—his twelve sons became, of course, the twelve patriarchs of the Jews. The Old Testament prophet Malachi saw God's reversal of primogeniture as proof of His special love for the chosen people—'Was not Esau Jacob's brother, said the Lord, yet I loved Jacob, and I hated Esau' (Malachi 1: 2–3)—but for Paul it teaches the Christian truth that election does not depend on age or right: 'As it is written, Jacob have I loved, but Esau have I hated. What shall we say then? Is there unrighteousness with God? God forbid. For he saith to Moses, I will have mercy on whom I will have mercy' (Romans 9: 13–15). This, Calvin's proof-text, was all the more powerful for Paul's inter-scriptural quotation of God's absolute judgement of election and reprobation.

Since Jacob was a type of the elect, he was also a type of what Protestants came to think of as the true or 'invisible' church: that unknown company of predestined souls which throughout history had preserved the true faith through countless persecutions, schisms, and the greater corruptions of Rome. But because only God truly knows the identities of the elect, this true church was necessarily invisible on earth and its members indistinguishable from the reprobate, as part of the mixed, visible

---

Reprobation in Esau, trans. J. Field (1579); Egeon Askew, *Brotherly Reconcilement, Preached in Oxford* (Oxford, 1605).

[70] See Ainsworth, *Annotations upon Genesis*, sig. ***2ʳ; Patrides, 'Jacob's Ladder', 414; Calvin, *Commentary upon Genesis*, 17–18; The Wisdom of Solomon 7: 17–18. The Wisdom of Solomon, which Vaughan had certainly read before 1650, describes how God gave Solomon 'knowledge of the things that are, namely to know how the world was made, and the operation of the elements. The beginning, endings, and midst of the times' (Vaughan alludes to Wisd. 7: 27 in the phrase 'prophets and friends of God', in 'Regeneration', l. 32.)

church.[71] Calvin recognized that Jacob, the father of the Jewish race and therefore Christianity's spiritual patriarch, represented the origin of true believers in one man. So while Jewish opinion held that God renamed Jacob as 'Israel' ('a prince of God' or 'prevailing with God') at the moment of racial maturity,[72] Christians saw this moment as the time when 'the blessed [race] began to take form and subsistency of the body in *Jacob* and his numerous family, under the new name of *Israel*; none of his Children being rejected, as some of the others were'—that is, in Protestant ecclesiology, the beginning of the invisible church.[73] In his *Commentary upon Genesis*, Calvin wrote of Jacob that 'in the order of this historie this especially is to be noted, howe the Lorde defended his Churche in the person of one man'.[74]

Being *with Jacob* is more than just being *like* Jacob, then. The strong preposition implies that by holding fast to their faith, the loyal Anglicans of the 1650s will show that they are members of the invisible church who shall one day be *with* the whole band of Jacob, the 'innumerable company' of the elect. Although being *with Jacob* is not the same as being at *Jacobs Bed*, two of Vaughan's prayers overtly identify 1650s 'Jacobites' as those, like himself, loyal to the church of king and Prayer Book. His 'Admonitions' on entering a church suggest that those who are *with Jacob* will put off their shoes before treading holy ground, a strongly Anglican idea in the mid-seventeenth century, as I have suggested already. Vaughan's warning leaves little doubt about who is Jacob and who Esau, coupling an attack on the Propagation Act with this beautiful and *instructive* account of how the patriarchs yearned for God's houses:

Such reverence and religious affection hath in all ages been shew'd towards these places, that the holy men of God detain'd either by Captivity, or other necessary occasions, when they could not remedy the distance, yet to testifie their *desire or longing for the Courts of the Lord*, Psal. 84. they would always worship towards them. (*V*, 147)

---

[71] The nature of the church is discussed by Anthony Milton, *Catholic and Reformed*, 128–31, 296–307; see also his 'The Church of England, Rome, and the True Church: The Demise of a Jacobean Consensus', 187–210 in Fincham (ed.), *The Early Stuart Church*.

[72] See Gen. 32: 28, 35: 10 and Augustine, 'What consideration caused Jacob to be given also the surname of Israel', in *The City of God*, 183–5; a note on 182 points out that the accepted senses of 'Israel' were disseminated by Philo, followed by Eusebius and Jerome.

[73] Diodati, *Pious Annotations*, sig. A4ʳ.

[74] Calvin, *Commentary upon Genesis*, 593; cf. *OED*, church militant, *sb.*, 4a.

Furthermore, the 'Admonitions when we prepare for any farre Journey' advise all who would be *with Jacob* to 'become two bands', an allusion to Genesis chapter 33, where Jacob and his travelling companions come under threat from Esau's murderous attentions. To save at least half of them from destruction, Jacob divides his band into two, so that if one half perish by the fratricidal reprobate, the remnant will yet go on. Vaughan may be remembering the exiled court of Charles II here, split from the main band of Jacob in Britain. To them and to other distressed conformists he offers a fragile and expensive hope in this startling sacrificial image of those who will be *with Jacob*.

Placed towards the end of *Silex* (1655), 'Jacobs Pillow and Pillar' remembers Vaughan's earlier meditations and in tones more sadly resigned confirms that Jacob's sufferings are the same, not merely analogically but *typologically*, as those of Vaughan and true Christians in the Interregnum. Though only a handful of those faithful to the Church of England actually went into exile in the 1640s, the languishing faithful who remained felt sharply the pain of *internal exile*, of being 'strangers and pilgrims' in their own land, and that suffering bridged the centuries separating them from their scriptural forebears. For Henry Vaughan, it brought a sense of commonality with the patriarch whose story penned that of his fellow 'Jacobites':

> blessed *Jacob* . . . thy sad distress
> Was just the same with ours, and nothing less;
> For thou a brother, and blood-thirsty too
> Didst flye, whose children wrought thy childrens wo.
>
> ('Jacobs Pillow, and Pillar', ll. 41–4)

Vaughan's unsteady but haunting poem begins with Jacob's desert church at Bethel—'I see the Temple in thy Pillar rear'd'—but quickly turns to the calamities of the present, neglecting the pillar until later in the poem (ll. 35–6) and not mentioning Jacob again until later still (after l. 41; the poem has fifty-four lines). Their return is delayed while Vaughan reveals what has happened to Britain and British religion in the 1650s by way of a series of allusions to Jacob's story in all its Reformed interpretations.

Like Herbert's 'The Church Militant', and Vaughan's earlier poems 'Mans fall, and Recovery' and 'Corruption', 'Jacob's Pillow and Pillar' operates on a cosmic time scale, spanning creation from religion's earliest stirrings until the uncertainties of the here-and-now, as it shapes a story about the past which can help understand the present. It opens with a swell of prophetic grandeur as Vaughan grafts Jacob's vision at Bethel onto his humbler scripture uses:

> I see the Temple in thy Pillar rear'd,
> And that dread glory, which thy children fear'd,
> In milde, clear visions, without a frown,
> Unto thy solitary self is shown.
> 'Tis number makes a Schism: throngs are rude,
> And God himself dyed by the multitude.
> This made him put on clouds, and fire and smoke,
> Hence he in thunder to thy Off-spring spoke;
> The small, still voice, at some low Cottage knocks,
> But a strong wind must break thy lofty rocks.
>
> (ll. 1–10)

At first it appears Vaughan has had a vision of Jacob's pillar as a type of *the* Temple—the first Temple at Jerusalem where Jehovah was worshipped 'with blood of beasts, and fat', as the poem later describes (l. 26). But the nesting of visions one within the other reminds the reader that Vaughan is seeing Jacob through the pages of his bible, cancelling any pretension to prophetic power of his own and reducing the visionary to the scriptural. Moreover, Vaughan's vision is more complex than it first appears:

> 'Tis number makes a Schism: throngs are rude,
> And God himself dyed by the multitude.

In his scriptural vision, Vaughan soberly remembers that the chief priest and elders of the Temple persuaded the 'multitude'—the very word used in Matthew 27: 20—to choose Barabas, rather than Jesus. Clearly Jacob's solitary pillar is not like this Temple, or its murderous crowd of worshippers.

Vaughan's second verse-paragraph narrates religion's progress from childhood to adolescence:

> The first true worship of the worlds great King
> From private and selected hearts did spring,
> But he most willing to save all mankinde,
> Inlarg'd that light, and to the bad was kinde.
> Hence Catholick or Universal came
> A most fair notion, but a very name.
>
> (ll. 11–16)

The alliteration and six stresses of Vaughan's opening line trumpet the seriousness of arguing that the Catholick or Universal church—the 'holy Catholique church' is the name for the earthly church of all believers in the Apostles' Creed[75]—has become no more than *a very name*. Five years before, in such poems as 'Faith' and 'The Law, and the Gospel', Vaughan had joyfully celebrated God's ancient widening of the 'private familie' of Judaism into the 'open house' of Christian churches ('Faith', l. 8). Now, in 1655, 'Jacobs Pillow, and Pillar' finds mankind condemned for ingratitude. Where 'Faith' rejoiced at the expansion of religion, 'Jacobs Pillow' sees even the initial change from Genesis to Exodus, from a time of solitary individuals to the time of Law, as a fatal widening of the spiritual franchise.

The hatred of mobs, crowds and multitudes evident in *Olor Iscanus* returns in 'Jacob's Pillow' to condemn the ignorance and pretended sanctity of mankind, offered life but returning only sullen ingratitude:

> Man slights his Maker, when familiar grown,
> And sets up laws, to pull his honor down.

> (ll. 19–20)

Accusing the law-giving Pharisees of Christ's day and of his own, Vaughan reveals a profound change of heart and a different focus for his hope. In 'Regeneration', *Jacobs Bed* was still a church; in *The Mount of Olives* it was where all true worshippers desired to worship and towards which they turned when absent or afflicted. In 'Jacobs Pillow, and Pillar', blaming the decay of religion on the ineluctable corruption of man, Vaughan sadly and defiantly concludes that *Jacobs Bed* has returned to the human heart, its primitive home in times before temples, churches and the expansion of faith:

> he foretold the place,
> And form to serve him in, should be true grace
> And the meek heart, not in a Mount, nor at
> *Jerusalem*, with blood of beasts, and fat.
> A heart is that dread place, that awful Cell,
> That secret Ark, where the milde Dove doth dwell
> When the proud waters rage: when Heathens rule
> By Gods permission, and man turns a Mule.
> .   .   .   .
> Thus is the solemn temple sunk agen

[75] *BCP*, 354.

Into a Pillar, and conceal'd from men.
And glory be to his eternal Name!
Who is contented, that this holy flame
Shall lodge in such a narrow pit, till he
With his strong arm turns our captivity.

(ll. 23–30, 35–40)

'Regeneration' was not, *pace* Summers and Pebworth, Vaughan's farewell to church worship; but 'Jacobs Pillow and Pillar' is. Since 'rule' is 'rage', religion has entered a new phase in which true worship will again be solitary and private like Christ's night-time prayers on Mount Olivet, or like the piety of Isaac, Ishmael and Elijah, all of whose devotions contribute to the prayers of Vaughan's *The Mount of Olives; or, Solitary Devotions* (1652).

'Jacobs Pillow, and Pillar' paints a picture of the 1650s as a *retrograde* stage in the history of religion rather than the bright new age of purified worship claimed by Puritans. Passionate and serious in defence of its cataclysmic vision, the poem is also a painfully sardonic comment on the Puritan belief that their style of worship—derived, in theory, entirely from the bible and the practice of the Apostles—was returning Christianity to its roots, purified in doctrine and discipline. This was the belief of John Cotton, who urged his congregation in Boston, Lincolnshire, in the 1620s to *live ancient lives*:

whatever comes from God . . . is always new, and never waxeth old, and as it is new, so it is always old, . . . All errors . . . are aberrations from the first good estate. . . . [In sum], *live ancient lives*, your obedience must be swayed by an old rule, walk in the old way.[76]

Dissenters like Cotton idealized the age of the Apostles—one reason why it pleased the Welsh Saints to be identified with them[77]—and decried the Fathers as the first corrupters of pure religion. Though Vaughan, too, looked back to a 'blessed', 'golden' or 'white' age of biblical times, seeing the patriarchs' days as a mythical 'strong time' in poems like 'Religion' and 'Corruption',[78] his conclusions are like a negative image of his ene-

---

[76] Quoted by Theodore Dwight Bozeman, *To Live Ancient Lives: The Primitivist Dimension in Puritanism* (Chapel Hill, NC, 1988), 14, 11.

[77] Discussed in Chapter 5, ''Tis a sad land'.

[78] All these adjectives are Vaughan's: see 'Begging [II]', l. 11 (and cf. 'Righteousness', l. 1 and 'The Shepheards', l. 9); 'The Search', l. 24; *The Consolation of Philosophy*, II. v (in *Olor Iscanus*), l. 1.

mies'. Motivated not by a belief in the possibility of swift reformation, but by a sorrowful recognition that the foundations of religion are shifting as mankind becomes ever more corrupt, Vaughan identified himself and his church with the solitary typological figure of Jacob, whose struggle to survive in the face of a fratricidal brother forced him into the wandering of exile. The closing accent of 'Jacobs Pillow' is strongly typological. Though Vaughan began the poem with his own vision ('I see the Temple'), the concluding volley of plural pronouns makes it clear that his concern is for the collected band of true Christians—all those who are *with Jacob*. It is their unhappy state which Vaughan typifies through the wanderings of the patriarch:

> blessed *Jacob*, . . . thy sad distress
> Was just the same with *ours*, and nothing less;
> For thou a brother, and blood-thirsty too
> Didst flye, whose children wrought thy childrens wo:
> Yet thou in all thy solitude and grief,
> On stones didst sleep and found'st but cold relief;
> Thou from the Day-star a long way didst stand
> And all that distance was Law and command.
> But *we* a healing Sun by day and night,
> Have *our* sure Guardian, and *our* leading light;
> What thou didst hope for and believe, *we* finde
> And feel a friend most ready, sure and kinde.
> Thy pillow was but type and shade at best,
> But *we* the substance have, and on him rest.

('Jacobs Pillow, and Pillar', ll. 41–54, my emphasis)

Those who are *with Jacob* must inevitably experience the same distress as the patriarch; but as antitypes, they 'finde | And feel' Christ's comforting presence as the pillow of true rest and the pillar of faith. Vaughan's faith, already strong through uncertainty, is marvellously reaffirmed across the line ending between 'finde' and 'feel' in the penultimate couplet above: a temporary uncertainty after the unpunctuated 'finde' (it is not yet clear *what* has been found, nor, given the poem's earlier despondency, that it has not been lost again) is resolved reassuringly in the alliterative *feel*, which suggests the almost physical comfort Vaughan took from the great friend Jacob believed in, and his spiritual descendants know as their father and saviour.

In retrospect, some noises of a return to the purity of *solitary* worship can be heard in Vaughan's earlier poems. Dissatisfaction with the vices and false piety of his age blooms angrily in 'Corruption', where Vaughan remembers that in the patriarchs' day mankind

> Was not all stone, and Earth,
> He shin'd a little, and by those weak Rays
> Had some glimpse of his birth.
>
> (ll. 2–4)

In 'Religion' Vaughan descants on mankind's further fall from God, taking his inspiration from Herbert's 'Decay', where the Old Testament figures have an enviable familiarity with God and easy access to His presence. Though the patriarchs' time was not perfect or immaculate, yet it could seem so, as when Jacob's sons

> In those calme, golden Evenings lay
> Watring their flocks, and having spent
> Those white dayes, drove home to the Tent
> Their *well-fleec'd* traine.
>
> ('The Search', ll. 24–7)

But this was, in Samuel Johnson's great phrase, an 'age that melts with unperceived decay'; for, as Cranmer wrote in the preface to both 1549 and 1552 Books of Common Prayer: 'there was never any thing by the wit of man so well devized, or so sure established, which in continuance of time hath not been corrupted'.[79] Like the child of 'The Retreate' and 'Childehood', Jacob's sons matured into depravity, losing their early innocence as 'weeping virtue parts with man' ('Childe-hood', l. 32). Vaughan can regain neither childhood nor the purity of the ancients, and unlike those who dreamed of a new Apostolic age, he counts the cost of failed attempts at so doing in the losses and scars of civil disorder, violence and church schism.

Viewed retrospectively, Vaughan's only patriarchal meditation in *Silex* (1650) begins to glimmer with the light of solitary holiness. '*Isaacs* Marriage', a serious, witty and curiously prim meditation on the nuptials of Jacob's father placed early in *Silex Scintillans* (1650), shows signs that Vaughan's thoughts were already moving toward the awful conclusions of 'Jacobs Pillow, and Pillar' when he prepared his first book of Christian poems. Though critics have tended to ignore '*Isaacs* Marriage', it is the

---

[79] Samuel Johnson, 'The Vanity of Human Wishes', l. 293, in *Samuel Johnson*, ed. Donald M. Greene, Oxford Authors Series (Oxford, 1984); Cranmer from the 1549 version (*BCP*, 321); the 1552 version is substantially the same.

only text which Vaughan decided to revise for the 1655 edition of *Silex*, suggesting that he continued to value and want to perfect it.[80] Its treatment of Isaac's story is certainly unusual. As a child sacrifice, Isaac appears—as a property, so to speak—in many unexceptional seventeenth-century poems about Abraham's faith;[81] but for the young Henry Vaughan, not yet 30 when *Silex Scintillans* was printed in 1650, Isaac's early manhood proved more interesting than his childhood.

'*Isaacs* Marriage' begins from the scene in Genesis 24: 63: Isaac goes out to pray in a field and sees the arrival of his wife Rebekah. Through this act of piety Vaughan reveals the holiness of the patriarchs, decries modern sophistication in a celebration of the ancient purity of the wedding, and praises the 'simplicity' of Rebekah.[82] He ends with a moving coda celebrating the *patriarchal* succession of spirit from Abraham to Isaac:

> Thus soar'd thy soul, who (though young,) didst inherit
> Together with his bloud, thy fathers spirit,
> Whose active zeal, and tried faith were to thee
> Familiar ever since thy Infancie.
> Others were tym'd, and train'd up to't but thou
> Diddst thy swift yeers in piety out-grow,
> Age made them rev'rend, and a snowie head,
> But thou wert so, e're time his snow could shed;
> Then, who would truly limne thee out, must paint
> First, a *young Patriarch*, then a *marri'd Saint*.
>
> (ll. 63–72)

Nicely inverting Donne's 'Goe, and catche a falling starre', where 'age [will] snow white haires on thee' by the time 'a woman true, and faire' can be found, Vaughan takes the opportunity of celebrating the conjunction of such a woman with Isaac's conspicuous lack of grey hairs.[83] Elsewhere, Vaughan calls the patriarchs 'the youthful world's grey fathers in a knot',

---

[80] The revisions, essentially refinements, are noted by *R*, 541. One change, 'day' for 'dayes' in line 18, seems to be a printer's error and is amended in *V*.

[81] Compare Francis Quarles, 'On Abraham', No. 48 in *Divine Fancies Digested into Epigrammes, Meditations, and Observations* (1632), or No. 61 'On the Sabboth', where Isaac is treated as a *type* of sacrifice; and Alexander Ross, *Three Decads of Divine Meditations* (1630), decad I.V 'Isaac Offered Up'.

[82] A more commonplace moralizing of Isaac and Rebekah's marriage is given in J. P., *Oeconimica Sacra; or, A Paranaetical Discourse of Marriage: Together with Some Particular Remarks on the Marriage of Isaac and Rebecca* (1685).

[83] 'Song', ll. 1, 13, 18 (in *Poems*).

and youth in this poem is also meant to suggest the pre-Christian world, unaware of the full glory of the gospel, but blessed with the proximate presences of God and his angels.[84] Vaughan's language here is steeped in that of the epistle to the Hebrews: Isaac has *inherited* his father's spirit whose faith was *tried* when God demanded Isaac as a sacrifice. In particular, he recalls two well-known texts: 'Be not slothful, but followers of them who through faith and patience *inherit* the promises' (6: 12); and 'By faith Abraham, when he was *tried*, offered up Isaac' (11: 17). Punning on 'familiar', Vaughan remembers that Isaac has inherited his father's piety by the line of blood, and also quietly acknowledges that Isaac had been *familiar* with faith since the time it led Abraham to offer his childhood blood.

A pious twenty-something when he wrote '*Isaacs* Marriage', Vaughan seems to have felt more familiar with the 'white days' of the patriarchs than with his own time. His words deride the '*Antick* crowd | Of young, gay swearers, with their needlesse, lowd | Retinue' who make merry at weddings, preferring, with Isaac, to meditate in solitude (ll. 21–3); there is a similar irritation with fashionable crews in Vaughan's '*To* Lysimachus, *the Author being with him in* London', published in *Thalia Rediviva* (1678), in which Vaughan views with obvious distaste the 'trim'd *Gallants*' and 'Fops' with their 'ill-got, ill-giv'n praise' (ll. 3, 12, 41). '*Isaacs* Marriage' is remarkable for a strange coincidence of Vaughan the young poet, and his older, greyer counterpart; it is an uncomfortable maturity which, to his credit, Vaughan shows every sign of recognizing in a series of tortuously ingenious ironies. 'Praying!' the poem begins,

> Praying! and to be married? It was rare,
> But now 'tis monstrous; and that pious care
> Though of our selves, is so much out of date,
> That to renew't were to degenerate.

('*Isaacs* Marriage', ll. 1–4)

The young man who wrote these lines felt out of date before he had reached 30. Even in the white days of Isaac it was *rare* to pray before a marriage; now it is not just unusual but verging on the unnatural to pray at all, indeed, it is *monstrous*. The same sense of ironic deformity produces the straight-faced, strait-laced and wonderfully perverse use of *degenerate* to mean changing from a normal type, shorn of its common sense of

---

[84] See 'The Rain-bow', l. 6.

debasement. Now it is Isaac, and Vaughan himself, who are the monsters, 'degenerating from bad to better'.[85]

THEN JOURNEY ON

That Vaughan remembers Isaac's pre-nuptial prayers as part of his 'Admonitions when we prepare for any farre Journey' in *The Mount of Olives* neatly suggests how important the patriarchs' solitary travels—and, indeed, their *travails*—were in shaping Vaughan's sense of being *with Jacob* in the 1650s. Yet Isaac's inclusion is initially puzzling. The 'Admonitions' remember him just after they advise the Anglican reader to be *with Jacob*, proposing Isaac's solitary prayer as a word for travellers under way: 'Nor must thou pray only at thy setting forth, but all the way, and at all times; Thus *Eliezer* prayed at the Well, *Isaac* in the field, and *Elias* (in his journey to *Mount Horeb*) under a *Juniper* tree in the Wildernesse' (*V*, 146). Isaac's inclusion here certainly appears a little incongruous, since his prayer was not part of an epic journey through the wilderness like those of Eliezer, Elijah, Abraham or Jacob. Indeed, Isaac was not much of a traveller at all: he was *prevented* from fetching himself a wife by the design of God, who instructs Abraham to send his oldest servant, Eliezer, on this mission. Artists of the early modern period neglected the eventual wedding of Isaac and Rebekah in favour of Eliezer's long journey, notably (the scene Vaughan remembers in the 'Admonitions') the moment when he meets Rebekah by a well. Claude Lorrain portrayed Isaac's marriage in 1648, Van den Eeckhout in 1665, but there are *twenty* pictures of Rebekah at the well surviving from this period, including works by Poussin, Bourdon and Francken the younger. Vaughan's closing comment that the artist who would truly 'limne out' Isaac must picture 'a young Patriarch then a married Saint' could hardly be more academic, since artists showed little or no interest in Isaac the bridegroom. They drew him as a child, being led to sacrifice by his father, and as an old man, blessing his son Jacob. But the groom's piety did not touch the artistic imagination like Rebekah's purity. She remained popular in the eighteenth century, from which time eighteen Rebekahs survive, but not a single picture of her spouse.[86]

[85]   *R*, 451, aptly notes *OED* degenerate, *v.* 3 'to show an alteration *from* a normal type' and *OED*'s citation from Gerarde's 1597 *Herbal*, 'It is altered . . . into Wheate it self, as degenerating from bad to better' (I. xlii. 62).

[86]   Details from the finding lists of *The World's Master Paintings: From the Early Renaissance to the Present Day*, compiled by Christopher Wright (1992); A. Pigler, *Barockthemen:*

Ultimately, though, Vaughan's memory of Isaac in the 'Admonitions when we prepare for any farre Journey' makes a good deal of dramatic sense. For as well as the patriarchs' travelling, it was their *solitude in the wilderness* which spoke to Vaughan, and from which he derived his sense of solitary internal exile. Seen in this light, Isaac is another type of the new 'patriarchal' style of worship Vaughan describes in 'Jacobs Pillow, and Pillar'; his withdrawal to a field alone figures the true Christian's need to wander apart from the crowd, to be alone with God and to sanctify those great parts of life—be it marriage or everyday prayers—which the age derides. Remembering the travails of the patriarchs' ancient 'selected hearts', Vaughan saw that the solitary worshippers of his day were also travelling hearts, forced out of their churches and homes into various wildernesses: exile from the country for some, including the patriarch Charles II; for the majority, internal exile from position, power, and the house of God. The suffering of the patriarchs returns me to the story of Jacob, whose flight from his brother Esau and long journey to Mesopatamia on foot was often seen by Renaissance commentators on Genesis (such as David Pareus and the Jesuit Pererius) as the first in a series of the 'sufferings of Jacob'; others included the death of Rachel and the sale of Joseph, his son.[87] To Vaughan, who also saw Jacob as a type of the invisible church, the patriarch's flight from Esau was thus a powerful type of the Church of England's situation in the 1650s; the more so, indeed, because of a prophecy from Revelation, extremely well known and influential in Protestant eschatology, in which a mysterious woman—conventionally understood as the church—flees into the wilderness to escape Satan:

And there appeared a great wonder in heaven; a woman clothed with the sun, and the moon under her feet, and upon her head a crown of twelve stars . . . And the woman fled into the wilderness, where she hath a place prepared of God, that they should feed her there a thousand two hundred and threescore days. (Revelation 12: 1, 6)

The prophecy has obvious similarities to the story of Jacob as it is read, typologically, by 'Jacobs Pillow, and Pillar' and by the travel prayers of *The*

Eine Auswahl von Verzeichnissen zur Ikonographie des 17. und 18. Jahrhunderts, 3 vols. (Budapest, 1974), i. 51–6.

[87] David Pareus, *In Genesin Moisis Commentarius* (1609; Geneva, 1614), cols. 2145–6; Benedictus Pererius, *Commentariorum et Disputationum in Genesin* (1589–98; Cologne, 1601), 1334; quoted by Williams, *Common Expositor,* 238–9.

Mount of Olives.[88] In these works, Jacob's travails become a prophetic type of the 1650s, revealing the inevitable persecution of the faithful in a new age of solitary worship. The Civil War and its consequences have driven a wedge between the desire of poems like Herbert's 'Decay', which admires and yearns after the age of the patriarchs, and Vaughan's sad acceptance that 'mad man I Sits down and freezeth on', complacent in corruption ('Corruption', ll. 29–30). The personal religion of the ancients, once desired with all Vaughan's heart in 'Religion' and 'Corruption', is now forced upon him in darker circumstances: Jacob's pillar has 'shrunk' back into the human heart, hardly an auspicious verb to use of the indwelling of God, and one which counts the horrible cost of the amassed sins which have forced God's hand.

Though he expressed his sense of the church's persecution through the patriarchs' travels, Vaughan was probably the worst-travelled poet of the seventeenth century. John Donne had sailed to Cadiz and the Azores as a young man, Milton had embarked on a continental tour and Andrew Marvell, Vaughan's contemporary, spent five years in Europe. In contrast, Vaughan spent his youth on the losing side of Royalist armies in the Welsh marches, followed by several years laid up with severe illness and whatever books he could obtain from his friends.[89] Given that he spent only four of his seventy-four years outside Wales, it is ironic that journeying and travel were a central metaphor in Vaughan's Christian writing. In an age of rapidly expanding communications, when friends and strangers alike greeted each other with the question 'do you have the news?', Vaughan stayed at home, aloof and disdainful, a spirit too refined for the times.[90] He must have read newsbooks, but is condescending about the importance of current events. His rather arch note 'To all ingenious lovers

[88]   The Protestant apocalyptic tradition surrounding Rev. 12: 6 is discussed by Richard Bauckham, *Tudor Apocalypse* (Abingdon, 1978), 119–21 and Milton, 'The Church of England', 190.

[89]   John Carey, *John Donne: Life, Mind and Art* (1981), 8–9, 50–3; William Riley Parker, *Milton: A Biography*, 2nd edn., rev. and ed. Gordon Campbell, 2 vols. (Oxford, 1996), 169–82; Pierre Legouis, *Andrew Marvell: Poet, Puritan, Patriot*, 2nd edn. (Oxford, 1968), 11–12; *Life*, ch. 4. On Vaughan's literary circles see Eluned Brown, ' "Learned friend and loyal fellow-prisoner": Thomas Powell and Welsh Royalists', *National Library of Wales Journal* 18 (1973–4), 374–81 and Alan Rudrum, 'Resistance, Collaboration and Silence: Henry Vaughan and Breconshire Royalism', 102–18 in Claude J. Summers and Ted-Larry Pebworth (eds.), *The English Civil Wars in the Literary Imagination* (Columbia, Mo., 1999).

[90]   Charles Carlton, *Going to the Wars: The Experience of the English Civil Wars, 1638–1651* (1992), 230.

of poesy' in *Poems, with the Tenth Satire of Juvenal English'd* (1646), participates in a gloomy Royalist attempt to rise above the troubled hills of England:

To you alone, whose more refined *Spirits* out-wing these dull Times, and soare above the drudgerie of durty *Intelligence*, have I made sacred these *Fancies*. I know the yeares, and what course entertainment they affoord *Poetry*. If any shall question that *Courage* that durst send me abroad so late, and revell it thus in the *Dregs* of an Age, they have my silence . . . My more calm *Ambition*, amidst the common noise, hath thus exposed me to the World . . . —It is for you only that I have adventured thus far, and invaded the Presse with *Verse*; to whose more noble *Indulgence*, I shall now leave it; and so am gone. (*V*, 2)

Gone back home, he might have said. Vaughan is inordinately careful here to excuse his stepping out of doors into the mud and mess of 'durty *Intelligence*', taking time to explain that he shares his readers' preference for staying at home, but has '*exposed*' himself for their benefit. Fear of the 'abroad' became a constant thread in his work, outliving his efforts to imp Royalist wings in *Poems* (1646). He included translations of Ovid's *Epistulae ex Ponto* in *Olor Iscanus* (1651) to express his sense of separation from the bright future as a lawyer and gentleman poet which he may once have foreseen for himself in England:

> 'Twas Fortune threw me hither, where I now
> Rude *Getes* and *Thrace* see, with the snowie brow
> Of Cloudie *Aemus*, and if she decree
> Her sportive pilgrims *last bed* here must be
> I am content; nay more, she cannot doe
> That Act which I would not consent unto.
>
> (ll. 25–30)

Rendering the poet as Fortune's pilgrim, a metaphor not in Ovid's original (which speaks only of the poet coming *ad extremum*), these lines anticipate the typological travels of the patriarchs Vaughan uses so skilfully in *Silex Scintillans* and *The Mount of Olives*. Here, though, the idea that the poet is on a pilgrimage to the holy places of Fortune only increases the bitterness of the stoic pill the poem must try to swallow.

Vaughan's own forced journey back to Wales drew him to the first of Jacob's many sufferings: the long, hard journey on foot to Mesopotamia undertaken to escape Esau's rage. Disabled by sickness for much of the early 1650s, Vaughan's travelling was spiritual rather than pedestrian, but his 'Jacobite' poetry remembers true Christians and Royalists whose journeys were wearisome on the feet as well as the spirits. Most importantly, of course, it remembers the young patriarch himself. On 1 January 1651, Charles Stuart, forced to flee to France for most of the 1640s, returned to Scone to be crowned King of Scotland. There is tantalizing evidence that Royalists may have connected him with the suffering Jacob. Did Vaughan know, for instance, the use of Jacob's story in *A Forme of Prayer Used in the King's Chappel upon Tuesdayes in These Times of Trouble and Distresse* published at The Hague in 1650? Tuesday services had been special to the Stuarts since 1606, when James I moved the practice of midweek sermons a day forward from Wednesday to commemorate his escape from the Gunpowder Plot.[91] The 1650 form used in Charles's chapel was an Anglican-style office for Morning and Evening Prayer which substituted Psalms and alternative readings for the Prayer Book's prescribed texts. The Morning Prayer lessons are both Old Testament readings. The second is Jehosaphat's appeal to God for help against the Ammonites, told in 2 Chronicles 20, which ends suggestively with the appointing of singers 'that should praise the beauty of holiness, as they went out before the army, and to say, Praise the Lord, for his mercy endureth for ever' (2 Chronicles 20: 21). The first reading is Jacob's sleep at Bethel, his divine vision and morning consecration ceremony.[92] Was there a Royalist connection between the exiled king and the travelling patriarch?

A stronger and indeed stranger connection between Jacob's stony desert pillow and the British monarchy suggests that there was, and that Vaughan's literary uses of Jacob float on a surface of loyalist associations invisible to the modern eye. When Charles was crowned at Scone in 1651, he could not sit on the famous Stone of Destiny which had once been used for all Scottish coronations because (now ironically) it had been taken to Westminster in 1297 by Edward I and used thereafter for English coronations. A web of legend surrounds the origin and power of the stone, but all myths begin by identifying it as the same one on which Jacob slept at Bethel. Its subsequent provenance makes a good story:

---

[91] James's commemorations of the Gunpowder Plot are discussed in Hugh Ross Williamson, *The Gunpowder Plot* (1951), 205–7. Parliament reassembled in 1606 on a Tuesday (21 Jan.) and the king ordered that the escape be remembered 'generally in the realm where sermons be on weekdays that the same might be transferred to a Tuesday, that a universal Thanksgiving might be on that day for this great work of God' (Lake to Salisbury, 27 Nov. 1605, Hatfield House MS, xvii, 516, quoted by Williamson, *Gunpowder Plot*, 207). I am grateful to Nicholas Cranfield for discussions of Tuesday worship.

[92] *A Forme of Prayer Used in the King's Chappel upon Tuesdayes in These Times of Trouble and Distresse*, 2nd edn. (1650; first published 1649), 10.

It was conveyed to Egypt, and after some marvellous wanderings partly conducted by the prophet Jeremiah, it reached Spain and Ireland, where it acquired the name of the 'Fatal Stone,' and was used as the coronation seat of kings in that country; . . . it subsequently reached the island of Iona, where it was the deathbed of Saint Columba; from thence it was brought to the mainland of Scotland, and was deposited for safety in Dunstaffnage Castle in Argyllshire, and was used there as the coronation seat of Scottish kings; then it was removed to the abbey of Scone, near Perth, by King Kenneth in the year 850, who caused it to be enclosed in a wooden chair.[93]

The legend was narrated by Holinshed and witnessed in Vaughan's day, albeit somewhat scornfully, by the account of James's coronation in Arthur Wilson's generally hostile *The History of Great Britain, Being the Life and Reign of King James the First* (1653): 'Which Stone some old *Sawes* deliver to be the same that *Jacob* rested his head on'.[94]

A further twist in this story of the stone is the 1651 coronation sermon delivered by Scotland's Moderator of the General Assembly Robert Douglas, which concerned the crowning of King Joash.[95] In 2 Kings 11, the Jewish boy-king is anointed in the Temple surrounded by Athaliah's troops: 'And when she looked, behold, the king stood by a pillar, *as the manner was*, and the princes and the trumpeters by the king' (11: 14). The Temple pillar was a kind of platform at the entrance to the Temple, the place where Josiah was later to make his covenant with the Lord (2 Kings 23: 3, 17); but to minds as providentialist and scriptural as Vaughan's, this manner or tradition of anointing kings in close contact with a Temple pillar must have been overpoweringly suggestive.[96] If he needed further proof of the cataclysmic times in which he was living, it was surely this: that Charles could not be crowned on Jacob's stone like his ancestors, disturbing the patriarchal line which had lasted from Jacob's day to the present. Now a new spiritual era was upon the holy nation of England and Wales, but it was not one of joy and new light, as Parliament and Puritan declared; rather, it is Vaughan's 'late and dusky age', the final chapter of

---

[93] James Hilton, 'The Coronation Stone at Westminster Abbey', *Archaeological Journal*, 54 (1897), 201–24 (201); see also Pat Geber, *The Search for the Stone of Destiny* (Edinburgh, 1992), 25 and *The Oxford Dictionary of the Christian Church*, ed. F. L. Cross, 3rd edn. ed. E. A. Livingstone (Oxford, 1997), 419, 855, 1471.

[94] The stone's appearance in Holinshed is noted by Hilton, 'Coronation Stone', 202–4; Arthur Wilson, *The History of Great Britain, Being the Life and Reign of King James the First* (1653), 5–6.

[95] *The Forme and Order of the Coronation of Charles the Second, As it was Acted and Done at Scoone* (Aberdeen, 1651).

[96] Geber, *Stone of Destiny*, 38.

history in which apostasy and sin would rule before being swept away by the Apocalypse.

One further 'Jacobite' connection deepens the patriarchal resonances of Vaughan's great complex word *Jacob*. Whilst Rebecca was the name of Thomas Vaughan's wife, there are no signs that Henry was writing obliquely about his twin brother and sister-in-law in the nuptials of '*Isaacs* Marriage'.[97] However, names and genealogy mattered to Vaughan, as they did to the Welsh gentry as a whole. Henry could trace the Tretower Vaughans back to some of the great houses of Wales such as the Earls of Pembroke and the Somerset Raglans, and as a native Welsh speaker he would have seen that the name *Vaughan* has an interesting resonance with Jacob's situation as the younger of two brothers. As Roland Matthias has noted in another context: 'Fychan was the original Welsh form of Vaughan. It meant "little" or "the lesser" and was used as an appendage to the name of the younger of two brothers who, though born of the same parents and therefore *full* brothers, had yet been given the same Christian name.'[98] Jacob was the lesser brother, the second-born twin; only his name, meaning 'He who usurps', revealed his essential greatness. Vaughan's own twinship is coincidental here. It is his diminutive surname which links him to Jacob, and his status as a son of Thomas Vaughan senior who was himself a younger son, one who did not inherit Tretower Court, the home of Henry's uncle Roger. 'It is important to register, when we visit Vaughan's father's childhood home at Tretower Court, that this imposing mansion was the home Henry Vaughan *did not* inherit.'[99] The Silurist's branch of the Vaughan family, now more famous through his poetry than its other limbs, was in his day the Jacobite branch.

[97]   Stevie Davies discusses the relations between Henry, Thomas and Rebecca in reference to one of Thomas's dreams, recorded in his notebook *Aqua vitae (TV*, 485–536); see Davies, *Henry Vaughan*, 41–4, 66–7.

[98]   Roland Matthias, 'In Search of the Silurist', in Rudrum (ed.), *Essential Articles*, 189–214 (214); see also T. J. Morgan and Prys Morgan, *Welsh Surnames* (Cardiff, 1985), 58–60; Patrick Hanks and Flavia Hodges, *A Dictionary of Surnames* (Oxford, 1988), 552; Charles Wareing Bardsley, *A Dictionary of English and Welsh Surnames* (1901), 780; A. R. Williams 'Welsh Names', *Folk-Lore: Transactions of the Folk-Lore Society*, 60 (1949), 392–3 and resulting correspondence in *Folk-Lore*, 61 (1950), 51–2.

[99]   Davies, *Henry Vaughan*, 29. Primogeniture is discussed by Joan Thirsk, 'Younger Sons in the Seventeenth Century', *History*, 54 (1969), 358–77; Louis Adrian Montrose, ' "The place of a brother" in *As You Like It*: Social Process and Comic Form', *Shakespeare Quarterly*, 32 (1981), 28–54; Jack Goody and E. P. Thompson (eds.), *Family and Inheritance: Rural Society in Western Europe, 1200–1800* (Cambridge, 1976).

CHAPTER THREE

Hezekiah and the hand of heaven

On 20 March 1655, the publisher and bookshop owner Lodowick Lloyd made his way to Stationers' Hall to register two new books.[1] A few months previously, he and his business partner Henry Crips had purchased The Castle, a bookshop near the north wall of Paul's Churchyard, from the widow of that well-known publisher of astrology and mysticism, Humphrey Blunden.[2] Unlike Crips, Lloyd shared Blunden's fascination with the arcane, and over the next few years would persuade his partner to sell works of mysticism and alchemy in their shop. It made good business sense, quite apart from nourishing Lloyd's personal fascinations. Richard Baxter later noted that Blunden had made something of a name for himself as the publisher of the German mystic Jacob Boehme, and everything suggested that there was a ready-made market for such works waiting to be exploited by The Castle's new owners.[3] Lloyd successfully

[1] This account is based on details from *A Transcript of the Registers of the Worshipful Company of Stationers from 1640–1708 A. D.*, ed. H. R. Plomer, 3 vols. (1913) and *A Catalogue of the Pamphlets, Books, Newspapers, and Manuscripts Relating to the Civil War, the Commonwealth, and Restoration, Collected by George Thomason, 1640–1661*, ed. G. K. Fortescue, 2 vols. (1908). The publishing records of Blunden, Lloyd and Crips are taken from *Index of Printers, Publishers and Booksellers in Donald Wing's Short-Title Catalogue*, ed. Paul G. Morrison (Charlottesville, Va., 1955).

[2] For the position of The Castle, see Peter M. W. Blayney, *The Bookshops in Paul's Cross Churchyard* (1990), 14 and cf. Mary D. Lobel, *The City of London from Prehistoric Times to c.1520* (Oxford, 1989), whose maps Blayney revises.

[3] Richard Baxter, *Reliquiae Baxterianae*, ed. and abr. J. M. Lloyd Thomas (1931), 13. Of the thirty-two books Blunden issued between 1648 and 1655, twelve were by the well-known astrologer William Lilly, eight were by Boehme, and four by Thomas Vaughan; between 1652 and 1655, Blunden published only Boehme and Lilly. For details of Blunden's professional career see *A Dictionary of Printers and Booksellers Who Were at Work in England, Scotland and Ireland from 1641 to 1667*, ed. H. R. Plomer (1907), 27; see also Colin Gibson's Introduction to *Witts Recreations: Selected from the Finest Fancies of Moderne Muses; A Facsimile Edition* (Menston, 1990), ix–xv and D. F. McKenzie, *Stationers' Apprentices 1605–40* (Charlottesville, Va., 1960), 123. Blunden's birth in Salop, Shropshire is noted on fo. 1ʳ of Bodleian MS Ashmole 386 (I am grateful to Ariel Hessayon for this reference) and a 'H. Blunden' translated Boehme's *Four Tables of Divine Revelation*, which Humphrey published in 1654.

published arcana until he ceased trading in 1674, including works such as Henry Vaughan's translation of Heinrich Nollius' *The Chymists Key* in 1657 and Samuel Pordage's long hermetical poem *Mundorum Explicatio* (1661).[4]

On 20 March 1655, Lloyd was to register Dr Sennertus' new five-volume Latin work of physic and a small octavo of religious poetry. The latter was a mix of newly printed poems and the unsold sheets of a book called *Silex Scintillans: Sacred Hymns and Private Ejaculations* (1650) that Lloyd and Crips had purchased as part of The Castle. These were the effusions of Henry Vaughan, whom Lloyd would almost certainly have known as the twin brother of that Eugenius Philalethes (Thomas Vaughan) whose alchemical works were noted in the Hartlib circle and had been published by Humphrey Blunden—some of the *Silex Scintillans* poems had themselves been touched by hermetical knowledge.[5] Now, in 1655, Vaughan had prepared a new collection of verses and agreed to issue them with the unsold sheets, as a two-part edition under the same title. The arrangement seemed to accord with his wishes. Indeed, he had revised the dedicatory verses to the first volume, addressed to God, so that the poem had a second part beginning, 'Dear Lord 'tis finished!', as if Vaughan had planned all along to make the work in two parts (*V*, 394).

Vaughan had requested that one poem, '*Isaacs* Marriage' be reset with alterations, but the bigger change to the new volume was that the engraved emblem of a stony heart and accompanying emblem poem which had prefaced the 1650 edition had been slashed out.[6] This was no great loss from a bookseller's point of view: the emblem had offered a graphic explanation of the book's title, but it was not an outstanding piece of engraving, and the lettering had been particularly poor.[7] And

---

[4] For details of Lloyd's career, see Morrison, *Index of Printers*, 126, Plomer, *Dictionary of Printers*, 119, who notes that catalogues of works printed for Lloyd can be found at the end of John Norton, *Abel Being Dead Yet Speaketh* (1658) and Samuel Pordage, *Mundorum Explicatio* (1661). For the elusive Henry Crips, see Plomer, *Dictionary of Printers*, 55–6, McKenzie, 'London Book Trade', ch. 1.

[5] See the Biographical introduction to *TV*, 11–15 for details of the alchemical circles in which Thomas was moving. For a survey of the hermetic influence in *Silex Scintillans*, see Holmes, *Vaughan and the Hermetic Philosophy*, *passim*; L. C. Martin, 'Henry Vaughan and "Hermes Trismegistus"'.

[6] My interpretation is based on internal evidence: no testimony survives as to how Vaughan's works reached the press, or who oversaw their printing. The debate surrounding the identity of the 'Friend' who brought *Olor Iscanus* to press is detailed below in Chapter 5, ' 'Tis a sad land'.

[7] The emblem, reproduced in *V*, *R* and most modern editions of Vaughan, shows signs

besides, the poet had offered a replacement: a prose apology for sacred poetry, some few pages of scripture, and a short poem called 'Vain Wits and eyes'.[8] The preface praised George Herbert, whose *The Temple* was still well known and universally admired, though it had been out of print since 1640. Humphrey Blunden would have approved: one of his earliest publishing ventures was Herbert's collection of *Outlandish Proverbs*, published as part of the popular *Witts Recreations* anthology of 1640.[9]

The last three months of the old year 1654 had seen quite a string of Royalist and Anglican books registered at Stationers' Hall; like Vaughan's poems, they appealed to those anxious to return to old ways. On 25 January, Richard Royston registered Jeremy Taylor's *The Golden Grove*, with its *Festivall Hymnes According to the Manner of the Auncient Church*, whilst Bishop Prideaux's *Euchologia* (Christian guidance for his daughters) was registered on 23 February, and Lancelot Andrewes's *Holy Devotions with Directions to Pray* on the 27th of that month.[10] George Thomason was in possession of Taylor's book by 12 March and Prideaux's by 24 May, but for whatever reason, he does not seem to have owned a copy of either edition of *Silex Scintillans*.[11] Though he was buying from Lodowick Lloyd and Henry Crips in 1655 (such works as John Goodwin's *Cata-baptism*), between 1646 and 1657, when Vaughan published eight books in total, Thomason only collected three of them: *Poems* (1646), *The Mount of Olives* (1652) and *Hermetical Physick* (1655).[12] The date on his

---

of hasty workmanship. Its lettering is particularly irregular, mixing scripts until the main title becomes hard to pick out: '*Silex Scintillans*' is boldest, but '*Sacred Poems*' is largest; and although '*Private Eiaculations*' is a subtitle, it is carved in the same script as the largest title words.

[8] *V*, 387–96.

[9] *Witts Recreations*, pp. ix–xi; *Outlandish Proverbs* was also issued separately [*STC* 13182]. Both versions were printed by T. P[aine] for Blunden. Blunden's apprenticeship was served with Philemon Stephens, who from 1640 held the rights to publish *The Temple* and Harvey's *The Synagogue*, works which Stephens sold bound together (Baxter, *Reliquiae Baxterianae*, 13; Stephens is also discussed by Birrell, 'Sevententh-Century Publishers', 163–6).

[10] *Stationers' Register*, ed. Plomer, 464, 466. This was another translation of Andrewes's Latin, Greek and Hebrew devotions *Preces Privatae*, which were published as *Private Devotions* (1647) and *A Manual of the Private Devotions* (1648) by Humphrey Moseley.

[11] *Catalogue of the Pamphlets, Books, Newspapers, and Manuscripts*, ed. Fortescue, E 1542(2) and E 1515.

[12] *Cata-Baptism* (E 849) is dated 21 July 1655. Vaughan's other works are catalogued as: *Poems* (1646) E 1178(3), undated 1646; *The Mount of Olives* E 1305(2), 16 Feb. 1652; *Hermetical Physick* E 1714(1), 25 June 1655.

copy of the latter is 25 June 1655, a full five months after it was registered by the Royalist publisher Humphrey Moseley.

While Vaughan's two-part *Sacred Hymns* went on sale in London's Cornhill, the poet was at work translating the Paracelsian treatise *The Chymists Key*, another follow-up of a sort, since the *Hermetical Physick* he had Englished in 1654 was from the same author, Nollius. Before *Silex* (1655) however, sequels were not Vaughan's style. His work had appeared under a series of different heads, without any revisions of, or additions to, earlier volumes: *Poems, with the Tenth Satyre of Juvenal Englished* (1646), *Silex Scintillans: Sacred Hymns and Private Ejaculations* (1650), *Olor Iscanus* (1651), *The Mount of Olives; or, Private Devotions* (1652), *Flores Solitudinis* (1654). Yet despite the fact that Vaughan's 'Poems 1650–55' show an undeniably different tone to *Silex* (1650), he allowed them to appear under an existing title.

Perhaps it had occurred to Lodowick Lloyd and Henry Crips that the leftover sheets from *Silex* (1650) could be put to good use in a two-part book. But from what Vaughan added to the untitled dedicatory poem first published in 1650, it is clear that wherever the idea came from, it was congenial to Vaughan's wishes: 'Dear Lord, 'tis finished! and now he | That copyed it, presents it thee' (1655 dedicatory poem, ll. 15–16). Vaughan had several precedents for adding to a work of devotional poetry in the style of Herbert, not least Christopher Harvey's sporadic expansions of *The Synagogue* (1640) and Crashaw's *Steps to the Temple*, which the author enlarged in 1648, only two years after its first publication.[13] These enlargements, like Vaughan's, were not prompted by any incompletion, fault or lack in the work as first published. When George Sandys expanded *A Paraphrase upon the Psalmes of David* (1636) into *A Paraphrase upon the Divine Poems* (1638), he could reasonably claim to have completed a project modelled on many existing Psalm commentaries which expanded to include Old Testament scriptural songs as honorary Psalms.[14] No such model governed the expansions undertaken by Harvey, Crashaw and Vaughan. Neither was theirs the tinkering of inveterate revisers like Daniel and Drayton, who altered the details of

---

[13] Ilona Bell, 'Herbert and Harvey: In the Shadow of The Temple', 255–79 in *Like Season'd Timber: New Essays on George Herbert*, ed. Edmund Miller and Robert DiYanni, Seventeenth-Century Texts and Studies (New York, 1987); A. C. Howell, 'Christopher Harvey's *The Synagogue* (1640)', *Studies in Philology* 49 (1952), 229–47; L. C. Martin, 'Textual Introduction' to *The Poems, English, Latin and Greek, of Richard Crashaw*, 2nd edn. (Oxford, 1957), pp. xliv–xlvii.

[14] See n. 56, below, for examples of these Psalm commentaries.

existing sonnets but maintained the overall shape and size of their sequences.

'Dear Lord, 'tis finished!' is the best testimony that what Lodowick Lloyd registered in March 1655 was intended as the whole collection of *Silex Scintillans*. One does not have to look far to see why. Vaughan was seriously ill from around 1652 until 1654, during which time he believed himself 'nigh unto death' (*V*, 392), and though he had recovered by the time he wrote 'The Authors Preface' to *Silex* (1655)—it is dated 30 September 1654—the notion that *all* his earthly works were finishing must have loomed over the writing of these great poems. His literary works offer only the most indirect witness to his physical state, providing no details of the sickness itself, or what sort of treatment he may have prescribed himself. Yet sickness and recovery lie at the very heart of the 1655 *Silex Scintillans*, and it was his sickness that led Vaughan to remove the hearty emblem from the new edition and to replace it with prefatory matter which reflected the lessons of his recent suffering.

The emblem had served its purpose well, introducing Vaughan as the poet of afflictive sparks and flashes just as the rustic emblem of grove, bees and eponymous swan which introduced *Olor Iscanus* (1651) had prepared the reader for a consolatory philosophy of country retreat. When Vaughan decided to change visual explanation for verbal in 1654, the result was no less introductory or original and was far from being, *pace* Louis Martz, a sign of weakening poetic power.[15] For although poets commonly added lengthy dedications to their works, and some, like Davenant and Cowley, engaged in literary-critical discussions in their prefaces, no other seventeenth-century devotional poet of the school of Herbert reflected quite as Vaughan did in September 1654.[16] The preface to *Silex* (1655) is one of the most important pieces of seventeenth-century literary criticism about writing what Vaughan, following George Herbert's usage, had come to call 'true hymns'. It consists of four parts. 'The Authors Preface to the following Hymns' represents Vaughan's mature views—it is sometimes hard to remember that he was only 32 in 1654—on sacred poetry, praising Herbert as a true poet and lamenting the

---

[15] Martz, *The Paradise Within*, 4. Positive readings of Vaughan's replacement of the emblem are given by Calhoun's Appendix, and by Rothberg.

[16] William Davenant, *Gondibert: An Heroick Poem, Written by Sr William D'Avenant* (1651), 'The Authors Preface to His Much Honour'd Friend Mr Hobs', 1–70, and Hobbes's reply, 71–88; Abraham Cowley, 'Preface' to *Poems* (1656), reprinted in *Critical Essays of the Seventeenth Century*, ed. J. E. Spingarn, 3 vols. (Oxford, 1908), ii. 77–90.

'most gross and studied *filthiness*' of contemporary verse (*V*, 391). Finishing with a two-paragraph introduction to his own work, 'The Authors Preface' is followed by three pages of scripture taken from the Old Testament books of Isaiah, Jonah and the Psalms; these are printed in a much larger fount than the Roman pica used for the poems, as is the expanded dedication 'To my most merciful, my most loving, and dearly loved Redeemer' and a short new poem, 'Vain Wits and eyes', which finishes Vaughan's attack on wits.

In choosing a preface to comment on his sickness and recovery, Vaughan implied a special relation between his dramatic alterations of health and the completed *Silex Scintillans*. In particular, he witnessed to God, his readers, and (not least) to other poets, that verse has a sacred purpose in returning thanks for mercies received; and he instanced his own work as the fruit of submission to God's trials and right use of His gifts. Throughout the preface, Vaughan complains that poets were much more Cain than Abel when it came to offering thanks: even among 'the principal or most learned Writers of *English verse*', he proclaims, there has been a marked tendency to prefer 'an idle or sensual *subject*' and even 'to dash *Scriptures*, and the *sacred Relatives* of God with their impious conceits' (*V*, 390). Records of published poetry in the years 1650–5 lend some credence to Vaughan's pious excoriations. When *Silex Scintillans: Sacred Poems and Private Ejaculations. The Second Edition, in Two Books* appeared on The Castle's shelves, some time in mid-1655, it entered a book market in which non-religious poetry outnumbered pious publications at least two to one. This was a significant change from 1650, when, as Joseph Frank has estimated, 35 per cent of published poetry was pious and 39 per cent secular.[17] If Vaughan had been receiving poetry books from London in the early 1650s—and copies of other books he received in these years survive—he would have noted that on average just over half of published poetry was explicity non-religious, whilst a little more than a quarter had a pious character.[18] And of that quarter, of course, much was overtly supportive

---

[17] The remaining 26% fall into one of Frank's miscellaneous categories, of which the largest is 'conservative' (*Hobbled Pegasus: A Descriptive Bibliography of Minor English Poetry, 1641–1660* (Albuquerque, 1968)).

[18] 53% (secular) and 28% (pious) are the average figures. Vaughan's surviving autograph books are listed by Edwin Wolf II, 'Some Books of Early English Provenance' and Margaret Munsterberg, 'The Swan of Usk, More Books'; Beal, *Index*, II. 2, 542–3. Three of these fourteen have 1650s autographs: Nicolaas Fonteyn, *Commentarius in Sebastianum Austrium . . . de Puerorum Morbis* (Amsterdam, 1642), signed on the title-page 'Henr: Vaughan Siluris, 1654 Salus mea ex Agno'; Hippocrates, *Aphorismi* (Marburg, 1650), signed

of Parliament (for instance, the celebratory hymns of the Presbyterian William Barton) or yet more radical and reformist, like the millenarian verses of the Welshmen Morgan Llwyd and Vavasor Powell.[19]

Only six copies of *Silex Scintillans* (1655) are known to survive, but the book was not as obscure as that figure suggests.[20] In 1658, the year Cromwell died, '*Silex Scintillans: two parts*' appeared on William London's list of the sixty most vendible books in London, as did 'Mr Vaughams [*sic*] Poems', which is almost certainly *Olor Iscanus*, the work for which Vaughan was best known to both his cousin John Aubrey and to Anthony Wood.[21] It was this 'finished' *Silex*—the only work on London's list noted as having two parts—that was in demand as the Commonwealth faltered and the principality of Wales generally breathed more easily at the prospect of monarchy restored.[22] It was this *Silex*, too, that influenced the 'Scintillulae Sacrae' of Nathaniel Wanley (better known as the author of *The Wonders of the Little World* (1678)), whose poetry is as indebted to Vaughan as was Vaughan's to George Herbert. The story of this chapter occurred at a turning point in Vaughan's life, four years before *Silex* was in such demand, or Wanley was reading it admiringly as a student at Interregnum Cambridge. Just beginning to recover from near-fatal illness, Vaughan saw the way to express thanks to God, through art, for mercifully extending his life: how he did so through the preface to *Silex Scintillans* (1655), and what this means for the way one should read the poems, is the substance of what follows.

'Vaughan' on the title page; and Jean Pecquet, *Experimenta Nova Anatomica* (Paris, 1651), inscribed 'Thomas Vaughan Deo Duce: Comite Natura. 1652°' on the flyleaf and 'H:V:S:' on 107. A six-line English translation of 'The famous Hexastic which Sannazarius made upon the City of Venice', written at the foot of a page in an exemplum of James Howell, *A Survay of the Signorie of Venice* (1651) has been ascribed to Vaughan by Beal on the basis of the hand.

[19] William Barton, *Hallelujah; or, Certain Hymns, Composed out of Scripture, to Celebrate Some Special and Publick Occasions* (1651); for Powell's and Llwyd's hymns see Smith, *Literature and Revolution*, 270–6.

[20] *Wing* lists copies in the British Museum, the National Library of Scotland, the Huntington Library, the University of Illinois at Urbana, Harvard, and Yale; seven copies of *Silex* (1650) are known to survive.

[21] William London, *A Catalogue of the Most Vendible Books in England*, 2nd edn. (1658); reprinted in Frank, *Hobbled Pegasus*, 463–5; Anthony Wood, *Athenae Oxoniensis, An Exact History of All the Writers and Bishops Who Have Had Their Education in the University of Oxford*, 3rd edn. with additions, ed. Philip Bliss, 4 vols. (1820), iv, col. 425 ('his *Olor Iscanus* was most valued'); *Aubrey's Brief Lives*, ed. Oliver Lawson-Dick (1949; repr. 1992), 303 ('one writt a Poeme called *Olor Iscanus* (Henry Vaughan, the first-borne)').

[22] Jenkins, *Protestant Dissenters*, 40.

COMFORTABLE WORDS

'The Authors Preface to the following Hymns' is by turns biting, confessional, uncomfortable for the reader (especially when Vaughan apologizes for his secular poetry) and perspicacious. Criticizing secular poetry makes Vaughan sound austerely pious, but his criticisms of sub-Herbertian verse are firm, useful and passionate, and the autobiographical hints of the last two paragraphs are included for the spiritual benefit of the reader of *Silex* (1655). The shadowy allusions to Vaughan's sickness that they contain have been used in F. E. Hutchinson's and Stevie Davies's fine critical biographies of the poet, but none of Vaughan's modern readers has seen how the allusions themselves act as a preface to the three pages of biblical text that follow. And this despite Vaughan's care to lead his reader into the arrangement of scripture with thanks that

the God of the spirits of all flesh, hath granted me a further use of *mine*, then I did look for in the *body*; and when I expected, and had (by his assistance) prepared for a *message* of *death*, then did he *answer* me with *life*; I hope to his *glory*, and my great *advantage*: that I may flourish not with *leafe* onely, but with some *fruit* also. (*V*, 392)

Fruit is the scriptural metaphor Vaughan had used in dedicating *Silex* (1650) to Christ: 'These thy deaths fruits I offer thee' ('The Dedication', l. 2); five years on, the poet hopes that his reprieve from sickness will be blessed with more fruit to offer back to the God that sent it. It is at this point, with the words of Vaughan's pious thanks and poetic offering ringing in the ears, that one turns over the leaf and is confronted by three pages of scripture without a title, marginal notes, or any other interpretative clue except the words themselves. Some lengthy quotation is necessary here, since these texts are the subject of the first half of this chapter. Below I have given the texts in full, with additional notes of their sources from L. C. Martin's revised Oxford edition of Vaughan's works, for which he consulted annotations in the copy of his earlier edition to Vaughan's biographer and the editor of Herbert's *Works*, Canon F. E. Hutchinson.[23]

O Lord, the hope of Israel, all they that forsake thee shall be ashamed; and they that depart from thee, shall be written in the earth, because they have forsaken the Lord, the fountain of living waters.

---

[23]   *V*, 728; Martin's notes are used by *R*, 528 and *George Herbert and Henry Vaughan*, ed. Martz, 517. *R* thinks Martin is citing the references from Hutchinson's *Life*, but in fact *Life* does not mention the scriptural prayer at all. See *V*, pp. iii–iv, xxviii on Canon Hutchinson's annotated copy of Martin's first edition of 1914.

Heal me, O Lord, and I shall be healed; save me, and I shall be saved, for thou art my health, and my great deliverer. [Jeremiah 17: 13–14]

I said in the cutting off of my days, I shall go to the gates of the grave; I have deprived my self of the residue of my years.

I said, I shall not see the Lord, even the Lord in the Land of the living: I shall behold man no more with the Inhabitants of the world. [Isaiah 38: 10–11]

O Lord! by thee doth man live, and from thee is the life of my spirit: therefore wilt thou recover me, and make me to live.

Thou hast in love to my soul delivered it from the pit of corruption; for thou hast cast all my sins behinde thy back. [Isaiah 38: 16–17]

For thy names sake hast thou put off thine anger; for thy praise hast thou refrained from me, that I should not be cut off. [Isaiah 48: 9]

For the grave cannot praise thee, death cannot celebrate thee: they that go down into the pit, cannot hope for thy truth.

The living, the living, he shall praise thee, as I do this day: the Father to the children shall make known thy truth. [Isaiah 38: 18–19]

O Lord! thou hast been merciful, thou hast brought back my life from corruption: thou hast redeemed me from my sin.

They that follow after lying vanities, forsake their own mercy. [Jonah 2: 6–8]

Therefore shall thy songs be with me, and my prayer unto the God of my life. [Psalm 42: 8]

I will go unto the altar of my God, unto God, the joy of my youth; and in thy fear will I worship towards thy holy temple. [Psalm 43: 4; 5: 7]

I will sacrifice unto thee with the voice of thanksgiving; I will pay that which I have vowed: salvation is of the Lord. [Jonah 2: 9]

Since the seventeenth century was exact in its worship and recognized many different kinds of verbal approaches to God, it is necessary to do more than identify Vaughan's biblical excerpts as a prayer. An explosion of vernacular prayer collections, catechisms and devotional handbooks during Elizabeth's reign meant that British devotional life in the seventeenth century was not short of examples of the many different ways of praying.[24] Worshippers would differentiate between public prayers and private prayers, prayers for everyday and those to be said on special occasions; some would put faith in set forms and decry extempore utterance,

[24] C. J. Stranks notes over eighty different collections of private devotions published during Elizabeth's reign (*Anglican Devotion: Studies in the Spiritual Life of the Church of England between the Reformation and the Oxford Movement* (1961), 27). Kinds of prayer elaborated in prayer books and instruction manuals are summarized by Helen C. White, *English Devotional Literature [Prose] 1600–1640* (Madison, 1931), 73–95 and 156 ff. For another poet's subtle awareness of kinds of prayer, see Adam and Eve's pre-lapsarian worship in *Paradise Lost*, ed. Alastair Fowler (1968), V. 142–52.

others vice versa; and all would offer thanksgivings, prayers for remission and petitions for forgiveness. For Vaughan and other conformists, one of the most unwelcome and powerful trends in seventeenth-century prayer was a general Puritan dislike of the Prayer Book liturgy on the grounds that it derived from the Mass. During the 1640s, Independent and Presbyterian divines clashed over what should replace the old style of public worship, but they were united in objecting to Common Prayer and would have recognized and objected to echoes of that service in Vaughan's devotional work *The Mount of Olives* (1652).[25]

The prefatory prayer, to give it a neutral name for the moment, is composed entirely of scriptures from Jeremiah, Isaiah, Jonah and the Psalms, and makes only minor changes to its texts, all of which are given from the Authorized Version.[26] This sets it slightly apart from the poems and prose of *Silex* (1650), *The Mount of Olives* (1652), and the poems of *Silex* Part 2, which mix scripture with liturgical and literary language. Even the most biblical poems in *Silex* or the extremely concentrated assemblages of scripture in *The Mount of Olives* are joined by Vaughan's own words, but here scripture rests against scripture uncemented.[27] The page layout of *Silex* (1655) also differentiates this prayer from its surroundings. The verso preceding the prayer is blank, and the prayer itself is set in a large italic fount rather than the standard roman pica used for the poems. Modern editions unfortunately tend to reduce the visual impact of the original printed edition by using an italic equivalent in size to their standard roman.[28] What to a reader of the 1655 volume looks like the climax of the preface can appear almost incidental to a reader of an Oxford or Penguin edition.

No literary key unlocks the secrets of these pages, which do not fall

---

[25] The debate over set liturgy versus extempore prayer is related to Vaughan's world and work by Wall, *Transformations of the Word*, 274–8.

[26] Vaughan changes 'my' to 'thy' in the text of Isa. 48.9, thus returning as prayer God's words to the house of Jacob.

[27] See 'A Meditation at the setting of the Sun, or the Souls Elevation to the true light' (in *The Mount of Olives*) for an example of the scripture-saturated style of Vaughan's original prose. In thirty-five lines, this meditation refers or alludes to, borrows from or paraphrases at least twenty-five biblical passages.

[28] Textual bibliography is applied to literary study by J. J. McGann, 'The Monks and the Giants: Textual and Bibliographical Studies and the Interpretation of Literary Texts', 180–99 in *Textual Criticism and Literary Interpretation*, ed. McGann (Chicago, 1985); D. F. McKenzie, 'Typography and Meaning: The Case of William Cowper', in Giles Barber and Bernhard Fabian (eds.), *Buch und Buchhandel in Europa im achtzehnten Jahrhundert; The Book and the Book Trade in Eighteenth-Century Europe* (Hamburg, 1981), 81–126; and Nicholas Barker, 'Typography and the Meaning of Words', *Buch und Buchhandel*, 127–65.

obviously into any of Vaughan's familiar poetic modes such as narrative ('Regeneration', 'The Ornament'), dramatic meditation ('The Lampe', 'Midnight'), or historical prophecy ('Mans fall, and Recovery', 'Jacobs Pillar, and Pillow'). Though the prose of *The Mount of Olives* (1652) is lined with scriptural passages and its prayers are virtually collections of scriptural texts on a devotional theme, Vaughan always gives his devotional reader a title or heading, such as 'A Prayer in the hour of Death' or 'Admonitions when we prepare for any farre Journey'.[29] The prefatory prayer provides no such signal, leaving the reader to decide how, if at all, the pieces of scripture may be linked together.[30]

Louis Martz has responded to this crux in the most recent edition of Vaughan by suggesting that the prayer is a '*catena* (chain) of biblical verses [which] follows an ancient tradition of creating a personal psalm out of an arrangement and adaptation of passages'.[31] This form, the *catena patrum*, is either a string of exegetical passages from the Fathers, or a string of extracts from both Old and New Testament assembled to prove that any doctrine is both ancient and enduring. Such compilations were a common exercise for medieval clerics, and reached a peak of popularity in the late Middle Ages.[32] Post-Reformation printed instances, such as Thomas Rogers's *A Golden Chaine, Taken out of the Psalmes of King David* (1579), are uncommon, though the noted biblical and patristic scholar Patrick Young published a folio *Catena Graecorum Patrum in Jobum* in 1628 on the basis of two Bodley manuscripts.[33] Among the priestly pedantries he mocks in *Areopagitica* (1644), Milton lists 'an English concordance and a *topic folio*, the gatherings and savings of a sober graduateship, a *Harmony* and a *Catena*, treading the constant round of certain doctrinal heads'.[34]

---

[29] The most extensive annotation of *The Mount of Olives* and the *The Life of Paulinus* is that of Hilary M. Day, 'A Study of the Use of the Bible and the Book of Common Prayer in the Prose Works of Henry Vaughan', Ph.D. thesis (London, 1986).

[30] How to attend to genre is the general subject of Alastair Fowler, *Kinds of Literature: An Introduction to the Theory of Genres and Modes* (Oxford, 1982); specific studies are collected as B. K. Lewalski (ed.), *Renaissance Genres: Essays on Theory, History, and Interpretation*, Harvard English Studies 14 (Cambridge, Mass. 1986); and for a critique of the methods whereby genre criticism attempts to reconstruct the artistic horizons of past ages and cultures, see Michael Baxandall, *Patterns of Intention: The Historical Explanation of Pictures* (New Haven, 1985).

[31] *George Herbert and Henry Vaughan*, ed. Martz, 517.

[32] *Oxford Dictionary of the Christian Church*, ed. Cross, 300; *A Dictionary of the Bible* (Oxford and New York, 1996), ed. W. F. Browning, 66; *OED*, catena, a.

[33] *Oxford Dictionary of the Christian Church*, ed. Cross, 1775.

[34] Milton, *Complete Prose Works*, ii. 546.

Vaughan's prefatory prayer is not really a *catena*, since it neither proves a doctrine or makes a typological point. Nevertheless, Martz is right to look for scripture uses in which biblical texts are linked together as Vaughan does in this prayer. Two of the devotional texts Vaughan knew best, the Book of Common Prayer and the sixteenth-century Church of England Primer, also contain chains of linked texts which offer more helpful models for the prefatory prayer. The first is the Prayer Book's Comfortable Words. As John Wall has shown, Vaughan was intimate with the Anglican liturgy and would almost certainly have known by heart the collection of eleven sentences, or Comfortable Words, which Cranmer placed in the 1552 revisions to the Prayer Book 'to hearten the penitent with "the comfortable salve of God's Word"' before Morning and Evening Prayer.[35] The minister is instructed to 'reade with a loud voyce some of these sentences of the scriptures that follow', which include verses from the Psalms, the prophets, two of the gospels and finally one from John's first epistle: 'Yf we saye that we have no synne, we deceyve ourselves, and there is no trueth in us.'[36] Although seldom read right through liturgically, the texts are thematically related, telling of man's sin, corruption, contrition, and repentance.[37] When Anglicans resorted to private reading of the Prayer Book following the 1645 Parliamentary Ordinance prohibiting its public use, these 'calls to worship' were transformed into calls to private devotion, Comfortable Words into comfortable reading.[38] They provided Owen Felltham's model for a call to worship in his *A Form of Prayer*, one of many alternative liturgies used during the Interregnum by Prayer Book conformists wishing to worship in a manner as close as possible to Cranmer's services.[39]

[35] Wall, *Transformations of the Word*, 273–89.

[36] *BCP*, 348; for similar Comfortable Words, see *The Order of the Communion* (1548), sigs. [B4]ᵛ–Ciʳ; and Herman von Wied, *A Simple, and Religious Consultation* (1548).

[37] See Samuel Leuenberger, *Archbishop Cranmer's Immortal Bequest: The Book of Common Prayer of the Church of England: An Evangelistic Liturgy* (Grand Rapids, Mich., 1990), 98–9; F. E. Brightman, *The English Rite: Being a Synopsis of the Sources and Revisions of the Book of Common Prayer*, 2 vols. (1915), i. p. clii; Frank E. Brightman and Kenneth D. MacKenzie, 'The History of the *Book of Common Prayer*', in *Liturgy and Worship: A Companion to the Prayer Books of the Anglican Communion*, ed. W. K. Lowther and Charles Harris (1932), 130–97, 178; *The Prayer Book Dictionary*, ed. George Harford and Morley Stevenson (1925), 222.

[38] An ordinance of 26 Aug. 1645 made use of the Prayer Book 'in any Private place of Family' illegal (*Acts and Ordinances*, ed. Firth and Rait, i. 755–7). A first offence against this ruling carried a £10 fine; a second offence £20; and a year in prison without the possibility of bail or remand awaited third-time offenders.

[39] 'Owen Felltham's *A Form of Prayer*', ed. Pebworth, 226.

As well as to Comfortable Words, the prefatory prayer looks to the scriptural sentences included in sixteenth-century Primers, devotional books based on the popular extra devotions appended to the Mass during the Middle Ages. Still popular after the Reformation, English Primers were issued with a purified doctrinal content until they fell out of use with the rise of the Prayer Book during Elizabeth's reign, though their traditional style of worship was much criticized as superstitious even before then. In 1627, the Master of Peterhouse John Cosin published his *Devotions* with a title-page announcing their descent from Elizabeth's 1559 Reformed Primer, outraging William Prynne and Henry Burton. Condemning the book, Prynne went so far as to accuse Cosin of employing canonical hours in the chapel at Peterhouse, then Cambridge's Laudian epicentre and later a centre of Loyalist support during the Civil Wars.[40]

It is the 'ejaculations' within the Primers and Cosin's *Devotions* which suggest a way of reading Vaughan's prefatory prayer. There were several different understandings of ejaculatory prayer in the mid-seventeenth century, but Vaughan's own examples in *The Mount of Olives* show that he approved of the kind recommended by the Primers: short, purposeful excerpts from scripture which the Christian might memorize for moments in everyday life as well as for special occasions. Ejaculations of this brief, scriptural kind also appeared in Jeremy Taylor's *Holy Living* (1650).[41] A good example of Vaughan's fifteen ejaculations in *The Mount of Olives* is that to be said 'When thou hearest that any is dead', brief and pregnant at only sixteen words: 'Teach me, O Lord, to number my dayes, that I may apply my heart unto wisdome' (Psalm 90: 2, 12; *V*, 154). Slightly longer at twenty-five words is Vaughan's choice of Psalms 61: 2–3, interspersed with Psalm 71: 5, to provide a word against fear:

Upon some suddaine feare.
O set me upon the Rock that is higher then I, for thou art my hope, and a strong tower for me against my enemy. (*V*, 153)

Scriptural ejaculations like Cosin's, Vaughan's and Taylor's were designed to be learned and remembered, and to be called upon instinctively

---

[40] John Cosin, *A Collection of Private Devotions in the Practice of the Antient Church: Called the Houres of Prayer*, ed. P. G. Stanwood (Oxford, 1967), pp. xvi–xxvi.

[41] My discussion is indebted to Elizabeth Clarke, 'The Ejaculatory Moment', a paper given to the Northern Renaissance Seminar (Nottingham Trent, 1995), a shorter account of which is given in her *Theory and Theology in George Herbert's Poetry: 'Divinitie and Poesie, Met'*, Oxford Theological Monographs (Oxford, 1997), 123–6.

when an appropriate response was required or demanded. But prayer treatises of the mid-seventeenth century show this style of ejaculatory prayer to have been the less popular. More favoured were ejaculations conceived of as outbursts of *improvised* prayer offered up in emergency; unlike the Primer tradition these utterances were neither memorized, nor need they be scriptural. Works like Thomas Cobbett's *A Practical Discourse of Prayer* (1654) and Charles Ducket's *Sparks from the Golden Altar* (1660) taught ejaculation by example, providing long, often laborious passages to imitate rather than memorable nuggets to be got off perfectly. Cobbett defined ejaculation as 'a short, yet serious and sincere lifting up of the heart', but *short* here means only shorter than his full-length prayers.[42] The 'Ejaculations to be used at the Lord's Table' from the popular devotional book *The Whole Duty of Man* are eighteen lines long, those of *Sparks from the Golden Altar* more than a whole page.[43] Often, 'ejaculation' seems interchangeable with 'short prayer', and it is possible that some ejaculations were intended to be read out: the engraved title-page to *The Whole Duty*, for instance, shows a kneeling figure praying by candlelight with a book open.[44]

The short, scriptural ejaculations favoured by Cosin, Taylor and Vaughan offer a model for the way the prefatory prayer to *Silex* (1655) gathers texts on a theme for a special occasion. Only in his ejaculations and the prefatory prayer does Vaughan omit all cementing prose: the other prayers in *The Mount of Olives* include scriptures within passages of original prose, often drawing attention to the shifts in and out of scripture with italics or chapter and verse citations.[45] One of these special prayers from *The Mount of Olives* seems, in hindsight, to be a trial run for the prefatory prayer to *Silex* (1655). Written in 1651 when Vaughan's illness may have seemed fatal, 'A Prayer when thou findest thy self sickly, or when thou art visited with any Disease' is included toward the end of the escha-tological treatise 'Man in Darkness'. Thanking God for the lessons of

---

[42]   Thomas Cobbett, *A Practical Discourse of Prayer* (1654), 31.

[43]   Richard Allestree (attrib.), *The Practice of Christian Graces; or, The Whole Duty of Man*, 2nd edn. (1659), 57. For another attribution, see *The Baronettage of England* (1720), ii. 202, where Dorothy, wife of Sir John Packington, is said to 'have the Reputation of being thought the Author of *the Whole Duty of Man*'. Charles Ducket, *Sparks from the Golden Altar; or, Occasional Meditations, Ejaculations, Observations, and Experiences* (1660), e.g. 'Ejaculation I' (77–8).

[44]   Allestree, *Whole Duty*, sig. xiᵛ.

[45]   Alan Rudrum notes that 'Vaughan's italics . . . are often significant, signalling a word used in a technical sense, a quotation of allusion, and so on' (*R*, 17); James Carscallen agrees ('Editing Vaughan', *University of Toronto Quarterly*, 47 (1978), 267–73).

affliction, it closely imitates the Prayer Book's 'Visitation of the Sick', right down to referring to sickness as a 'visitation' which 'we shoulde paciently and with thankesgeving beare';[46] but while the Prayer Book uses Christ's long-suffering as an exemplar, Vaughan turns vividly—garishly, almost—to the sufferings of the martyrs: 'Thou that didst give to thy blessed and faithful *Martyrs* such a glorious *measure* of thy Almighty *spirit*, as encouraged them for thy sake to be *sawed* asunder, to be *burnt*, *stoned and beheaded*, give unto me now such a gracious *portion* of the same *Comforter* as may leade me through *death* unto *life*' (*V*, 189). Celebrating Christian endurance through the pain of martyrdom, Vaughan forgets himself and his ostensible topic of the lessons of sickness. He may already have been assembling materials for the *Life of Paulinus* which he included in *Flores Solitudinis* (1654), materials which were to include Paulinus' meditation on martyrdom, unflinchingly translated by Vaughan:

> Burne me alive, with curious, skilfull paine
> Cut up and search each warme and breathing vaine:
> When all is done, death brings a quick release,
> And the poore mangled body sleeps in peace.
> Hale me to prisons, shut me up in brasse:
> My still free Soule from thence to God shall passe;
> Banish or bind me, I can be no where
> A stranger, nor alone; My God is there.
>
> (ll. 97–104)[47]

'A Prayer when thou findst thyself sickly' wanders from sickness to affliction, from affliction to endurance, and finally reads less like a prayer during sickness than it does the two prayers for the persecuted which end the first part of *The Mount of Olives*. Though Vaughan draws on the bible for the prayer's exhortations to faith and to the Christian virtue of patience— citing notable texts including Romans 5: 4, 15: 4, and Colossians 3: 2—he relies entirely on echoes of the Prayer Book's 'Visitation of the Sick' to relate these virtues to the experience of sickness. Yet in compassing the possibility of a God-sent recovery, the prayer suggests the direction of

---

[46] *V*, 188; 'The Ordre for the Visitacion of the Sicke', *BCP*, 417–21 (418).

[47] For the Latin text of Paulinus, see *S. Paulini Opera Omnia*, in *Patrologia Latina*, ed. J.-P. Migne (Paris, 1847), LXI, *Appendix . . . Opera Dubia*, Poem I ('Age, iam precor mearum'). Vaughan read Paulinus in the 1621 edition of Eucherius' letters published at Amsterdam by Rosweydus and Ducaeus along with a Latin *Life of Paulinus*; the following year they published an edition of Paulinus' works, with a reprint of the *Vita* (see *V*, 722–3).

Vaughan's thoughts during the early 1650s and begins to explore the theme of the scriptural prayer which prefaces *Silex Scintillans* (1655). The Old Testament word *enlarge*, used of all God's gifts of increase and plenty in the Pentateuch and Psalms, resounds in Vaughan's humble petition: 'Or if thou wilt in mercy restore me again, and enlarge my time, give me, I beseech thee, a thankful *heart*, holy *resolutions*, and a stedfast *spirit* to performe them' (*V*, 189).[48]

HE WAS SICKE, AND THEN HE PRAYED

As Canon Hutchinson's scriptural annotations show, the most important text in the prefatory prayer to *Silex Scintillans* (1655) is Isaiah 38: 1–8, the story of the sickness, recovery and thanksgiving of Hezekiah, king of Judah. The book of Isaiah tells how Hezekiah, already 'sick unto death', is informed of his imminent death by the prophet. Weeping sorely, the king prays to God, who grants him another fifteen years of life and turns back the shadow on his sundial as a sign of this. The rest of chapter 38 is 'the writing of Hezekiah king of Judah, when he had been sick, and was recovered of his sickness' (verse 9).[49] 'The Authors Preface' to *Silex* (1655) prepares the way for the use of the story through a fleeting allusion to Hezekiah's belief that he was sick 'unto death' (Isaiah 38: 1): 'By the last *Poems* in the book (were not that *mistake* here prevented) you would judge all to be *fatherless*, and the *Edition* posthume; for (indeed) *I was nigh unto death*, and am still at no great distance from it' (*V*, 392). As Louis Martz has observed in another context, the boundary between physical and spiritual sickness is often unclear in Christian devotional writing: 'The occasion . . . may be one of actual sickness . . . but the ills of sin provide occasions for every moment'.[50] In Vaughan's world, a Christian's sickness could never be understood in purely medical terms, since physical ailments were thought to be the spiritual lesson or punishment of Providence. But whatever Vaughan believed to be the causes of sickness, his symptoms were real enough. 'The Epistle Dedicatory' to Sir Charles Egerton which prefaces *Flores Solitudinis: Certaine Rare and Elegant Pieces*

---

[48]   For *enlarge*, see Gen. 9: 27, Exod. 34: 24, Deut. 12: 20, Pss. 4: 1, 119: 32, Isa. 54: 2; cf. 2 Cor. 6: 13.

[49]   The story is repeated in 2 Kgs. 20: 1–6, 8–11, but *without* the return of praise important to Vaughan's use of Hezekiah; John Prideaux used the shorter version as the text for his sermon *Hezekiah's Sicknesse and Recovery, A Sermon Preached before the King's Majestie at Woodstocke*, part of *Certaine Sermons Preached by John Prideaux* (Oxford, 1637).

[50]   Martz, *Poetry of Meditation*, 140.

. . . *Collected in His Sicknesse and Retirement* (1654) complains of the 'incertainty of life' and of the 'peevish, inconstant state of health', which was threatening to cut short its author's literary endeavours (*V*, 215).

Hezekiah's name appears in seventeenth-century Christian discussions of sickness more often than any other biblical figure except Job.[51] His story and his song were traditionally invoked by sickness prayers in many devotional manuals, most notably the first official English Primer, the 'King's Primer' published in 1545, which reached for Isaiah 38: 10–20 to express 'Thanks for recovery'. It was retained in Elizabeth's updated and purified Primer, where it is referred to as the 'Thanks for recovery of health, Psalm Esaie.xxxviii'.[52] In 1619, Lewis Bayly included it as 'A Thanksgiving to bee said of one that is recovered from sicknesse' in the best-selling manual of Christian duty *The Practice of Piety*, a work Vaughan knew well.[53] In *The Rule and Exercises of Holy Dying* (1651), Jeremy Taylor alludes in passing to Hezekiah when he advises the sick man to 'set his house in order before he die'—Isaiah 38: 1 being the only occurrence of the phrase 'set his house in order' in the English bible.[54]

---

[51] For Job, see Antonie Batt, 'A Prayer To Be Said by One That is Sicke, for the Recoverie of His Health' in *A Hidden Treasure of Holie Prayers and Divine Meditations Newly Found Out in Holie Scripture* (Paris, 1641), sigs. Qii'–Qiii'. Poetical versions of Hezekiah's sickness include Alexander Hume, 'Thanks for the Deliverance of the Sicke', in *Poems Edited from the Text of Waldegrave*, ed. Alexander Lawson (Edinburgh, 1902), 41–6 (cf. ll. 95–103), an account which is followed by a passage on Job (ll. 107–12); Edward Buckler, 'Profitable and Pious Thoughts of Death', in *Midnight Meditations of Death; With Pious and Profitable Observations, and Consolations: Perused by Francis Quarles a Little before his Death* (1646). Eighteenth- and nineteenth-century poets continued to versify Hezekiah's sickness and recovery: Isaac Watts, 'Hymn 55 (C.M.) Hezekiah's Song; or, Sickness and Recovery. Isaiah xxxviii.9,&c', in *The Works of Isaac Watts, Containing, besides his Sermons and Essays on Miscellaneous Subjects, Several Additional Pieces*, 6 vols. (1810–11); Samuel Wesley the younger, 'Hezekiah's Thanksgiving for His Recovery from Sickness, Isaiah 38. A Pindarick Ode', in *Poems on Several Occasions*, 2nd edn. (Cambridge, 1743); Christopher Smart, 'A Hymn to the Supreme Being on Recovery from a Dangerous Fit of Illness', in *Christopher Smart: Selected Poems*; ed. Karina Williamson and Marcus Walsh (Harmondsworth, 1990); William Thompson, 'Sickness: A Poem in Five Books', in *Poems* (Oxford, 1757).

[52] *Private Prayers Put Forth by Authority During the Reign of Queen Elizabeth* [The Primer of 1559, the Orarium of 1560, the Preces Privatae of 1564, the Book of Christian Prayers of 1578, with an appendix containing the Litany of 1544], ed. William W. Clay (Cambridge, 1851), 65.

[53] Lewis Bayly, *The Practice of Piety: Directing a Christian How to Walke That He May Please God* (first published 1611; 1640), 574–80. On Bayly see Stranks, *Anglican Devotion*, 35–56 and for Vaughan's reading of him Watson, 'Two New Sources'.

[54] Jeremy Taylor, *The Rule and Exercises of Holy Dying*, in *Holy Living and Holy Dying*, ed. P. G. Stanwood, 2 vols. (Oxford, 1989), 'Sect. IX. Of the Sick Mans Practise of Charity

The king's song of thanksgiving was extremely popular in other contexts, particularly with those who, like Vaughan, were drawn to the 'poetical' section of the bible, that is, the Psalms, Proverbs, Ecclesiastes, the Song of Solomon, and usually Job.[55] It featured regularly in collections of versified biblical passages and commonly in the 'In Sacrae Scripturae Cantica' sections of Psalm commentaries as one of the extra songs belonging with the Psalms along with the songs of Daniel, Deborah and other biblical figures.[56] English verse adaptations begin with 'The Song of Ezechia' in John Hall's *The Court of Virtue* (1565) and appear regularly until Vaughan's own day, including a notable appearance in Sandys's *A Paraphrase upon the Divine Poems* (1638), the enlarged version of his *A Paraphrase upon the Psalmes of David* (1636).[57] Among the seventy-one entries for Isaiah listed by Rous's catalogue of scriptural commentaries held by the Bodleian library in 1620, chapter 38's seven entries make it the only section of Isaiah to be listed more than once.[58]

It would, then, have been relatively easy for seventeenth-century readers of the bible and other devotional literature to identify the texts at work in Vaughan's prayer: as well as Isaiah 38 these are Psalms 42 and 43, the book of Jonah, and Jeremiah 17, which was topical in the 1650s for being

---

and Justice, by Way of Rule' (167). The allusion to Isaiah is not noted in Stanwood's critical apparatus.

[55] Division of the bible into sections is discussed by Lewalski, *Protestant Poetics*, 32.

[56] See Jacob Janson, *In Psalterium, et Cantica Quibus per Horas Canonicas Romana Utitur Ecclesia, Expositio* (Lovanii, 1597), 798–802; Francis Titelman, *Elucidatio in Omnes Psalmos* (Antwerp, 1531), sigs. f377ʳ–f378ᵛ; Cornelius Janson, *Paraphrasis in Psalmos Omnes Davidicos* (Leiden, 1586), 321–3. Other popular scriptural songs were those of Moses, Habakkuk, Isaiah, Anna and Judith.

[57] John Hall, *The Court of Virtue* (1565), ed. Russell A. Fraser (1961; preserves 1565 pagination), 138–41; George Sandys, 'Esay 38', *A Paraphrase upon the Divine Poems*, 2nd edn. (1638), sigs. 3C4ʳ–3C4ᵛ; cf. No. 10, 'Jonah 1'. See also: George Wither, *Britains Remembrancer* (1628), Canto 2, 60ʳ⁻ᵛ, and 64ᵛ; and Wither, *Hymnes and Songs of the Church* (1623), which versifies Hezekiah's prayer from Isa. 37: 15; Nathaniel Richards, 'Teares Triumph' in *Poems Sacred and Satyricall* (1641), ll. 27–8; Nicholas Billingsley, 'Of Chattering', in his *A Treasury of Divine Raptures, Consisting of Serious Observations, Pious Ejaculations, Select Epigrams* (1667); Samuel Woodford, 'The Song of Hezekiah', in *A Paraphrase upon the Canticles, and Some Select Hymns of the New and Old Testament, with Other Occasional Compositions in English Verse* (1679); cf. Samuel Wesley, *The History of the Old Testament in Verse: with One Hundred and Eighty Sculptures in Two Volumes* (1715), ii. ch. CCI, 461–4.

[58] Rous also compiles bibliographies for chs. 1–7, 12, 16, and 52–3 (*Catologus Interpretum S. Scripturae juxta Numerorum Ordinem, quo Extant in Bibliotheca Bodleiana*, 20–2, appended to Thomas James, *Catalogus Universalis Librorum in Bibliotheca Bodleiana Omnium Librorum*, 2nd edn. (Oxford, 1620)).

the source of the phrase 'the hope of Israel', the title of Manassah ben Israel's petition for Jewish repatriation.[59] None of Vaughan's texts was obscure to an age which attended to the farthest reaches of scripture, nor would his readers have been ignorant of the range of interpretative opinion which surrounded them. Hezekiah's kingship was also important, of course. Although Vaughan does not compare Charles I with Hezekiah, other poets had done so in 1649. In his elegy for the dead king, which appeared soon after the execution, Bishop Henry King wrote that 'Hezekiah he exceeds in zeal'; and thirty-five years later the same comparison was made on the death of his son Charles II: 'All *Isra'l* when good *Hezekiah* Di'd | To his last Breath, true Loyal Honour pey'd'.[60]

But it was the double applicability of Hezekiah's story to his own life which most appealed to Vaughan: that is, the king's sickness and his singing of thanks. The relations between sickness and writing were discussed in a 1626 sermon by Robert Harris during his incumbency at Hanwell in Oxfordshire, when he noted the 'double condition and behaviour of King *Hezekiah*, 1. he was sicke, and then he prayed: 2. he is recovered, and now he gives thankes'.[61] Always a typological thinker, Vaughan recognized this pattern in his own experience and allowed it to shape his view of the act of writing divine poetry. Like Hezekiah, Vaughan was 'sick unto death' (Isaiah 38: 1); and although the prophet did not come to tell him so, Isaiah's book did. This is the '*message of death*' expected in the 1655 Preface: 'and when I expected, and had (by his assistance) prepared for a *message* of *death*, then did he *answer* me with *life*' (*V*, 392). This 'prepared' calmness contrasts strongly with Hezekiah's weeping into the wall, in shock and grief. The king's troubled reaction divided interpreters: some, like Calvin, saw signs of rebellion against God's will and a fear 'that his

---

[59] Edward Spencer's *A Brief Epistle to the Learned Manasseh ben Israel in Answer to His, Dedicated to the Parliament, by E.S.* (1650) reproduces lines from Vaughan's 'The Shepheards', one of the few pieces of evidence for Vaughan's readership.

[60] Henry King, 'An Elegy upon . . . Charles. the I' (1649), l. 39 (*Poems*, ed. M. Crum (Oxford, 1965)); Patrick Ker, *An Elegy on the Deplorable, and Never Enough to be Lamented Death, of Charles the II* (1685), ll. 15–16.

[61] Robert Harris, *Hezekiah's Recovery; or, A Sermon, Shewing What Use Hezekiah Did, and All Should Make of Their Deliverance from Sicknesse, to Which is Annexed a Particular Postscript to the Citie of London*, 2nd edn. (1626), 1. Harris's parsonage at Hanwell was 'a favourite resort for Oxford students', despite his support of Parliament. Later a member of the Westminster Assembly, then 'one of the six divines commissioned to preach and invade any pulpit they pleased', Harris eventually became Master of Trinity, Oxford, and was much satirized by Royalists as a pluralist (*DNB*).

sinnes had bereaved him of his life'; for others, weeping was a normal display of emotion: 'Tis not unlawfull to pray in mirth, to sing in miserie, ordinarily; but tis simply necessary in afflictions to be prayerful, in the midst of mercies to be thankfull, and to entertaine several conditions with different behaviours.'[62] Any panic or fear Vaughan may have felt at the approach of death is expunged, with hindsight, from his carefully modulated account. But there is an inevitable tension between that calmness and a broader identification with the weeping king. The witness of other poems, particularly the anxious questions of the Body in 'Death. *A Dialogue*' and 'Resurrection and Immortality', reveals Vaughan's familiarity with the fear of leaving this life and points up the contrast between the 'prepared' Vaughan of 'The Authors Preface' and the man who recognized himself in the figure of the weeping king. (I shall return shortly to the significance of Hezekiah's weeping for Vaughan.)[63]

The second part of Hezekiah's condition—'he is recovered, and now he gives thankes'—also reveals something about Vaughan's poetry and his view of it. Preachers and commentators often used the king's song of thanksgiving and praise to remind their audience that prayer is a sacrifice of worship as well as a petition. 'Not to be forward with our praises as prayers, argues base self-love and servilitie, and makes it appeare that wee love not God but his gifts', urged Harris.[64] Adam Littleton went further, seeing Hezekiah's act of praise as virtually synonymous with faith itself:

Again, *praising* and *celebrating God*, and *hoping for his truth*, (*his mercy*, say the LXX; *his salvation*, the Chaldee Paraphrast) are here made *Synonyma's*, to mean the same thing. If so, then a generous trust in God's mercy is the right celebration of it. *To trust in God is to praise him.* I have been afflicted; God has deliver'd me; I praise him for it: how? by trusting that he will still deliver me.[65]

---

[62] Calvin, *A Commentary upon the Prophecie of Isaiah* (1609), 392; Harris, *Hezekiah's Recovery*, 2. In *The Way to True Peace and Rest, Delivered at Edinburgh in XVI Sermons: on the Lords Supper: Hezekiahs Sicknesse: and Other Select Scriptures* (1617), Robert Bruce suggested that Hezekiah, a good Christian, did not fear death, as Isaiah's fierceness ('for thou shalt die, and not live') has sometimes suggested. Bruce diagnoses Hezekiah's disease as the plague, and since plague is always fatal, he sees Isaiah's annunciation as rather pointless. On the probable nature of Hezekiah's sickness, see Julius Preuss, *Biblical and Talmudic Medicine*, trans. and ed. Fred Rosner (New York, 1978), 143, 341–2.

[63] Vaughan's eschatological dialogues are discussed in Rosalie Osmond, *Mutual Accusation: Seventeenth-Century Body and Soul Dialogues in Their Literary and Theological Context* (Toronto, 1990), chs. 5, 6.

[64] Harris, *Hezekiah's Recovery*, 4.

[65] Adam Littleton, *Hezekiah's Return of Praise for His Recovery* (1668), 34.

Thus Hezekiah becomes a type of the Reformed Christian, for whom 'an earnest and vehement Prayer' is a sign of true faith and perseverance.[66] Littleton glosses Isaiah 38: 18 as '*Life itself is a blessing to be spent in the giver's praise*': 'For the grave cannot praise thee, death cannot celebrate thee: they that go down into the pit, cannot hope for thy truth.' Of this passage Calvin notes disapprovingly that while it is good to desire life in order to praise God, 'the faithfull glorifie God no lesse by their death'.[67] Underlying this judgement is Calvin's strongly anti-somatic reading of Paul, particularly his advice in Romans 8 that Christians look always away from this life to the next and 'walk not after the flesh, but after the Spirit' (Romans 8: 4); texts like this influenced Calvin profoundly and led him to suspect a strong desire for fleshly life. For Vaughan's 'The Authors Preface', Hezekiah's story relates more simply to what one should do on continuing to live. In theory, it matters little to the contented soul Vaughan presents there whether it live or die, since either eventuality is according to God's will. But in the case of life, it is Hezekiah's story that teaches the poet that he should spend his days in praise of God: 'see the Lord, even the Lord in the Land of the living' (38: 11). Though Vaughan makes no allusion to Romans in the prefatory prayer, its teaching underlies the entire preface: 'For whether we live, we live unto the Lord; and whether we die, we die unto the Lord: whether we live therefore, or die, we are the Lord's' (Romans 14: 8).

The sickbed has always provided an opportunity for withdrawal from the affairs of the world and proper reflection on the life to come. This was Robert Bruce's explanation, in writing of Hezekiah's sickness in *The Way to True Peace and Rest* (1617), for why Providence brought sickness, namely to 'bid the Patient lay aside the worldly part: and next, to prepare for the heavenly part'.[68] The Book of Common Prayer's 'Order for the visitation of the sick', which Vaughan quotes from in *The Mount of Olives'* sickness prayer, enumerated many possible causes for God's 'visitation' of sickness upon us:

And for what cause soever this sickenesse is sente unto you; whether it be to trie youre patience for the example of other, and that your fayth may be found in the day of the lord laudable, glorious, and honorable, to the encrease of glory, and endless felicitie: Or else it be sent unto you to correct and amend in you, whatsoever doeth offend the eyes of our heavenly father.[69]

[66] Taylor, *Holy Living*, 177.   [67] Calvin, *A Commentary upon Isaiah*, 392.
[68] Bruce, *True Peace and Rest*, 163.   [69] *BCP*, 418.

Sickness could be a blessing in disguise, then, which might tend 'to our great profite and commodity; to wit, that we being corrected here, should not perish hereafter with the wicked world'.[70]

Just as Providence was seen as the source of sickness and affliction, sent 'no doubt for blessed ends', so recovery could be understood as a providential sign that God willed the sufferer's earthly life to continue.[71] Most seventeenth-century Britons understood coincidental or dramatic events as acts of God.[72] But to Calvinists, who were taught to watch for special signs of their spiritual election, 'every happening, catastrophe or trivial, was held to be relevant to the quest for assurance that one numbered among the "saints", a signpost concerning the Lord's soteriological intentions'.[73] Henry Vaughan seems to have shared the general habit of relating important, disturbing or joyous events to his own spiritual life. For instance, in 'Thou that know'st for whom I mourne', probably an elegy for his younger brother William, Henry tells God that he knows it was his sin that 'forc'd thy hand | To cull this *Prim-rose* out' (ll. 9–10).

Such unabashed selfishness may now shock, but it was an inevitable consequence of the providentialist world-view of that Reformed Christianity which in its most extreme form produced the 'experimental' Puritan practice of sifting every event in one's life for a sign of election (or, indeed, reprobation). Reading misfortunes as providential signs was also one way of explaining and coping with calamity. In his diary for 1 March 1650, the Puritan clergyman Ralph Josselin thanked 'Gods

---

[70] Bruce, *True Peace and Rest*, 159. Jeremy Taylor is reluctant to emphasize the profits of sickness: 'God's providence is not so afflictive and full of trouble as that it hath placed sicknesse and infirmity among things simply necessary; and in most persons it is but a sickly and effeminate vertue which is imprinted upon our spirits with fears and the sorrowes of a feaver, or a peevish consumption. It is but a miserable remedy to be beholding to a sicknesse for our health', *Holy Dying*, III. iv, 'Advantages of Sickness' (97).

[71] Nathaniel Wanley, 'Upon his Sicknesse and Paine', stz. 4, in *The Poems of Nathaniel Wanley*, ed. L. C. Martin (Oxford, 1928), 49.

[72] Providential thought of the period is best entered through Alexandra Walsham, *Providence in Early Modern England* (Oxford, 1999); William R. Elton, *'King Lear' and the Gods* (San Marino, Calif., 1966), ch. 2, 'Renaissance Concepts of Providence', 9–33; Thomas, *Religion and the Decline of Magic*, 78–112; Blair Worden, 'Providence and Politics in Cromwellian England', *Past and Present*, 109 (1985), 55–99; Worden, 'Oliver Cromwell and the Sin of Achan', 125–45 in D. Beales and G. Best (eds.), *History, Society and the Churches: Essays in Honour of Owen Chadwick* (Cambridge, 1985), 125–45; Barbara Donagan, 'Understanding Providence: The Difficulties of Sir William and Lady Waller', *Journal of Ecclesiastical History*, 39 (1988), 433–44.

[73] Walsham, *Providence*, 15.

hand'—a providential emblem, of course, as it is on the title-page of *Silex Scintillans* (1650)—for the recovery of his children from an eye sickness. Two months later, as his daughter lay near to death, he thanked God for her life and drew what comfort he could from her death in providential terms:

> my litle Mary, very weake, wee feared shee was drawing on, feare came on my heart very much, but shee is not mine, but the Lords, and shee is not too good for her father . . . shee was: 8 yeares and 45 dayes old when shee dyed, my soule had abundant cause to blesse god for her, who was our first fruites, and those god would have offered to him, and this I freely resigned up to him, it was a pretious child, a bundle of myrrhe, a bundle of sweetnes; . . . Lord I rejoyce I had such a present for thee.[74]

When Vaughan, prepared for death, was faced with finding an explanation for his recovered health, Hezekiah's song provided a providential lead: 'The living, the living, he shall praise thee, as I do this day' (Isaiah 39: 19, as given, slightly varied from the Authorized Version, in the prefatory prayer). If God gives life, it is fit that life should return thanks in a way that only the living can. For Hezekiah, a song; for Vaughan, poetry. This, then, is the frame into which Vaughan placed his poetry's renewed offering in the preface to *Silex Scintillans* (1655). His verses of praise and thanksgiving are the 'fruits' for which he hopes in 'The Authors Preface'—'that I may flourish not with *leafe* onely, but with some *fruit* also' (p. 392)—and in the first part of the 'Dedication': 'My God! thou that didst dye for me, | These thy deaths fruits I offer thee' (ll. 1–2).

The fruits Vaughan offers back are his poems, but also his life. For since the greater fruit of Christ's death is the redemption of mankind, Vaughan's sacrifice of 'fruits' extends to include his life and removes the distinction between living and writing. With a paradox learnt from Herbert, Vaughan makes the offering as if his life and poetry were both the immediate product of Christ's death.[75] At the end of the shorter, 1650 'Dedication', he offers *Silex Scintillans* to God as 'thy Tenants Rent' (l. 14), precisely the same metaphor with which Robert Harris explains the song of Hezekiah: 'wee owe God thankes, 1. in point of Law and covenant; Tis

---

[74] *The Diary of Ralph Josselin 1616–1683*, ed. Alan MacFarlane, Records of Social and Economic History, NS, III (1976), 191, 201, 203.

[75] Vaughan is remembering the 'Dedication' of *The Temple*: 'Lord, my first fruits present themselves to thee; | Yet not mine neither: for from thee they came, | And must return.' (ll. 1–3).

our profession, our promise, our cheefage and rent that is due to him'.[76]
Debt to God is a recurring image of covenant or agreement with God in
the seventeenth century, used by Josselin of his dead daughter and with
great delicacy by Ben Jonson, of his dead son Benjamin:

> Farewell, thou child of my right hand, and joy;
>   My sinne was too much hope of thee, loved boy,
> Seven yeeres thou wert lent to me, and I thee pay,
> Exacted by thy fate, on the just day.[77]

Death is a one-off payment which cancels all debts. Recovery demands
more, calling not for one 'just day', but for continuous instalments in a
life of prayer and praise. So Vaughan reads Hezekiah's tale, and so he will
produce a 'holy life and verse' worthy of a Christian-sacred poet.

Reformed Christians relished the literary virtues of Hezekiah's thanksgiving, as the naming of the passage in various translations suggests: 'The
writing of Hezekiah', '*Hezekiah*'s Song of Thanksgiving', 'The songe of
Ezechia' and so on.[78] Even Robert Harris, whose concern was the story's
moral uses, notes 'the nature of it, a Poem written . . . The writing is
Poeticall, and delivered in Verse, for the help both of memory & affection'.[79] Most commentators make something of the fact that Hezekiah is
supposed to have written down his song. Clearly this writtenness would
have moved a bookish man like Henry Vaughan, whose entire spiritual
life, from the first epiphany to his last farewell—'O book! lifes guide! how
shall we part, | And thou so long seiz'd of my heart!'[80]—was spent in the
company of other literary-spiritual fruits. Having begun by commending
poetry as an aid to memory, Robert Harris later urges his educated audi-
tor to consider the purpose and power of writing, in a passage which
speaks touchingly to many of the preoccupations of Vaughan's 1655
Preface and poems:

for singular mercies we must doe some singular thing, set apart some time, some
Present, some gift, doe some thing that may seale up our humblest acknowledgement of Gods goodnesse . . .

---

[76] *V*, 394, l. 14; Harris, *Hezekiah's Recovery*, 4. *OED*, chevage ('Capitation or poll-money paid to a lord or superior') cites twice from Harris.

[77] ('On my first sonne', *Epigram* 45, ll. 1–4) from *Epigrammes* (1616); see *Ben Jonson*, ed. C. H. Herford, Percy and Evelyn Simpson, 11 vols. (Oxford, 1925–52), VIII [The Poems, The Prose Works] (1947), 41.

[78] Harris, *Hezekiah's Recovery*, 1; Littleton, *Hezekiah's Return of Praise*, 11; John Hall, *The Court of Virtue*, 138.

[79] Harris, *Hezekiah's Recovery*, 16.   [80] 'To the Holy Bible', ll. 18–21.

Art thou learned? doe good that way, as *Hezekiah* did. Some conceive him well seene in the Mathematicks . . . however, wee have his Epistle and Poeme extant, and they hold out instructions to the worlds end. If God had given thee sufficiencie in this kinde, thou mayest speake thy minde to men yet unborne, and convey to them that light which God hath reached to thee. Be not too curious in this way; thou seest that some in this scribling age set forth their owne wits, some their owne folly: doe thou set forth Gods praise, and ayme at mans good; write something (as thy gift is) that may doe posteritie good.[81]

This strikes deep chords with Vaughan's attacks on the idle scribbler and the hurt he does himself and others by making 'for himself another *body*, in which he always *lives*, and *sins* (after *death*) as *fast* and as *foul*, as ever he did in his *life*' (*V*, 390). But if that body can live and sin, so can it live and work at 'mans good'. Harris's exhortation to emulate Hezekiah in setting forth God's praise finds the same strong justification as Vaughan's faith in sacred poetry: that literary works go on after their authors' deaths, transmitting faith and wonder to generations unborn. Or, in Vaughan's adaptation of Hezekiah's words: 'the living, the living, he shall praise thee, as I do this day: the Father to the children shall make known thy truth'. Each person, as Harris advises, has a special gift of thanksgiving, which they should return to God as they are able, special monuments of God's victories like Goliath's sword and Gideon's 'Ephod-like present, what ever it was'.[82] Each to his own. If a special talent is yours, you also have a duty to use it—'as thy gift is'.

FIRE TO ME

The purpose and power of holy verse is the subject of the short lyric with which Vaughan concludes the preface to *Silex* (1655), 'Vain Wits and eyes'. This ingenious, patient and restful poem is a word in the ear of all those 'ingenious persons, which in the late notion are termed *Wits*':

> Vain Wits and eyes
> Leave, and be wise:
> Abuse not, shun not holy fire,
> But with true tears wash off your mire.
> Tears and these flames will soon grow kinde,
> And mix an eye-salve for the blinde.
> Tears cleanse and supple without fail,

---

[81] Harris, *Hezekiah's Recovery*, 15, 22.   [82] Ibid. 18.

> And fire will purge your callous veyl.
> Then comes the light! which when you spy,
> And see your nakedness thereby,
> Praise him, who dealt his gifts so free
> In tears to you, in fire to me.

As well as Vaughan's characteristic blend of scientific and scriptural ideas about the nature of light, these lines also call upon seventeenth-century medical terms to represent spiritual sickness.[83] Though there is no allusion to a single passage or disease, *mire, supple, purge*, and *callous* are words commonly collocated in sixteenth- and seventeenth-century medical books, where receipts for eye-salves and eye-bright mixtures (and even an unrelated complaint called the 'holy-fire') can also be found.[84] The terms all feature, for instance, in John Hartman's translation of Oswald Crollius' *Bazilia Chymica, & Praxis Chymiatricae; or, Royal and Practical Chymistry in Three Treatises* (1670); and with Quercetanus, Crollius is the most frequently cited authority in Heinrich Nollius' *Hermetical Physick*, the work Vaughan translated at the same time he was working on *Silex* (1655) and which was published a few months before it.[85]

Wit is famously a complex word.[86] In 'Vain Wits and eyes', Vaughan flourishes it with conventional irony at the writers of '*vitious verse*' he has already identified in 'The Authors Preface' (*V*, 389). But also, by bringing together *Wits* and *eyes*, he recalls the ancient psychological theory according to which man has five outward or bodily wits (the modern senses) and

---

[83] For Christian discussions of the divine light of John ch. 1: see Calvin, *Commentary on the Gospel According to John*, trans. by William Pringle (Edinburgh, 1847), 33–7, 324; Augustine Marlorate, *A Catholike and Ecclesiasticall Exposition of the Holy Gospell after S. John* (1575), 10; George Hutcheson, *An Exposition of the Gospel of Jesus Christ According to John* (1657), 5 and cf. Andrew Willet's discussion of first light in *Hexapla in Genesin; that is, A Sixfold Commentarie upon Genesis* (1632), 3; cf. Margaret Llasera, 'Concepts of Light in the Poetry of Henry Vaughan', *Seventeenth Century*, 3 (1988), 47–61; Joseph Anthony Mazzeo, 'Light Metaphysics in Dante's *Convivio*', *Traditio*, 14 (1958), 191–229.

[84] 'Purgation' was standard medical practice, though often overused—'Whether vacuations come spontaneously by Nature, or be caused by Art, there must be a mean and measure used therein. And hereby are confuted those ignorant Physicians who think a man is never well purged but when he is abundantly purged' (*The Aphorismes of Hippocrates, Prince of Physicians* (1655), 15). Vaughan's autograph Latin edition of the *Aphorismi* (Marburg, 1650) survives in Philadelphia (Edwin Wolf II, 'Some Books of Early English Provenance').

[85] John Hartman, *Bazilica Chymica, & Praxis Chymiatricae; or, Royal and Practical Chymistry in Three Treatises* (1670), Part I, 30 ('A water profitable against Scabs, Fistula's, and malignant Ulcers'), 160–6 ('Externals. Vulnerary (*a*), Ulcerous, Pustulous . . .'), Part II, 2 ('Of the Eyes'), Part III, 40 ('Affects of the Eyes').

[86] William Empson, 'Wit in the Essay on Criticism', in *The Structure of Complex Words* (1951), 84–100; C. S. Lewis, 'Wit', in *Studies in Words* (Cambridge, 1960), 86–110.

five inward or ghostly wits: memory, estimation, fancy, imagination and common wit.[87] Since the inward wits were held responsible for artistic and creative acts including poetry, Vaughan's collocation 'Wits and eyes' can be seen as an act of poetic renovation, revivifying the compacted idea Wits (Scribblers) by suggesting an underlying metonymic origin in the idea Wits (Users of inward wits).

To caution Wits against an improper use of their gifts, Vaughan has written a riddling, witty poem, whose simple rhythm, unthreatening monosyllables and Herbertian brevity bely a strong web of interconnecting conceits. Most importantly, the witty reader has to spot the origin of Vaughan's *eye-salve* metaphor in the story of the blind man who was cured by Christ's spittle; then he or she must also work out that the inner Wits' proper job is not to make light with witty words, but to receive the light of God.[88] The best gloss on 'Vain Wits' is provided by 'Easter-day' from *Silex* (1650), which alludes to the same story:

> Arise, arise,
> And with his healing bloud anoint thine Eys,
> Thy inward Eys; his bloud will cure thy mind,
> Whose spittle only could restore the blind.

> (ll. 13–16)

Margaret Llasera has explained the Neoplatonic distinction Vaughan accepted (if he did not always hold closely to) between the divine light *lux* and *lumen*, the light of the senses.[89] This notion of two different but related lights makes it clear that Vaughan's attempt to return the Wits' wits ('thy inward Eys', receptors of *lux*) to their proper task will be achieved by stopping them writing '*vitious verse*'; repentant tears will then wipe clean their inner eyes to admit *lux* once more. This spiritual process is figured by what happens to the real eyes, receptors of *lumen*; the outer wit, but also the vehicle of Vaughan's conceit. Like the inward, ghostly senses which are being put to ill use, so too the eyes have been turned to corrupt use by writers, who observe the transitory beauties of the world, rather than weep for sin. Their tearless eyes are sore, dried up and covered over with calluses.

Though these conceits are simple enough to grasp, 'Vain Wits and eyes' is complicated because inner cleansing is figured by outer cleansing— weeping—which is itself more than merely metaphorical. Vaughan is

---

[87] *OED*, wit, *sb.*, 3a; cf. Lewis, 'Wit', 87–8.

[88] The biblical accounts in question are John 9: 1–14 and Mark 8: 22–6.

[89] Llasera, 'Concepts of Light', 47–53.

playing on the necessity of representing inward movements by external ones in order to suggest the holistic experience of true repentance. The tears Vaughan urges are not internal, 'spiritual' tears but also real ones, a brine which will also work the inner suppling of the ghostly wits. True repentance is simultaneously an inward and outward weeping, a double cleansing action.

The *holy fire* which mixes with tears in Vaughan's eye-salve suggests the appearance of the Holy Ghost after Christ's Ascension, when the Apostles were crowned with tongues of fire; in a more general way, it recalls God's fiery manifestations in the Old Testament, and seems, therefore, to be a metaphor for the action of grace.[90] Many poems in *Silex Scintillans* figure divine power as a fire or flame through biblical images, among which Vaughan lingers over Malachi's prophecy of an apocalyptic Refiner and the fire of Revelation which tries and purifies the faithful.[91] The *holy fire* of 'Vain Wits and eyes' is certainly a manifestation of the Spirit, but it has a less direct form of action than the Pentecostal fires:

> Abuse not, shun not holy fire,
> But with true tears wash off your mire.
> Tears and these flames will soon grow kinde,
> And mix an eye-salve for the blinde.

> (ll. 3–6)

In a lesser poem, *these flames* would simply be a synonym for *holy fire*, but in Vaughan's the shift from the single *fire* to plural *flames* opens a possibility that *these flames* are the poems in the reader's hand; *these*, the poem's only deictic, is carefully deployed to create this fruitful ambiguity. The last couplet urges repentant sinners to 'Praise him, who dealt his gifts so free | In tears to you, in fire to me': could it not be that Vaughan, who saw '*vitious verse*' as a 'soul-killing Issue' had come to see holy poems as fiercely medicinable, potent with Spiritual care?

Vaughan's *holy fire* has burst from several sparkles in *Silex* (1650). A

---

[90] See Chapter 5 for a full discussion of Acts 2. Instances of divine fire in *Silex Scintillans* include 'This made him put on clouds, and fire and smoke' ('Jacob's Pillow and Pillar', l. 7); the 'fiery Law' ('The Law, and the Gospel', l. 2); 'Nay thou thy self, my God, in *fire*, | *Whirlwinds*, and *clouds*, and the *soft voice* | Speak'st there so much' ('Religion', ll. 17–19).

[91] Mal. 3: 1–3 and 'Ascension-hymn', ll. 25–36; Rev. 3: 18 and Heb. 11: 17 and '*Isaacs Marriage*', l. 65; on Mal. 4, see Erwin Panofsky, *Meaning in the Visual Arts: Papers in and on Art History* (Garden City, NY, 1955), 286–8.

humbler version appeared in 'The Lampe' (*Silex* Part 1), where Vaughan saw his poems as lamp-light passed on:

> Yet, burn'st thou here, a full day; while I spend
> My rest in Cares, and to the dark world lend
> These flames, as thou dost thine to me.

> (ll. 5–7)

The flames George Herbert lent to the world are also a source of *holy fire*. In 'The Match', Vaughan addresses a 'Dear friend! whose holy, ever-living lines | Have done much good | To many, and have checkt my blood' (ll. 1–3). On the evidence of the 1655 Preface, where Vaughan praises 'Mr. *George Herbert*, whose holy *life* and *verse* gained many pious *Converts* (of whom I am the least) and gave the first check to a most flourishing and admired *wit* of his time' (*V*, 391), and with the further clue of a strong echo of Herbert's 'Obedience', the friend is normally identified with the poet of *The Temple*:

> Dear friend! whose holy, ever-living lines
> Have done much good
> To many, and have checkt my blood,
> My fierce, wild blood that still heaves, and inclines,
> But is still tam'd
> By those bright fires which thee inflam'd.

> (ll. 1–6)

Vaughan gives a glimpse here of the ongoing process of restraint and guidance begun by his first reading of *The Temple* and continued by 'those bright fires which thee inflam'd', a conflagration which can only be the power of the Holy Spirit. There is a strong suggestion that Herbert's poetry speaks to Vaughan in the language of the Spirit, and that its words act as a channel for divine power and force in the task of converting sinners and sustaining their new-found faith.

The conceit of *holy fire* was frequently employed by late sixteenth-century poets to describe their inspiration, and was afterwards borrowed by divine poets to talk about theirs. Donne's Sappho begins her letter to Philaenis by enquiring 'Where is that holy fire, which verse is said | To have?'; and Ben Jonson, one of the influences on Vaughan's early *Poems, with the Tenth Satyre of Juvenal Englished* (1646) wrote:

> This morning, timely rapt with holy fire,
> I thought to forme unto my zealous *Muse*,

> What kinde of creature I could most desire,
> To honor, serve, and love; as *Poets* use.[92]

Christian poets of the seventeenth century seized on this sense of being overtaken by a divine power to use the phrase, like George Daniel, of a God 'who didst inspire I My frozen Spirits with this holy fire'.[93] *Holy fire* almost always features in their thanksgivings or requests for the Spirit's literary inspiration: Giles Fletcher the Younger praised God as 'thou that didst this holy fire infuse' and Francis Quarles asks Him several times to 'inflame my frozen tongue with holy fire', a phrase which glances at the coal with which a seraph touched Isaiah's lips (Isa. 6: 6–7).[94] Praising George Sandys's *A Paraphrase upon the Divine Poems* (1638), Dudley Digges raised holy fire above a mere secular flame: 'Let others wanton it, while I admire I Thy warmth, which doth proceed from holy Fire'; and Arthur Wilson told Edward Benlowes that the poet was 'Loves *Flamen*, and with Holy Fire I Refin'st thy *Muse*, to make her mount the Higher'.[95]

In the prefatory texts to *Silex Scintillans* (1655), Vaughan, too, saw the Christian poet as God's scribe, a passive receptor of *holy fire* like the writers of the bible. The dedicatory poem to that volume extends the 1650 version with two new stanzas, beginning:

> Dear Lord, 'tis finished! and now he
> That copied it, presents it thee.
> 'Twas thine first, and to thee returns,
> From thee it shin'd, though here it burns;

---

[92] John Donne, 'Sappho to Philaenis', ll. 1–2; Ben Jonson, Epigram 76 'On Lucy Countess of Bedford', in *Ben Jonson*, viii. 52; cf. William Habington, 'In Praise of the City Life, in the Long Vacation' (ll. 1–8), in which *holy fire* is the gift of knowledge (*The Poems of William Habington*, ed. Kenneth Allott (Liverpool, 1948)).

[93] George Daniel, 'numero *Deus* impure gaudet' following Ecclesiasticus 51 in *The Poems of George Daniel*, ed. Alexander B. Grosart (Edinburgh, 1878), ll. 49–50.

[94] Giles Fletcher the Younger, *Christs Victorie in Heaven*, in *Giles and Phineas Fletcher: Poetical Works*, ed. F. S. Boas (Cambridge, 1908), l. 19; Francis Quarles, *Divine Poems* (1632), 'To the Most High, His Humble Servant Implores His Favourable Assistance', l. 12; cf. 'Job Militant', ll. 119–20.

[95] Digges, 'To My Worthy Kinsman Mr George Sandys, in His Excellent Paraphrase upon Job', l. 10 (in Sandys, *A Paraphrase upon the Divine Poems* (1638)); Arthur Wilson, dedication to Edward Benlowes, *Theophila; or, Loves Sacrifice* (1652), ll. 105–6. For other 1650s examples see Robert Aylett, *Divine and Moral Speculations in Metrical Numbers, upon Various Subjects* (1654), III, Meditation 2 'Of Zeal and Godly Jealeusie', ll. 1–4, 69 f. and 163 f.; also 'Joseph, or Pharoah's Favorite', II, ll. 399–400; Thomas Baines's dedication to the William Cartwright folio (1651), ll. 35–40; William Davenant, *Gondibert*, II. 5. 203 f.

> If the Sun rise on rocks, is't right,
> To call it their inherent light?
> No, nor can I say, this is mine,
> For, dearest Jesus, 'tis all thine.

> (ll. 15–22)

A humble disclaimer on Vaughan's part, but a far-reaching one, since *'twas thine first* and *'tis all thine* offer back *Silex Scintillans* to God as His own Word. Vaughan uses another deictic ambiguity, this time in *here*, to great effect: God's light not only shines *here* in the poems, but *here* on *rocks*—suggesting, of course, the rocky heart at the centre of both poet and poetry, while also glancing at the discarded emblem of *Silex* (1650). *Holy fire*, it seems, can not only burn within the Christian poet's heart (inflamed there by Herbert's poetry) but also *through* poetry: the poet can set that fire aflame in the crucible of other souls. Repentance, in 'Vain Wits and eyes', is an alchemical fusion of the power of the Holy Spirit (flowing through the poetry of *Silex Scintillans*) with the true, penitent tears of both inner and outer eye.

A SAD BLUBBER'D STORY

With his scriptural prayer presiding over the two-part *Silex Scintillans*, Vaughan had sealed a new understanding of sacred poetry as a return of prayer and praise, given his 'finished' book shape and purpose, and made his first offering of thanks in doing so. But he had also laid an ever greater responsibility on himself to be like Hezekiah in offering poetic sacrifices free from self-interest, ambition and pride. Like the poems which follow, Vaughan's prefatory texts are quietly alive to the dangers of wit even as they propose the imagination as a spiritual gift capable of responding appropriately to divine grace. 'Vain Wits and eyes' affirms poetry's power and duty to be the *holy fire* of true hymns, a co-agent in the production of spiritual eye-salve; but it also knows that all too often poetry becomes the vanity of jigging Wits, those '*lascivious fictions*' which 'The Authors Preface' abhors as a 'soul-killing Issue' (*V*, 388). The final lesson of the 1655 preface, then, is how to ensure that poetry is of the former kind, and not the latter; that it was *holy fire*, and not the bad sight of callused eyes.

The eye-salve that Vaughan prescribes is a briny one. Throughout *Silex Scintillans*, and especially in the 1655 poems, tears are a complementary offering to prayer and poetry and an important check on creativity. This complementarity is most beautifully expressed through another biblical story in Vaughan's 'St. Mary Magdalene', but it also informs the prefatory texts, particularly 'Vain Wits and eyes'. Vaughan hopes that the repentant tears of the Wits will participate in a spiritual eye-salve which will let God's light back in and show them their nakedness. This light is a saving illumination only, and not that *holy fire* which burns in Vaughan's poetic furnace; but although repentant tears will not yet help Wits write their own true hymns, there is a suggestion that they one day might. After all, as Vaughan confesses, he too had turned away from the follies of secular verse through tearful repentance and, finally, a new dedication of his work to God.

In the two-part *Silex Scintillans*, tears enable Vaughan to defend artistic praise against the thought that sin and vanity lurk within every act of poetic creation, a fear shared by Marvell's 'The Coronet', which examines the poetic garland its author has weaved for God only to find

> the Serpent old
> That, twining in his speckled breast,
> About the flow'rs disguis'd does fold,
> With wreaths of Fame and Interest.
>
> (ll. 13–16)[96]

Deciding that art must be intrinsically corrupt, Marvell's poet-speaker calls on God to 'shatter' and 'tread' his poetic garland and the Devil with them; only thus can the poem conceive that it will partake in a meaningful sacrifice. After such a conclusion, which remembers the utter depravity which for Calvinists renders all human actions unacceptable to God, Marvell seems to have dropped the practice of poetic devotion.[97] While he lived with his own uncertainties about the worth of art, Vaughan found hope and encouragement in weeping, and particularly in the biblical tears of Mary Magdalene, whose 'Cheap, mighty Art! her Art of love' he esteemed. The example of Mary's incessant tears, like Hezekiah's constant returns of praise, gave Vaughan strength for his artistic endeavours and the confidence to struggle for purity of intention. Her inarticulate

---

[96] *The Poems and Letters of Andrew Marvell*, ed. H. M. Margoliouth, 3rd edn. rev. by Pierre Legouis with Elsie Duncan-Jones, 2 vols. (Oxford, 1971).

[97] The theology of 'The Coronet' and its place in Marvell's writing are discussed by Barbara Lewalski, 'Marvell as Religious Poet', ch. 12 of *Approaches to Marvell*, The York Tercentenary Lectures, ed. C. A. Patrides (1978), esp. 255–7, and by Legouis, *Andrew Marvell*, 37–8.

message of love reminded the sophisticated poet that the simplest groan could be more powerful than his 'arted string', but it also heartened him to pursue his own divine gift—poetry—in imitation of Mary's divine art of tears, an art which she gathered from the dregs of her past sins.

That we should both pray and weep together is lesson implicit in the preface to *Silex* (1655): for it is not Hezekiah's prayer alone, but the combination of that prayer and his tears, 'wept sore' into the wall, which move God to lengthen the king's life. As one Middle English dialogue of the soul's confession explains with a disarming simplicity, tears have a special advocacy with the Almighty:

> We find nowhere that God denied anything for which any man besought Him with tears . . . Therefore God heard him [Hezekiah] and said to His prophet, who was homeward: 'Turn again,' quoth He, 'and say to the king: *Vidi lacrimam tuam*, "I saw" quoth He, "thy tears, and I heard thy prayer. Thou shalt live fifteen years; so much have I increased thy life." '[98]

The king's prayers and tears *together* move God to send back His homeward prophet with a message of life. The lesson was not lost on either of the Vaughan twins. Recording the dreams of one April night in 1659, Thomas Vaughan wrote in his notebook *Aqua Vitae*: 'I went to bed after prayers, and hearty teares'.[99] *Silex Scintillans* witnesses the great extent to which, like Thomas and Hezekiah, Henry felt tears should be the constant companions of prayer; his poetic pairings of prayer and tear are more frequent than those of any other devotional poet of the period. Early in *Silex* (1650), 'The Call' issues a self-command to seek God with weeping *and* praying:

> Come my heart! come my head
> In sighes, and teares!
>
> .   .   .   .   .
>
> Who never wake to grone, nor weepe,
> Shall be sentenc'd for their sleepe.
>
> (ll. 1–2, 8–9)

These dry-wet pairings—the chiasmic quartet heart, head, sighs, tears, and the pair groan, weep—remember the first of the penitential Psalms, a

---

[98] 'Of Teares', from *Vices and Virtues: Being a Soul's Confession of its Sins with Reason's Description of the Virtues; A Middle-English Dialogue of about 1200 A.D.*, ed. Ferdinand Holthausen (1886), 146–7.

[99] Thomas Vaughan, *Aqua Vitae* [British Library, Sloane MS 1741], repr. in *TV*, 585–96 (593).

famous verse of which Vaughan paraphrases in the first section of the 'Admonitions for Morning-Prayer' in *The Mount of Olives*: '*I am weary of my groaning, every night wash I my bed, and water my Couch with my tears*' (*The Mount of Olives* (*V*, 143), quoting Coverdale's translation of Psalm 6). In the same way Hezekiah promises God praise 'in the land of the living', so the Psalmist David tells God: 'in death there is no remembrance of thee: in the grave who shall give thee thanks?' and implores Him to deliver the faithful from suffering. The end of Psalm 6 warns enemies to flee, because God is sure to hear both the weeping *and* the prayers of his children: 'Depart from me, all ye workers of iniquity, for the Lord hath heard the voice of my weeping. The Lord hath heard my supplication; the Lord will receive my prayer' (Psalm 6: 8–9).

The speaker of 'The Call' is not alone when he feels that his soul has lain 'dead | Some twenty years'; other poems by Vaughan at this time—he was in his late twenties—share the belief that childhood's end is a catastrophe in the spiritual life.[100] In 'The Call', those twenty years of sin must now be repented by filling a glass—Vaughan's final stanza is instructingly shaped rather like one—with penitent tears:

> Yet, come, and let's peruse them all;
> And as we passe,
> What sins on every minute fall
> Score on the glasse;
> Then weigh, and rate
> Their heavy State
> Untill
> The glasse with teares you fill;
> That done, we shalbe safe, and good,
> Those beasts were cleane, that chew'd the Cud.

(ll. 20–9)

The hourglass must first be marked off with the sins of every minute of the past twenty years, scoring higher and higher up the glass; then whilst meditating on them—this is to 'weigh, and rate | Their heavy State'—the

---

[100] Stevie Davies puts the age of the Vaughan-child in poems such as 'The Retreate' and 'Childe-hood' at less than 10 (Davies, *Henry Vaughan*, 47); cf. Leah Marcus, *Childhood and Cultural Despair: A Theme and Variations in Seventeenth-Century Literature* (Pittsburgh, 1978), 153–75. Vaughan's translation of Nieremberg's 'Of Life and Death' (in *Flores Solitudinis* (1654)) speaks of a child's 'nine monthes in a thick darknesse, and more then nine years (perhaps all the years of their sojourning) [spent] in hallucinations, and the darknesse or ignorance' (*V*, 282).

penitent will begin to weep, and then will cry a whole bottle of tears. Vaughan's more gnomic closing couplet alludes to the Levitical commandment that 'whatsoever parteth the hoof, and is cloven-footed, and cheweth the cud among the beasts, that shall ye eat' (Leviticus 11: 3); true penitence, then, is an active regurgitation of sins past, a painful reliving of them in the new knowledge of their shamefulness after 'weep[ing] night and day for my infinite trangressions' ('A Prayer for the grace of repentance', in *The Mount of Olives*, V, 159).

George Herbert's line 'What is so shrill as silent tears?'[101] reappears in Vaughan's poem 'Thou that know'st for whom I mourne' to celebrate the speechless power of tears and groans:

> A silent teare can peirce thy throne,
>> When lowd Joyes want a wing,
> And sweeter aires streame from a grone,
>> Than any arted string.
>
>> (ll. 49–52)

When words fail, tears fill the penitent's hourglass. Groans, it seems, are more articulate because less artful; the cries of the afflicted better music to God's ears than an 'arted string'. Equated here with hollow ostentation, art is kept in constant check throughout *Silex Scintillans* by the power of simple acts of worship, and especially by the copresence of speechless acts like groaning and, most importantly, weeping. This repeated partnership of tears and words both vents Vaughan's honourable suspicions of artistic vanity and itself produces some of his most moving affirmations of faith.

The power for good or bad that Vaughan ascribes to art in 'The Authors Preface' to *Silex* (1655) is also on show in that volume's poems. Satan, for instance, teaches children to spoil their innocence by imparting 'the black art to dispence | A sev'rall sinne to ev'ry sence' ('The Retreate', ll. 17–18); and his infernal art also brings despair to weak-minded man: 'For 'tis our foes chief art | By distance all good objects first to drown' ('Sure, there's a tye of Bodyes!', ll. 18–19). Corrupted by the fall of Adam, men devise arts to lead each other from true beauty to fleeting pleasures: 'soft, kinde arts and easie strains | Which strongly operate, though without pains' ('The hidden Treasure', ll. 21–2). Yet art is not essentially bad; bad users make it so. God was an artist when he planned and built the Creation:

---

[101] 'The Familie', l. 20.

> Sure, mighty love foreseeing the discent
>   Of this poor Creature, by a gracious art
>   Hid in these low things snares to gain his heart,
> And layd surprizes in each Element.
>
> ('The Tempest', ll. 21–4)

As well as architecturally, He is also artful in repair, tuning 'disorder'd man' by a 'sacred, needful art' in 'Affliction [I]'; and in 'Begging [I]', which ends *Silex* Part 1, divine artistry brings the stony human heart back to life: 'O it is thy only Art | To reduce a stubborn heart' (ll. 13–14). In an etymological pun, Vaughan mingles the humbling sense of *reduce* with its etymological root *reducere*, to lead back: like seventeenth-century surgeons, who were said to *reduce* organs or limbs by putting them back into their right place and use, God brings man's heart back to life and at the same time humbles it; a sacred, needful art of spiritual surgery. Another common seventeenth-century usage, was 'to lead or bring back from error in action, conduct, or belief, *esp.* in matters of morality or religion'.[102]

Contrasting with its praise for divine artistry, *Silex Scintillans* characterizes man's artistic achievements as fraught with pride, lust, greed and fame. 'The Daughter of *Herodias*' continues what 'The Authors Preface' began, grimacing at the damage '*vitious verse*' does to poets' souls:

> Vain, sinful Art! who first did fit
> Thy lewd loath'd *Motions* unto *sounds*,
> And made grave *Musique* like wilde *wit*
> Erre in loose airs beyond her bounds?
>
> What fires hath he heap'd on his head?
> Since to his sins (as needs it must,)
> His *Art* adds still (though he be dead,)
> New fresh accounts of blood and lust.
>
> (ll. 1–8)

Salome's 'soft arts' (l. 16) and (especially) her accompanying music are plainly in need of redirection. Though 'The Daughter of *Herodias*' is one of Vaughan's most unattractive poems in some ways, it establishes within the 'finished' book a contrast between the arts of the 'yong Sorceress', Salome, and those of other biblical women who make rarer and more pleasing appearances: Rebekah, Rachel, and finally Mary Magdalene. In

---

[102] See *OED*, reduce, *v.*, I. 6, 8.

poetry which perceives these women as either artless or gifted with sacred arts, Vaughan puts weeping and writing onto a new, less antipathetic footing, and then seeks to reconcile them in a vision of Mary's weeping which does not denigrate his own art of poetry, the skill with which, like Hezekiah, he has chosen to make his returns of praise.

Mary's poem is in the second volume of *Silex Scintillans*. Early in the first, '*Isaacs* Marriage' attacks the 'art | Of these our dayes' which coins 'oathes, and Complements (too) plenty'[103]—note the delicious ambiguity of that *too*, both *also* and *too many*—as it heaps praise on Rebekah for her simplicity:

> All was plain, modest truth: Nor did she come
> In *rowles* and *Curles*, mincing and stately dumb,
> But in a Virgins native blush and fears
> Fresh as those roses, which the day-spring wears.
> O sweet, divine simplicity! O grace
> Beyond a Curled lock, or painted face!
>
> (ll. 33–8)

Free from worldly arts, Rebekah has that 'divine simplicity' which Paul urges Christians to cling to lest 'as the serpent beguiled Eve through his subtilty, so your minds should be corrupted from the simplicity that is in Christ' (2 Corinthians 11: 3). Unlike her original mother, Rebekah has not fallen prey to Satan's beguiling. Her 'native' blush is recalled in the Part 2 poem 'The Ornament', which decries the world's 'gorgeous Mart and glittering store' in contrast with the stark purity of Rachel:

> Quite through their proud and pompous file
> Blushing, and in meek weeds array'd
> With native looks, which knew no guile,
> Came the sheep-keeping *Syrian* Maid.
>
> Whom straight the shining Row all fac'd
> Forc'd by her artless looks and dress,
> While one cryed out, We are disgrac'd
> For she is bravest, you confess.
>
> (ll. 13–20)

As he continued to meditate on the wilderness prayers of Isaac and Jacob, Vaughan also found scriptural and spiritual warrants for sacred poetry in

---

[103] '*Isaacs* Marriage', ll. 14–17.

the stories of their wives, Rachel and Rebekah. Reusing the idea of simple beauty (Rachel has a touch of the rustic shepherdess as well as an innate and untouched beauty), 'The Ornament' continues Vaughan's earlier reflections and enforces the sense of guileless and artless beauty suggested in Rebekah's 'native blush'.

Though he admired artless, native purity, Vaughan was a man of arts whose conscience had forced him to beg forgiveness for his secular verse, those *'greatest follies'* which no apology could excuse ('The Authors Preface', *V*, 390). However much he desired to return to childhood purity, Vaughan could not reach it, and knew that his gift was not the artlessness of Rebekah and Rachel, but rather, to recall Robert Harris's gloss on Hezekiah, the gift to 'speake thy minde to men yet unborne, and convey to them that light which God hath reached to thee'.[104] Gifted with artistry, Vaughan turned to the bible to see himself as a giver of thanks for recovery like Hezekiah; and also, in other poems from *Silex* Part 2, to consider how art can overcome corruption and indulgence in the story of a biblical woman. The youthful purity of the Old Testament world having died with Rebekah, Rachel and the patriarchs, Vaughan turned to the New Testament stories, and importantly, to a weeper like Hezekiah; indeed, to 'The Weeper', as she is called in Crashaw's *Steps to the Temple* (1646); to Mary Magdalene. Vaughan's lachrymal poetry takes some time to reach Mary, who is scripture's most celebrated weeper as well as literature's. 'The Call' saw weeping as a penitent reliving of sins past; 'Thou that know'st' celebrated tears as a power equal to, and sometimes above, words; and the story of Hezekiah witnessed to Vaughan the power of true tears, which God never ignores. In 'St. Mary Magdalen', positioned half way through *Silex* (1655), tears at last come into their own as a lesson and example of how to sanctify one's gifts for use in artful prayer and praise.

Luke's gospel tells of the unnamed woman 'which was a sinner', normally identified with the Magdalene, who came to Jesus with a box of expensive ointment 'and stood at his feet behind him weeping, and began to wash his feet with tears, and did wipe them with the hairs of her head, and kissed his feet, and anointed them with the ointment' (Luke 7: 38). Unlike the dutiful figures of Rebekah and Rachel whose stories begin with an idea of their purity, Mary emerges from a sinful past, when like Salome she used her eyes to tempt, rather than weep, and costly ointment to

---

[104] Harris, *Hezekiah's Recovery*, 22.

entice, not to salve. But for Vaughan, the tears, hair and ointment of the Magdalene become emblems of a specially powerful penitential offering precisely because they were the tools of her past sins: her eyes, now weeping, were once 'sins loose and tempting spies' (l. 58); her hair and ointment used for lascivious profit. This makes them all the more acceptable to the New Testament God of mercy and forgiveness. Similarly, Vaughan's art was once taken with an 'idle and sensual *subject*' and spurred on by desire for name and reputation; but now, like Mary, he has put the tools of his trade to a better use, washing and annointing the feet of the Lord:

> How art thou chang'd! how lively-fair,
> Pleasing and innocent an air,
> Not tutor'd by thy glass, but free,
> Native and pure shines now in thee!
>
> .   .   .
>
> Why lies this *Hair* despised now
> Which once thy care and art did show?
> Who then did dress the much lov'd toy.
>
> ('St. Mary Magdalen', ll. 5–8, 15–17)

Mary's tears have set her free from the glass she once used, with *care and art*, to dress her hair; now she is *native*, like Rebekah and Rachel, and tears are her proper ointment. It is this purity, possible only by giving to God the very means of one's previous sins, and washing His feet with floods of tears, that Vaughan sought in his *Sacred Hymns and Private Ejaculations*. For only the soul which is broken by awareness of its own sins—the 'nakedness' which Vaughan hopes the vain Wits see—will make a proper sacrifice:

> Why is this rich, this *Pistic* Nard
> Spilt, and the box quite broke and marr'd?
>
> .   .   .   .
>
> Dear *Soul*! thou knew'st, flowers here on earth
> At their Lords foot-stool have their birth;
> Therefore thy wither'd self in haste
> Beneath his blest feet thou didst cast.
>
> (ll. 21–2, 27–30)

This act made Mary 'one of the supreme examples in Christian story and iconography of the repentant sinner, who turned from a life of depravity to devote herself to the service of Christ'.[105] Cast down and broken at her Lord's feet, she is like the box of ointment which she has spilt, each an emblem of each other: 'Refuse it not! for now thy *Token* | Can tell thee where a heart is broken' ('The Dedication', ll. 45–6). The image of Mary cast down recalls the climax of Vaughan's offering of the finished *Silex Scintillans* to God, where the poet owns that he has nothing else to give but the fruits of Christ's death—his poems, witnesses of the repentant and broken heart of their human author.

Mary's story shows that God is especially pleased with the penitent who transforms the means of sins past into the means of praise and prayer, and it is surely significant for Vaughan that some of his early poems, particularly 'Song' from *Poems* (1646) concerned the power of female tears to enrapture men's souls. Having written of the 'sacred dew' that Chloris weeps, 'her Art' that kills 'Mens joyes . . . with griefes and feares', he was able finally, like Mary, to repent best by recapitulating his former sins in a sanctified key ('Song', ll. 14, 17–18). What Vaughan recommends for the witty scribbler in 'Vain Wits and eyes' is what has already happened to Mary: penitential sacrifice has recovered her eyes from a debased use of tempting men, and brought them back to their original, God-sent, purpose of weeping 'true tears'; her precious ointment has now been spent on the feet most precious to her. In contrast, Salome, whose coy spirits taught her 'to please his eyes' (Herod Antipas), failed to turn her 'soft arts' into the 'Cheap, mighty Art' of divine love; she was too pleased by her *ars amatoria* to change for *amor dei*.

The Vaughan of *Silex* Part 2 can reach no easy conclusion about art, but 'St. Mary Magdalen' acknowledges that it must be simple, pure, cheap and mighty, and art brought up from corruption by the power of repentance and sanctified by a flood of *true tears*. As the poem draws its lesson, Vaughan sounds the word Art over and over like a mantra:

> Cheap, mighty Art! her Art of love,
> Who lov'd much and much more could move;
> Her Art! whose memory must last
> Till truth through all the world be past,
>
> .   .   .   .   .   .
>
> Her Art! whose pensive, weeping eyes,
> Were once sins loose and tempting spies,

[105] Robert Wilcher, *Andrew Marvell*, British and Irish Authors Introductory Critical Studies (Cambridge, 1985), 17.

> But now are fixed stars, whose light
> Helps such dark straglers to their sight.
>
> ('St. Mary Magdalen', ll. 49–52, 57–60)

'Cheap, mighty Art!' is one of Vaughan's most casually surprising collocations: it celebrates the power of inarticulate groans and their availability to all, whilst also, by lauding Mary's weeping as an art—'Her Art!'—affirming Robert Harris's advice to the learned Christian in *Hezekiah's Recovery*: 'Art thou learned? . . . write something (as thy gift is)'. Mary's art is tears, Vaughan's is poetry: each to his, or her, own.

In 'St. Mary Magdalen' Vaughan found belief that art may be purified and returned to its original purpose, the purpose of Hezekiah in thanking God for his life and health which breathes life into *Silex Scintillans*' 1655 prefatory prayer. In conclusion, it is tempting to wonder whether Vaughan's familiarity with Jesuit literature extended to a work which touches these artistic concerns at many points, the *Marie Magdalens Funerall Teares* (1609) of Robert Southwell. Published eighteen years after Southwell's execution, this book introduced into English the late sixteenth-century literature of weeping which had produced important continental works such as Valvasone's *Le Lagrime della Maddalena* (1580) and Tansillo's influential *Lagrime di San Pietro* (1585). Like Vaughan, Southwell composed a literary-critical preface to his work; and like Vaughan's, it is concerned with the interactions between life and poetry, between the poet's devotions, the devotions he might inspire in others, and the ends and purposes of writing. There is a stunning congruence of opinion with 'The Authors Preface' to *Silex* (1655):

For as passion, and especially this of love, is in these dayes the chiefe commaunder of most mens actions, and the Idol to which both tongues and pennes doe sacrifice their ill bestowed labours: so is there nothing now more needful to be intreated, than how to direct these humours unto their due courses, and to draw this floud of affections into the right channel. Passions I allow, and loves I approve, onely I would wish that men would alter their object, and better their intent.[106]

---

[106] Robert Southwell, *Marie Magdalens Funerall Teares* (1609), sigs. A3ʳ–A3ᵛ. On Southwell and Counter-Reformation literature of weeping, see Pierre Janelle, *Robert Southwell the Writer: A Study in Religious Inspiration* (Mamaroneck, NY, 1971), 184–97; Wilcher, *Andrew Marvell*, 13–20; Thomas F. Healy, *Richard Crashaw*, Medieval and Renaissance Authors Series (Leiden, 1986), 35–9; Austin Warren, *Richard Crashaw: A Study in Baroque Sensibility* (1939), 77–134. Other early lachrymal works in English include Thomas Nashe, *Christs Teares over Jerusalem* (1593), in *The Works of Thomas Nashe*, ed. Ronald B.

As well as these foreshadowings of Vaughan's corrective lecturing in 'The Authors Preface', Southwell's preface urges the proper use of eyes for weeping, as Vaughan did in 'Vain Wits and eyes'—'it is both the salve and smart of sinne, curing that which it chastiseth with true remorse, and preventing need of new cure with the detestation of the disease'; and furthermore, he complains, like Vaughan, that 'the finest wits loose themselves in the vainest follies, spilling much Art in some idle fansie, and leaving their workes as witnesses how long they have been in travaile, to be in fine delivered of a fable'.[107]

Passions I allow and loves I approve. Vaughan's great approval of poetry in *Silex* (1655) stems from two great scripture uses: the prefatory prayer's identification with Hezekiah, king of Judah, and 'St. Mary Magdalen''s celebration of Mary, from whose transformations Vaughan took heart and an example. Vaughan's sickness and recovery led him to one, his artistic conscience to the other. Together, they helped him to place the poetry of *Silex Scintillans* in a new frame of worship, a frame fastened securely by the prefatory materials to his 'finished' thanksgiving and strewn throughout with the true tears of a clear eye.

McKerrow, 5 vols. (Oxford, 1958), ii. 1–177; Thomas Lodge, *Prosopopeia* (1596) and Gervase Markham (attrib.), *Marie Magdalens Lamentations for the Losse of her Master Jesus* (1601).

[107] Southwell, *Marie Magdalens Teares*, sigs. A3ᵛ, B1ʳ.

CHAPTER FOUR

Holy living, hourly living

The Mount of Olives; or, Solitary Devotions (1652) takes its title from Luke's account of how Jesus taught one day in the temple and then afterwards 'went out and abode in the mount that is called the mount of Olives' (Luke 21: 37).[1] In that place, Vaughan writes in his 'Admonitions for *Morning-Prayer*', Christ 'continued all night in prayer', as was his manner, 'sometimes in a Mountain apart, sometimes among the wild beasts, and sometimes in solitary places' (*V*, 143). Such dutiful, incessant devotion in the night presides over Vaughan's book of instructions for holy living, instructions which derided and defied an age in which (as he believed) public shows of piety prevailed above unseen holiness of *solitary devotions*, 'Glory, the Crouds cheap tinsel' above a true Christian's 'secret growth'.[2]

The Mount of Olives distinguishes those who noisily profess Christian lives from those true Christians whose holy living excludes such self-publicity. Its heroes are lonely men of faith like the patriarchs, but more specifically those Christians who live wholly for Christ: hermits and saints, rejectors of the world, regular worshippers who maintain 'appointed times to offer up a Spiritual sacrifice' (*V*, 150). Nowhere is dissembling clearer for Vaughan than in the apocalyptic hopes expressed by the '*friends of this world*':

It is a sad observation for true Christians to see these men who would seem to be Pillars, to prove but reeds and specious dissemblers. For what manner of livers should such *professors* be, seeing they expect and beleeve the dissolution of all things? With what constant holinesse, humility and devotion should they watch for it? How should they *passe the time of their sojourning here in fear, and be diligent that they may be found of him in peace, without spot, and blamelesse?* What preparation should they make against the evill day? What comfort and treasures

---

[1] Luke 21: 36–7, given on the title-page of *The Mount of Olives* as 'Luke 21. v. 39, 37' (the inverted 6 suggesting a compositor's error).

[2] 'The Seed growing secretly', ll. 37, 45.

should they lay up for that long voyage? For what a day of terrors and indignation is the day of death to the unprepared? (*V,* 170)

Between specious *seeming* and a true *being,* between sly *professing* and holy *living,* is a great difference in this world, and a much more dreadful one in the world to come. 'Christians should neither wander, nor sit down, but goe on', wrote Nieremberg, whose 'Of Temperance and Patience' Vaughan translated for *Flores Solitudinis* (1654), and it is a principle of his prose works throughout the 1650s that Christians can be best distinguished from dissemblers by their constant, directed labour. In fact, shows of holiness are antithetical to the Christian manner of living Vaughan circumscribes in *The Mount of Olives,* where Christians are constant, watching, diligent, and always preparing, passing their time in fear as they lay up treasure for their posthumous lives.

'What manner of livers should such *professors* be?' According to the *Oxford English Dictionary,* a *liver* is 'one who lives, is alive', and the word has been used from the fourteenth century until the end of the nineteenth, when it became rare. *Liver* is a familiar term in seventeenth-century didactic writing, particularly appearing in works of practical divinity concerned to teach a manner of life; Bunyan's Wiseman and Attentive sigh over that 'wicked liver' Mr Badman, for instance.[3] The exceptional frequency of its appearance in Vaughan's poetry and prose has gone ignored by his critics and by the *OED,* despite its prominence in the first line of 'The Shepheards', from *Silex Scintillans* (1650)—'Sweet, harmles livers!'—and despite the fact that Vaughan's coupling of *liver* with a preceding adjective is the commonest stylistic form of the word.[4] That form is worth pondering: as in Spenser's 'The damned ghosts doen often creep | Backe to the world, bad livers to torment' or in the travels of William Lithgow, quick to moralize on 'the Turke, and the Irish-man [as] the least industrious, and most sluggish livers under the Sun'. [Adj.] + *liver* creates a significant charge of adverbial force between *liver* and its qualifying adjective, the power of which is to suggest that its subject is not merely *bad* but responsible for a whole *life of badness,* or possessed of a character-defining sluggishness. To be a *sluggish liver* implies routine, cultivation even, accuses its subject of a *way of life* as the adjective alone does

---

[3] John Bunyan, *The Life and Death of Mr. Badman,* ed. James F. Forrest and Roger Sharrock (Oxford, 1988), 160.

[4] *Liver* appears, for instance, in Vaughan's translation of 'Psalm 104', l. 28; in 'The Shepheards', l. 36; 'The Praise and Happinesss of the Country-Life', 124, 127, and 'Of Temperance and Patience', 260, 261.

not. To be 'Sweet, harmles livers!' is something more than being sweet and harmless.[5]

Liver dropped out of use just as psychology began to encroach upon the vocabulary of ethics and morals. Its summary force survived for a time in the psychological term *life-style*, coined by the neurologist Alfred Adler in 1929 to denote a person's basic character as established in the first four or five years of childhood. Since it purported to essential knowledge of a person, the 'unitary life-style behind this ostensible duplicity', this word recalled the way in which [adj.] + liver used to sum up a person's moral character.[6] In the later twentieth century, though, *life-style* dropped its hyphen and become a slang term for a deliberately chosen combination of career, personal life, place of habitation, and other variable factors of modern living. The *OED* instances the *Guardian* of 21 March 1961: 'The mass-media . . . continually tell their audiences what lifestyles are "modern" and "smart".' The deterministic summarizing force of Adler's *life-style*, then, has been replaced by a sense of acquirable, one might even say consumer, *stylishness*. Since the 1960s the word has been assimilated by a modern ideal of social and economic mobility according to which living is about style, not necessity. Lacking the phrase *lifestyle magazines* (those glossies which claim to single out the materials of a desirable life), the second edition of the *OED* (1989) is already behind the times. Its next edition may be able to assess how the rise of *lifestyle* has affected use of older expressions, notably the Shakespearian coinage *way of life*, which now tend to be reserved for past eras and other people. We choose our lifestyle, they knew a way of life.[7]

The 1640s saw an explosion of lives and an explosion of old ways of living. Change was often discussed in the vocabulary of religious reformation, but events were to demonstrate that religion, politics and society in seventeenth-century Britain were inextricably connected. 'The great misfortune of Religion [is to be] made the pretence to ruin Monarchy', complained John Nalson, whose Royalist polemics were sharpened by teenage years spent under the Protectorate.[8] What Anglicans and Royalist conformists had once assumed to be the given *way of life* could

---

[5]   *OED*, liver, *sb.* 2, 1, 1b.

[6]   *OED*, lifestyle; quotation is the *OED*'s 1939 illustration.

[7]   *OED*, way, *sb.*, 1, 14h. The first recorded use of 'way of life' is *Macbeth* v. iii. 24.

[8]   John Nalson, *The Common Interest of King and People: Shewing the Original, Antiquity and Excellency of Monarchy, Compared with Aristocracy and Democracy, and Particularly of Our English Monarchy* (1677), sig. [A4]ʳ.

no longer be easily walked. Many found themselves suddenly relocated to the edges of power and religious life both national and local, making them an oppressed band of the faithful (as they saw it) in a time of rebellion and exile. With the king dead and his church and its liturgy banned, maintaining one's beliefs took more than a desire not to change. Change itself had to be understood. The second Civil War and the regicide had put an end to the confidence with which Vaughan's *Poems* (1646) had confidently addressed its readers as those who '*out-wing these dull Times, and soare above the drudgerie of durty* Intelligence' (*V*, 2).

A more resolved determination was necessary, and it was to provide the appropriate helps to loyal, faithful *livers* that Anglicans and Royalists went into print in the early 1650s. As a gentleman-poet, Vaughan had half apologized for his early *Poems*, excusing their appearance with a Latin shrug 'Languescente seculo, liceat aegrotari': 'When the age is languishing, one is permitted to be sick' (*V*, 2). But like other traditions, such conventional expressions of modesty were being increasingly left behind in the late 1640s. The immediate occasion of Jeremy Taylor's *The Rule and Exercises of Holy Living*, as its Epistle Dedicatory to the Earl of Carbery states through a wealth of biblical allusions, was seeing

Religion painted upon Banners, and thrust out of Churches, and the Temple turned into a Tabernacle, and that Tabernacle made ambulatory, and covered with skins of Beasts and torn Curtains, and God to be worshipped not as he is the *Father of our Lord Jesus* (an afflicted Prince, the King of sufferings) nor as the *God of peace* (which two appellatives God newly took upon him in the New Testament, and glories in for ever:) but he is owned now rather as the *Lord of Hosts*, which title he was pleased to lay aside when the Kingdom of the Gospel was preached by the Prince of peace.[9]

Taylor's plea for the God of peace was entered into the Stationers' Register on 7 March 1650, three weeks before the first edition of Vaughan's *Silex Scintillans*.[10] Over the next five years, Taylor continued to console the displaced and distressed in works such as *The Rule and Exercises of Holy Dying* (1651), *A Short Catechism* (1652) and *The Golden Grove; or, A Manuall of Daily Prayers and Letanies, Fitted to the Dayes of the Weeke* (1655). The latter, as the Stationers' Register noted, included 'Festivall hymnes according to the manner of the auncient church', a rejoinder from Taylor to the then widespread belief that Puritan forms of worship

---

[9] Jeremy Taylor, *The Rule and Exercises of Holy Living*, ed. Stanwood, 5.
[10] *Stationers' Register*, ed. Plomer, i. 339, 341.

were returning Christianity to its primitive or apostolic style.[11] Taylor's hymns celebrated the banned festivals of Christmas, Easter, and Whitsun, remembering and so sustaining the established church, whose episcopal structure Taylor had earlier defended (in its Laudian form) as directly descended from Christ.[12] Other defenders of the established church waded in to join Taylor, including Joseph Hall, who made further contributions to the nourishment of Anglicans in *Cheirothesia; or, The Apostolique Institution* (1649) and in *The Holy Order; or, Fraternity of the Mourners in Sion, Whereunto is Added, Songs in the Night; or, Cheerfulnesse under Affliction* (1655), adding to his energetic defence of the ecclesial status quo in the early 1640s.

The voices of the holy dead echoed up from the presses to succour the faithful. Lancelot Andrewes's *Preces Privatae* were printed for Humphrey Moseley in 1648; John Cosin's *Private Devotions*, the book which provoked William Prynne to outrage in 1627 at its use of the Catholic hours, was republished in 1655; as were the late Bishop Prideaux's instructions to his daughters in *Euchologia; or, A Doctrine of Practical Praying*. Another Englishing of Lancelot Andrewes's prayers appeared as *Holy Devotions with Directions to Pray*, as did several other of his works; and alongside them on London's bookshelves could be found defences and rationales of the Anglican liturgy like John Spark's *Scintillulae Sacrae* (1654) and Lionel Gatford's 1655 *Petition for the Publique Use of the Booke of Common Prayer*. Christopher Harvey's poetic defence 'Common Prayer' added its mite to the collection (in *The Synagogue*), an offering preserved in the amber of Isaac Walton's *The Compleat Angler; or, The Contemplative Man's Recreation* (1653), another eloquent lay defence of our 'good old Service book' and the church that used it.

It can seem strange now that Parliament allowed these works to be published, for, as the Preface to *Silex Scintillans* (1655) notes, suppression of books was at least partly 'in the power of the *Magistrate*' (*V*, 391). Yet Anglicans and Royalists continued to see their literary acts of resistance through the press. In the Puritan-dominated London of the 1650s, it was still Royalist poets who produced most of the published verse, and though the pro-Anglican devotional books I have mentioned were outnumbered by a flood of literature by, for and against Quakers, Independents and Presbyterians, the Royalist flow never dried up. Joseph Frank

[11] Ibid. 464.
[12] In his *Of the Sacred Order and Offices of Episcopacy by Divine Institution Apostolicall Tradition & Catholike Practice* (Oxford, 1642); see Milton, *Catholic and Reformed*, 491–4.

has suggested that pro-Royalist booksellers were greatly 'abetted by the laxity in enforcing censorship statutes', though it is also true that censorship was tightened by an Act of 1649 which took control back from the army (which had been the official censor since 1647) and returned it to the state. Booksellers' motives ranged from loyalty to king and church (in the case of Richard Royston, for instance) to good business sense and economic opportunism, as Lois Potter has shown in several detailed studies.[13]

How to be a true *liver* in a 'sad Land' ('Death. A Dialogue', l. 1) is an abiding interest of all Vaughan's major works from 1648, when he had finished *Olor Iscanus*, to 1655, when the two-part *Silex Scintillans* appeared. For the last prose work in *Olor* (a book dominated by Boethian stoicism, tinged with Christianity), Vaughan translated *The Praise and Happinesse of the Countrie-Life* from a Latin version of Antonio de Guevara's *Menosprecio de Corte y Alabanza de Aldez* (1539), the work urging retreat as an honourable option for the defeated and frustrated.[14] Though it is not primarily devotional, *Countrie-Life* seeks to attract the devout, noting that '*Pietie and Religion* may be better Cherish'd and preserved in the Country than any where else' (*V*, 125). There are passages which would have spoken comfortingly to Interregnum Anglicans, particularly those which stress the country's observance of the turning year: 'Whereas in *Towns* and populous *Cities* neither the *Day*, nor the *Sun*, nor a *Star*, nor the *Season* of the *Year* can be well perceived. All which in the Country are manifestly seen, and occasion a more exact care and observation of *Seasons*, that their *labours* may be in their appointed time, and their *rewards* accordingly' (*V*, 129). Religion, too, is purer in the country, administered 'according to the *sacred rules* and *Ordinances* of *Religion*' by which Vaughan means that 'The *Temples* and *Communion tables* are drest, and the *beauty of holinesse* shines every where' (*V*, 131). With its translations of Boethius and its swipes at Puritan and Parliament, *Olor Iscanus* is not

[13] Frank, *Hobbled Pegasus*, 20–2; Potter, *Secret Rites*, ch. 1.

[14] For details of contemporary Spanish translations including Vaughan's, see A. F. Allison, *English Translations from the Spanish and Portuguese to the Year 1700: An Annotated Catalogue of the Extant Printed Versions (Excluding Dramatic Adaptation)* (1974); see 84–5 for Vaughan, where Allison notes that Vaughan used Egidius van der Myle, *Oblectatio Vitae Rusticae* (1633), an abridgement of Guevara. Vaughan and Guevara are discussed by Anthony Low, *The Georgic Revolution* (Princeton, 1985), 24–8 and Maren-Sofie Røstvig *The Happy Man: Studies in the Metamorphoses of a Classical Idea*, 2 vols. (Oslo, 1954), i. 195–211; an ample scholarly discussion of the intellectual and literary background is provided by Brian Vickers, 'Leisure and Idleness in the Renaissance: The Ambivalence of Otium', *Renaissance Studies*, 4 (1990), 1–37 and 107–54.

a devotional work about how to be a *holy liver*; but it demonstrates that Vaughan's first thoughts after the early secular *Poems* (1646) were of how the defeated or distressed should be *faithful livers*; constant in their lives to principles, friends, church and king.

There are signs that, after *Olor Iscanus*, Vaughan passed through a transitional phase in which he increasingly sanctified the philosophy of retirement through allusions to Old Testament country livers. Like other poems from the late 1640s and 1650s, 'Retirement' was not published until *Thalia Rediviva* (1678), but its echoes of Vaughan's translation of Guevara support a date of around 1648. Both *The Praise and Happinesse of the Country-Life* and 'Retirement' also use the word *liver*, and both affirm that 'Whoever Loves the *Country*, and Lives in it upon his owne Estate, . . . I shall not feare to affirme, That such a liver is the *wisest of men*' (*V*, 124). The advantages of country life are enumerated one by one: country contentedness, piety, beauty, and an innocence and purity greater than can be found in the city:

> Fresh *fields* and *woods*! the Earth's fair *face*,
> God's *foot-stool*, and mans *dwelling-place*.
> I ask not why the first *Believer*
> Did love to be a Country liver?
> Who to secure pious content
> Did pitch by *groves* and *wells* his tent;
> Where he might view the boundless *skie*,
> And all those glorious *lights* on high.
>
> ('Retirement', ll. 1–8)

Strong echoes of Guevara mix in these lines with a broad allusion to Abraham, the country *liver* and 'first *Believer*' from Genesis. Between the country retreat of *Olor* and the sparks of *Silex*, Vaughan's 'Retirement' promotes country living with the authority of scripture as well as philosophy. It is a marked change from the 'usuall Retyrement' of the 'Henry Vaughan, Gent.' who wrote *Poems, with the Tenth Satyre of Juvenal Englished* (1646). Then, in that volume's penultimate number 'Upon the Priory Grove, His usuall Retyrement', the young poet wrote of the 'sacred shades' and 'coole, leavie House' of Colonel Herbert Price's house.[15]

After the poems and translations of *Olor Iscanus*, Vaughan turned his attention to what it meant to be a Christian *holy liver*. As well as offering

[15] On Price and Priory Grove, see *Life*, 52–3.

poetic witness to his own struggle to live well, Vaughan looked to George Herbert's exemplary use of poetry as a didactic tool for instruction in holy living—'A verse may find him, who a sermon flies'—but with the added frisson that, like Jeremy Taylor's, Vaughan's was also an effort to sustain and instruct loyal followers of the established church during Puritan rule. 'The Authors Preface' to Vaughan's completed volume of *Sacred Poems and Private Ejaculations* hints at its functional role in the title 'The Authors Preface to the following *Hymns*'. *Hymn* derives from the Latin word *hymnus* used to translate the Septuagint's ὕμνος (hymnos), a rendering of various Old Testament words meaning a song in praise of God.[16] In the New Testament epistles, hymns are made part of a Christian duty of 'speaking to yourselves in psalms, and hymns and spiritual songs' to be used by Christians to teach and admonish one another. St Paul gives hymns a didactic and exhortatory function as well as one of praise, two of the purposes uppermost in Vaughan's mind when he conceived of his poems.[17] The *Private Ejaculations* of Vaughan's title refers to his habit of assembling and learning by heart appropriate scriptural responses to events during each day and in his life, examples of which are given in *The Mount of Olives*. It is easy to see that the scripture-rich poems of *Silex Scintillans* or *The Temple* could themselves be learned in a similar fashion and repeated from memory to sweeten and guide the day-to-day lives of their readers.

Certainly the habit of reading daily from *The Temple* and quoting it from memory are well documented in the mid-century, for instance in the life and ministry of the noted Nonconformist minister, John Bryan, or those of his more famous correspondent Richard Baxter.[18] Bryan's pattern of reading is mentioned towards the end of his funeral sermon, *Peace and Rest for the Upright* which was preached in 1678 by his closest friend and one of the few known contemporary readers of Vaughan's poems, Nathaniel Wanley.[19] It is also clear from Baxter's correspondence that he understood *The Temple* as a book of practical divinity as well as of poetry.

---

[16] See *OED*, hymn, *sb.*, 1.

[17] Eph. 5: 19, Col. 3: 16. For a contrasting interpretation of these widely cited verses, see William Barton, *A View of Many Errours and Som Gross Absurdities in the Old Translation of the Psalms in English Metre* (1650), sig. A2ʳ.

[18] Many examples are traced in Helen Wilcox, 'Something Understood: The Reputation and Influence of George Herbert to 1715', Ph.D. thesis (Oxford, 1974); Robert Ray, 'The Herbert Allusion Book', *Studies in Philology*, 83 (1986), 1–82; C. A. Patrides (ed.), *George Herbert: The Critical Heritage* (1983).

[19] Nathaniel Wanley, *Peace and Rest for the Upright* (1678), 19.

A spiritual doctor to many, Baxter was eventually led to prescribe a dose of Herbert to one of his spiritually distressed correspondents, Katherine Gell, which he did by sending her a copy of *The Temple* (perhaps the new 1656 edition published by Philemon Stephens) in 1657. Their three-year exchange of letters concerning her spiritual doubts had not managed to alleviate her obsessive self-examination, and it is to Baxter's and to Herbert's credit that Gell was 'put . . . into a very good praying frame which I seldom am \in/' on reading some of Herbert's hymns.[20]

Vaughan, too, thought that *Sacred Hymns and Private Ejaculations* should be useful. 'The Authors Preface to the Following Hymns' reserves harsh criticisms for those imitators of *The Temple* whose poems are not only witless, but also offer no help to a Christian's daily prayers:

those wide, those weak, and lean *conceptions*, which in the most inclinable *Reader* will scarce give any nourishment or help to *devotion*; for not flowing from a true, practick piety, it was impossible they should effect those things abroad, which they never had acquaintance with at home; being only the productions of a common spirit, and the obvious ebullitions of that light humor, which takes the pen in hand, out of no other consideration, then to be seen in print. (*V*, 391)

Success as a 'Christian-sacred *Poet*' (as Vaughan calls Prudentius earlier in this passage) depends on a 'true, practick piety' underlying its production, since only a writer dedicated to the practice of piety knows the trials and glories of a Christian life '*in detail, from hour to hour*, & feels Christianity as a Life, a Growth, a Pilgrimage thro' a hostile Country'.[21] To be a holy writer, it would seem, one must first be a *holy liver*. Vaughan's translation of the *Life of Paulinus* makes a similar connection (between the Saint's life and his letters) when it quotes Augustine's approbation of 'those letters of an unfained faith, those letters of holy hope, those letters of pure Charity!' (*V*, 359–60). Vaughan's three *ofs* do not distinguish between man and his work, and so connect the virtues equally to both, and each to other, just as Vaughan's praise of Herbert attaches itself equally to his 'holy *life* and *verse*' (*V*, 391).

Both need rules. The two volumes of *Silex Scintillans* (1650, 1655), *The Mount of Olives* (1652) and the prose translations of *Flores Solitudinis*

---

[20] *Calendar of the Correspondence of Richard Baxter*, ed. N. H. Keeble and G. F. Nuttall (Oxford, 1991), I, letter 489.

[21] S. T. Coleridge, notebook entry for Feb. 1826, discussing *The Temple* (*Samuel Taylor Coleridge*, 556).

(1654) exhort their reader to become a holy liver according to a pattern of rules and certain habits of mind. The first rule is not mistaking rules for their practice: 'The *Doctrine* of good living is short, but the *work* is long and hard to be perswaded', as Vaughan translated at the very beginning of 'Of Temperance and Patience' (part of *Flores Solitudinis* (1654), *V*, 220). Vaughan urges a particular effort to obey St Peter's advice that men spend 'every minute of our time that we might make *our calling and election sure*' (*The Mount of Olives* (*V*, 180)). A rigorous and ascetic conception of holy living is promoted by the poems of *Silex*, notably in the twenty-four-stanza daily rule 'Rules *and* Lessons' (1650); that poem is complemented by the daily devotions and other special prayers of *The Mount of Olives* (1652), which instruct their reader first and foremost in the nature and practice of order, obedience and patience. Supporting Vaughan's duties are practical meditations on the proper use of one's time, seen most clearly in Vaughan's two translations from the Jesuit Nieremberg in *Flores*; both laud the benefits of an active Christian life as they decry sloth and laziness with meditations on 'Of Temperance and Patience' and 'Of Life and Death'. Hence Vaughan's *holy living* is also fundamentally *hourly living*, an incessant rule and order of daily prayers and devotions with which to structure every day.

Vaughan's devotions take heart in difficult times from ideas of Christian *order* and *obedience* and the virtues of patience and steadfastness which he derives from scripture, liturgy and Anglican apologetics. Of course, Anglicans did not have a monopoly on order and obedience. Until the late 1650s, most books of practical divinity—after sermons perhaps the seventeenth century's foremost source of advice on how to be orderly livers—were authored by Puritans. Arthur Dent's *The Plaine Mans Path-way to Heaven* (1601), Lewis Bayly's *The Practice of Piety* (1611), John Preston's *The Saints Daily Exercise* (1629) and Robert Bolton's *Some Generall Directions for a Comfortable Walking with God* (1626) all offered advice on the moment-to-moment management of one's actions from a Puritan point of view. But such works were far from abhorrent to Vaughan, who knew and borrowed from Bayly and Bolton's works. Rather than rejecting their teaching as contributory to the collapse of order in the 1640s, Vaughan mingled it with that of devotional texts stemming from older traditions (John Cosin's *Devotions*, for example), and subordinated the whole to a reading of God's Two Books which proclaimed the consolation of order in a time of confusion and incoherence.

DISORDER'D MAN

Silex Scintillans (1650), *The Mount of Olives* (1652) and *Silex* (1655) want to mould their reader into a regular, pious *liver* such as Vaughan became during the years of his greatest literary productivity, 1648–55. In a state of shock after his brother William's death in 1648, Vaughan fell seriously ill in the early 1650s, complaining in 'The Epistle Dedicatory' to *Flores Solitudinis* (1654) that a 'peevish, inconstant state of health would not suffer me to stay for greater performances, or a better season' (*V*, 215). With such an expectancy, Vaughan seems to have focused ever more closely on the way to order time profitably, his poetry becoming correspondingly aware of time passing, of the hours and minutes wasted through the constant irritations of distraction and disorder, and of the need 'to number my dayes, that I may apply my heart unto wisdome' (*V*, 154).

Vaughan's poetry of disorder is already one of the keynotes of *Silex* (1650). A fine instance of Vaughan's liking for pairs of poems, 'Distraction' and 'The Pursuite' together lament the time wasted as a result of man's freedom to choose rightly or wrongly. If one reads *Silex Scintillans* cover to cover (rather than by means of 'The Alphabetical Table', say), these two poems are the earliest instance in which Vaughan makes nature the mark of stability and wholeness against which to measure man, a role which stars, rocks, birds and trees play more and more powerfully as the collection continues:

> Hadst thou
> Made me a starre, a pearle, or a rain-bow,
> The beames I then had shot
> My light had lessend not,
> But now
> I find myself the lesse, the more I grow;
> The world
> Is full of voices; Man is call'd, and hurl'd
> By each, he answers all,
> Knows ev'ry note, and call,
> Hence, still
> Fresh dotage tempts, or old usurps his will.
>
> ('Distraction', ll. 5–16)

Heavy, unhappily irregular rhythms, ever-changing line lengths, and staccato, unsatisfying rhymes hurl Vaughan's Man around like the voices of the world, while he desires order, but can possess none. As often for

Vaughan, such disorder has increased with maturity; 'The Retreate', coming a few poems after 'Distraction', measures the loss of childish innocence partly by the increasing power of worldly voices to tempt man away from inner contemplation and other duties. With a glance at Genesis 6: 6, where God grieves that he ever made man at all (the flood soon follows), Vaughan grieves that God did not make man differently by clipping his wings, that is, denying him free will:

> I grieve, my God! that thou hast made me such.
> > I grieve?
> O, yes! thou know'st I doe.
>
> > > > ('Distraction', ll. 26–8)

'The Pursuite' places man's abuse of free will in a more optimistic light by remembering that the first disobedience of Adam and Eve led eventually to the Redemption and salvation through Christ. But the poem also admits that the right choices do not come easily:

> Hadst thou given to this active dust
> > A state untir'd,
> The lost Sonne had not left the huske
> > Nor home desir'd;
> That was thy secret, and it is
> > Thy mercy too,
> For when all failes to bring to blisse,
> > Then, this must doe.
> Ah! Lord! and what a Purchase will that be
> To take us sick, that sound would not take thee?
>
> > > > (ll. 9–18)

Behind these lines lies the *felix culpa*, the idea that man fell to God's greater glory and so that He could show his love through Christ's Incarnation and sacrifice. But like Milton in Book XII of *Paradise Lost*, Vaughan eschews the paradoxical aspects of the fortunate fall, and concentrates instead on its cost. 'The Pursuite' foregrounds an ungrateful mankind which, like the Prodigal son, will journey home to its father only when no other choice remains, and not before. Small words carry a heavy weight in Vaughan's terse, slim poem. The modal ambiguity of 'Then, this must doe' (l. 16), for instance, sounds much too much like scraping home (*will have to do*) to suggest fortunate success (*will definitely do*). And with a ghostly reminder of the redemption in the final couplet—

Christ is 'the earnest of our inheritance until the redemption of the *purchased* possession' in Ephesians 1: 14 (my emphasis)—Vaughan hushes his tones as the poem confesses the enormous cost of 'thy mercy' (l. 15).

'The Pursuit''s swiftly humbled attempt to think well of man is uncharacteristic of *Silex Scintillans'* generally pessimistic outlook. Poems such as 'And do they so?', 'Misery' and 'The Constellation' feel with more abiding disappointment man's stubborn refusal to choose God's glory and his own good: 'mad man | Sits down, and freezeth on' is the horrified observation of 'Corruption' (ll. 29–30). Already met in the title of 'Distraction', the prefix *dis-* appears like a bad penny in *Silex* (1650), where it cancels, even before Vaughan can fully name, those prelapsarian qualities of obedience, order and harmony which fallen man can recover only with God's help. Vaughan's excoriation of human restlessness in 'Distraction' continues in 'Affliction [I]', which admits the need for God's wrath to make ungrateful livers value God and their souls:

> All flesh is Clay, thou know'st; and but that God
>   Doth use his rod,
> And by a fruitfull Change of frosts, and showres
>   Cherish, and bind thy *pow'rs*,
> Thou wouldst to weeds, and thistles quite disperse,
>   And be more wild than is thy verse.

> (ll. 11–16)

Distraction leads to a dispersal of man's powers—though here, as Vaughan would have known, the etymological root is the Latin verb *di-spergere* (to scatter about, to disperse). The same poem likens man to a colour, noting that '*whites* that rest | Something of sickness would disclose', and it celebrates God's capacity to assist man with the most important and habitual *dis-* prefix in *Silex Scintillans*:

> Thus doth God *Key* disorder'd man
>   (Which none else can,)
> Tuning his breast to rise, or fall.

> (ll. 35–7)

The negative prefix *dis* becomes a sign for Vaughan of the fallen state, a reminder of the failure implicit in all human actions. Midway through *Silex* (1650), 'Disorder *and* frailty' uses the very Herbertian metaphor of musical alignment at its climax, where Vaughan asks God, in Christ's name, to 'tune to thy will I My heart, my verse' (ll. 59–60).[22] To follow the Prodigal Son's journey home, Vaughan's corrupted Man must undergo regular repairs and constant tuning; left alone, he will inevitably fall further out of key.

Silex Scintillans characterizes the path to heaven as one of order and rule, urging disordered man to find it, with God's help, by becoming a *holy liver*. This was not in itself an unusual plan. Reformed devotional manuals from the mid-sixteenth century on had recommended an order, or pattern, of daily prayers, and in the seventeenth century *The Practice of Piety* and *The Plaine Mans Path-way* (Bunyan's two books) both proffered a step-by-step guide to sanctifying every moment of the day with prayer.[23] Vaughan's own *The Mount of Olives* exhorts in a somewhat traditional vein when it warns the lukewarm: 'Be not regular and holy for a day or two, but all the dayes of thy life, and number thy dayes, that thou mayst apply thy heart unto wisedome' (*V*, 164).

What is new and different about Vaughan's sense of order is that it derives largely from observing and meditating on the natural world, as viewed particularly through the scriptures, and especially Paul's epistle to the Romans. Whereas man cannot sit still, and needs to beg God to control him—'Lord, bind me up, and let me lye I A Pris'ner to my libertie ('Misery', ll. 1–2)—Creation possesses an order, harmony and sustaining joy which man cannot achieve in his lapsed and hardened state. Stars, stones, trees and birds are the touchstone by which *Silex Scintillans* measures mankind's 'infidélité au dessein de la création', in Robert Ellrodt's phrase; they are a lesson for man's pride in his freedom and intellect, a check on his sense of worth.[24] It is to misunderstand Vaughan's attraction to nature to argue, as William Empson did in 1929, that Vaughan does not 'seem anxious to remember what the lessons [of nature] were', and that he thought only of 'a state of melancholy peace experienced when he was out walking, and implying that it did him good, without conscious effort of his will'.[25] To attend to the biblical senses of Vaughan's natural imagery, as his contemporary reader could have done almost instinctively, is to learn the very *specific* lessons Vaughan drew from nature

---

[22] The whole poem is one of Vaughan's closest imitations of Herbert.

[23] Stranks, *Anglican Devotion*, 45.

[24] Robert Ellrodt, *L'Inspiration personnelle et l'esprit du temps, chez les poètes métaphysiques anglais*, 3 vols. (Paris, 1960), ii. 186.

[25] William Empson, 'An Early Romantic', 260–3 in *Argufying: Essays on Literature and Culture*, ed. John Haffenden (1988).

about prayer, constancy and holiness; above all, about the *discipline*, the practice of holy living, and how nature instructs the poet in his quest to be a holy liver.

The interest shown by Vaughan's poems in religious *discipline* helps to explain a famous crux in *Silex Scintillans* (1650). In 'And do they so?', Vaughan not only wishes that he had the orderliness and single-minded devotion of stones, trees and flowers, but explicitly rejects the idea, gleaned from his books, that the creatures of nature cannot worship God and yearn to be with Him. With an epigraph from Romans 8: 19, which it cites in Latin from Beza's translation of the New Testament, 'And do they so?' holds that the creatures *are* sentient, capable of prayer and of desire for God: *Etenim res Creatae exerto Capite observantes expectant revelationem Filiorum Dei* (For the creatures, watching with lifted head, wait for the revelation of the sons of God) (*V*, 432).[26] The teaching of Romans chapter 8, that 'the whole creation groaneth and travaileth in pain together' provoked interpretation and counter-interpretation from Patristic times until Vaughan's own day, as Alan Rudrum has shown. Vaughan's view of the sentience of the creatures was an unorthodox one in the eyes of most Reformed Christians, but not without precedent in Reformed theologians such as Peter Martyr.[27]

Rudrum's essay tries the unusual beliefs of 'And do they so?', which are shared by Vaughan's 'The Book' (*Silex* Part 2), against the heresies listed in Thomas Edwards's infamous catalogue of heterodoxy *Gangraena* (1646) and the more moderate *A Discoverie of the World to Come* (1650) written by the Devon minister, John Seager. Both of these men identify the resurrection of the creatures and potential universalism (the idea that God would make everything new again) as the strongest heresy stemming from Romans chapter 8. Rudrum makes the very plausible suggestion that Vaughan was aware of the anti-predestinarian, anti-Calvinist implications of these beliefs, and deliberately cited Beza's translation of Romans to make what is 'almost like a *comic* comment'[28] on the Calvinist doctrines of election and reprobation:

> And do they so? have they a Sense
> Of ought but Influence?

---

[26] Translation from *R*, 557.

[27] Alan Rudrum, 'Henry Vaughan, the Liberation of the Creatures, and Seventeenth-Century English Calvinism', *Seventeenth Century*, 4 (1989), 33–54.

[28] Ibid. 48.

> Can they their heads lift, and expect,
>   And grone too? why th'Elect
> Can do no more.
>
> (ll. 1–5)

This is a valuable point (first made in Rudrum's edition of the poems), but Stevie Davies is also right to note that Vaughan's joke is curiously humourless, his poem's desire to be a rock, stone or tree quite innocent of the wit which powers George Herbert's line from 'Affliction [I]': 'I reade, and sigh, and wish I were a tree'.[29] Critical uncertainty over the tone of Vaughan's lines can be dispelled, I think, by reading the poem as part of Vaughan's ongoing meditation on creaturely order and obedience. The undeniable echo of Beza's *exerto Capite observantes* in line 3—'Can they their heads lift, and expect?'—suggests that Vaughan preferred Beza's translation for its small but metonymically powerful detail of 'watching with lifted head', something which is quite lacking in the Authorized Version's 'For the earnest expectation of the creature waiteth for the manifestation of the sons of God'. Constant watchfulness, expressed in the dutifully lifted heads of birds, beasts and even plants, is nature's example to mankind of the proper degree of duty.

Rudrum's article falters only where it tries to read for doctrine poems whose emphasis is firmly on *discipline*. Herbert's and Vaughan's poetry leans toward practical rather than controversial topics in theology, often approaching controversies—the soul's progress after death, its pre-existence, the future course of the Church Militant—without urging or adopting any particular view. And although many lines in *The Temple* and *Silex Scintillans* are helpfully glossed from works of controversial theology, the reader who attempts to separate out entire theological positions is easily frustrated.

Vaughan writes confidently of the self-regulation of nature and its worship of God, disagreeing with the view of Herbert's 'Providence' that:

> Beasts fain would sing; birds dittie to their notes;
> Trees would be tuning on their native lute
> To thy renown: but all their hands and throats
> Are brought to Man, while they are lame and mute.
>
> (ll. 9–12)

---

[29] 'Affliction [I]', l. 57; Davies, *Henry Vaughan*, 97.

When Vaughan, by contrast, calls man nature's 'high-priest' in 'Christs Nativity', his very next stanza yearns to be 'some *Bird*, or Star' that could offer a 'Shining, or singing' sacrifice (ll. 11, 13, 18). Capable but irregular, man may be inherently more able to glorify God, but in Vaughan's writing he often fails to do so; Herbert's picture of 'A beast, yet is, or should be more' is still too optimistic for Vaughan ('Man', l. 9). The '*birds* and inferiour *creatures*' may be lesser beings, yet, as Vaughan noted in *The Mount of Olives*, 'not so contemptible, but they may serve us for noble instances' (*V*, 177). *Silex Scintillans* particularly celebrates creaturely prayer. When Vaughan writes, in 'The Morning-watch', that 'Birds, beasts, all things | Adore him [God] in their kinds', he praises the creatures' kindness as well as their different kind of worship. For Herbert, 'Trees *would* be tuning'; for Vaughan, 'The world' is 'in tune'.[30]

Like 'Distraction', 'And do they so?' imagines divine restraint by contemplating the creatures' limited freedom. If Vaughan were a stone, or tree or flower,

> Then should I (tyed to one sure state,)
>   All day expect my date;
> But I am sadly loose, and stray
>   A giddy blast each way;
> O let me thus not range!
>   Thou canst not change.

                              (ll. 15–20)

Man's disorder is a meditative theme to which *Silex* (1650) returns with a regularity almost equal to the creatures' devotional returns. As it lauds the order and regularity of the heavens, Vaughan's well-known stellular poetry continues the creaturely meditations of 'And do they so' and the debate over man's freedom begun in 'Distraction' and 'The Pursuite'. The greatest star poem in *Silex* (1650), 'The Constellation', draws on the translations of Boethius Vaughan made for *Olor Iscanus*, particularly 'Lib. 1 Metrum 5':

> O thou great builder of this starrie frame
> Who fixt in thy eternall throne dost tame
> The rapid Spheres, and lest they jarre
> Hast giv'n a law to ev'ry starre!
> Thou art the Cause that now the Moon

---

[30] Herbert, 'Providence', l. 6; Vaughan, 'The Morning-watch', l. 19.

> With full orbe dulls the starres, and soon
> Again growes dark, her light being done.
>
> .   .   .   .
>
> Thus by Creations law controll'd
> All things their proper stations hold
> Observing (as thou didst intend)
> Why they were made, and for what end.
> Only humane actions thou
> Hast no Care of, but to the flow
> And Ebbe of Fortune leav'st them all,
> Hence th'Innocent endures that thrall
> Due to the wicked, whilst alone
> They sit possessours of his throne.
>
> (ll. 1–7, 25–34)

Whether Vaughan had translated this passage by 1647 (the Preface to *Olor Iscanus* is dated 17 December that year) or whether it was added before the book's eventual publication in 1651, Boethius' words speak powerfully to the translated Royalists of the day. Boethius' stars, law-abiding and tamed once-and-for-all, divinely controlled by the God who put them in their proper stations, cast a poetic light on the obliquely Royalist sense of order and obedience which informs the regular stanzas of 'The Constellation':

> Fair, order'd lights (whose motion without noise
>   Resembles those true Joys
> Whose spring is on that hil where you do grow
>   And we here tast sometimes below,)
>
> With what exact obedience do you move
>   Now beneath, and now above,
> And in your vast progressions overlook
>   The darkest night, and closest nook!
>
> (ll. 1–8)

Through the etymological root of 'exact'—*agere*, to drive—Vaughan links the stars' *order* with their *obedience*, which consists, as it does in Boethius I: 5, in *driving*, unjarringly, round the heavens in the order God set them in. Their orderly living is precisely what man could not achieve in 'Distraction' and 'The Pursuit'.

Vaughan explores man's response to divine orders and commandments through a group of words with related Latin etymologies. *State* and *sta-*

tion share a root in *status* (posture, position, attitude; state, condition) and the related *statio* (a place of abode, a post or station), while *order* and *ordain* both derive from *ordo* (right order, regular succession). 'The Pursuite' struggles hard to make the most of man's 'state untir'd', and in 'And do they so?' the speaker wants to be 'tyed to one sure state' like the creatures; while Vaughan's choice of *station* to translate Boethius' 'Nihil antiqua lege solutum | Linquit propriae stationis opus. | Omnia certo fine gubernans', emphasizes the creatures' fixed place within a cosmic order: 'Thus by Creations law controll'd | All things their proper stations hold'.[31] With the exception of Ecclesiastes, in which the 'the estate of the sons of men' is their vain and beastly nature (3: 18), the bible does not use *state* in this way. But the Prayer Book does, famously, speaking of the 'honourable estate' of marriage in 'The fourme of solemnizacyon of matrymonie' and in the revised version of 1662 prayers are offered for 'the good estate of the Catholick Church'.

It is with relief that Vaughan casts his poetic eye upward (and backward in time), away from man's *disorder*, to let the unprefixed, positive *order* ring out in celebration of the creation. The opening phrase of 'The Constellation'—'Fair, order'd lights!'—highlights the double sense of order—to command and to put into order—and rolls them together, connecting the stars' present orderliness with God's original fiat. The verb *ordain* cannot muster a similar sense of patterning, since its noun form *ordinance* carries only the sense of command; and indeed, the Authorized Version uses it for God's decrees and sanctifications. 'Man', third from last in *Silex* (1650), uses both *order and ordain* to describe man's *state*, with a conceit Vaughan adopts from Herbert's 'The Pulley':

> Man is the shuttle, to whose winding quest
>   And passage through these looms
> God order'd motion, but ordain'd no rest.

('Man', ll. 26–8)

This is an instance of Vaughan's black humour, since although God has verbally *order'd motion*, *order'd motion* is just what man lacks, while slothful rest is a familiar sin.[32] The world is a gloomy and boundless playpen for man's endless wandering in Vaughan's 'Man', a poem which darkens considerably the picture of a bountiful and navigable home from

---

[31] *The Consolation of Philosophy* I. 5, l. 25; Vaughan's translation, ll. 15–16.
[32] For another poet's hatred of sloth, see John L. Klause, 'Donne and the Wonderful', *English Literary History*, 17 (1987), 41–66.

Herbert's poem of the same name. Again, Vaughan's creatures reveal how restless is man's *state*:

> Weighing the stedfastness and state
> Of some mean things which here below reside,
> Where birds like watchful Clocks the noiseless date
> And Intercourse of times divide,
> Where Bees at night get home and hive, and flowrs
> Early, aswel as late,
> Rise with the Sun, and set in the same bowrs;
>
> 2.
> I would (said I) my God would give
> The staidness of these things to man! for these
> To his divine appointments ever cleave
> And no new business breaks their peace;
> The birds nor sow, nor reap, yet sup and dine,
> The flowres without clothes live,
> Yet *Solomon* was never drest so fine.
>
> 3.
> Man hath stil either toyes, or Care,
> He hath no root, nor to one place is ty'd,
> But ever restless and Irregular
> About this Earth doth run and ride.
>
> ('Man', ll. 1–18)

In the birds, bees and stars, Vaughan found a perfect example of the *stedfastness* (l. 1) that St Paul preached to the primitive churches: 'Man' redirects Paul's words to the Colossians—'am I with you in the spirit, joying and beholding your *order*, and the *stedfastness* of your faith in Christ' (Colossians 2: 5)—to the creatures, whilst remembering St Peter's warning to endure in faithfulness: 'beware, lest ye also, being led away with the error of the wicked, fall from your own *stedfastness*' (2 Peter 3: 17).[33] *Staidness* is in fact the opposite of sloth, since it requires an active constancy man does not possess naturally in his fallen condition; it is that 'one sure state' dreamed of in 'And do they so?', the peculiarly *ecclesiastical* helps to which are suggested by the biblical associations of *staidness* (l. 9). Lacking the persistency of the creatures, man needs *stays* to keep him constant, and the best stay (also Vaughan's most likely use) is the Authorized Version's alternative reading at 1 Timothy 3: 15, where the church is called 'the pil-

---

[33] For other uses of *stedfast* and its cognates in this sense, see: 1 Cor. 7: 37, 15: 58; Heb. 3: 14, 6: 19; 1 Pet. 5: 9.

lar and stay of the truth'. Pillars certainly form part of the meditative background to Vaughan's 'Man': *steadfastness*, the quality Paul admired in the Colossians and which Vaughan reapplies to nature, was a word originally used of the fixity of pillars and foundations.[34] Some men, Vaughan had lamented in 'Man in Darkness' 'would seem to be Pillars', and 'prove but reeds and specious dissemblers'; and he had gone on to use with approval passages from Ralegh's *History* and Casaubon's Polybius that note how speedily such pillars totter: 'A day, an hour, a minute . . . is sufficient to over-turn and extirpate the most settled Governments, which seemed to have been founded and rooted in Adamant. Suddenly do the high things of this world come to an end' (*V*, 171). Against time's violent uprootings, Vaughan opposes a steadfast lowliness that is itself rooted in the second chapter of Paul's advice to the Colossians: the sorrow expressed in stanza 3 of 'The Constellation', that man has 'no root', surely recalls Paul's approval that the Colossians are 'Rooted and built up in him, and stablished in the faith' (Colossians 2: 7).

Though Vaughan's images of holiness are frequently of solitary devotion, then, they lean for support on scriptural affirmations of the church's power to guide and regulate human life. The later stanzas of 'The Constellation' find those *stays* under desperate attack:

> Since plac'd by him who calls you by your names
>   And fixt there all your flames,
> Without Command you never acted ought
>   And then you in your Courses fought.
>
> But here Comission'd by a black self-wil
>   The sons the father kil,
> The Children Chase the mother, and would heal
>   The wounds they give, by crying, zeale.

(ll. 33–40)

The first of these stanzas alludes to the bible's most famous poetical images of stars—'He telleth the number of the stars: he calleth them all by their names' (Psalm 147: 4)—and to the accounts of the creation in Genesis and Job 38, and to the song of Barak and Deborah in Judges 5, in which 'the stars in their courses [or paths] fought against Sisera', an extraordinary image of the creation fighting on the side of

---

[34] *OED*, pillar, *sb.*, 1, 2. Onians notes that Paul calls James, Peter and John 'columns' (Gal. 2: 9) in his discussion of 'Architecture and Christian Morality', 112–29 (112) in his *Bearers of Meaning* (Princeton, 1988).

righteousness.[35] The stars' order, obedience and fixity (words used in the penultimate stanza of the poem) shame the zealous *Commissions* of men—not least, one supposes, those Parliamentary Commissions charged with reforming British religion, most notably for Vaughan the Westminster Assembly and the Commission for Propagation in Wales.[36] Thus the dead *father* is Charles, the wounded *mother* the Church of England, and the wounds themselves include the dismantling of episcopacy, banning of the Prayer Book, and ejections of the existing clergy. As J. Sears McGee has noted in another context, offences against one's mother and father were often construed by the forces of the early modern establishment as a sin against God's Fifth Commandment:

> Anglicans were fully agreed that the duty of obedience to the powers that be was implied in this law. The king was the father of the nation, and the church was often referred to as the holy mother of its members . . . Hammond, in his widely used *Practical Catechism*, simply assumed that 'honor of father and mother, obedience to superiors, magistrates, etc' were part and parcel of the Fifth Commandment's meaning. Sanderson said in 1640 that 'to disobey lawful authority in lawful things is a sin against the Fifth Commandment'. Taylor asserted the same in his famous tract, *Holy Dying*, saying that 'to obey kings and all that are in authority' was a duty of the Fifth Commandment.[37]

The unusually forthright denunciation of Puritanism in 'The Constellation' gathers strength from its awareness of community with clergymen like Hammond and Taylor, and with those conformist believers whose religion was nurtured by their ministry and writings.[38]

The stars of 'The Constellation' teach man the true *obedience*, as well as *order*, by which he should live. Through the Word, God reveals to man that his worship must be obedient, like the creatures'; but also, since Paul describes perfect *obedience* as the power which redeems mankind, devotion should be like that of Christ, the great exemplar: 'For as by one man's disobedience many were made sinners, so by the obedience of one shall many be made righteous' (Romans 5: 19). Though men cannot hope to

---

[35] For Donne's exegesis of this text, see *Sermons of John Donne*, iv. 179–209.

[36] Pettet, *Of Paradise and Light*, 206; noted by *R*, 582, who also notes the stellular passages from the bible apart from the Job.

[37] J. Sears McGee, *The Godly Man in Stuart England: Anglicans, Puritans and the Two Tables, 1620–1670* (New Haven, 1976), 148; see also Ian Green, *The Christian's ABC* (Oxford, 1996), 451–60.

[38] On obedience as the key note of Henrician religion, see Richard Rex, 'The Crisis of Obedience: God's Word and Henry's Reformation', *Historical Journal*, 39 (1996), 863–94.

emulate Christ's holiness, they may learn ideal obedience from his example. 'The Mutinie' makes this point, versifying closely from Hebrews 12: 2, towards the end of *Silex* (1650):

> though in this vale
> Of sin, and death I sojourn, yet one Eie
> May look to thee, To thee the finisher
> And Author of my faith.

> (ll. 20–3)

That *Eie* fixed on Christ is a metonymic extrapolated from the indexical verb in Hebrews 11: 2, which simply advises Christians that they should be always 'Looking unto Jesus'.[39] Adding it, Vaughan gets the exemplary sense of *look up to* as well as the emblematic suggestion of *look at*; his head is raised 'Up to those bright, and gladsome hils | Whence flowes my weal, and mirth,' ('Psalm 121', ll. 1–2) as well as in contemplation of the *author-*ity of Christ, who has set the pattern of obedience by which men should live, and is the 'author and finisher of faith', as Hebrews 12 teaches.

'But seeks he *Obedience, Order, Light*, | Your calm and wel-trained flight?' asks 'The Constellation' (ll. 29–30). *Trained* is Vaughan's metaphor in '*Isaacs* Marriage' for how some men are 'tym'd, and 'train'd up' to holiness, in contrast to Isaac who, having *inherited* Abraham's faith, needed no training. 'But seeks he your *Obedience, Order, Light* . . . ?' Such *seeking* recalls the many other narratives of spiritual questing in Vaughan's writing: the pilgrim of 'Regeneration' seeking a true Spring to replace the frost of the world; Nicodemus seeking Jesus by cover of darkness in 'The Night'; and in 'The Retreate', the unreachable 'ancient track' that would return the Christian to childish and heavenly simplicity (l. 22).

If Christ is Vaughan's ideal and nature his spur and inspiration, then it is the holy lives of other Christians that provide a guide and pattern. Some of these he found, unsurprisingly, in scripture. 'To the Holy Bible', the penultimate poem in the finished *Silex Scintillans*, wonders how to leave behind the guidebook which has been like a lover—the poem is a sacred parody[40]—through thick and thin:

> O book! lifes guide! how shall we part,
> And thou so long seiz'd of my heart!

---

[39] For a discussion of index and indexical verbs, see John Lyons, *Semantics*, 2 vols. (Cambridge, 1977), i. 106–9.

[40] Discussed by Freeman, 'Parody as a Literary Form'; Malcolmson, 'George Herbert and Coterie Verse'; Martin, 'George Herbert and Sacred "Parodie"'.

> Take this last kiss, and let me weep
> True thanks to thee, before I sleep.
>
> ('To the Holy Bible', ll. 1–4)

How to part from the bible is uncertain, but *when* is clear: as near to the 'sleep' of death as possible—and the poem is spoken as from the deathbed—when the bible's rules for *holy living* are overshadowed by those for *holy dying* (to adopt Jeremy Taylor's two famous titles). Until death, the bible offers a plethora of guides to show the way, ancient holy livers whose lives planted an avenue all along the way to heaven:

> Fair, solitary path! Whose blessed shades
> The old, white Prophets planted first and drest:
> Leaving for us (whose goodness quickly fades,)
> A shelter all the way, and bowers to rest.
>
> ('Righteousness', ll. 1–4)

As well as reading the stories of the prophets and patriarchs as a typological and prophetic lesson for his own time, yearning too for that immediacy with which God directed their lives, Vaughan also remembers the ancients as exemplary holy livers, part of whose holiness is to have survived in the story of scriptures to guide the Christian 'still homeward' ('Righteousness', l. 17).

Next best are those modern *livers* whose lives most resemble the ancients in purity. In their preface to Lancelot Andrewes's *XCVI Sermons*, William Laud and John Buckeridge suggest that the dead Archbishop's virtue 'was comparable to that which was want to be found in the *Primitive Bishops* of the *Church*. And had he lived among those *ancient Fathers*, his Vertue would have *shined, even amongst those vertuous men*'.[41] Vaughan, too, speaks of light shining from the recently deceased. 'Joy of my life!', an elegy most likely written for Henry's younger brother William, likens the deceased to a star, a fixed point for the soul's navigation, and then to the pillar of fire by which God guided the Jews out of Egypt:

> 2.
> Stars are of mighty use: The night
>   Is dark, and long;
> The Rode foul, and where one goes right,
>   Six may go wrong.

---

[41] Andrewes, *XCVI Sermons* (1629), sig. A3^v.

One twinkling ray
Shot o'r some cloud,
May clear much way
And guide a croud.

3.

Gods Saints are shining lights: who stays
Here long must passe
O're dark hills, swift streames, and steep ways
As smooth as glasse;
But these all night
Like Candles, shed
Their beams, and light
Us into Bed.

4.

They are (indeed,) our Pillar-fires
Seen as we go,
They are that Cities shining spires
We travell too.

(ll. 9–28)

This twinkling star might seem to be the one celebrated in the children's rhyme, but in fact Vaughan's useful stars are probably the spirits of the saints, widely thought to inhabit stars through a posthumous process of 'stellification'.[42] The pillar of fire in the wilderness and the candle shining on Job's head, like the path of the 'white Prophets' from 'Righteousness', are characteristic of Vaughan's preference for Old Testament images of guidance. He also found the Old Testament law a force for control and guidance, the covenant of grace notwithstanding. The opening stanza of 'The Law, and the Gospel' (*Silex* Part 1) at first appears, like the earlier 'Faith', to be a celebration of the 'open house' of Christianity, remembering the thunder and threats which echoed down from Mount Sinai as a time of fainting and fear:

How did poor flesh (which after thou didst weare,)
Then faint, and fear!
Thy Chosen flock, like leafs in a high wind,
Whisper'd obedience, and their heads Inclin'd.

('The Law, and the Gospel', ll. 7–10)

---

[42] Stellification is the topic of Alastair Fowler, *Time's Purpled Masquers: Stars and the Afterlife in Renaissance English Literature* (Oxford, 1996); for later traditions of stellular poetry, see J. H. Prynne, *Stars, Tigers and the Shape of Words*, The William Matthews Lectures 1992 (1993), Lecture 1, 'Stars'.

However, although the 'Chosen flock' may have fainted and feared, they also 'Whisper'd obedience'; and in the distracted, disordered world of poems like 'The Pursuite', obedience is Vaughan's answer and corrective to destructive freedom. After a stanza in praise of the Redemption, 'The Law, and the Gospel' reaches back again, unconfident of the 'filial Confidence' (l. 13) of the previous stanza, and begs for the rod and well as divine love:

3.

Yet since man is a very brute
And after all thy Acts of grace doth kick,
Slighting that health thou gav'st, when he was sick,
Be not displeas'd, If I, who have a sute
    To thee each houre, beg at thy door
      For this one more;
O plant in me thy *Gospel*, and thy *Law*,
    Both *Faith*, and *Awe*;
So twist them in my heart, that ever there
I may as wel as *Love*, find too thy *fear*!

(ll. 21–30)

For the Vaughan of 'And do they so?' and 'The Pursuite', man's perversity is to run from the shadow of truth rather than to stand in its light, to need to be chased into Christ's arms rather than to walk there himself. Such pessimism stood in emotional and political opposition to the enthusiastic claims Vaughan heard around him in the late 1640s for the Revolution of the Saints, a glorious last age of the world in which the truth—and Christ himself—was soon to be fully revealed on earth. For Vaughan, incredulous at these claims as he counted the high costs of civil war, holy living according to a rule attested to the madness of a times of 'persecution and Heresie', when since God's 'Service and thy Sabbaths, thy own sacred Institutions and the pledges of thy love are denied unto us', the true holy liver must find other means to worship the God of peace (*V*, 166).

HOLY, HOURLY

Order, obedience, steadfastness, law: in a rebellious age, *Silex Scintillans* sounded these words as witness to the counter-rebellious conformity of its author's holy living, and a prompt to others to follow his example. Yet the Christian living Vaughan describes in *Silex Scintillans* and *The Mount of Olives* is not Anglicanism as Donne, Herbert, Laud or Evelyn would have known it; even the Silurist's formidable linguistic skills could not recreate the spiritual effect of common prayer and church ceremony in poetry confined to solitary or personal settings. While the cadences of the Prayer Book haunt *The Mount of Olives* and its daily services are remembered in some of the poems from *Silex Scintillans*,[43] Vaughan's instructions for a holy life do not so much enjoin strict obedience to Cranmer's liturgy as succour those dismayed by its passing.

In a disordered world, Vaughan sought out and offered his reader a means to create Christian *staidness* without the *stays* of the church, to live an *ordered*, holy life without the holy orders of Anglican worship 'now trodden under foot, and branded with the title of *Antichristian*' ('Man in Darkness', *V*, 186). The order which Vaughan offers imitates those regularities of nature his poems celebrate, but it is also designed strongly to resist and to reject the changes of the 1640s. Vaughan's profound admiration of the creatures' *order* and his belief that man's *descent* from order had reached its lowest point in the present-day rebellion of the Civil War years, led him to evolve a substitute: an hourly rule for everyday living, a pattern of piety which would keep the faithful *steadfast* on the funambulatory way of faith in difficult times. This rule, established most clearly in the poem 'Rules *and* Lessons', uses the hours of the day as a framework for devotion; it sees a dutiful and regular disposition of hours as the essential task of holy living. In other words, it considers *hourliness* an essential ingredient of *holiness*.

Vaughan's prescription for mankind's chronic disorder is rule and regularity, his treatment the poetry of *Silex Scintillans* (1650). Although *The Mount of Olives* (1652) is ostensibly Vaughan's most instructive work, its preface directs those who would be regular in their lives and worship to the less evidently didactic *Silex*:

Neither did I thinke it necessary that the ordinary Instructions for a regular life (of which theere are infinite Volumes already extant) should be inserted into this small Manuall, lest instead of Devotion, I should trouble thee with a peece of Ethics. Besides, thou hast them already as briefly delivered as possibly I could, in my *Sacred Poems*. (*V*, 140)

---

[43] For a discussion of the Prayer Book in Vaughan's writing, see Wall, *Transformations of the Word*, 274–8; Day, 'Prose Works of Henry Vaughan', *passim*. The morning and evening services of the Prayer Book are recalled by Vaughan's 'The Morning-watch' and 'The Evening-watch'.

The Mount of Olives is, of course, a practical book, commended to its readers' 'practise' in the preface, and consisting of prayers for many regular occasions such as 'When thou dost awake' and 'A Prayer before thou goest to Church'. Thus far it resembles the dozens of other popular instruction manuals of the day. Yet Vaughan insists that he has not written a 'peece of Ethics', and refers the reader seeking instruction to *Silex Scintillans*, a book which to modern readers has seldom been considered *practical.* Vaughan even allows himself a small swell of pleasure in his having delivered poetical instructions 'as briefly . . . as possibly I could', aware, no doubt, that brevity was scarce among the 'infinite' manuals of the day.

'In my *Sacred Poems*': I have suggested above that many poems in *Silex* (1650) are richly laden with exemplars of devotion (in the form of the stars, the moon, the creatures, and the dead), and that they ring with appeals to rise above disorder and disobedience. As well as this general sense, though, 'in my *Sacred Poems*' is also thinking particularly of 'Rules *and* Lessons', the one poem in *Silex* (1650) which specifically teaches 'ordinary Instructions for a regular life'. The etymological root of *regular* is the Latin *regula*, 'rule', and it is a ruled life that Vaughan sought to describe in 'Rules and Lessons', one at an opposite extreme from that distracted, disordered restlessness lamented in *Silex* (1650), 'a life having form, structure, operating on a definite principle, marked by steadiness, pursuing a definite course'.[44] Instilling this regularity, and provoking active admiration for order and obedience, is the task of Vaughan's instructive poem, which is one of the most productive fruits of his own habitual approval of constancy. (In '*To* Etesia *looking from her Casement at the full* Moon' (published in *Thalia Rediviva*) that habit led him to look with a fresh eye at the moon, so often a Renaissance symbol of all that is inconstant, and to see her as a creature with her own 'Rules', in the form of the lunar cycles.)[45]

'Rules *and* Lessons' is the longest poem in either edition of *Silex Scintillans* and is placed thirty-eighth out of seventy-three poems, at the very heart of the 1650 edition. Although 'The Match', Vaughan's reply to Herbert's 'Obedience', is the central poem numerically,[46] 'Rules *and* Lessons' occupies the *physical* centre of Vaughan's book, that is signatures D3ᵛ to [D5]ᵛ (pages 54–8 of the book's 110), and so announces typographically

[44] *OED*, regular, A. *adj.*, 1, 2, 3.
[45] '*To* Etesia *looking from her Casement at the full* Moon', l. 16.
[46] On this positioning, see the comments of Post, *Henry Vaughan*, 117.

the central importance of holy, hourly living in Vaughan's holy writing. Though the Silurist may have deprecated over-lengthy instruction manuals, he was manifestly unafraid to use the 'brief' instructions of 'Rules *and* Lessons' as the keystone of his broadly lyrical collection. He was right to have confidence in the poem. 'Rules *and* Lessons' is a fascinating hybrid of the lyric and the didactic, both less proverbial and more compact than its model, George Herbert's seventy-seven-stanza 'The Church Porch', and also written in verse which is never less than accomplished, and which bursts with Vaughan's characteristic concerns—death, worship, time, and the veils between man and God—in a manner which never seems nakedly didactic.

One might ponder the fact, too, that 'as briefly delivered as I could' means no fewer than twenty-four stanzas: no fewer, no more. Thus 'Rules *and* Lessons' counts off one by one the most important period of instruction and the period of dutiful worship throughout *Silex Scintillans*: the hour. Driving the comparison between man and creature in 'The Tempest', for instance, is Vaughan's disgust that man should refuse the lessons of one hour spent listening to the creation:

> How is man parcell'd out? how ev'ry hour
>   Shews him himself, or somthing he should see?
>   This late, long heat may his Instruction be,
> And tempests have more in them than a showr.
>
>   .   .   .   .   .
>
> O that man could do so! that he would hear
>   The world read to him! all the vast expence
>   In the Creation shed, and slav'd to sence
> Makes up but lectures for his eie, and ear.
>
> (ll. 1–4, 17–20)

Part of 'The Tempest''s own instruction lies in the opportunity to notice that the poem has just as many lines as an hour has minutes. Vaughan, like nature, is giving a *lecture*, albeit to an audience whose hearing is constantly called into question.[47]

Not in lines, but in stanzas, 'Rules *and* Lessons' bodies forth the hours of the day which wind through the poetry of *Silex Scintillans*. Though

---

[47] *OED*, lecture, *sb.*, 4b; and for an example of the convention that a lecture took one hour, see Thomas Carew, 'An Elegie upon the death of the Deane of Pauls, Dr. John Donne', ll. 3–8, esp. l. 6, 'short liv'd as his houre' (*Poems, by J. D. with Elegies on the Authors Death* (1633), 385).

the poem has no other formal divisions, it splits into five chronologically arranged sections beginning at dawn and ending at bedtime. They are: early morning duties (stanzas 1–5); a Christian's duties and conduct in the world (stanzas 6–14); constancy in devotion when moving in the world (15–17); meditations on the day's dying as a reminder of mortality (18–21); and three last stanzas which draw the poem to a close with instructions for sleep (22), waking again (23) and finally a 'brief' exhortation to love God and one's neighbour which remembers the two Great Commandments singled out by Christ.[48] This chronological structure is the most striking difference between 'Rules *and* Lessons' and Herbert's 'The Church Porch', and emphasizes Vaughan's creation of a *rule* rather than a summary of advice or adages.[49] Whereas 'Perrirhanterium' offers general moral warnings and advice for a pious life—'Be sweet to all', 'Laugh not too much' (ll. 211, 229)—the devotions of 'Rules *and* Lessons' begin with the dawn and progress through the day until sleep; only the last stanza proffers more general advice. Thus hours are the vertebrae of Vaughan's day, forming the regular—rigid even—backbone of 'Rules *and* Lessons', a strong core around which a holy, hourly life can take shape.

Hours are the measure of Christian duty in *Silex Scintillans*; how they are spent says much about the 'manner of *liver*' who spends them. The second section of 'Rules *and* Lessons' advises on the Christian's duties in the world (his morning pursuits) and recommends that a holy liver waste not one hour in pointless grief: 'Spend not an hour so, as to weep another, | For tears are not thine own' (ll. 67–8). Like coins, then, hours may be spent for good or bad. The penultimate act of the day is to spend an hour in grave preparation for the final sleep:

> Thy Accounts thus made, spend in the grave one houre
> Before thy time; Be not a stranger there
> Where thou may'st sleep whole ages.

> (ll. 121–3)

---

[48] 'Love the Lord thy God with all thy heart' and 'love thy neighbour as thyself' (Matt. 22: 37–40; cf. Luke 10: 27).

[49] Herbert's epigrammatic style is the basis of Nathaniel Wanley's most frequently revised and copied poem 'Advice' (sometimes called 'Alphabet'), included in *Poems*, ed. Martin. In 1674 Thomas White appended alphabetized selections of advice from Herbert's 'The Church-Porch', to the London edition of his *A Little Book for Children* (Ray, 'Herbert Allusion Book', 117–18), calling them 'Youth's Alphabet; or, *Herbert's* Morals'.

These timely pieces of advice proceed from Vaughan's stark observation (the burden of 'And do they so?') that man struggles to offer even an occasional hour's worship:

> Sometimes I sit with thee, and tarry
> An hour, or so, then vary.
> The other Creatures in this Scene
> Thee only aym, and mean.
>
> ('And do they so?', ll. 21–4)

That admission 'or so' swells all the more painfully from the depths of Vaughan's guilty conscience—where he knows that mankind is 'Each day, and *houre* . . . on wing | Rests not a span'[50]—for its being so small, as if it were trying not to be noticed. The ambiguity of 'or so' ('An hour or more', 'an hour or less') is resolved to man's discredit by Vaughan's desire to quit human shape for unreasoning animal, vegetable or mineral, to aim more as the creatures do, to '*only* aym, and mean'.

Like the purity of '*Isaacs* Marriage' and the Old Testament commerce of man and God, hourly devotion was once intuitive; but unlike the purity of Rachel, celebrated in the *Silex* Part 2 poem 'The Ornament', such 'native', holy intuition has been rusted over with sins. The easy, intimate devotion Vaughan ascribes to the patriarchs in poems like 'Religion', 'Corruption' and 'Jacobs Pillow and Pillar' is further characterized as a *regular* devotion and watchfulnesse in 'The Rain-bow' (*Silex* Part 2), which imagines how '*Terah, Nahor, Haran, Abram, Lot*' would hourly look to the skies for a sign from God:

> The youthful worlds gray fathers in one knot,
> Did with intentive looks watch every hour
> For thy new light, and trembled at each shower!
>
> (ll. 6–8)

Every hour: only a dim awareness of the patriarchs' hourly watch for the divine remains, and that only of *God's* faithfulness hour-by-hour, not distracted man's. Wondering at the spiritual mechanics of the afterlife, 'Buriall' marvels that

> nothing can, I hourely see,
> Drive thee from me,

---

[50] 'The Pursuite', ll. 3–4.

> Thou art the same, faithfull, and just
> In life, or Dust;
>
> (ll. 21–4)

and 'The Agreement' realizes that the *hourly* awareness of God, once achieved, gives a better measure of his marvellousness:

> But while time runs, and after it
> Eternity, which never ends,
> Quite through them both, still infinite
> Thy Covenant by *Christ* extends;
>   No sins of frailty, nor of youth
>   Can foil his merits, and thy truth.
>
> And this I hourly finde, for thou
> Dost still renew, and purge and heal.
>
> (ll. 49–56)

To *finde* divine faithfulness hour by hour, constantly to be rediscovering it, is to be spurred on to the hourly devotions of 'Rules *and* Lessons'; but it is also to need those spurs, and it is to be ashamed at the memory of a time when man fulfilled his end of the bargain, too, and was not a 'truce-breaker', like the confused, tormented man of Vaughan's 'Religion'.[51]

Intuitive regular worship was a loss whose worst effects Vaughan saw around him in the disorders of the mid-seventeenth century. Having condemned man's disuse of the hours by looking to the creatures, Vaughan also finds in nature a devotion of *hours* which recalls the liturgy of the medieval church:

> As leafs in Bowers
> Whisper their hours,
> And Hermit-wells
> Drop in their Cells:
>   So in sighs and unseen tears
>   Pass thy solitary years,
> And going hence, leave written on some Tree,
> *Sighs make joy sure, and shaking fastens thee.*
>
> ('Joy', ll. 23–30)

The hours of medieval worship were a set of daily offices to be read at seven times—matins, prime, terce, sext, nones, vespers and lauds—

---

[51] 'Religion', l. 21 ('Is the truce broke?'); the eschatological hints of this phrase are discussed below in Chapter 5, 'A tainted sink we have'.

as part of a tradition which reached back to the Fathers but which became an institution following its inclusion in the Benedictine Rule. The hours persisted in Reformed Britain in sixteenth-century English Primers,[52] and made a controversial presence in devotional works of the late 1620s and 1630s, notably in the *Devotions* of John Cosin.[53] The lesson of nature's *hours* in 'Joy' is sharpened by its dialogue with 'The Call', one of Vaughan's earlier poems from the start of *Silex* (1650). Opening with a summons to 'Come my heart! come my head | In sighes, and teares!', this poem weeps a penitential offering of tears into an hourglass on which its sinning speaker has notched up the hours of 'every minute' past, so measuring out the floods of tears required to show true penitence (if not fully to make amends). 'Joy' continues where 'The Call' leaves off: it is now *hourly* sighs and tears (still filling the glass, but now hour by hour, not in one penitential downpour) that can 'make sure' the hermit-like holy liver in his monk's cell. 'Who never wake to grone, nor weepe, | Shall be sentenc'd for their sleepe' warned 'The Call'; and once awakened, the holy liver must also be an hourly liver to be truly fastened to God.

An air of the monastery hangs about Vaughan's devotional attachment to the hours, a monkish sense of solitary contemplation which the poet himself recognized, but which his critics have often overlooked. A plain admission of this ascetic atmosphere opens the dedication to *Flores Solitudinis* (1654), where Vaughan tells Sir Charles Egerton, his dedicatee, that the ensuing prose pieces will lead 'from the Sun into the *shade*, from the open *Terrace* into a private grove, & from the *noyse* and *pompe* of this world into a silent and solitary *Hermitage*' (*V*, 213). Robert Ellrodt sensed the same attraction to pious solitude when he characterized Vaughan's writing as a hermit-like withdrawal into silence:

[52] The liturgical history of *hours* and *primers* is discussed by P. G. Stanwood, *The Sempiternal Season: Studies in Seventeenth-Century Devotional Writing*, Seventeenth-Century Texts and Studies, 3 (New York, 1992), 103–23; Martin Thornton, *English Spirituality* (1963), 263–70; H. C. White, *The Tudor Books of Private Devotion* (Madison, 1951), chs. 3–4; E. Bishop, *Liturgica Historica* (Oxford, 1918); C. C. Butterworth, *The English Primers* (Oxford, 1918); E. C. Ratcliff, 'The Choir Offices', in *Liturgy and Worship*, ed. Lowther and Harris; C. Wordsworth and H. Littlehales, *The Old Service Books of the English Church* (1904); E. Hoskins, *Horae Beatae Mariae Virginis* (1901).

[53] For early seventeenth-century *hours* in verse, see John Wilson, *The Treasury of Devotion, Containing Diverse Pious Prayers . . . Together with the Seaven Little Offices in Latin and English* (1622); *The Primer According to the Last Edition of the Roman Breviarie* (1617); Cosin, *A Collection of Private Devotions*; Hieremias Drexelius, *The Angel-Guardian's Clock Translated out of Latin into English* (1630).

Ce pieux Anglican se plaît à évoquer la vie des anciens hermites qui vivaient dispersés dans le désert, éloignés les uns des autres afin que rien ne vint troubler le silence de leur retraite ni détourner leur esprit de la contemplation des choses célestes.[54]

As Ellrodt suggests, Vaughan sought to achieve the hourly worship of nature and the ancients by a conscious spiritual detachment from all affairs outside the individual's inner life. To do this, the holy liver must observe the hours, and like a monk or nun adhere to a religious *rule*; which, as an Englished Benedictine rule of 1632 urged, was instruction sufficient for a whole life: 'neither add you any thinge to itt, nor take any thinge away; for itt hath that which sufficeth, and is in nothing defective'.[55]

In 1627, John Cosin outraged William Prynne by including the hours in his *Devotions*, a book to which Vaughan's *The Mount of Olives* owes a debt, especially in its 'Ejaculations', as does the *Scintilla Altaris* of Edward Sparke (1652).[56] The association between the hours and Roman Catholicism was clearly still strong in the 1650s, yet Vaughan's devotions are not intentionally provocative. His writing includes glimpses of Anglican and Roman liturgies, but it also frequently dwells on the primitive and Apostolic church and its practices, not to mention devotional exempla of the Old Testament. Thus references to specific liturgies need not be read as enigmatically partisan, even in the coded world of Royalist writing. As a group, Vaughan's liturgical echoes are unstudiedly broad: their breadth avoided giving his poetry or its rules the appearance of a Prayer Book patchwork, and enabled him to avoid the sorts of political controversy (not least, with the censor) which his preferred style of holy living shunned.

Regular acts of worship often recall the Book of Common Prayer, as when 'Praise' promises God that 'Day, and night, not once a day | I will blesse thee', a remembrance of the daily Morning and Evening Prayer services. But when Vaughan writes, in 'Rules *and* Lessons' and 'The Bird', of the morning songs of creation, he thinks of both the hymns of Anglican Morning Prayer and of a Roman matins:

> There's not a *Spring*,
> Or *Leafe* but hath his *Morning-hymn*;
>
> ('Rules *and* Lessons', ll. 14–15)

---

[54]   Ellrodt, *L'Inspiration personnelle*, 179.

[55]   *The Rule of the Most Blissed Father Saint Benedict, Patriarke of all Munkes*, trans. A. Gray (Gant, 1632), title-page.

[56]   See Chapter 3, 'Comfortable Words', for more on the Primer tradition.

> But as these Birds of light make a land glad,
> Chirping their solemn Matins on each tree.

('The Bird', ll. 23–4)

Other poems celebrate regulations of prayer so small—'Not one minute in the year | But I'l mind thee'[57]—that they escape specific liturgical association. Vaughan's protest in the translator's note to *Hermeticall Physick* (1655) that he 'honour[ed] the truth where ever I find it, whether in an old, or a new Booke', is supported by his rule of holy living, which is essentially syncretic (*V*, 548). But also, of course, he developed it particularly for those true (that is, Anglican) worshippers whose '*Brittish Church* . . . [was] trodden under foot' (*V*, 186). Questions about which church best enshrines the qualities of order and obedience, or can lead the holy liver to an easy recovery of them, were beside the point in a land which, as Vaughan saw it, had rebelled against God's church and was perhaps destined never to recover its lost status as the chosen nation.

No church can claim the creatures, and again it is the creatures through whom Vaughan effects a powerful reordering of man in 'Rules *and* Lessons'. Like *The Mount of Olives*' first two prayers, meant to be said before leaving one's bedroom in the morning, the opening lines of 'Rules *and* Lessons' manifest Vaughan's devotional attraction to the still hours before 'the world's up'. These moments, when the creation, too, shakes off night and unveils itself before God in an act of worship, are man's great opportunity to achieve regular worship throughout the day by attuning himself to the natural rhythms of worship all around him:

> When first thy Eies unveil, give thy Soul leave
> To do the like; our Bodies but forerun
> The spirits duty; True hearts spread, and heave
> Unto their God, as flow'rs do to the Sun.
> > Give him thy first thoughts then; so shalt thou keep
> > Him company all day, and in him sleep.
>
> Yet, never sleep the Sun up; Prayer shou'd
> Dawn with the day; There are set, awful hours
> 'Twixt heaven, and us; The *Manna* was not good
> After Sun-rising, far-day sullies flowres.
> > Rise to prevent the Sun; sleep doth sins glut,
> > And heav'ns gate opens, when this world's is shut.

(ll. 1–12)

---

[57] 'Praise', ll. 17–18.

Two purposeful ambiguities in these lines connect activity and hour to establish a *rule* according to which acts of devotion and worship are linked to specific moments. The comparative *as* in 'True hearts spread, and heave | Unto their God, as flow'rs do to the Sun' means both *like* ('True hearts open to God, turn to face him') and *when* ('True hearts do this at dawn, when the flowers do') and so delicately reveals that true devotional acts consist of timing as well as manner. The same ambiguity moves in the instruction 'Prayer should | Dawn *with* the day': Vaughan's *with* suggests both *at the same time as* ('True hearts first pray at dawn') and *in harmony with* ('The day's dawning is a regular act of worship which true hearts should join'). In both cases, regular living begins by joining the rhythms of the creation, and so setting the human clock to run once more to natural time.

'Rules *and* Lessons', for all its hourliness, does not instruct hour by hour, devoting one stanza to one hour of the day; the only single stanza whose actions last one hour is the twenty-first, whose advice is to 'spend in the grave one hour'. But the poem's order is chronological, and its progression marks the passing of the day:

> High-noon thus past, thy time decays; provide
> Thee other thoughts; Away with friends and mirth.
>
> (ll. 103–4)

As midday approaches it becomes clear that the pattern established in the early morning is crucial to the whole day's devotions. As soon as the Christian's worldly business is taken care of, Vaughan immediately instructs him (the poem's Christian is a man (l. 82)) to return to that regulated devotional state begun in the early morning, when prayer dawned with the day, and the souls opened, like flowers, to the sun:

> That done, speed
> And bring the same man back, thou wert at first.
> Who so returns not, cannot pray aright,
> But shuts his door, and leaves God out all night.
>
> (ll. 81–4)

And after eight stanzas where the only mention of the creatures comes in the 'vip'rous thought' which our holy liver would do well to smother (l. 70)—remembering that Jesus called the Sadducees a 'generation of vipers'[58]—Vaughan delightfully turns for encouragement in hourly living to the active, intuitive worship in the creatures' every movement:

> To highten thy *Devotions*, and keep low
> All mutinous thoughts, what busines e'r thou hast
> Observe God in his works; here *fountains* flow,
> *Birds* sing, *Beasts* feed, *Fish* leap, and th' *Earth* stands fast;
> Above are restles *motions*, running *Lights*,
> Vast Circling *Azure*, giddy *Clouds*, days, nights.
>
> .   .   .   .   .   .
>
> Thou canst not misse his Praise; Each *tree*, *herb*, *flowre*
> Are shadows of his *wisedome*, and his Pow'r.
>
> (ll. 85–90, 95–6)

The singing, feeding, leaping, and steadfast standing of the sublunary creation, and the exact, obedient, incessant motion of the heavens, act as an example and as an object for praise in themselves: 'Thou canst not misse his Praise'.

WHEN THE CLOCK STRIKES

When Vaughan thought of time passing, he thought primarily in hours, and of the striking of a clock. 'When the clock strikes', the first of fifteen ejaculations for various moments of the day in *The Mount of Olives*, thinks in the same hourly way: 'Blessed be the houre in which my Lord Jesus was borne, and the houre in which he died! O Lord Remember me in the houre of death!' (V, 153). The spiritual use of observing time passing is the subject of a miscellaneous poem by Vaughan not collected in *Thalia Rediviva* (1678), his translation of Thomas Campion's epigram *de Horologio Portabili* (*V*, 681). The translation was published by Thomas Powell, the friend and neighbour Vaughan addresses in 'To his learned Friend and Loyal Fellow-Prisoner, *Thomas Powel* of *Cant.* Doctor in Divinity' (printed in *Thalia*), in his 1661 history of the manual arts, *Humane Industry*.[59] Vaughan's translation appears in Powell's first section, on timekeeping:

> Times-Teller wrought into a little round,
> Which count'st the days and nights with watchful sound;

---

[58] Matt. 3: 7.
[59] Powell is discussed by Brown, '"Learned friend and fellow prisoner"', *passim* and Rudrum, 'Resistance, Collaboration and Silence', 104–5.

> How (when once fixt) with busie Wheels dost thou
> The twice twelve useful hours drive on and show.
> And where I go, go'st with me without strife,
> The Monitor and Ease of fleeting life.[60]

Vaughan's 'watchful sound' is a good reminder that watches were first so called in the late sixteenth century for their *watchfulness*, one of the supreme qualities of the creatures praised over and over in *Silex*: 'birds like watchful clocks' in 'The Bird', the watchful heads of the expectant creatures in Romans 8 and 'And do they so?'[61] Powell's history of 'The Invention of *Dyals, Clocks, Watches,* and other *Time-tellers*' encourages an altogether more worldly engagement with practical business than Vaughan's 'Rules *and* Lessons', and eschews the vehemence of Vaughan's ejaculation for 'When the clock strikes'. But Powell, too, valued clocks and watches as instruments for the better disposition of one's available time, and his book praises 'the ancient *Sages* of the word' for having devised a way to divide the day into hours, quarters and minutes, 'that by this *Horometry*, they might mete out and proportion business to the time, and time to the business in hand'.[62]

Vaughan's admiration for the creatures is shadowed in Guevara's 'The Praise and Happiness' (translated in *Olor*), which admires the country liver for a perceived closeness to natural order and a greater harmony with the divine. If Guevara and Powell moralize regularity in a less fretful (and less liturgical) way than the poet of *Silex Scintillans*, all three men share an essentially figurative view of nature, seeing the creation anthropomorphically and *usefully*, and extracting lessons from observing the world around them. According to Powell's history of ΏΡΟΛΟΓΙΚΗ, for instance, the *original* of all clocks was a creature, an Egyptian beast called *Cynocephalus*, which:

did make water twelve times in a day, and so often in the night, and that regularly, at even spaces of time; from the observation whereof they divided the natural day

---

[60] Thomas Powell, *Humane Industry; or, A History of Most Manual Arts, Deducing the Original, Progress, and Improvement of Them* (1661), 11 (repr. *V*, 681).

[61] *OED*, watch, *sb.*, 21a. 1588 is the earliest citation. Renaissance horology is discussed by Carlo Cipolla, *Clocks and Culture 1300–1700* (1967), 37–75; David Landes, *Revolution in Time: Clocks and the Making of the Modern World* (Cambridge, 1983), esp. ch. 4; Samuel L. Macey, *Clocks and the Cosmos: The Time in Western Life and Thought* (Hamden, Conn., 1980), chs. 1, 6 (esp. 136–40); Stuart Sherman, *Telling Time: Clocks, Diaries, and English Diurnal Form, 1660–1785* (Chicago, 1996).

[62] Powell, *Humane Industry*, 2.

into twenty four hours; and that Beast was their Clock and Dyal, both to divide the day, and reckon the hours by.[63]

Such strange natural histories placed man firmly at the centre of the cosmos. A hundred years later, Gilbert White's letters containing his observations of *The Natural History of Selborne* (published 1788) are quite differently amazed by natural phenomena:

For many years past I have observed that towards Christmas vast flocks of chaffinches have appeared in the fields; many more, I used to think, than could be hatched in any one neighbourhood. But when I came to observe them more narrowly, I was amazed to find that they seemed to be almost all hens . . . Now I want to know, from some curious person in the north, whether there are any large flocks of these finches with them in the winter, and of which sex they mostly consist. For, from such intelligence, one might be able to judge whether our female flocks migrate from the other end of the island, or whether they come over to us from the continent.[64]

The breed of bird, its yearly movements, sex groupings, the ornithologist's observation, the curiosity and amazement at the facts of a bird's physical life: all these are absent in seventeenth-century creaturely meditations of Vaughan, Powell and Guevara. The regularity in which their writings interested themselves was not—not *yet*, one might say—that of migratory habits.

Yet the desires Vaughan expresses through the creatures are real enough. It is only natural that he should have responded to Guevara's *Menosprecio*, which dwells in many passages on the importance of life's rhythms, how in the country, unpolluted by business, distraction or noise, time could return to its purer uses:

He that lives in his own *fields* and *habitation*, which God hath given him, enjoys true Peace . . . He busieth not himself in a *search* of pleasures, but in regulating, and disposing of his family; in the education of his Children, and Domestick Discipline. No violent tempestuous motions distract his *rest*, but soft gales, and a silent aire refresh and breath upon him. He doth all things commodiously, ordereth his life discreetly, not after the the opinion of the people, but by the rules of his own certain experience . . .

The day it self (in my opinion) seems of more *length* and *beauty* in the Country, and can be better enjoyed than any where else. There the *years* passe away calmly,

---

[63] Ibid. 6–7.
[64] Gilbert White, *The Natural History of Selborne*, ed. Richard Mabey (Harmondsworth, 1977), 39–40.

and one *day* gently drives on the other, insomuch that a man may be sensible of a certaine *satietie* and *pleasure* from every *houre*, and may be said to feed upon *time* it self . . .

The Husbandman is alwaies up and drest with the morning, whose dawning light at the same instant of time breaks over all the Fields and chaseth away the darknesse (which would hinder his early labours) from every *valley*. If his days task keep him late in the *fields*, yet *night* comes not so suddenly upon him, but he can returne home with the *Evening-star*. Whereas in *Towns* and populous *Cities* neither the *Day*, nor the *Sun*, nor a *Star*, nor the *Season* of the *Year* can be well perceived. All which in the Country are manifestly seen, and occasion a more exact care and observation of *Seasons*, that their *labours* may be in their appointed time, and their *rewards* accordingly. (*V*, 125, 129)

The Husbandman, like Vaughan's hourly liver, is 'alwaies up and drest *with* the morning', beginning his day with the day's own beginning, his prayer 'dawn[ing] with the day' ('Rules and Lessons', l. 8). His life is *regulated, disciplined,* and *ordered* in its conformity to a rule, so that by performing all tasks and duties in 'their appointed time' he draws closer to the rhythms by which nature praises God with joy in order and obedience.

Since Vaughan's holy liver is protected from distractions and disorder by the regularity of hourly prayer, the basis of holy living is the repairing and careful use of man's internal clock, Times-teller, which was damaged by the Fall and has since rusted further by sin. An internal clock is what regulates the creatures in 'Man':

> Weighing the stedfastness and state
> Of some mean things which here below reside,
> Where birds like watchful Clocks the noiseless date
> And Intercourse of times divide,
> Where Bees at night get home and hive, and flowrs
> Early, aswel as late,
> Rise with the Sun, and set in the same bowrs;
> 2.
> I would (said I) my God would give
> The staidness of these things to man!
>
> (ll. 1–9)

These 'birds like watchful Clocks' recall the 'watchful sound' made by the watch of Thomas Campion's *Horologia* epigram. Vaughan's lines are thinking of the cockerel, of course, the bird whose eyes 'watch for the morning hue' in the magnificent *Silex* Part 2 poem 'Cock-crowing'—

> Their eyes watch for the morning hue,
> Their little grain expelling night
> So shines and sings, as if it knew
> The path unto the house of light
>
> (ll. 7–10)

—and of the 'Matins' dawn chorus of birds in 'The Bird'. The birds' internal clocks divide 'the noiseless date | And Intercourse of times' so that their 'prayer dawn[s] with the day' as naturally as the stars circle the heavens.

Becoming a natural clock is the first and crucial step in becoming a holy liver. Christ is the best exemplar Vaughan can point to, but it is his moving eulogy of George Herbert's patterned life in *The Mount of Olives* that should conclude any discussion of Vaughan's holy, hourly living. Above all of the poet's other achievements, in Vaughan's eyes, came his devotion to meditating on the hour of death and ordering his life's time accordingly:

Let us look always upon this *Day-Lilie* of life, as if the *Sun* were already *set*. Though we *blossome* and *open* many *mornings*, we shall not do so always, *Soles occidere & redire possunt*; but *man* cannot. *He hath his time appointed him upon earth, which he shall not passe, and his days are like the days of an hireling.* Let us then so husband our time, that when the *flower* falls, the *seed* may be preserved. We have had many blessed Patterns of a holy life in the *Brittish Church*, though now trodden under foot, and branded with the title of *Antichristian*. I shall propose but *one to you, the most obedient *Son* that ever his *Mother* had, and yet a most glorious true *Saint* and a *Seer*. Heark how like a *busie Bee* he *hymns* it to the *flowers*, while in a handful of *blossomes* gather'd by himself, he foresees his own *dissolution*.

*Mr George Herbert of blessed memory

(*V*, 186)

The manifold meditations on time and living which impinge on this passage reveal the passion with which Vaughan contemplated holy, hourly living. He knew that *he hath his time appointed*, like Job, whose lamentation is borrowed here: 'Is there not an appointed time to man upon earth? are not his days also like the days of an hireling?' (Job 7: 1) And from Catullus, in a passage often translated in the Renaissance, Vaughan adapts the *carpe diem* phrase *soles occidere, & redire possunt*: 'Sunnes, that set, may rise again | But if, once, we loose this light, | 'Tis with us perpetuall night' as Ben Jonson succinctly translated; or, in the more expansive 1601 version of Thomas Campion:

> heavn's great lays do dive
> Unto their west, and strait againe revive,
> But, soone as once set is our little light,
> Then must we sleepe one ever-during night.[65]

In Vaughan's application, Catullus' words become an exhortation to wise disposition of time. To imitate the *pattern* of Herbert's life, its regularity and order, is to think always on fleeting life. Clocks are a help to this, and portable clocks, rightly called watches; but the *hourly liver* should attempt a life like the whispering bush, or the hermit-well, sighing and weeping the hours of life in recognition of the world's disorder which he cannot otherwise repulse.

[65]   *The Oxford Book of Classical Verse in English Translation*, ed. Adrian Poole and Jeremy Maule (Oxford, 1995), 248a–e [Ben Jonson, from *Volpone*; Thomas Campion, 1601].

True lights and new lights: Vaughan's 'White Sunday' and the false prophets of the 1650s

In 1652, filled with visions of Christ's Second Coming at the return of Charles II, the Welsh tailor Arise Evans remembered the May morning when, aged 14, he had awaited the dawn atop *Gole Ronnw*, the hill whose name means 'they will give light',

hearing some say that whatsoever one did ask of God upon Whit-Sunday morning at the instant when the Sun arose and play'd, God would grant it him . . . And seeing the Sun at its rising, skip, play, dance, and turn about like a wheel, I fell down upon my knees, lifting up mine eys, hands, and heart unto God; I cried, saying, O Lord most high, that hast made all things for thy glory, give me grace, wisedome and understanding that I may glorifie thee as this Instrument doth now before all the world.[1]

Grace, wisdom and understanding duly received that Whitsun, Evans began a career of prophecy in England, during which he was treated with a good deal of licence by the authorities, who seemed to have thought the 'holy imbecile' no threat. He was even allowed to publish his prophecies and visions once they began to favour the exiled monarch and an episcopal church after 1649.[2]

Had Evans been a more charismatic figure, his joyous pronouncement in *An Eccho to the Voice of Heaven* (1652) that Christ and Charles were about to return to Britain together, might have provoked official retribution. As might his Whit Sunday story, which attributed deep—and deeply superstitious—significance to one of the most prominent festivals

---

[1] Arise Evans, *An Eccho to the Voice from Heaven* (1652), 9.
[2] Christopher Hill, 'Arise Evans, Welshman in London', 48–77 in his *Change and Continuity in Seventeenth-Century England*, rev. edn. (New Haven, 1991).

of the old Church of England, festivals whose observance Parliament had begun to prohibit in 1645, when traditional celebration of Christmas was forbidden; by June 1647 Easter, Whitsun and Rogationtide had followed Christmas into the Act book. These prohibitions were accompanied by such other measures as the replacement of the Prayer Book by the West-minster Assembly's *Directory for Public Worship* in 1645, as Parliament tightened its grip and tried to purge Christianity in England and Wales of the vestiges of Anglican tradition tainted (as they saw it) by its Roman roots.[3]

For all its legislation, though, Parliament could not erase the religious calendar of the past hundred years at a stroke: its anti-festival ordinances were commonly ignored by parishes reluctant to forgo popular celebra-tions, and use of the Prayer Book also continued, at varying levels of se-crecy. Nevertheless, festival observance was undeniably declining. In the ten years between the 1645 anti-Christmas ordinance and the publication of Part 2 of Henry Vaughan's *Silex Scintillans* in 1655, festivals were legally prohibited, less and less publicly observed, and replaced in law by a regu-lar series of fasts.[4] Only when restoration of the monarchy seemed in-evitable do records show a dramatic rise in festivals and other traditional activities such as Sunday games, dancing and festival ales—by which time the Silurist's career as a publishing Christian poet had substantially ended.[5]

Like the *Festivall Hymns* which Jeremy Taylor attached to *The Golden Grove* (1655), Vaughan's calendrical poems celebrate the forbidden days against this background of Parliamentary prohibition.[6] Most of Vaughan's remembrances of the church year are doubled: in Part 1, 'Christ's Nativity' has two distinct parts and there are two separate Easter poems; in Part 2 there are two poems on the Ascension, as well as one each on 'White Sunday' and 'Trinity Sunday'. Together, they form a very visi-ble part of Vaughan's contribution to what John Morrill has called 'An-

[3] Ronald Hutton, *The Rise and Fall of Merry England: The Ritual Year 1400–1700* (Oxford, 1984), 121; Corns, *Uncloistered Virtue*, 102–14.

[4] David Cressy, *Bonfires and Bells: National Memory and the Protestant Calendar in Eliz-abethan and Stuart England* (1989), chs. 1–3; Hutton, *Rise and Fall*, 213–14; Morrill, 'The Church in England, 1642–9', 89–114; Maltby, *Prayer Book and People*, chs. 3, 5. Charles I's controversial reissue of the Jacobite *Book of Sports* (which prescribed Sunday games after church) is discussed by Kevin Sharpe, *The Personal Rule of Charles I* (New Haven, 1992), 351–9.

[5] Hutton, *Rise and Fall*, 214.

[6] See Jeremy Taylor, *Works*, ed. R. Heber and C. P. Eden, 10 vols. (1847–52), vii, 649–62.

glican Survivalism'.[7] Faced with a seemingly interminable future of Puritan rule, demoralized adherents to the established national church developed covert ways of worshipping according to the rite of the Book of Common Prayer or with alternative liturgies which partially concealed their Anglican forms. By soaking up the words of the Prayer Book and writing hymns for the key feasts of the church year, Vaughan's poems sought to preserve what they could of the church of his youth and his king by keeping faith with the words of true religion and singing the Lord's songs in a land where the captors had commanded silence.

One such song remembering a forbidden festival is the locus of Vaughan's major confrontation with the radical prophesying of the 1650s. 'White Sunday' greets the day appointed by the church to remember the spiritual inspiration of the Apostles after Christ's Ascension. Like Arise Evans, Vaughan knew the account in Acts 2 of how the Apostles

were all with one accord in one place. And suddenly there came a sound from heaven as of a rushing mighty wind, and it filled all the house where they were sitting. And there appeared unto them cloven tongues like as of fire, and it sat upon each of them. And they were all filled with the Holy Ghost, and began to speak with other tongues, as the Spirit gave them utterance. (Acts 2: 1–4)

Vaughan's poem is angry and sad that this great light is claimed (counterclaimed, as he saw it) by contemporary prophets, with their message of further reformation towards the kind of gathered churches and religion of the Spirit inimical to the established church. In a language at once direct and allusive it asks Christ:

> Can these new lights be like to those,
> These lights of Serpents like the Dove?
> Thou hadst no *gall*, ev'n for thy foes,
> And thy two wings were *Grief* and *Love*.

> ('White Sunday', ll. 9–12)

Even among Vaughan's bookish and allusive poems, 'White Sunday' stands out as a particularly intertextual creation, fashioned out of snippets of other texts, strands of New Testament epistles, and parodies of Puritan language; these are deftly reworked into a blanket rejection of the creed

---

[7] Morrill, 'The Church in England', 90; the term is applied to Vaughan in Wall, *Transformations of the Word*, ch. 4 and Claude J. Summers, 'Herrick, Vaughan, and the Poetry of Anglican Survivalism', 46–74 in *New Perspectives on the Seventeenth-Century English Religious Lyric*, ed. John R. Roberts (Columbia, Mo., 1994).

that new prophetic inspiration had descended on Britain during the revolution.[8] 'White Sunday' asks to be tugged and examined, its strands leading to their Interregnum contexts: the experience of defeat, the bitter factionalism of Interregnum Breconshire, the baleful presence of people Vaughan was forced to call enemy, and his attempts to understand and temper his own feelings towards them. 'White Sunday' is carved out of Vaughan's negative emotions: hatred, enmity, bitterness, revenge, a strong dark side of Vaughan's poetry which was long overlooked as an embarrassing slip in artistry, but which Jonathan Post, Stevie Davies and others have reinstated at the heart of his poetry.[9] As James Simmonds suggested some time ago, the secular satire of Vaughan's early work (his translation of Juvenal and Royalist sniping at Puritans) did not simply disappear when he became a Christian poet.[10] Rather, it was transformed. 'Religion', 'White Sunday' and 'The Men of War' show the path of this transformation, and record how, as Vaughan persistently refused to hate his 'haters', the Puritan revolution instead became evidence for him that the Last Days and their false prophets were finally at hand in God's chosen nation.

'TIS A SAD LAND

The years of Civil War and Parliamentary rule were the darkest time of Henry Vaughan's life. At the outbreak of war in 1642, the 22-old law student travelled home from London to his native Breconshire, where he served as a secretary to Sir Marmaduke Lloyd, Chief Justice of the Welsh South-West circuit. His legal career over before it had started, Vaughan soon lost his job and employer too, as Parliament tightened its grip in south Wales by removing Lloyd (an active Royalist) and replacing him with an Englishman and sympathetic secretaries.[11]

War brought faction and emnity to Brecon, and sent the literate to

---

[8] 'White Sunday' is related to prophecy by Prineas, 'Dream of the Book', 336, and by Esther Gilman Rickey, '"Prophets and friends of God": Prophetic Discourse in Andrewes, Herbert and Vaughan', Ph.D. thesis (Los Angeles, 1990), 241–3 (a reading mostly based on the glosses of *R*).

[9] Post, *Henry Vaughan*, ch. 6, 'Spitting out the Phlegm: The Conflict of Voices in *Silex Scintillans*'; Davies, *Henry Vaughan*, 152–8.

[10] James D. Simmonds, *Masques of God; Form and Theme in the Poetry of Henry Vaughan* (Pittsburgh, 1972), ch. 5A, 'Satire: Anti-Puritanism', 85–116.

[11] *Life*, 48–50. The circuits of the Great Sessions are shown on map 57 of William Rees, *An Historical Atlas of Wales from Early to Modern Times*, 2nd edn. (Cardiff, 1972).

their books to learn what it meant to be set against their countrymen. Scripture abounds with lessons about war and the triumph of enemies, especially the Old Testament where defeat is God's way of showing his displeasure at the sins of His children. 'The ways of Zion do mourn', sighs the book of Lamentations (in a passage Vaughan alludes to in *The Mount of Olives*[12]), 'her adversaries are the chief, her enemies prosper; for the Lord hath afflicted her for the multitude of her transgressions' (Lamentations 1: 5). Conversely, Israel's triumph shows God's love: 'I will sing unto the Lord, for he hath triumphed gloriously', sing Moses and the children of Israel on the banks of the Red Sea, 'the Lord is a man of war: the Lord is his name . . . Thy right hand, O Lord, is become glorious in power: thy right hand, O Lord, hath dashed in pieces the enemy' (Exodus 15: 1–6).

Vaughan's conversion to writing religious poetry occurred after 1647. Before then, he professed his loyalties to King and Country, rather than to God, Church and King; little is known of his religious observance at the time of his return from London, though his later poems paint a conventionally exaggerated picture of a callow and unreligious youth.[13] Henry played his part in the Royalist campaign, enlisting in the forces of the Royalist Colonel Herbert Price, the local MP and governor of Brecon Castle; with Price's forces he fought at the battle of Rowton Heath, near Chester, in September 1645. Two months earlier, Price had entertained the king at Brecon Priory, less than 3 miles from Vaughan's home, as he toured Wales drumming up men and support. The royal effort was to prove in vain: the New Model Army, formed earlier the same year, crushed the Royalist forces, and by the following spring even the obstinate western counties had fallen to Parliament.[14]

During the first Civil War, Vaughan assembled his first book of poetry, *Poems, with the Tenth Satyre of Juvenal Englished*, a collection of love poems in the style of William Habington's *Castara*. They show, as Stevie Davies has wryly remarked, 'devastating competence' in their affections, though the translation of Juvenal is accomplished. A group of Royalist elegies also written during this period were not published until 1651 in *Olor Iscanus*.[15] Much less conventional and much more angry, these

---

[12] 'A Prayer in Time of Persecution and Heresie' (*V*, 160).

[13] See especially 'The Garland', 'To the Holy Bible', ll. 9–17 and 'The Authors Preface' to *Silex* (1655).

[14] *Life*, 57–71; Jenkins, *Foundations*, 9–19.

[15] On the coming-to-press of *Olor Iscanus*, see William R. Parker, 'Henry Vaughan and

poems contrast the honour of Royalist loyalty with the blackness of Parliamentary ambition. 'So much wing is given | To my wild thoughts,' Vaughan grieves, 'that they dare strike at heav'n' ('An elegy on the death of Mr. *R. W.* slain in the late unfortunate differences at *Routon* Heath, neer *Chester*, 1645', ll. 1–2). Despite notable successes by the armies of Rice Powell, the king's cause again floundered in 1648, Colonel Horton's Ironsides decisively smashing Royalist resistance at St Fagan's in the largest battle of the Civil War in Wales.[16] The following years brought no relief to the Vaughans of Tretower. In 1648, Henry's younger brother William died, perhaps fighting for the king. The following December, a special High Court of Justice (among whose members were two Welshmen) sent Charles I to his death on 30 January 1649.

At this time of Parliament's supreme triumph Vaughan began to publish his greatest work. *Silex Scintillans; or, Sacred Poems and Private Ejaculations*, his first book as a Christian poet, was entered in the Stationers' Register on 28 March 1650. During the next seven years, Vaughan's output was prodigious, averaging a volume a year.[17] Like the oppressed palm tree of many an emblem book, the Silurist seems to have grown taller and straighter for being weighed down and oppressed; the quieter years after the Restoration added few enough sparks from the flint of *Silex Scintillans* that Vaughan waited another eighteen years to publish them in *Thalia Rediviva* (1678). In the late 1640s, Vaughan's attention turned sharply to the problem of Christian conduct in the face of a triumphant enemy. He badly needed to come to terms with the humiliation and frustration of defeat. A son of the Vaughans of Tretower, one of the ancient families of Wales, Henry was fiercely proud of his loyalty to Crown and Church, and appalled by treachery, an attitude he shared with much of the Welsh gentry, which looked beyond its own island to the damage done to central

his Publishers', *Library*, 20 (1940), 401–11; Harold R. Walley, 'The Strange Case of *Olor Iscanus*', *Review of English Studies*, 18 (1942), 27–37; E. L. Marilla, '"The Publisher to the Reader" of *Olor Iscanus*', *Review of English Studies*, 24 (1948), 36–41; James D. Simmonds, 'The Publication of *Olor Iscanus*', *Modern Language Notes*, 76 (1981), 404–8; John Curtis Reed, 'Humphrey Moseley, Publisher', *Oxford Bibliographical Society Proceedings and Papers*, 2 (1930), 57–142 (esp. 70–1).

[16] Jenkins, *Foundations*, 19–21; Geraint H. Jenkins, 'The Early Peace Testimony in Wales', *Llafur*, 4: 2 (1975), 10–19.

[17] After *Silex Scintillans* (1650), Vaughan published six substantial works in a row: *Olor Iscanus* (1651), *The Mount of Olives* (1652), *Flores Solitudinis* (1654), *Hermetical Physick* (1655), *Silex Scintillans, The Second Edition in Two Books* (1655), *The Chymists Key* (1657). As the dated poems in *Thalia Rediviva* suggest, Vaughan produced more poetry than could be readily accommodated even in these volumes.

Europe by the Thirty Years War and feared the coming of what Sir Thomas Salisbury of Llewini called 'perpetual war'.[18]

The Church of England was foremost among the hierarchies of power threatened by Civil War. Unifying the variety of Puritan calls for further reformation during the 1640s was a shared belief that church worship should be purged of 'antichristian' relics (as they were seen) of the Roman church; bishops, church ceremonies, and church decorations were all progressively decried and removed. In 1643 the Long Parliament set up the Westminster Assembly of Divines, whose *Directory for Public Worship* (1645) and *Westminster Confession* (1648) embodied the Presbyterianism which for a time looked to have established itself as a stable and viable alternative.[19] But the Assembly's influence waned after the second Civil War and the regicide, and while the members of the Rump Parliament considered ways to reconcile Independent and Presbyterian positions, radical sects proliferated across the nation.[20] In 1653, Cromwell dissolved the Rump and brought in a Parliament of Saints elected by the gathered churches and Council of Officers. This was a scheme particularly urged by Major-General Thomas Harrison, commander of the New Model Army in England and a known supporter of the Fifth Monarchists, a radical group for whom the events of the Civil War proclaimed the imminent thousand-year rule of Christ and the Saints on earth.[21] For this coming millennium, all remnants of antichristian religions, especially Anglican 'statism', needed to be swept aside.[22]

---

[18] Jenkins, *Foundations*, 4. Michael Walzer comments: 'news of the Thirty Years' War circulated in England and when the time for her own civil war drew near, the metaphor was used more and more intentionally and its surface meaning became increasingly significant' (*The Revolution of the Saints: A Study in the Origins of Radical Politics* (1966), 278). The Vaughans of Tretower are discussed by C. A. Ralegh Radford, 'Tretower: The Castle and the Court', *Brycheiniog*, 6 (1960), 1–17 (16–17) and Ithiel Vaughan-Poppy, 'The Homes of the Vaughans—Part I', *Brycheiniog*, 18 (1978–9), 103–9 (106).

[19] 'An Ordinance for Taking away the Book of Common Prayer and for Establishing and Putting in Execution of the Directory for the Publique Worship of God', 4 Jan. 1644/5, in *Acts and Ordinances*, ed. Firth and Rait, i. 582–607. On the failures of this project, see Morrill, 'The Church in England, 1642–9', 92–4, 103–8, 111–12.

[20] Blair Worden, *The Rump Parliament 1648–1653* (Cambridge, 1974), 120–6; Bernard Capp, *The Fifth Monarchy Men: A Study in Seventeenth-Century Millenarianism* (1972), 99. On developments in millenarian faith see Chapter 6; an outline of its importance for radical Christianity is offered by Nigel Smith, *Perfection Proclaimed*, 9–10.

[21] Hill, *World Turned Upside-Down*, chs. 1, 2, 6; Thomas, *Religion and the Decline of Magic*, 166–73; Bernard Capp, *The Fifth Monarchy Men* (1972), ch. 2.

[22] Robert South, sermon on 1 Kings 13: 33–4, in *Forty-Eight Sermons and Discourses on Several Subjects, and Occasions*, 4 vols. (1715), 150–1: 'Hence it is, that the Enemies of God take occasion to blaspheme, and call our Religion *Statism*.'

Millenarian views were both propagated and satirized in the pamphlet wars of the 1640s and again in the Restoration. Since Vaughan's earliest anti-Puritan murmurings pre-date his religious awakening, they tend directly to attack crimes against society and status, rather than investigating their basis in radical belief. *Olor Iscanus* accuses Parliament and Puritan of self-seeking, nest-feathering and false piety, a litany of complaint familiar from other well-known attacks on religious novelty as Thomas Edwards's infamous heresiography *Gangraena* (1646) and Alexander Griffith's *Strena Vavasoriensis* (1654), a New Year's gift of personal abuse presented to the most important Welsh Puritan preacher of the day, Vavasor Powell.[23] Vaughan takes an opportunity to mock the Westminster Assembly in his poem printed in the 1647 Beaumont and Fletcher folio; the '*Eares*' of the Assembly, he tells the playwrights, will 'think't fit | Their *Synod* fast, and *pray*, against thy wit' ('Upon Mr. *Fletchers* plays, published, 1647', ll. 33–4). This folio, published by Humphrey Moseley, was something of a Royalist manifesto, boasting thirty-four obviously partisan dedications.[24] In 1647, Vaughan was no doubt unquestionably pleased by his inclusion in as illustrious a volume; a year or so later, though, he was to renounce both the Cavalier wit of *Poems* (1646) and the kinds of satirical hit achieved by *Olor*.

Vaughan's brushes with Royalist propaganda were to prove useful to his Christian writing even after he renounced the satirical edge of his earlier work. One popular topic of Cavalier merriment in the 1640s was 'new light', the widespread Puritan belief that the Holy Spirit was making a fresh revelation of God to man, perhaps as a prologue to Christ's Second Coming.[25] While many held this belief in a mild form, others agreed that the Spirit was bringing a new and urgent message to the elect through a band of new Apostles touched by the prophetic fire of the Holy Ghost. Vavasor Powell thought that 'no generation since the Apostles daies had such powerful preachers and plenty of preaching as this generation', and

---

[23] Edwards, *Gangraena*; Alexander Griffith, *Strena Vavasoriensis, a New-Years-Gift for the Welch Itinerants; or, A Hue and Cry after Mr Vavasor Powell* (1654). On Griffith, see Jenkins, *Protestant Dissenters*, 18–19.

[24] Potter, *Secret Rites*, 21; on Moseley, see ibid. 19–21 and Reed, 'Humphrey Moseley, Publisher', 57–142; Arthur F. Marotti, *Manuscript, Print and the English Renaissance Lyric* (Ithaca, NY, 1995), 259–63, 266–7; Ann Baynes Coiro, 'Milton and Class Identity: The Publication of *Areopagitica* and the 1645 *Poems*', *Journal of Medieval and Renaissance Studies*, 22 (1992), 277–89.

[25] See the authoritative study of Geoffrey Nuttall, *The Holy Spirit in Puritan Faith and Experience* (Oxford, 1946).

Oliver Cromwell that Wales was experiencing a wave of holiness 'hardly to be paralleled since the primitive times'.[26]

The preaching of Powell and his fellow 'Welsh Saints' (as they quickly became known) brought new light even to the remoter parts of Breconshire, those 'dark corners of the land' identified by Parliament as needing urgent reformation. Vaughan would probably have seen the phrase 'new light' in print in 1651, when it appeared among the dedications to yet another Royalist publishing venture by Humphrey Moseley, this time the *Comedies and Tragi-Comedies* of William Cartwright. The folio has fifty-two Royalist dedications, including one by Vaughan, as Moseley, a bookseller noted for his oppositional views, continued to risk the censor in order to rally Royalist spirits.[27] The eighth dedicator, Jasper Mayne, was an ejected Anglican clergyman whose poem praises Cartwright as a symbol of the golden past of the Church of England. Anti-Puritan sentiment gradually sours into a ridiculing of their beliefs. 'Thou wert not like our New-light men', Mayne tells the dead Cartwright, with their 'Shopboard Revelation'.[28]

Perhaps Mayne himself saw the phrase in the title *A True and Perfect Picture of Our Present Reformation; or, The Christians Prospective, To Take a Short View of the New Lights That Have Brake Forth Since Bishops Went Downe* (1648).[29] It seems to have stuck as a handy term of abuse. Abraham Wright's compiler's preface to *Parnassus Biceps* (1655), a Royalist miscellany of university poetry, complains of 'those glaring New Lights that have muffled the Times and Nation with a greater confusion and darknes, then ever benighted the world since the first chaos'.[30] By the time of the Restoration, 'new lights' was a buzz-word for anti-Puritans, turning up several times in *Hudibras*, for instance, where the narrator comments on the squire Ralpho's gift of unriddling mysteries: 'What e'er men speak by

[26] Both quoted in Jenkins, *Foundations*, 53, taken from Christopher Hill, 'Propagating the Gospel', in H. E. Bell and R. L. Ollard (eds.), *Historical Essays 1600–1750* (1963), 45–6; but the first is given more accurately in Nuttall, *Holy Spirit*, 28, quoting it from Thomas Richards, *A History of the Puritan Movement in Wales 1639–1653* (Cardiff, 1920), 171.

[27] Potter, *Secret Rites*, 21; see also Louis B. Wright, 'The Reading of Plays during the Puritan Revolution', *Huntington Library Bulletin*, 7 (1934), 73–108.

[28] William Cartwright, *Comedies, Tragi-Comedies, with Other Poems* (1651), sig. b6ᵛ. Mayne later became a Canon of Christ Church and chaplain to Charles II (*DNB*).

[29] *Wing* T 2538. The imprint describes this work as published 'in the first yeare of King CHARLES His Imprisonment, 1648'.

[30] *Parnassus Biceps; or, Several Choice Pieces of Poetry, Compiled by the Best Wits That Were in Both the Universities before Their Dissolution*, compiled by Abraham Wright (1656), sigs. [A4]ᵛ–[A5]ʳ.

this *New Light* | Still they are sure to be i'th right'.[31] Puritans themselves used *new light* as a handy tag for those whose views they thought unorthodox, as for instance in the Baptist John Tombes's 1660 attack on Quakerism, *True Old Light Exalted above Pretended New Light.*[32] Robert South picked up the term to fling it back sarcastically at the 'New lights, Sudden Impulses of the Spirit [and] Extraordinary Calls' of the Revolution, and the Restoration polemicist John Nalson, too, complained of 'the late discovery of New Regions of Fath, and New Lights of Religion, [which] has given such disturbance to the old'.[33]

For South, lecturing in 1665, the rise of Independency was an aberration the more swiftly forgotten the better; for Vaughan it must have had all of the appearance of an unending nightmare. Welsh Independency was born in the large towns of the South, but the enthusiasm and energy of its itinerant preachers ensured a rapid evangelizing. The bearers of 'new light' in Wales were barely older than Vaughan himself—he was 28 in 1650—but they had been sequestrating Breconshire clergymen, with the Army's authority, since 1645.[34] In the increasingly millenarian atmosphere following the king's death, their rash of local evictions became a country-wide operation to purge the church. In February 1650, the Rump Parliament passed an 'Act for the Better Propagation and Preaching of the Gospel in Wales' which, for the next three years, was to authorize the eviction of some 278 Welsh clergy by a group of seventy-one regional Commissioners; an elite body of twenty-five 'Approvers' was licensed to find suitable replacements. Among the 'Approvers' were many of the Welsh 'new lights' including Vavasor Powell, Walter Cradock and Morgan Llwyd, men increasingly respected in Parliamentary circles for their zeal and piety.[35]

The Propagation stung Henry Vaughan directly. His twin brother

[31] Samuel Butler, *Hudibras*, Part 1, Canto 1, ll. 497–8 (*Samuel Butler's 'Hudibras'*, ed. by John Wilders (Oxford, 1967)); 'new light' in *Hudibras* is discussed briefly by James Sutherland, *Restoration Literature 1660–1700: Dryden, Bunyan and Pepys*, Oxford History of English Literature VIII (1969; Oxford, 1990), 297–300.

[32] On Tombes's and John Owen's opposition to Fox, see Nuttall, *Holy Spirit*, 13, 42.

[33] Robert South, *Forty-Eight Sermons*, 151; John Nalson, *The Common Interest of King and People*, 168.

[34] In 1650, Vavasor Powell was 33, Morgan Llwyd was 31 and Walter Cradock, an elder statesman, at 39. See Nuttall, *The Welsh Saints, 1640–1660, passim*.

[35] 'An Act for the Better Propagation and Preaching of the Gospel in Wales', in *Acts and Ordinances*, ed. Firth and Rait, ii. 342–8. 'Propagation' was the standard term in contemporary acts and ordinances for spreading news of the gospel; see Worden, *Rump Parliament*, 120–1.

Thomas, ordained by Bishop Mainwaring in 1645, was removed from his living as rector of the Vaughans' local parish of Llansantffraed and his £60 a year confiscated.[36] He was charged with being a drunkard, a common swearer, no preacher, a whoremaster, and 'in armes personally against the Parliament'.[37] The incumbent of the next parish, Rowland Watkyns, responded in angry verses to his own ousting, scolding radical belief in 'The new, illiterate Lay-Teachers' as so much 'Hocus-Pocus'. Like Jasper Mayne, Watkyns also alludes to the origin of many 'new light' preachers among the labouring and merchant classes to which he wishes they would return; his sense of the desecration of the nation's pulpits perhaps recalls Christ's ejection of the traders from the Temple.[38] Watkyns was far from alone in his fury. For Henry Vaughan, however, led by his new-found faith to read affliction as a providential trial, the literary venting of anger became unacceptable at precisely this moment of greatest trouble. To rail against misfortune now, as he urges in 'Affliction [I]', would be to 'miscall | Thy Physick' (ll. 1–2).[39] Vaughan had also begun to reflect on New Testament warnings against corrupt communication or the utterance of hasty words, pondering Christ's well-known monition that 'every idle word shall be accounted for'.[40] Since even the best-intentioned satire might be twined about with the desire for vengeance or fame, a Christian poet (Vaughan felt) has to do something different with his or her enemies than score satirical hits.

The contrast between Vaughan and Watkyns is a salutory reminder of the broad range of reactions to war, violence and suffering that fall under the umbrella term 'Royalist'. Vaughan's literary responses often feel closer in spirit to George Fox's renunciations of violence than to postponements of revenge like Watkyns's—though of course Fox would have ranked

[36] *V*, 688 (letter to John Aubrey); *Life*, 92–3; cf. Biographical Introduction to *TV*, 7, n. 3, 'it was common for the actual care of souls to be paid at £10 or £20 a year or even less' (see A. H. Dodd, *Studies in Stuart Wales* (Cardiff, 1952, 41). The £100 (maximum) stipend laid down in the Propagation Act (*Acts and Ordinances*, ii. 346) is therefore a somewhat inflated figure, though it was notoriously awarded in full to the Itinerants.

[37] *Life*, 93.

[38] Watkyns, *Flamma sine Fumo*, 43–4. On the stylistic and temperamental differences between Watkyns and other contemporary Christian poets, see P. C. Davies, 'Rowland Watkyns and the Simple Style', in William Tydeman (ed.), *The Welsh Connection: Essays by Past and Present Members of the Department of English Language and Literature, University College of North Wales, Bangor* (Llandyssul, 1986), 54–66.

[39] Herbert, of course, included no less than four 'Affliction' poems in *The Temple* (1633).

[40] Matt. 12: 36, cited in 'The Authors Preface' to *Silex Scintillans* (1655), where Vaughan also cites Eph. 4: 29: 'no corrupt communication should proceed out of our mouths' (*V*, 389).

alongside the Propagators in Vaughan's list of 'new lights'.[41] By the time Fox passed through Brecon in 1657, Vaughan's publishing career was entering its twenty-year hiatus, so there is no record of whether he was among the angry Welsh-speaking crowd who, as Fox noted in his journal, 'if ye Lords power had not prevented ym they might have pluckt doune ye house & us to peices'.[42]

A TAINTED SINK WE HAVE

The transformation of Vaughan's satirical energies is visible as early in *Silex* (1650) as 'Religion', placed fifth in the collection. Instead of dismissing the Puritan view that British religion has become corrupt, Vaughan here agrees to recognize a crisis. At which point he lays out a powerful, gloomy and resolutely *anti-Puritan* version of why this is so, in which he returns fire on those who blame the national church and who believe that separation from it could engineer a return to the purity of apostolic worship. Since the 1630s, separation from the national church had been justified by characterizing Anglicanism as incurably corrupt, its roots sunk too deep in a mire of Catholic superstition for the spiritual health of the elect. In its place, separatists urged gathered churches, improvised services and a much looser church organization, claiming that these represented a return to the pure, primitive worship of the Apostles which God had once again revealed to his children.[43] For those unhappy with the established religion it was a powerful and practical myth, whilst for Anglicans, it quickly grew from the ridiculous to the abhorrent. Yet in *Silex* Vaughan chose not to mock Puritan primitivism with the wit he had flourished in *Olor Iscanus*. Rather, 'Religion' is in agreement with the general observation of primitivist views—that contemporary religion was horribly corrupt—and it, too, contrasts primitive purity with modern-day corruption to discover this. The difference lies in the way Vaughan's poem

---

[41]   On Fox's peace testimony, see Jenkins, 'The Early Peace Testimony in Wales', 13–14. In March 1655 Fox told Cromwell, 'I, who am of the world called George Fox, do deny the carrying or drawing of any carnal sword against any. My weapons are not carnal but spiritual, and my kingdom is not of this world' (see P. Brock, *Pacifism in Europe to 1914* (Princeton, 1972), 260–61)—a sentiment (if not a style) echoed by Vaughan's 'The Men of War', discussed below and in Chapter 6, 'The patience of the saints').

[42]   *The Journal of George Fox, Edited from the MSS*, ed. Norman Penney, 2 vols. (Cambridge, 1911), I, 271.

[43]   See the finely argued account of Theodore Dwight Bozeman, *To Live Ancient Lives: The Primitivist Dimension in Puritanism* (Chapel Hill, NC, 1988).

apportions blame and goes on to deny the possibility of something better.

As they celebrate God's fresh, familiar and intimate commerce with the Old Testament patriarchs, the opening stanzas of 'Religion' gradually begin to discern, to their unpleasant surprise, that staleness and corruption engulf modern religion:

> Here *Jacob* dreames, and wrestles; there
> *Elias* by a Raven is fed,
> Another time by th'Angell, where
> He brings him water with his bread;
>
> In *Abr'hams* Tent the winged guests
> (O how familiar then was heaven!)
> Eate, drinke, discourse, sit downe, and rest
> Untill the Coole, and shady *Even*;
>
> Nay thou thy self, my God, in *fire*,
> *Whirle-winds*, and *Clouds*, and the *soft voice*
> Speak'st there so much, that I admire
> We have no Conf'rence in these daies.
>
> (ll. 9–20)

'O how familiar then was heaven!': such yearning for the holiness and intimacy of the ancient past haunts many others poems in *Silex Scintillans*, such as 'Corruption', 'The Rain-bow' and 'The Brittish Church'. 'Religion' holds back its devastating lesson until scripture reading ('Here . . . ; there' turning the leaves of Genesis) has built up desire in the reader ('O how familiar') to the point of making an 'admir[ing]' application to the present 'daies'. This studied passage from Word to world knows exactly where it is going, but Vaughan delays further. Now the speaker returns to the leaves of the Old Testament, worrying that man has broken some treaty (ll. 21–4) or misunderstood the Gospel, afraid that God may have left the world to its own devices (ll. 25–8). Nathaniel Wanley, whose poems pay homage to *Silex Scintillans* in style and content, understood these thoughts in 'The Invitation' (from the late 1650s):

> Lord what unvallu'd pleasures crown'd
>   Those times of old?
> When thou wer't so familiar found
>   Those daies were gold.
>
>   .   .   .   .

> What shall thy people be so deare
>   To thee no more?
> Or is not heav'n to Earth as neare
>   As heretofore?
>
> ('The Invitation', ll. 1–4, 13–16)[44]

Had man so offended God that the 'truce' is broken, Vaughan wonders ('Religion', l. 21)?[45] Such precise questions about the state of British religion imitate, in order to mock, those over-precise diagnoses of many who proceeded to blame its degeneration on the Roman church and its episcopal Anglican offspring. Vaughan's mimicry prepares for a devastating rejection of such beliefs. The eighth stanza seems to laugh off the theological worries the poem has raised, and to be about to answer them in the positive. But rather than assuring man that God is watching over him and will soon resume intercourse with His creatures, the poem paints a damning picture of mankind's inexorable corruption of religion and rules out recapturing the purity of the Apostles or patriarchs:

> No, no; Religion is a Spring
> That from some secret, golden Mine
> Derives her birth, and thence doth bring
> Cordials in every drop, and Wine;
>
> But in her long, and hidden Course
> Passing through the Earths darke veines,
> Growes still from better unto worse,
> And both her taste, and colour staines,
>
> (ll. 29–36)

This gradually corrupted stream of British religion sinks rapidly into the last two stanzas, where British religion is no more spiritually quenching than the dry well of Jewish faith:

> Just such a tainted sink we have
> Like that *Samaritans* dead *Well,*
> Nor must we for the Kernell crave
> Because most voices like the *shell.*
>
> (ll. 45–8)

---

[44] *Poems*, ed. L. C. Martin (Oxford, 1928).

[45] A subtle eschatological hint may reside in the word 'truce'. 2 Tim. 3, discussed below in reference to 'White Sunday', describes the evil men of the last days as 'without natural affection, trucebreakers, false accusers' (v. 3). This is the only use of 'trucebreakers' or cognates in the Authorized Version.

Jacob's well returns a few poems later in 'The Search', where the well's bubbles whisper that '*Jesus had been there* | But *Jacobs children would not heare*' (ll. 31–2). Both poems allude to chapter 4 of John's gospel, where Jesus stops by the well dug by Jacob at Sychar and asks a Samaritan woman to draw him a drink. When she refuses, Jesus interprets the well's water as a symbol of the Law, which has lost its ability to refresh the soul as the Jews have grown careless of God. In place of the dead well, Jesus speaks of a new water which 'springs up into eternal life'. Like the Jews, Vaughan warns, British Christians have become attached to the form and appearance of piety rather than to true religion, the shell rather than the kernel.[46] 'Religion' ends not with a Puritan vision of church reformation, but with God as apocalyptic physician. 'Heale then these waters, Lord' begins the final stanza, which adds a foot to the iambic tetrameter of the first twelve but can say nothing more that might suggest that Britons can help to clear their 'tainted sink'. Vaughan's pentameters lift reformation out of man's hands and look to God to end the apostasy of his country-men. Following three heavy caesurae, the last line moves irresistibly to its ultimate request without pause, expressing a hope which after the poem's twisting stanzas seems more rapturous than assured: 'And turn once more our *Water* into *Wine*!' ('Religion', l. 52).

'Religion' is the first poem in which Vaughan accounted for the state of 1640s Britain in terms derived almost solely from the bible. In its refusal to lay the blame for religious corruption at any one door except that of all mankind, the poem shows a new providentialist emphasis. Rather than blaming Puritans as a *cause* of corruption, this poem begins to understand them as a *symptom* of a larger malaise, the increasing corruption of mankind as a whole, and of God's meting out punishments for apostasy. Vaughan did not always maintain providentialist patience in the face of dispiriting events. *Silex* (1650) sometimes falls back on tougher satire, especially where poems address aspects of religion which had become long-running disputes, such as the posture for receiving communion ('Dressing', ll. 31–42) or the Parliamentary ban on church festivals ('Christ's Nativity [II]', ll. 15–18). In 'The Constellation', which celebrates the steadfastness of the faithful remnant of true Christians,[47] Vaughan loses his patience and lashes out at the Propagators of the Gospel in a moment of loyal anger:

---

[46] Donald R. Dickson, *The Fountain of Living Waters: The Typology of the Waters of Life in the Poetry of Herbert, Vaughan, and Traherne* (Columbia, Mo., 1987), 138–55.

[47] Discussed in Chapter 4, 'Disorder'd man'.

> But here Commission'd by a black self-wil
>   The sons the father kil,
> The Children Chase the mother, and would heal
>   The wounds they give, by crying, zeale.

(ll. 37–40)

The Commission for Propagation, representing Parliament's control over the Welsh religion, was a few months old when Vaughan's outburst appeared in print in 1650. Its satirical and bitter edge was something which he came increasingly to reject and control during the writing of *Silex Scintillans* Part 2.

A new, more patient way to endure the elevation of enemies is already visible in *The Mount of Olives; or, Solitary Devotions* (1652). Manuals of the devotional life, such as the much-reprinted *The Practice of Piety* (1611), abounded in the seventeenth century, as Vaughan notes in the Preface to this, his one essay in the genre.[48] *The Mount of Olives* is split into three sections, beginning with a series of prayers and 'ejaculations' for everyday living and instructions in preparation for the Eucharist. Two treatises follow: 'Man in Darkness; or, A Discourse of Death', an original prose composition, and 'Man in Glory', which translates a set of meditations on the heavenly life to come often wrongly attributed to Anselm.[49] 'Man in Darkness' is not only written *about* Vaughan's enemies, but also *for* them, a concerted effort by Vaughan to flourish the rod at Puritan religion: not, for Vaughan, a violent act, but one which channelled divine force.[50] Like a shepherd's crook, which can be used both to hook in the flock, or as a rod with which to encourage the more stubborn sheep, Vaughan's approach is both gentle and threatening. He is quick to defend God's use of force throughout *Silex*, reserving a special affection and reverence for the power of the Old Testament Law to impose the lingering guilt that accompanies regeneration. The stony heart must be cracked open with the chisel of the law before the medicinable gospel can work on the fleshly

[48]   Helen C. White, *English Devotional Literature* provides an overview of the different kinds of manual. On Vaughan's reading of Bayly see Hilary M. Day, 'Bayly's *The Practice of Piety:* A New Source for Henry Vaughan's *The Mount of Olives*', *Notes and Queries*, 233 (1988), 163–5, and 'Vaughan and the Seventeenth Century—Religious Prose', ch. 9 of her 'Prose Works of Henry Vaughan', esp. 408–20.

[49]   Vaughan follows his Latin source text, *S. Anselmi . . . de Felicitate Sanctorum Dissertatio; Exscriptore Eadinero* [*sic*] *Anglo Canonico Regulari* (Paris, 1639), in attributing the discourse to 'the most Revered and holy Father Anselmus' (191).

[50]   A similar rhetorical strategy often underlies Milton's prose exhortations (Corns, *Uncloistered Virtue*, chs. 1–2).

heart: 'O plant in me thy *Gospel,* and thy *Law*' ('The Law, and the Gospel', l. 27).

Like Petrarch's *De Contemptu Mundi,* parts of which Vaughan translates into his text, 'Man in Darkness' is in the tradition of Christian contempt for the world of which the Welsh poet was extremely fond.[51] And like Erasmus, who also wrote *De Contemptu Mundi,* Vaughan's text reaches outside the Christian tradition, calling upon a wide range of knowledge from across the disciplines to carry out its aim: to provoke in the 'new lights' and their followers a dramatic revelation of their grand delusion.[52] Vaughan begins by undermining the view that his age was a special era of spiritual enlightenment, raiding Ralegh's *History of the World* for stories of the rise, and more importantly the fall, of other revolutions. The perspective of eternity is used repeatedly to belittle mortal life, that 'meere apparition, [which] differs but very little from a dream'.[53] Earthly life is strenuously renounced: Vaughan draws copious evidence for its worthlessness from over forty authorities besides the bible, including natural history from Pliny, hermetical lore from Agrippa and poetry from Saint Paulinus and the Welsh bard Aneurin.

Thus far the discourse offers the lost sheep an attractive picture of the pen. In the second part of the 'Discourse', however, the shepherd's crook is reversed to become a rod, threatening the proud and the mighty with a terrible fate: 'Seeing then it is so, that eternal pleasures or eternal pains do inavoidably and immediately overtake us after our dissolution, with what unwearied care and watchfulnesse should we continue in well-doing, and *work out our salvation with fear and trembling?*' (*V,* 180)[54] As such threats

---

[51]   L. C. Martin notes Vaughan's borrowings as 171 (note 1), 183 (note 2), 186 (note 1), 187 (ll. 1–41, loose translation); Vaughan also quotes from Petrarch's *De Otio Religiosorum,* 172, ll. 22 f. and 173, ll. 7–22.

[52]   On Erasmus' innovations in the genre see Erica Rummel, 'Quoting Poetry instead of Scripture: Erasmus and Eucherius on *Contemptus Mundi* ', *Bibliothèque d'Humanisme et Renaissance,* 45 (1983), 503–9.

[53]   *V,* 174. Vaughan acknowledges Chrysostom as his source here, *Homily on Matthew,* xii [*V* 's note]. It is also quoted earlier by Vaughan: 'I can conclude my present *being* or state . . . to be nothing else but an *apparition*', unacknowledged this time (*V,* 169). The homily also features in Traherne's *The Kingdom of God.*

[54]   The assertion here that eternal pains 'immediately' overtake the damned after death is conspicuously orthodox in the age of growing Mortalism, the belief that the soul and body slept after death until the Last Judgement (see N. T. Burns, *Christian Mortalism from Tyndale to Milton* (Cambridge, Mass., 1972), ch. 1). However, poems such as 'Death. A Dialogue', 'Resurrection and Immortality' and 'Buriall' do suggest a period of liminal sleep for the body before Judgement Day, and it is fair to say that Vaughan refused to speculate consistently on the mechanics of the afterlife.

shoo the reader towards a change of heart, Vaughan rains stinging attacks on the superficiality of modern religion. Ancient piety is again Vaughan's touchstone, but this time he looks to early Christians rather than to the patriarchs who exemplify holiness elsewhere in *Silex Scintillans*;[55] in comparison to these ancient saints '*the painted* and *illuding appearance* of [holiness] *in these of our times*' makes Vaughan again wonder if religion in Britain is nearing its end (*V*, 181). Lest we repent, he warns, 'we shall have just cause to fear that our *Candlestick* (which hath been now of a long time under a Cloud) is at this very instant upon removing' (*V*, 181). The topos of the candlestick, as used in many seventeenth-century sermons, was based on John's prophetic warning to the church of Ephesus: 'Repent . . . or else I will come unto thee quickly, and will remove thy candlestick out of his place' (Revelation 2: 5). Vaughan's use of it flings the apocalyptic text at millenarians, for whom such texts were a rallying cry for reform. Typically quick to spot a simple scriptural riposte, Vaughan turns their interpretation upside-down: their beliefs are the sickness, not the cure.[56]

Having dug a purposeful channel for his anger, Vaughan releases a torrent of rebuke on the new religion:

This was the *old way*, and whether we are *in it*, or *out* of it, is not hard to be decided. A pretended *sanctity* from the teeth outward, with the frequent *mention* of the *Spirit*, and a presumptuous assuming to our selves of the stile of *Saints*, when we are within full of *subtilty, malice, oppression, lewd opinions*, and *diverse lusts*, is (I am sure) a convincing argument that we are not onely *out* of it, but that we have no mind to returne. (*V*, 182)

Against this modern style, Vaughan describes an ascetic vision of the Christian life which totally rejects spiritual ascendancy and earthly contentedness, just those rewards which millenarians saw as signs of their special favour in the run-up to the end of the world. 'To be short', Vaughan concludes, 'acquit thee *wisely* and *innocently* in all thy Actions, live a

---

[55] A special reference to the Apostles may be intended by Vaughan's use of the biblical adjectives 'fervent and shining', which appear frequently in the Acts of the Apostles, but not elsewhere in the bible.

[56] Sampson Price's *Ephesus' Warning before Her Woe* (1616) parades Rev. 2: 5 as a fearful monition to the nation, teaching urgent repentance. (I am grateful to Mary Morrissey for this reference). John's exhortations to the churches in his portrait of religious hypocrisy come up again later in the 'Discourse', 180 ff.: 'Methinks I see the remisse, lukewarme *professour*, and the *hypocritical, factious pretender of sanctity*'. 'Lukewarme' is John's judgement on the church of the Laodiceans in Rev. 3: 16.

Christian, and die a *Saint*' (*V*, 188). Here is Vaughan's credo, and it is one implicitly opposed to the ecstatic religion of his day.

THESE NEW LIGHTS

Typical of Vaughan's subtly oppositional writing is the double instruction to 'live a Christian and die a *Saint*'. In contrast, Puritans frequently adopted the name of Saint *before* death, living in conscious sainthood, persuaded of their election. One of the foremost Welsh Puritan preachers of the 1640s, Walter Cradock, was famed for his celebration of the blessedness of *The Saints Fulnesse of Joy* on earth (the title of his 1646 sermon before Parliament); 'A Saint O! how full of joy he is,' he wrote in *Gospel-Holinesse*, published in 1651.[57] By contrast, Vaughan was deeply sceptical of the possibilities of spiritual advancement before death. The impenetrable veil between man and God became especially important to him as he wrote the second part of *Silex Scintillans*. Historians and literary critics have tended to pigeonhole Vaughan as a mystical poet, whether in contrast to the churchier George Herbert or under the tow of Thomas Vaughan's alchemical tracts, also published in the 1650s;[58] but although he was familiar enough with hermetical and mystical writings to borrow from them images of spiritual transformation, Henry Vaughan was not a mystic. He seems to have made a principled decision *against* the possibility of knowing God in this life.[59]

The poems Vaughan added to the 1655 edition of *Silex Scintillans* begin with a meditation and hymn for the festival of the Ascension in which his anti-inspirational views take shape. First 'Ascension-day' joyously pictures the scene of Christ's return to heaven and thinks longingly of the Day of Judgement, when the Ascension will be replayed in reverse and Christ will return to separate the sheep from the goats. In contrast, 'Ascension-Hymn' then considers the sacrificial purpose of Christ's death,

---

[57] Walter Cradock, *Gospel-Holinesse* (1651), 73, quoted by Nuttall, *Welsh Saints*, 24.

[58] On 'mystic' as a term applicable to Herbert, Vaughan and Traherne see Evelyn Underhill, *The Mystics of the Church* (1925), ch. 11 'Some Protestant Mystics'.

[59] Jacob Boehme's influence on the brothers Vaughan is traced by Davies, *Henry Vaughan*, 50, 130–3 and Smith, *Literature and Revolution*, 267–75; cf. Smith, *Perfection Proclaimed*, ch. 5. Boehme's influence on the Welsh Saint Morgan Llwyd is discussed by E. Lewis Evans, 'Morgan Llwyd and Jacob Boehme', *Jacob Boehme Society Quarterly*, 1, part 4 (1953), 11–16 and further connections between mysticism and politics in this period by J. Andrew Mendelsohn, 'Alchemy and Politics in England, 1649–1655', *Past and Present*, 135 (1992), 30–78.

resurrection and Ascension into heaven, lingering over the sins for which He atoned. Here begins a strong vein of anti-inspirational, anti-mystical poetry, which prepares the way for Vaughan's anti-radical masterpiece, 'White Sunday', two poems later.

'Ascension-Hymn' remembers how once man could

> Like the Sun shine
> All naked, innocent and bright,
> And intimate with Heav'n, as light.
>
> (ll. 22–4)

But this intimacy was lost at the Fall, and will only be restored at the General Resurrection when Christ comes as the Refiner prophesied by Malachi, to scrub clean man's corruption.[60] Glossing the poem's second stanza, Vaughan's editors have suggested parallels with Behmenist mysticism:

> And yet some
> That know to die
> Before death come,
> Walk to the skie
> Even in this life; but all such can
> Leave behinde them the old Man.
>
> (ll. 7–12)

Alan Rudrum glosses this sky-walking as either the 'orthodox Christian' mystic experience in the prayer of union, or the hermetic view that man could be 'deified' in this life, and live permanently in Paradise.[61] While this is a useful contrast, it is a misleading comparison. The very idea of attaining Paradise on earth is quite clearly at odds with the rest of the poem, where it is clear that Christ

> alone
> And none else can
> Bring bone to bone
> And rebuild man,
>
> (ll. 37–40)

lines which evince an orthodox belief in the bodily resurrection as the first moment of man's Redemption and the beginning of a new existence. In

---

[60] Mal. 3: 3. Malachi is discussed at length in Chapter 6, 'Smiles of the Day-star'.
[61] *R*, 590.

Vaughan's view here, it is only at the Resurrection that body and soul will reunite to put on incorruption; until then, man cannot be fully glorified with the knowledge of God.[62] The other possibility—that man can periodically glimpse God—has been frequently associated with Vaughan's aching remembrance of the 'bright shootes of everlastingness' he saw as a child. Poems such as 'The Retreate' and 'Childe-hood' remember glimpses of something eternal or mysterious; yet these are utterly lost with the passing of childhood, which for Vaughan meant as soon as the ability to reason and speak appears.[63] From then on, as the speaker of 'They are all gone into the world of light!' knows, man is imprisoned in a 'world of thrall', from which only God can retrieve him (l. 35). Most Protestants would have understood a 'walk' to God simply as the pilgrimage of an elect soul through the stages of regeneration, justification, sanctification and glorification; one influential guidebook to this journey, by Robert Bolton (a writer whose works Vaughan knew well), was called *Some Generall Directions for a Comfortable Walking with God.* And besides, to talk of *walking* to the sky seems rather pedestrian for a mystical experience.

A better source for the lines is Colossians 3: 9, 'ye have put off the old man with his deeds'. This image of redressing also appears in Ephesians 4, a chapter which begins with the Ascension and turns, as do both Colossians and 'Ascension-Hymn', in order to discuss how Christians should become purified so that they may walk with God in the spiritual body of Christ. Those that 'know to die' in this life are therefore those who die *to sin* by casting off their Old Man: then their path is ever to God, and they can walk to the sky by leaving behind their old concerns and desires. Spiritual walking, like dying to sin, is a powerful metaphor in the epistles, appearing at least a dozen times. (Bunyan was later to write *The Heavenly Footman,* and *The Pilgrim's Progress* is also unalterably pedestrian.) Like all of God's ways, this spiritual walking is in part a mystery, but it is no more mystical than the power of a church service, or of private prayer. 'Ascension-hymn' is an important addition to Vaughan's anti-mystical,

---

[62] In 'Death. *A Dialogue*', second poem in *Silex* (1650), the Soule states that while the Body will sleep in the earth, it will 'each minute grone to know | How neere Redemption creepes' (ll. 29–30), an anti-mortalist vision of the deceased Soule's longing watch for the Last Day. The ultimate transformation of man does not occur after death, but at the very end of creation itself. Until then, dead souls are not given this final glorification, the union with and knowledge of God; little chance for living souls, therefore, however holy they may appear.

[63] For a possible dating of Vaughan's childhood's end, see Chapter 3, 'A sad blubber'd story'.

anti-Puritan poetry in *Silex* (1655), rather than an awestruck intimation of earthly sainthood.

None of Vaughan's poems wish to escape the recognition that man's mind is fallen, his senses confused, and his perception radically flawed. They return in horror and fascination to linger on this worst of all the consequences of the Fall, the distancing of Man from God in a nature prone to greed, hatred and enmity. Similarly, *The Mount of Olives* characterizes the sinful mind as *distracted* and wandering: 'the very *fowles of the aire*, and their own *horrid guilt* either in time of *distraction* (which they are always subject to) or in their *sleep* (which is always fraught with *penal visions* and *spiritual tumults*)' (*V*, 181).

A marginal note quotes Phaedra's speech of guilty conscience from Seneca's *Hippolytus* and the 'Discourse' instances to the Parliamentary reader plenty of powerful men torn apart by their inner voice: the emperor Hadrian, who died without faith, and Henry IV admitting his lack of right.[64] In *Silex Scintillans*, poems about enemies and oppression lead inexorably into reflections on the partial and limited human perception of God and divine truth in a fallen world. 'The Rain-bow' pictures man and God gazing from different directions at the token of Noah's covenant. But whereas God sees all creation beneath Him, mortal vision is bounded by the visible:

> When I behold thee, though my light be dim,
> Distant and low, I can in thine see him,
> Who looks upon thee from his glorious throne
> And minds the Covenant 'twixt *All* and *One*.

> (ll. 15–18)

The calm of Vaughan's poem wells from its contentment with the beauty of *the sign* of God's promise, its peace from accepting what mystics deny, that fallen man can gaze at God only through signs and symbols. Common metaphors in Vaughan for this partial knowledge are the effect of a veil across the eyes, or like seeing in half-light; in 'The Timber', also from the 1655 volume, Vaughan turns to the Johannine water of life to express the same idea:

> But these chaste fountains flow not till we dye;
> Some drops may fall before, but a clear spring

---

[64] *V*, 181, ll. 162–4; 173; 183; cf. 'Distraction' (*Silex*, 1650), and Post's comments on its mimetically chaotic form (*Henry Vaughan*, ch. 6).

And ever running, till we leave to fling
Dirt in her way, will keep above the skie.

(ll. 53–6)

Such pertinent reminders of the limits of mortality often follow a meditation on the joys of heaven, or, as in 'The Rainbow', adjoin a passage on sin; they frown at the possibility of worldly joy and the belief in 'new light', ideas which Vaughan's lines implicity react against, arguing the fallen partiality of man's vision.

The seventeenth poem of the 1655 collection again focuses Vaughan's warnings about the end of religion in Britain through a comparison with God's first chosen people. 'The Jews', like George Herbert's poem of the same name, imagines the conversion to Christianity which was traditionally supposed to herald the Last Judgement. Millenarians like the Welsh mystic William Erbery and the self-elected high-priest Theauraujohn Tany actively sought the readmission of the Jews to England as if to bring about the Last Days by beginning their conversion.[65] As in 'Religion' and 'The Brittish Church', 'The Jews' sees its subject as a type of lost blessing and apostasy. The poem figures the Holy Spirit in its conventional guise of a dove:

> When the fair year
> Of your deliverer comes,
> And that long frost which now benums
> Your hearts shall thaw; when Angels here
> Shall yet to man appear,
> And familiarly confer
> Beneath the Oke and Juniper:
> When the bright *Dove*
> Which now these many, many Springs
> Hath kept above,
> Shall with spread wings
> Descend, and living waters flow
> To make drie dust, and dead trees grow.

(ll. 1–13)

---

[65] Tany is the subject of Ariel Hessayon, ' "Gold tried in the fire": The Prophet Theauraujohn Tany and the Puritan Revolution', Ph.D. thesis (Cambridge, 1996); see also Nigel Smith, *Perfection Proclaimed*, 299–307 and *Parnassus Biceps* (1655), where 'Theorau Johns *Revelations*' are scorned as 'new lights' (sig. [A4]'). Erbery's philo-Semitism is discussed below, Chapter 6, 'Vaughan's expectancies'.

As often, Vaughan looks forward to the Last Day while keeping one eye firmly on the present; here, in order to urge repentance. The moments of Creation and Apocalyptic Re-creation are overlaid in the image of the spread wings of the Dove, which recalls the Spirit of God moving on the face of the waters in the first moments of Genesis.[66] On the Last Day the power which once shaped creation will return and the everlasting waters of God will flow again. But not, the poem stubbornly announces, until that day. Once more, Vaughan denies the extraordinary activity of the Spirit in the world.

Geoffrey Nuttall's classic study of *The Holy Spirit in Puritan Faith and Experience* (1946) explores the many ways seventeenth-century Puritans conflated passages from the Acts of the Apostles into beliefs about the extraordinary ministry of the Holy Ghost.[67] Vaughan's 'White Sunday' begins to question these beliefs of Spiritual light by lingering on the actions and behaviour of those who, in the 1650s, believed they saw by it:

> Can these new lights be like to those,
> These lights of Serpents like the Dove?
> Thou hadst no *gall*, ev'n for thy foes,
> And thy two wings were *Grief* and *Love*.
>
> (ll. 9–12)

These *new lights* did indeed claim allegiance with the Holy Dove. The Welsh Saints' particular claim is witnessed in the writings of Morgan Llwyd, a friend of Vavasor Powell and Walter Cradock, a member of the 1653 Parliament of Saints, and the major literary figure of Welsh mysticism at this time. Llwyd was much influenced in his writing by the German mystic Jacob Boehme and his English disciples, but his best-known work, *Llyfr y Tri Aderyn* (*The Book of the Three Birds*) (1653) was a more straightforward allegory concerning the spiritual revolution under way in Britain. It represented Cromwell as an eagle, the episcopal church as a raven (the bird which did not return to the ark) and the Puritan Saints as a dove.[68]

Vaughan's rejoinder in 'White Sunday' is to liken the *new lights* to Serpents. There is something bluntly, almost absurdly, straightforward about

---

[66] Gen. 1: 2: 'And the Spirit of God moved upon the face of the waters'.

[67] Nuttall, *Holy Spirit*, 1–19.

[68] Jenkins, *Protestant Dissenters*, 24, 82–3. Ravens are, by contrast, positively remembered in Vaughan's writing, which recalls the bird which fed Elijah in the desert (*The Mount of Olives*, 184 and 'Religion', l. 10).

this riposte, which holds Puritan pretensions up to the reasonable light of Anglican common sense with the broadest of scriptural allusions to Satan as the slippery seducer of souls. But reasonable satire is seldom the mode of *Silex Scintillans*, which as a collection looks to the scripture-using culture of its time to propel and sharpen every blunt force. The same is true here. For as well as the obvious Satanic serpent, 'White Sunday' remembers Christ's words to his Disciples about the proper manner of a Christian evangelist: 'Behold, I send you forth as sheep in the midst of wolves: be ye therefore wise as serpents, and harmless as doves' (Matthew 10: 16). Through this allusion, Vaughan recalls Christ's advice to his lieutenants, as well as the Pentecostal inspiration of the Apostles recorded in Acts; and by underplaying the reference, Vaughan leaves the reader to work out that the *new lights* have perverted the calling of Christian ministers, becoming *serpents* whilst forgetting to be *doves*. For those who grasp the point, Vaughan's poem quickly presses home what it means to be truly dove-like, reusing an observation already made in *The Mount of Olives*, that the turtle-dove is 'always groning, and Naturalists say, she hath no gall' (*V*, 182). The warlike Saints of the revolution, already branded soldiers and schismatics, are, by contrast, far from gall- (or guile-) less.

Clustered in the next stanzas are further accusations against *new lights*, and the suggestion that their misuses of scripture add up to powerful and palpable proof that they are false prophets, deceiving and self-deceived:

> Though then some boast that fire each day,
> And on Christs coat pin all their shreds;
> Not sparing openly to say,
> His candle shines upon their heads:
>
> Yet while some rays of that great light
> Shine here below within thy Book,
> They never shall so blinde my sight
> But I will know which way to look.
>
> (ll. 13–20)

Worst of the *new lights'* sins is that they combine boastfulness—St Paul warns 'boasters and inventors of evil things' (Romans 1: 30)—with brutal misappropriation of scripture. Here Vaughan has in mind chapter 29 of the book of Job, where Job famously expresses his wish that 'I were as in months past, as in the days when God preserved me; When his candle shined upon my head' (Job 29: 2–3). Vaughan was fond of this image (and he was of many moments from Job) as instancing Christian patience and the affliction of a virtuous life; longing for God's candle to shine on him, Job is a broken, suffering soul, his memories of a better time a piteous lament. For the *new lights*, however, Job's candle became a symbol of their supposed special bond with God. As Walter Cradock put it, the Christian Saint is always 'full of joy, and sweetenesse, and comfort . . . the reason is . . . the Lord shines upon his soul'.[69] Vaughan's lines protest in a tone of quiet outrage that to make a present claim of candlelight is to commit a sin of presumption, and to do so as the basis of a revolutionary ministry is to court catastrophe with pride. It was with the sorrow of hindsight (and only with that sorrow) that the patient Job realized how he had once been favoured. Boasting in the present is a clear sign for Vaughan that these *new lights* care enough for scripture only to acquire scraps with which to delude themselves about the true nature of their enterprise.

Though the Spirit has kept above, 'White Sunday' acknowledges that some of the Apostolic fire has outlasted Acts, having been drawn into the text of scripture, a correct reading of which can provide enough light to see the pitfalls of the world, if not the truths of heaven. Vaughan is drawing on the traditional Christian view that the scriptures were divinely inspired by the Spirit when he imagines its Ghostly light shining out of the book's pages:

> For though thou doest that great light lock,
> And by this lesser commerce keep:
> Yet by these glances of the flock
> I can discern Wolves from the Sheep.
>
> (ll. 21–4)

These lines share with 'The Jews' a belief the Holy Spirit has not ministered in an extraordinary way since the Apostles' days. In 'Whitsunday', Herbert had asked God to 'Restore this day, for thy great name, | Unto his ancient and miraculous right', and lamented the day when the Dove of the Holy Spirit 'shutt'st the door, and keep'st within', thus closing what had been an 'open house, richly attended' (ll. 21, 6–7). Twenty years later, with Whitsun proscribed and the Apostolic fire assumed by new prophets, Vaughan changes Herbert's conceit of divine hospitality withdrawn for one of continued guardianship: 'thou dost that great light lock' significantly uses the continuous present to describe an action (locking) that would usually be expressed in the perfect tense as a completed single

---

[69] Cradock, *Gospel-Holinesse*, 73 (quoted by Nuttall, *Welsh Saints*, 24).

action; for God, Vaughan implies, once locked is always locked. But no prophetic light is needed to spot that something is wrong among God's flock. The new Apostles may come disguised as sheep, but they are the wolves about whom Christ warns the Disciples in Matthew chapter 7, 'false prophets, which come to you in sheep's clothing, [who] inwardly are ravening wolves' (Matthew 7: 15).

This reference to Matthew's gospel begins a series of biblical allusions designed to identify Puritan *new lights* as these false prophets. Although Vaughan's allusion to Matthew does not include the phrase 'false prophet', it is clear that he assumed his readers would either recognize or seek out the larger context of his partial quotations. To such a scripture-using readership, even single words might change the sense of a whole poem by implying framing scriptural contexts, as 'wolves' and 'sheep' do in the opening stanzas of 'White Sunday' by alerting the reader to the Sermon on the Mount. Since Vaughan chose many of the passages he works with on account of their popularity with his scripture-using opponents, he could also be partly sure that they would be recognized through notoriety. His allusion to Matthew 7: 15, for instance, probably stems from that text's popularity in anti-clerical literature of the earlier seventeenth century, the classic exposition being Stephen Denison's sermon on *The White Wolfe* (1629).[70]

Lest its anti-illuminist feelings be read as scepticism or lukewarm piety, 'White Sunday' preventatively argues that wishes can only be fulfilled according to scripture and not to whim, to God's timetable, not to man's:

> Not, but that I have wishes too,
> And pray, *These last may be as first,*
> *Or better*; but thou long ago
> Hast said, *These last should be the worst.*
>
> (ll. 25–8)

To readers alive to the age's millennial shorthand, 'these last' meant the *last days*, that is, the final age of creation preceding the Apocalypse. Belief in a 'last age' of the world had warmed steadily in Protestant Europe since the mid-sixteenth century and reached boiling point in England and Wales following the king's execution. Only twelve or thirteen of the 140

---

[70] Stephen Denison, *The White Wolfe* (1627) is discussed at length in Peter Lake, *The Boxmaker's Revenge: Orthodoxy, Heterodoxy, and the Politics of the Parish in Early Stuart London* (Stanford, Calif., forthcoming).

members of the Nominated Parliament of 1653 were Fifth Monarchists, but many shared their aspirations, and the proclamations issued by the Parliament expected Christ's 'glorious coming, who is King of kings, and Lord of lords'.[71] It is the rashly enthusiastic scripture use of millenarian enthusiasts that Vaughan questions in the wish that '*These last may be as first*', a phrase which remembers two distinct biblical passages concerning the end of the world. The first is Christ's teaching that the Day of Judgement will see a great reversal where 'many that are first shall be last, and the last shall be first' (Matthew 19: 30); the second is Paul's prophecy that 'in the last times perilous times shall come . . . evil men and seducers shall wax worse and worse, deceiving, and being deceived' (2 Timothy 3: 1, 13). Christ's 'last' are of course the lowly, Paul's the ages of creation. In 'White Sunday', Vaughan first contrives to wish, millenarian-fashion, that the Last Days might be as glorious as the first; but he immediately turns to another scripture to put down this hope. Those for whom the revolution of the Saints introduces a glorious last era, the lines argue, deny Paul's apocalyptic prophesy and so twist scripture to their own ends. Biblical manipulation of this nature was especially rife among Welsh millenarians; in one passage, William Erbery concluded that Saint Paul was, among other things, a Welshman, because Tarsus, where he was born, was a sea town, 'and so is *Cardiffe in Wales*'.[72]

Vaughan certainly disapproved of unscriptural millennial prophecies, but he frequently yearns after the Day of Judgement itself.[73] Part 1 of *Silex* includes at least ten poems with a strong eschatological content, notably 'Day of Judgement' and 'The Dawning', and many more which touch on the four last things; in Part 2, poems like 'The Bird', 'The Rain-bow' and 'The Seed growing secretly' end in a mood of unbearable longing to see 'the white winged Reapers come' ('The Seed growing secretly', l. 48). With Saint Paulinus, his chosen model of ascetic piety, Vaughan held it a Christian duty to live every day as if it were the last. Writing to his wife Therasia in the last days of the Roman Empire, Paulinus supposed the last times to be upon him (although not the last day). As Vaughan translated in 1654:

---

[71] Capp, *Fifth Monarchy Men*, 68 (quoting *Severall Proceedings*, 199 (14–21 July 1653), 3142); Mark Kishlansky, *A Monarchy Transformed: Britain 1603–1714* (Harmondsworth, 1996), 205.

[72] William Erbery, *The Bishop of London, the Welsh Curate, and Common Prayers, with Apocrypha in the End* (1652), sig. [B2]ʳ.

[73] A desire discussed further in Chapter 6, 'Smiles of the Day-star'.

An Universall discord mads each land,
Peace is quite lost, the last times are at hand.

('St Paulinus to his wife Therasia', ll. 27–8)

Like Vaughan's lines 'but thou long ago | Hast said *These last should be the worst*', Paulinus is thinking of Paul's warning to Timothy about the 'evil men and seducers [who] shall wax worse and worse' and of Christ's apocalyptic predictions of 'false Christs, and false prophets, and shall shew great signs and wonders; insomuch that if it were possible, they shall deceive the very elect' (Matthew 24: 24). With these texts as his witness, Vaughan reveals Puritan *new lights* as the object of scriptural warnings about the wolfish last times. 'White Sunday' then returns to its Herbertian model, praising God's unchanging love for the creation and anticipating the glorious Last Day. As a coda, the final stanza remembers Balaam, the prophet who was offered honour and riches by the King of Moab if he would curse the Israelites. Here, and in the next poem 'The Proffer', Vaughan writes as though he had received offers of reward for his loyalty from the new powers. 'I'le not stuff my story | With your Commonwealth and glory' (ll. 35–6) he tells the black parasites of 'The Proffer', with a glance at the Propagators of the Gospel and their Parliamentary stipends, which were notoriously drawn from ministerial tithes.[74]

Unravelling the popular prophecies of *new light*, 'White Sunday' weaves a daring poetic fabric in which true scripture uses correct false ones through careful cross-referencing of popular millenarian texts with their scriptural nemeses. The parody that 'White Sunday' has learnt from the Part I poem 'Religion' (and perhaps also 'The Brittish Church') is thus thickened with scriptures from the larger seventeenth-century debate on apocalyptic chronology, a debate from which Vaughan remained knowledgeably distant. But he reused the techniques of 'White Sunday' in several other Part 2 poems, nowhere less impressively perhaps than in 'The Men of War', a poem toward the end of that volume. Its title is a great example of Vaughan's ability to fix on a scripture whose interpretation divided radical from conformist in the mid-century. The 'men of war' it refers to are the soldiers of Herod's who mock Christ during his interrogation: 'And Herod with his men of war set him at naught, and mocked him, and arrayed him in a gorgeous robe, and sent him again to Pilate'

---

[74] Jenkins, *Foundations*, 59–60, discusses the financial redistributions of the Propagation movement.

(Luke 23: 11). But the poem is also aware that Moses calls God 'a man of war' in his famous thanksgiving song after the crossing of the Red Sea (Exodus 15: 3). Just as 'White Sunday' is angry at those who identify their *new light* with the light of Job's candle, so 'The Men of War' is aimed at those who trumpet the victories of the Old Testament man of war—God as victor—whilst ignoring the greater lesson of the New Testament: that most *men of war* are persecutors and that God's fuller revelation of himself was made not on the field of war but on the cross.

Again, the bible's Spiritual light of the bible is Vaughan's sure defence against the optical illusions of *new light*:

> For in this bright, instructing verse
> Thy Saints are not the Conquerors;
> But patient, meek, and overcome
> Like thee, when set at naught and dumb.
>
> ('The Men of War', ll. 17–20)

'Overcome', a strong word to use about Christ's silence during Pilate's interrogation, is repeated eight lines later to describe His sacrifice:

> The sword wherewith thou dost command
> Is in thy mouth, not in thy hand,
> And all thy Saints do overcome
> By thy blood, and their Martyrdom.
>
> (ll. 25–8)

Christ's sacrifice is the source of the faith of saints and martyrs, faith which Saint John calls 'the victory that overcometh the world'. In a reversal of the world's victory over Jesus, Christian victories are martyrdoms and sacrifices, not martial glories. Christ may have announced that he came 'not to send peace, but a sword' (Matthew 10: 34), but to understand that scripture in isolation from the rest of the bible was not, Vaughan's poem complains, to give proper respect to God or his Word. Demonstrating a more thorough reading, Vaughan collocates two *other* mentions of the divine sword (in Revelation 19: 15 and Hebrews 4: 12) to make the point that in the bible God's sword is most often a figurative one: His eternal Word, whose edge will divide the sheep from the goats at the Last Judgement.[75] Driving home these military preoccupations

---

[75] Rev. 19: 15, 'And out of his mouth goeth a sharp sword that with it he should smite the nations'; Heb. 4: 12, 'For the word of God is quick, and powerful, and sharper than any two-edged sword'.

of the new Saints, Vaughan elides the centuries with a slight change of
tense that brings the soldiers of the 1650s together with their ancient
counterparts:

> But seeing Soldiers long ago
> Did spit on thee, and smote thee too;
> Crown'd thee with thorns, and bow'd the knee,
> But in contempt, as still we see,
> I'le marvel not at ought they do
> Because they us'd my Savior so.

> (ll. 29–34)

Men like Herod's soldiers are still at large, the poem tells its reader with a
penetrating glance: and they are still soldiers.

The prayer for patience which ends 'The Men of War' recalls both the
prayers of *The Mount of Olives* and the exhortations to patience and faith
of Saint Paul in Hebrews and Titus. 'Let us run with patience the race that
is set before us' Paul writes famously in Hebrews 12, and in the epistle of
James, the trying of faith is said to 'work patience'. The influence of James
and of Job,[76] whom he holds up as an example of faith, is felt in Vaughan's
closing prayer:

> Dear *Jesus* give me patience here,
> And faith to see my Crown as near
> And almost reach'd, because 'tis sure
> If I hold fast and slight the *Lure*.
> Give me humility and peace,
> Contented thoughts, innoxious ease,
> A sweet, revengeless, quiet minde,
> And to my greatest haters kinde.
> Give me, my God! a heart as milde
> And plain, as when I was a childe;
> That when *thy Throne is set*, and all
> These *Conquerors* before it fall,
> I may be found (preserv'd by thee)
> Amongst that chosen company,

---

[76] Job is present in the parenthesis '(preserv'd by thee)' in l. 49 of the quotation following, reminding the reader of *Silex Scintillans* of a favourite text of its author, Job chapter 7
(here verse 20: 'I have sinned; what shall I do unto thee, O thou preserver of men?' Compare the Part 1 poem 'Buriall', l. 7, 'O thou great Preserver of all men!' and Lancelot
Andrewes' devotions for Monday in the *Preces Privatae*).

> Who by no blood (here) overcame
> But the blood of the *blessed Lamb.*
>
> (ll. 37–52)

The prayer for patience *overcomes* the need for satire and enmity without losing its awareness of right and wrong or its sense of the hypocrisy and treachery of its enemies. It is, after all, one thing for Vaughan to pray to be 'sweet', but quite another to ask for '*in*noxious' ease and a 'revenge*less*' mind. In the understatement of a prayer for peace, the privative prefix and suffix admit what is in need of repression and control by the stronger force of Vaughan's faith in God's promises.

Turning the idiom of its times against its propagators, *Silex* Part 2 subordinates its urges toward enmity to a vision of Puritans as the false prophets of the Last Days and their minions, an enemy that do not need to be overcome since their fate has been prophesied since the days of Christ. Adopting a quietist position, Vaughan discovers suitable scriptural support in a pair of meditations on the tears of Christ. Whereas previous poems had focused wonder on Christ's Incarnation and Passion, asking 'Lord! what couldst thou spye | In this impure, rebellious clay, | That made thee thus resolve to dye' ('The Incarnation, and Passion', ll. 13–15), Part 2 of *Silex* turns to instances of divine love at once more imitable and more mysterious. In the first of two poems called 'Jesus Weeping', Vaughan asks:

> My dear, Almighty Lord! why dost thou weep?
>
> .   .   .   .
>
> Since the same sacred breath which thus
> Doth Mourn for us,
> Can make mans dead and scatter'd bones
> Unite, and raise up all that dyed, at once?
>
> (ll. 1, 5–8)

In reply, Vaughan finds a revelation of divine grief and pity: 'Thou griev'st, man should himself undo, | And lov'st him, though he works thy wo' (ll. 24–5). Though the saving of man is nothing to God's omnipotence, that power does not define the Godhead nor the fullness of divine love: He cannot do it without suffering and sorrowing for His creature as well. 'Dear Lord! thou art all grief and love' (l. 22), Vaughan cries, in one of the typically terse ejaculations which burst out of his poems at moments of profound mystery.[77]

Christ's tears are an emblem of true holiness, innocent of hatred, enmity or the sword. The final lines draw the use directly:

> Then farewel joys! for while I live
> My business here shall be to grieve:
> A grief that shall outshine all joys
> For mirth and life, yet without noise.
> A grief, whose silent dew shall breed
> Lilies and Myrrhe, where the curs'd seed
> Did sometimes rule. A grief so bright
> 'Twill make the Land of darkness light;
> And while too many sadly roam,
> Shall send me (*Swan-like*) singing home.
>
> (ll. 44–53)

In these lines, the resonant *griefs* of Vaughan's suffering again touch those of the book of Job, this time to Job's achingly sorrowful third expostulation. 'Are not my days few?' he asks: 'Cease then, and let me alone, that I may take comfort a little before I go whence I shall not return, even to the land of darkness and the shadow of death; a land of darkness, as darkness itself; and of the shadow of death, without any order, and where the light is as darkness' (Job 10: 20–2). In his suffering, Vaughan saw Britain as that very 'Land of darkness' which Job awaited. Yet his possession of a Christian 'business'—that regular, active worship Vaughan learnt from the busy Creation—will turn faith into light, and the shadow of death into a valley of lilies.

Tears that breed lilies and myrrh recall the Song of Solomon chapter 5, verse 13, 'his lips like lilies, dropping sweet smelling myrrh'. Christ is once more the great exemplar, this time in his allegorical role as the bridegroom of the triumphant church of the elect. Like Christ, Vaughan will spend his life in tears of grief and pity for the sins of man, and lilies and myrrh will grow in the soil of the 'curs'd seed' of Adam's fault. As the Preface to the 1655 *Silex Scintillans* makes clear, Vaughan had come to understand his poetry as the special gift with which he was to spend his days on earth writing hymns of thanksgiving. In the face of the *new lights* of the 1650s,

---

[77] See Chapter 3, 'Comfortable words' on the nature and occasion of Ejaculation in Vaughan's writing and spiritual life.

a new old song entered his repertoire: the grief and sorrow of God at man's inconstancy and capacity for self-deception felt in the affliction and suffering of the elect when 'the heathen rage and the people imagine a vain thing'.

CHAPTER SIX

Perfection postponed

The years between the first publication of *Silex Scintillans* (1650) and its second appearance in a larger, expanded edition in two parts (1655) witnessed the high point of apocalyptic and millenarian fervour in England and Wales. Never before had the nation seen so many prophets, saints and preachers of an imminent parousia as walked the land in the last years of the Civil War and Interregnum; never had British faith in a thousand-year rule of Christ on earth been so fervent or so widespread.[1] Though millenary belief held particularly well among the army and the gathered churches, its zeal had reached all levels of society in England before Vaughan had published a single poem. Many Parliamentarians were also convinced. Oliver Cromwell and Henry Vane had strong millennial ideals, while the Welsh Major-General Thomas Harrison was directly involved with the most radical and active proclaimers of Apocalypse, the Fifth Monarchists.[2] The Nominated or 'Barebones' Parliament which

[1] Millenarian religion in Britain and Europe is discussed by Hill, *World Turned Upside-Down*, chs. 1, 2, 6; Thomas, *Religion and the Decline of Magic*, ch. 5; Capp, *Fifth Monarchy Men*, ch. 2; Hill, *Antichrist in Seventeenth-Century England* (1971); Paul Christianson, *Reformers and Babylon: English Apocalyptic Visions from the Reformation to the Eve of the Civil War* (Toronto, 1978); William M. Lamont, *Godly Rule: Politics and Religion 1603–60* (1969). For the medieval and sixteenth-century background see Norman Cohn, *The Pursuit of the Millennium: Revolutionary and Mystical Anarchists of the Middle Ages*, rev. edn. (1970); Richard Bauckham, *Tudor Apocalypse*, Katherine R. Firth, *The Apocalyptic Tradition in Reformation Britain, 1530–1645* (Oxford, 1979). A good recent discussion of Gerard Winstanley's revolutionary millenarianism is Andrew Bradstock, *Faith in the Revolution: The Political Ideologies of Müntzer* (1997), 108–25. The literary heritage is explored in C. A. Patrides and Joseph Wittreich (eds.), *The Apocalypse in English Renaissance Thought and Literature: Patterns, Antecedents and Repercussions* (Ithaca, NY, 1984), esp. chs. 1 [Bernard McGinn, Marjorie Reeves] and 2 [Jaroslav Pelikan, Bernard Capp] and Madeleine Forey, 'Language and Revelation: Protestant Apocalyptic Literature 1500–1660', D.Phil. thesis (Oxford, 1994).

[2] Ian Gentles, *The New Model Army in England, Ireland and Scotland, 1645–1653* (Oxford, 1992), ch. 4. On Cromwell, see Capp, *Fifth Monarchy Men*, 40–1, 66–7, and for Harrison, chs. 3–5 and 251; also C. H. Firth, *The Life of Thomas Harrison* (Worcester, Mass., 1893), C. H. Simpson, *Thomas Harrison* (1905). Capp also details powerful millenarians (40–2) and the extent of millennial ideas among publishing ministers (46–9).

replaced the Rump in 1653 was strongly urged by Harrison on Cromwell, who closely oversaw the nomination of its 140 members from the 'Saints' of the gathered churches. At its first meeting Cromwell told the Parliament that it had been 'called by God to rule with Him and for Him', and the house responded by declaring in print its expectancy of Christ's glorious coming.[3]

While Barebones sat through the turbulent months of 1653, Henry Vaughan lay 'sick unto death' in his downstairs study-bedroom at Sketh-rock.[4] But though weak in body, Vaughan's mind stole abroad to confront some of the leading millenarians of the day, and in particular to resist the threat of Parliament's evangelical 'Act for the Better Propagation and Preaching of the Gospel in Wales', legislation passed by the Rump in February 1650, largely at the behest of Harrison, to authorize and resource the preaching of the Puritan revolution. Seventy-one chosen Commissioners had the power to remove unfit ministers, while an elite body of twenty-five 'Approvers' scouted for suitably godly replacements. The impossibility of their task led the Approvers (Harrison included himself and his friends the 'Welsh Saints', Vavasor Powell, Morgan Llwyd, and Walter Cradock) to establish instead a team of itinerant ministers. Eventually numbering around ninety, this team preached mostly in the southern counties of Wales, spurred on by Vavasor Powell's own travelling ministry, which often brought him to Brecon, Montgomery and Radnor.

The millenarian message of the Propagators staggered Vaughan. His guidebook for holy living, *The Mount of Olives* (1652) reserves particular animus for those who 'expect and beleeve the dissolution of all things', calling them 'reeds and specious dissemblers', '*hypocritical, factious pretender*[s] of sanctity' whose behaviour shows up their outward pretence of piety (*V*, 170, 180). Vaughan had previously expressed a rather impotent disgust at all things revolutionary, mocking 'new fine *Worships*' in whose midst 'the *Crosse* looks sad' in *Olor Iscanus* ('To his retired friend, an Invitation to *Brecknock*', ll. 19, 21); but by the early 1650s his criticisms had turned from the deplorable visible effects of the Puritan revolution to their causes. This change corresponds with a more steely attempt by Vaughan to discredit millenarian preachers on their own ground rather than to scorn them from a position of defeat, and it coincides with his

---

[3] Capp, *Fifth Monarchy Men*, 66–7; cf. Jenkins, *Protestant Dissenters*, ch. 3.
[4] Vaughan's study is discussed by Davies, *Henry Vaughan*, 31 and *Life*, 18.

regeneration as a poet in *Silex Scintillans*. As part of that regeneration, Vaughan's anti-millenarian scripture uses fired some of the great poems of *Silex Scintillans* Part 2 (1655)—including 'Ascension-day', 'They are all gone into the world of light!' and 'The Palm Tree'—and fired a resistance which glitters incidentally through many others as well.

In recent years, the Apocalypse has presented Vaughan's scholarly readers with one of their best approaches to his great poems. From Christopher Hill to Stevie Davies, critics have argued that *Silex Scintillans* is permeated—dominated, even—by meditations on the Four Last Things, apocalyptic ejaculations, and innumerable allusions to the book of Revelation. Eschatological thoughts, spilt in profusion across the pages of *Silex Scintillans* and *The Mount of Olives*, have helped distinguish Vaughan from Herbert, whose own meditations on the Four Last Things—'Death', 'Dooms-day', 'Judgement' and 'Heaven'—sit neatly at the end of the 'The Church' section of *The Temple*, in formal and temperamental contrast with the Silurist's compulsive returns. And while Marvell and Milton (among others) have received proper attention as scripture users of Revelation in their own right, Vaughan's intense five- or six-year period of lyric apocalypse continues to provoke much of the most interesting critical debate on seventeenth-century apocalyptic writing.[5]

Despite this increasing familiarity with Vaughan's Apocalypse, close attention has not been brought to the scriptural *anti-millenarian* thrust of the second volume of *Silex* or to its subtle strikes at the interpretative foundations of Vavasor Powell's Propagation movement and the

---

[5] Critical discussion of Vaughan's Apocalypse begins with Calhoun, *Henry Vaughan*, chs. 5–6 and Noel Kennedy Thomas, *Henry Vaughan: Poet of Revelation* (Worthing, 1986); Post (*Henry Vaughan*, ch. 7) successfully integrates modern historical scholarship; John Wall (*Transformations of the Word*, ch. 4) offers an intelligent reading of Vaughan's 'homiletics of expectancy'; and Madeleine Forey's accomplished Oxford thesis includes a chapter subsequently published as 'Poetry as Apocalypse: Henry Vaughan's *Silex Scintillans*', *Seventeenth Century*, 10 (1996), 161–86. See also Mark Anthony Patrick Houlahan, 'Writing the Apocalypse 1649–1660', Ph.D. thesis (Toronto, 1989), ch. 4, 'Winding the Horn: Lyric Apocalypse'; Stevie Davies's well-informed chapter 'Christ Coming in Triumph to Brecon'; and the remarks of Nigel Smith, *Literature and Revolution*, 267–73. Milton's and Marvell's Apocalypse is best entered through the work of Michael Fixler, 'The Apocalypse within *Paradise Lost*', 131–78 in Thomas Kranidas (ed.), *New Essays on 'Paradise Lost'* (Berkeley, Calif., 1969); Stella P. Revard, *The War in Heaven: 'Paradise Lost' and the Tradition of Satan's Rebellion* (Ithaca, NY, 1980), 108–28; Leland Ryken, '*Paradise Lost* and Its Biblical Epic Models', 43–81 (esp. 72–9) in James H. Sims and Leland Ryken (eds.), *Milton and Scriptural Tradition* (Columbia, Mo., 1984); Margarita Stocker, *Apocalyptic Marvell: The Second Coming in Seventeenth-Century Poetry* (Brighton, 1986).

Barebones Parliament which enacted it. Such poems as 'Ascension-day', 'Ascension-hymn', 'The Palm-tree' and 'The Men of War' achieve much of their greatness (and scriptural density) by meditating on the Apocalypse in the light of Vaughan's understanding of the religious and political changes of the 1640s. Vaughan's resistance takes two forms. To overcome the almost overwhelming radical claims on the Apocalypse, his later poems deploy among their lines key millenarian texts drawn from the gospels, epistles and the book of Revelation; juxtaposing these with other texts and Vaughan's own arguments for passive resistance, the poems of *Silex* Part 2 attempt a careful defusing of millenarian zeal. Alongside such corrective sorties into the millenarian scriptures, Vaughan's poems also search for apocalyptic metaphors from scripture whose logic resists millenarian interpretation; among his most powerful defences of this kind are images of daybreak and purification from the book of Revelation. Together, these two sorts of textual resistance enable Vaughan to inscribe the Apocalypse in a profoundly anti-radical vision of the Last Day throughout the completed *Silex Scintillans*.

Revelation is the text Vaughan was most keen to preserve from the hands of abusive rapists and pillagers of the Word, those whose vain wits have been so wilfully misemployed as to force the meaning of scripture for self-ends:

> But what is highest sin and shame,
> The vile despight done to thy name;
> The forgeries, which impious wit
> And power force on Holy Writ,
> With all detestable designs
> That may dishonor those pure lines.
>
> ('The day of Judgement', ll. 33–8)[6]

This complaint is from the last verse-paragraph of 'The day of Judgement', a poem steeped in Revelation and Christ's apocalyptic prophecies from John's gospel.[7] Vaughan was especially incensed by radical appropriation of Revelation and shared Richard Haytor's observation, made in his 1676 commentary *A Meaning to the Revelation*, that 'a great in-let to our

---

[6] cf. 'Holy Scriptures' and, in particular, the 'sacred parody' of 'To the Holy Bible': 'O book! life's guide! how shall we part, I And thou so long seized of my heart! I Take this last kiss' (ll. 1–3) in which the scriptures take the place of the profane lover; cf. 'Lovesick', where the object of Vaughan's adoration is Christ.

[7] See Rev. 12: 12, John 4: 35, 5: 28–9 (*R*, 635). Not all scripture abusers in *Silex* are pillagers of Revelation: cf. 'The Agreement', ll. 25–30.

late civil wars, hath been the misinterpretation of the Revelation'.[8] Like Haytor, Vaughan knew that John's visions were an important source of inspiration and scriptural authority for those who sought to stir up religious militancy and a violent, zealous reformation of the church.[9] Vaughan's greatness as an apocalyptic poet lies in finding a way of expressing faith in the Last Judgement while also defending the bible's last book against the misinterpreters who made the 1650s Britain's most millenarian decade.

There was no winner in the interpretative struggle between Vaughan and Powell, nor is it necessary to adjudicate between Vaughan's and Vavasor Powell's Apocalypses. No doubt Vaughan was every bit as sure that true Christians should resist and overcome through passive resistance as Powell was that the Saints must prepare for Christ's second coming by whatever action was required, even the drawn sword.[10] Powell's apocalyptic faith gives his life some of the heroic shape of Milton's: an energetic period of service to the revolution, followed by a turn in fortunes (in Powell's case beginning with his disillusionment with the Protectorship) and a later term of enforced quietism. Vaughan's apocalyptic faith, on the other hand, survives entirely in his writing. He also has no fifth act to compare with Powell's: his subsequent life as a country doctor adds little to our understanding of his apocalyptic poems, nor is it certain how often he put pen to paper after 1657. As a result, his moving literary ripostes to the Propagation have become obscured by the very medium of their achievement: their scripture uses. For Vaughan's contemporary reader, this great inwardness with scripture made the poetry of *Silex Scintillans* a sensitive, penetrating and intellectually dazzling Comforter in times of affliction. For later readers, ironically, subtleties of resistance can often be mistaken for the very faith they sought to scrutinize and correct.

Imprisoned two months after Charles II's Restoration in May 1660, Vavasor Powell remained in gaol until his death, aged 53, in October 1670. He had composed just one prison work, *Bird in the Cage, Chirping* (1661).[11] Yet Vaughan, too, published nothing during the 1660s, and

---

[8] Haytor, *A Meaning to the Revelation*, cited by Lamont, *Godly Rule*, 21. See *OED*, inlet, *sb*, 1. Letting in, admission. 2. A way of admission; an entrance. Sense 1 is older, recorded from 1300 to the mid-nineteenth century; sense 2 is recorded from 1624.

[9] Hill, *World Turned Upside-Down*, 94, 321; Christianson, *Reformers and Babylon*, 179–243.

[10] The claims of conformist and dissenter are weighed with admirable impartiality by Jenkins, *Foundations*, 43–83.

[11] Jenkins, *Protestant Dissenters*, 41. Powell was released once, for ten months. Of the

when he did return to print, it was with *Thalia Rediviva* (1678), a galli-
maufry of miscellaneous pieces partly by his late brother Thomas, and not
with another *Silex Scintillans*.[12] The greatest achievements of both men—
Powell in lighting new fires of faith, Vaughan in nursing the embers of old
ones—had been their time of greatest enmity.

VAUGHAN'S EXPECTANCIES

Vaughan's interest in the Apocalypse was unusual. Most mid-century Anglicans found it difficult to take inspiration from a study whose keenest
exponents were responsible for their discomfort and straitened condition. Among the few exceptions were two pillars of the church, James
Ussher and Joseph Hall. Ussher's chronological *Annales Veteris Testamenti*
(1650) drew on millenarian interpretative tools developed by his friend
Joseph Mede's *Clavis Apocalyptica* (1627), a book which influenced millennial opinion during the middle third of the century more than any
other. The *Clavis* was translated into English in 1633 and again, by order
of Parliament, in 1643. Its popularity with millenarians was one prompt
for Joseph Hall's *The Revelation Unrevealed* (1650), a work which dis-
paraged the Fifth Monarchist claims of John Archer's influential
The Personal Reign of Christ on Earth (1643) and sought to defuse such
instrumental commentaries as the *Clavis* and Thomas Brightman's *A Revelation of the Revelation* (1615). Like Ussher, Hall was friendly with some
millenarians, but his loyalties were first and foremost to the church; *The
Revelation Unrevealed* is resolutely aware that those who zealously awaited
the Apocalypse had also branded British episcopacy antichristian and
brought about the execution of its patriarch. Hall's title-page holds out its
challenge in Lancelot Andrewes's estimation of man's ability to understand God's ways: '*My friend, I am not comme so far*'.[13] It is a view whose
deflationary power and appeal for humility echoes through Vaughan's
poems and prose of the 1650s.

Most supporters of church and king chose to reject and deride radical

other Welsh saints, William Erbery died in 1654, Morgan Llwyd in 1659 (aged 40), and
Walter Cradock in 1649 (aged 49).

  [12] Aside from a few translations from Latin in Thomas Powell's *Humane Industry* (1661)
reprinted in *V*, 681–4.

  [13] Joseph Hall, *The Revelation Unrevealed* (1650), sig. B2ʳ. Hall entries into apocalyptic
debate are discussed by Richard A. MacCabe, *Joseph Hall: A Study in Satire and Meditation*
(Oxford, 1982), 316–20; Andrewes is cited on 316; on Ussher's chronological studies see
Trevor-Roper, *Catholics, Anglicans and Puritans*, 159–61.

teachings, not engage with them. A typical Anglican response of this sort came from the Vaughans' clergyman neighbour, Rowland Watkyns of Llanfrynach. Like Thomas Vaughan, Watkyns was ejected by the Propagation, and once removed he took up the pen to lambast Puritan and Propagation in verses published (from the safety of the Restoration) as *Flamma sine Fumo; or, Poems without Fictions* (1662). Specializing in eulogies to desirable patrons (including Jeremy Taylor's patron the Earl of Carbery), Watkyns pulled no punches.[14] His satire on 'The new illiterate Lay-Teachers', for instance, begins with a Greek epigram—Ἕκας, ἕκας ἔστε βέβηλοι (Far off, far off, O profane ones)—which is a much better insult than it is a warning, since clearly none of those Watkyns purports to address could understand him. *Flamma* leaves its educated reader in no doubt that it fully endorses the Anglican view of ignorant 'tub-preachers' and lay-preachers as fit only to return to the manual trades they had left to invade the pulpit.[15]

A more conventional poet and man than Vaughan (he scorns hermetic and Paracelsian learning[16]), Watkyns follows many Royalists (including Vaughan) in recommending retirement from public life.[17] But having distanced himself from the world, Watkyns is not interested in understanding the millennium or its powerful advocates in poetry; the 1650s were 'bad times' (so called in 'Lay-teachers', l. 43) but not, for him, the *last* times ('Affliction [I]', l. 24). The poems of affliction in *Flamma sine Fumo* lack those imploring climactic appeals for Apocalypse which quicken Vaughan's afflictive poetry: 'Lord haste, Lord come, | O come Lord *Jesus* quickly!'; 'But hark! what trumpets that? what Angel cries | *Arise! Thrust in thy sickle*' ('Buriall', ll. 39–40, 'Corruption', ll. 39–40). For Watkyns, the Grand Rebellion was a period of trial and punishment for the faithful

---

[14] Watkyns, *Flamma sine Fumo*, ed. Davies; Paul C. Davies, 'Two Breconshire Contemporaries: Henry Vaughan and Rowland Watkyns', *Poetry Wales*, 11 (1975), 98–115; Rudrum, 'Resistance, Collaboration, and Silence', esp. 105–8.

[15] *Flamma sine Fumo*, 43; Davies notes that the Greek is 'a formula recited at the beginning of the Mysteries to warn off the uninitiated' (158). See *OED*, tub *sb.* 4 and tub-preachers, both of which are recorded from 1643 on. The social origins of Puritan leaders and prophets are discussed by Hill, *Upside-Down*, 92–3 and ch. 14; Hessayon, ' "Gold tried in the fire" ' chs. 1–2 on Thomas Tany's ingenious mutation of his trade as a goldsmith into an integral part of his prophetic calling.

[16] For Watkyns's conventional views on medicine, see his 'A *Looking-glasse* for the sick: or, the cause and symptoms, or signs of several diseases, with their cures and remedies'; his other scepticism is noted by Rudrum, 'Resistance, Collaboration, and Silence', 106.

[17] P. C. Davies, suggests a Horatian flavour to Watkyns's verse ('Rowland Watkyns', 55; cf. his remarks in 'Two Breconshire Contemporaries').

which would pass away, like others before it, when God willed; then the upstarts would fall like 'little streams' which 'do swell, | And rise above their banks, and then have fell | And sunk into their channels' ('The prosperity of the wicked', ll. 3–4). In 'The Changes'—not, as Vaughan might have written, ' *The* Change'—Watkyns wrote:

> Sometimes the sea doth ebb, and sometimes flow,
> Now with, anon against the tide we row;
> No haven's so secure but some ill blast
> May toss the ship, and break the stately Mast
>
> .   .   .   .   .   .
>
> The sweetest comfort I do feel, or find,
> Though fortune change, is not to change my mind.
>
> ('The Changes', ll. 9–12, 17–18)

This classical idea of destiny recalls the poetic interludes from *The Consolation of Philosophy* which Vaughan translated for *Olor Iscanus*, most notably in its fragile hope that man should not 'By casual evils thus bandied, be | The sport of fate's obliquity' (I. 5, ll. 51–2). Vaughan preserved elements of Boethius' consolation in poems like 'The Retreate' and 'The Constellation', while his 'Man in Darkness' criticizes aetheists with an excerpt from Juvenal's thirteenth satire, admonishing those who imprudently believe that 'all things succeed | By chance or fortune' rather than by the hand of Providence (*V*, 178).

'Man in Darkness' also cites Ralegh's view, in the *History of the World*, that in time all kingdoms rise and fall. C. A. Patrides has observed that generations of Christian exegetes found no contradiction between a view of history influenced by Greek philosophy and the teleological model Christianity inherited from Judaism: they simply conflated the two in an image of time as a *succession* of cycles rolling forwards towards an eventual end.[18] Although cyclical time had its uses—Vaughan wields it in 'Man in Darkness' as a tool for encouraging *contemptus mundi*[19]—it is the teleological view which is most important to Christianity. Only

---

[18] On Christian conceptions of time, see Achsah Guibbory, *The Map of Time: Seventeenth-Century English Literature and Ideas of Pattern in History* (Urbana, Ill., 1986), 12–15, 226–31; C. A. Patrides, *The Grand Design of God: The Literary Form of the Christian View of History* (1972); id. (ed.), *Aspects of Time* (Manchester, 1976), Introduction, 1–8.

[19] See *V*, 171. Curiously, Vaughan is known to be quoting Ralegh here from an eschatological work, Robert Bolton's *Last and Learned Work of the Four Last Things* (1632): Oliver Jonson, 'Robert Bolton and Henry Vaughan's "Man in Darkness" ', *Notes and Queries*, 229 (1984), 331–4.

if time runs like a stream into the sea of infinity can there can be an estuarine Last Time; and only if there is such a Time can millenarians posit a last age and Vaughan see their fervour as a bleak sign of lastness and corruption.

Such urgent scriptural interpretation is quite unlike the brittle, victorious mockery hurled at millenarianism by Restoration satirists. Vaughan's abiding fascination with the Apocalypse is most obvious, perhaps, in *The Mount of Olives*' regular quotations from contemporary eschatological literature such as Robert Bolton's *Last and Learned Worke of the Four Last Things* (1632) and Drexelius' *De Considerationes Aeternitatis*, a work translated into English by Ralph Winterton in 1632 (it reached its fifth edition by 1650).[20] 'Man in Darkness' urges contemplation of death, judgement and eternity as a powerful force for conversion to a holy life: 'Upon our little inch of time in this life, depends the length and breadth, the height and depth of Immortality in the world to come: even two eternities, the one infinitely accursed, the other infinitely blessed' (*V*, 178). Vaughan's conversion, like St Augustine's, was spurred on by these 'two eternities', which between them led him to meditate on the relations between time and eternity, and the changes from corruption to incorruption, from separation to union with God, which mark the boundary.[21] The callow youth shamefully displayed by poems like 'The Garland' needed the stick of damnation to drive him to consider the state of his soul; one is reminded how grateful the regenerate Vaughan is (in 'The Law and the Gospel', for instance) for the Law's punitive power, as though terrified of his too ample freedom under the gospel.

Like Joseph Hall, Vaughan must have kept abreast of the Apocalyptic tradition, if only in order to refute it successfully.[22] He shows little interest in universal chronology or synchronisms, two of the techniques developed by commentators like Thomas Brightman, Heinrich Alsted and Joseph Mede.[23] Rather, Vaughan used the Apocalypse to humble

[20] Bolton, *Mr Boltons Last and Learned Worke of the Foure Last Things, Death, Judgement, Hell and Heaven* (1632); Hieremias Drexelius, *The Considerations of Drexelius upon Eternitie*, trans. Ralph Winterton (1632).

[21] See the preface to Christopher Love, *Heavens Glory, Hells Terror* (1653) for a contemporary version of Augustine's conversion from Epicure to Christian; cf. 'The hidden Treasure', ll. 23–4.

[22] MacCabe, *Joseph Hall*, 317.

[23] The major millenarian commentaries in English are: Thomas Brightman, *A Revelation of the Revelation* (1615), Joseph Mede, *Clavis Apocalyptica* (1627), translated as *The Key of the Revelation* (1633), and Johannes Alsted, *The Beloved City; or The Saints Reign on Earth a Thousand Yeares* (1643). On these works and their authors, see Firth, *Apocalyptic Tradition*,

himself in pious meditations on death, judgement and heaven (in *Silex* Part 1) and to stimulate thoughts of eternity by attending to the mysterious changes of the Last Day (in *The Mount of Olives*).[24] His uses of Revelation were thus more like those of medieval piety than the revolutionary political readings of the 1650s. For medieval eschatologists, as Marjorie Reeves notes, 'the climax of history had already been reached and passed in the life and death of Jesus . . . For all future generations what remained of the time-process was a period of waiting until the End was consummated in the second coming. The only movement was that of individual souls on their pilgrimage.'[25] This notion of indefinite waiting agrees exactly with Vaughan's view of an indefinitely postponed Apocalypse and with Joseph Hall's beautiful vow to 'wait at the threshold of grace untill my changing come; with a trembling joy, with a longing patience, with a comfortable hope'.[26]

Like Joseph Hall, Henry Vaughan believed both that the world was in a last age, and also, crucially, that the time of its end was known only to God. This strongly anti-millennial idea inspires several of the biblical end-texts Vaughan appends to poems in Part 1 of *Silex Scintillans*. To 'Day of Judgement', the fourth poem of *Silex* (1650), Vaughan adds St Peter's advice to the primitive church: 'Now the end of all things is at hand, be you therefore sober, and watching in prayer' (1 Peter 4: 7). The end-text to 'The Lampe', which speaks deeply to Vaughan's anti-millennial concerns and to Joseph Hall's vow of waiting, is Christ's powerful warning that 'you know not when the master of the house commeth, at Even, or at midnight, or at the Cock-crowing, or in the morning' (Mark 13: 35). And in

ch. 7; Christianson, *Reformers and Babylon*, 124–31; David Katz, *Philo-Semitism and the Readmission of the Jews to England 1603–1655* (Oxford, 1982), 91–4; Capp, *Fifth Monarchy Men*, 28–31; Michael Murrin, 'Revelation and Two Seventeenth-Century Commentators', 125–46 in Patrides and Wittreich (eds.), *Apocalypse* [on Pareus and Mede]. Mede was the teacher of Henry More, Thomas Vaughan's pamphleteering opponent in the 1650s.

[24] Eschatological meditation features notably in 'Death. *A Dialogue*', 'Resurrection and Immortality', 'Day of Judgement', 'The Evening-watch', 'Buriall', 'And do they so?', 'Sure, theres a tye of Bodyes', 'Rules and Lessons' (ll. 121–44), 'Corruption', 'The Check', 'The World', 'I walkt the other day', 'Ascension-day', 'Ascension-Hymn', 'They are all gone into the world of light!', 'White Sunday', 'Cock-crowing', 'The Palm-tree', 'The Bird', 'The Timber', 'The Jews', 'The Rain-bow', 'The Seed growing secretly', 'As time one day', 'Fair and yong light!', 'The Stone', 'The Men of War', 'The Night', 'Jacobs Pillow, and Pillar', 'The day of Judgement', 'The Throne', 'Death', 'The Book', 'L'Envoy'. In *The Mount of Olives*, see particularly 'Man in Darkness' (168–90).

[25] Marjorie Reeves, 'The Medieval Inheritance', in Patrides and Wittreich (eds.), *Apocalypse*, I. 2, 40–72 (41).

[26] Joseph Hall, *Susurrium cum Deo, Together with the Souls Farewell* (1651), 419.

'The Dawning', Vaughan prayed that he would 'all my busie age | In thy free services ingage', so that

> when that day, and hour shal come
> In which thy self wil be the Sun,
> Thoul't find me drest and on my way,
> Watching the Break of thy great day.
>
> (ll. 45–8)

The poems of *Silex Scintillans* cry out for the quick coming of Christ, and beg Him belligerently to come and judge the world and wipe away the tears of the Saints; certainly, too, they wonder when the Bridegroom will return (in 'The day of Judgement', for instance). Yet it is not the proximity of the Apocalypse that guides the writing of these poems, but simply its inevitability. Millenarian timetables of the imminent are useless to someone who urges that 'Incertainties we cannot know', and is sure only of the eventual apocalyptic consummation of Creation revealed by scripture.[27] Vaughan's poetry revolves around the thought encapsulated in Joseph Hall's exhortation to his readers that they should 'fix not their belief upon any Kingdome of Christ our Saviour, but spirituall and heavenly'.[28]

Just as sure as his antagonists that the world was in its last age, Vaughan says so twice in *Silex Scintillans*: once in 'White Sunday', which speaks of '*These last*' days and 'this last and lewdest age' (ll. 26, 39) and once in 'The Jews', where British apostasy parallels Israel's rejection and persecution of Christ. The conversion of the Jews at the Last Judgement is another important locus of Vaughan's anti-millenarianism in *Silex* (1655). Belief in the Jewish conversion, traditionally a signal of the Second Coming, arose from apocalyptic readings of Romans 11: 25–6: 'blindness in part is happened to Israel, until the fullness of the Gentiles be come in and so all Israel shall be saved'. Vaughan made a familiar interpretation of this verse, then, when he wrote in 'The Jews' that the Apocalypse was near since 'by all signs | Our [British Christians'] fulness too is now come in' (ll. 26–7).[29]

Silex Part 2 reads the Jews' loss of the birthright as a monition for Britons: the two poems entitled 'Jesus Weeping' style Britain as an antitype of Jerusalem, that 'blessed, unhappy City' over which Christ weeps

---

[27] 'Sure, there's a tye of Bodyes!', l. 23.   [28] Quoted by MacCabe, *Joseph Hall*, 320.
[29] On importance of this prophecy in the revolutionary decades, see Katz, *Philo-Semitism*, 90–1.

in Luke 19: 41; and 'The Stone' (nine poems later) fears that in this last and lewdest age the British, like the Jews, have 'promis'd much, but did refuse | Performance' (ll. 46–8). Vaughan's typologies cast doubt on the privileged spiritual status which seventeenth-century Puritans assumed for the nation, puncturing the growing millenarian hope that the Jews would return to Britain for conversion before Christ's Second Coming.[30] Among the notable champions of such philo-Semitism was the Welshman William Erbery, a millenarian and mystic who preached extensively in south-east Wales in the early 1650s.[31] Erbery had repeatedly petitioned Parliament to readmit the Jews so that their pre-apocalyptic conversion might occur soon and in what he and others believed to be the chosen place.[32] His *Apocrypha: The Second Epistle of Paul to the Church of Laodicea* (1652) prophesied that the millennium would begin in Wales, having heard the same view in 'Mr. [Peter] *Sterry's* sermon to the Northern Presbytery, proposing it strongly to the brethren'.[33] His conviction shares its nationalistic edge with the chiliastic rhetoric of those other prominent Welsh Saints Morgan Llwyd and Vavasor Powell, both of whom evolved myths of pure Ancient British religion to bolster their hopes for Puritanism in Wales.[34] Erbery taught that the Welsh were 'pure *Britaines*' while the English were 'of kin to the Dutch, that dull and muddy people' and he propagated the idea—extremely powerful as a justification and inspiration for the Propagation—that the Welsh were descended from the Jews: 'Besides, 'tis of the opinion of some, that the *Britaines* are of the *Iewes*, but the old *Dutch* and *Germanes* are mere *Gentiles*, and so are the *English* still'.[35]

As well as likening the Welsh to the Jews, William Erbery had also promulgated the idea of the English race as a reprobate Esau to the elect Welsh nation of Jacob.[36] Vaughan's awareness of philo-Semitic speculation among the Welsh Saints spikes his reference to the story of Jacob and Esau in the penultimate stanza of 'The Jews':

---

[30] On the readmission and conversion of the Jews, see ibid., 89–126, 'The Calling of the Jews'; and P. Toon (ed.), *Puritans, the Millennium, and the Future of Israel: Puritan Eschatology, 1600 to 1660* (Cambridge, 1970); Hessayon, '"Gold tried in the fire"', 125 and nn. 114, 115.

[31] Jenkins, *Protestant Dissenters*, 21–2.

[32] Hill, *World Turned Upside-Down*, 193; Capp, *Fifth Monarchy Men*, 59–60.

[33] Erbery, *Bishop of London*, sig. E2ʳ.

[34] Smith, *Literature and Revolution*, 271–5.

[35] Erbery, *Bishop of London*, sig. [D4]ᵛ.

[36] Erbery, *Bishop of London*, sig. [D4]ᵛ. Esau and Jacob as types of the elect are discussed extensively in Chapter 2.

You were the *eldest* childe, and when
Your stony hearts despised love,
The *youngest*, ev'n the Gentiles then
Were chear'd, your jealousie to move.

(ll. 42–5)

Both Erbery and Vaughan are using Jacob and Esau as types of the elect nation, but whereas the Welsh Saint sees England as a race of Esaus, the Silurist likens the whole nation to the crucifiers of Christ. Vaughan welcomes the imminent Apocalypse, saying in 'The Jews' that it is but 'few hours hence' (l. 30), but for him the conversion of the Jews is a threat and a warning to British Christians, not perfection proclaimed:

Thus, Righteous Father! doest thou deal
With Brutish men; Thy gifts go round
By turns, and timely, and so heal
The lost Son by the newly found.

(ll. 46–9)

This punning attack on the British is aimed at the whole nation, but it also singles out those ancient Britons, the Welsh.[37] 'The Jews' closes by turning upside-down the millenarian optimism of the Welsh Saints and introducing a hint of menace in the closing thought of 'The Jews' that God will 'heal | The lost Son by the newly found'. This could suggest that Britons will save the Jews, a cherished opinion of Erbery, Theauraujohn Tany and other millenarians; but a more sinister reading of 'heal . . . by' is *take the place of*, a strong warning that the British have become less worthy of salvation than the Jews were when God altered the spiritual franchise by sending his only Son. Since Vaughan looks forward to seeing the conversion of the Jews himself: 'O then that I | Might live, and see the Olive bear | Her proper branches!' there is hope for some—but the hard of heart are duly warned.

---

[37] Vaughan uses *British* to mean Ancient Britons in 'Man in Darkness', *V*, 174 (Aneurin is 'The *Brittish Bard*'). Vaughan's use there avoids anachronism, as does James Howell's in a 1645 letter cited by *OED*: 'He calls . . . Helen an English woman; whereas, she was purely British, and that there was no such nation upon earth called English at that time' (from Howell's *Letters*, published 1650); see *OED*, British *a.* (*sb.*) 1a, 1b, which records the word in use throughout the seventeenth century. Vaughan's other most prominent use of 'Brittish' is in the title of 'The Brittish Church' (*Silex* Part 1).

SMILES OF THE DAY-STAR

Silex Scintillans Part 2 opens with a pair of dazzlingly anti-millenarian poems, 'Ascension-day' and 'Ascension Hymn', in which Vaughan apprehends the Apocalypse, the Second Coming of Christ and the purification of man at the Last Judgement in a non-millennial and anti-radical vision. Here, too, Vaughan begins to deploy the means of resistance I outlined above, defusing verses of Revelation often cited by millenarians and invoking the Apocalypse through scriptural images which together resist the idea of a thousand-year rule. 'Ascension-day' reflects on the meaning of the Ascension for a Christian liver, both in this life—

> Lord Jesus! with what sweetness and delights,
> Sure, holy hopes, high joys and quickning flights
> Dost thou feed thine!
>
> (ll. 1–3)

—and, more importantly, in the time after time, at the end of all things, at the 'last great day' (l. 29). What Christ's Ascension at Bethany means most of all to 'Ascension-day' is that He shall one day return there to judge the world; thus the Ascension becomes a locus for Vaughan's apocalyptic meditations. In the following 'Ascension-Hymn', Vaughan further strengthens the anti-radical arguments of 'Ascension-day' by alluding to a series of Old Testament prophecies which postpones until the Last Judgement those changes which millenarians were proclaiming on earth.

'Ascension-day' challenges Nigel Smith's theory that Vaughan's Apocalypse can be distinguished in two ways from the Welsh Saints' millennium: 'The Apocalypse is the Day of Judgement, not the Second Coming of Christ. The millennium is subjugated to the always present, gradual slowing down of the world; the apocalypse becomes the poetic mode of apprehending final purification and resurrection.'[38] The second part of this remark is acute and worth pursuing through Vaughan's poems in order to show how Vaughan's images of purity have anti-millenarian implications (something I shall come to in a moment). The first part, however, oddly denies those many rapturous calls to Christ in *Silex Scintillans* to 'come Lord *Jesus* quickly!' ('Buriall', l. 40). Both parts of *Silex Scintillans* yearn passionately for the Second Coming, so that to correct Smith, one must say that Vaughan's Apocalypse is *both* the Second Coming of Christ *and* the day of Judgement. It is this togetherness of the Son's return

---

[38] Smith, *Literature and Revolution*, 269.

and His Judgement Day, in fact, which denies the millennium and dissolves the possibility of a thousand-year rule between Christ's coming and his eventual judgement of man. Once eternity has begun, there can be no thousand-year rule of the Saints.

This anti-millenarian force of *Silex Scintillans* resides largely in its scriptural metaphors, which establish that Christ's Second Coming will mark the start of eternal life and not the beginning of an earthly millennium. In particular I am thinking of Vaughan's fondness for the apocalyptic 'Sun of Righteousness, risen with healing in his wings' from the prophecy of Malachi 4: 2, 'the Sunne [that will] never set' ('Death. *A Dialogue*', l. 32) and the 'all-surprizing light' which might break at any hour (even midnight) but whose arrival is the certain herald of the New Jerusalem:

> O the *new worlds* new, quickning Sun!
> Ever the same, and never done!
> The seers of whose sacred light
> Shall all be drest in shining white.
>
> ('L'Envoy', ll. 1–4; my italics)

Just as often, Christ is 'that morning-star' from Revelation 22: 16, whose early beams signal the Last Judgement in 'The Dawning' (ll. 5, 23–4) and for which Vaughan waits, with patience, at the end of 'The Bird': 'Brightness and mirth, and love and faith, all flye, | Till the Day-spring breaks forth again from high' (ll. 31–2). In coupling these two prophetic metaphors with that of the Last Day, *Silex Scintillans* evolves an ongoing apocalyptic conceit in which Christ's Second Coming is the first event of the last, eternal day of the *new world*; his powerful confluence of metaphors washes away the thousand-year rule of Christ and the saints, and looks forward to His Coming just after the end of time, not before it.[39]

The distinction between time and timelessness reaffirms Vaughan's opposition to the millennium. 'Buriall' tells Christ that Time 'Thy servant is, and waits on thee' and implores him to 'Cutt then the summe, | Lord haste, Lord come, | O come Lord *Jesus* quickly!' When there is no

---

[39] Apocalyptic images of dawning find their complement in Vaughan's other favourite conceit of life as a 'neast of nights', for which see 'Death. *A Dialogue*', 'The Night' and especially 'The Pilgrimage', where the pilgrim admits 'I may | Have yet more days, more nights to Count', where 'more days, more nights' means 'nights as well as days' but also 'nights (my days are only nights)' (ll. 25–6).

time, no 'hours, days, years' but only a '*Ring* of pure and endless light',
then there can be no thousand years, and so no rule of Christ on earth
('The World [I]', ll. 4, 2). In 'The Evening-watch', the Body explains to
the Soul that

> Heav'n
> Is a plain watch, and without figures winds
> All ages up; who drew this Circle even
> He fils it; Dayes, and hours are *Blinds*.
>
> (ll. 11–14)

Judgement and eternal life begin as soon as He comes, at which time even
the very notion of a millennium is lost. A trace of Vaughan's stubborn resistance to the millennium therefore lies within every mention of the Sun
of Righteousness or the Morning Star in *Silex Scintillans*.

'Ascension-day' holds a special place in Vaughan's corpus because as
well as applying scriptural metaphors of Christ as the Morning Star, it relates His return to the purification of man. It is an anti-millenarian combination. Nigel Smith begins to recognize this in the second part of his
observation that Vaughan's Apocalypse is 'the poetic mode of apprehending final purification and resurrection'. This is correct, but it does miss the
point that this purification is the locus of anti-millenarian resistance in
'Ascension-day' and 'Ascension-Hymn', and that both poems focus on a
single scriptural image of purity: the white garments which will be given
to the Saints on the Last Day. The white-clad host of angels which flies up
with the ascending Christ in the opening of 'Ascension-day' reminds
Vaughan of the resurrected saints on the Last Day, when they will be re-
warded with white robes signifying their new purity. In Revelation, St
John reveals to all that: 'He that overcometh, the same shall be clothed in
white raiment . . . And white robes were given unto every one of them
. . . These are they which came out of great tribulation, and have washed
their robes, and made them white in the blood of the lamb' (Revelation 3:
5; 6: 11; 7: 14). White was the robe of the martyr, and to mid-seventeenth-
century Anglicans was also the robe of their murdered king, Charles, who
had chosen to be crowned in 1625 wearing white rather than the traditional purple. Compounding the coincidences, he had also requested to
have his coronation sermon that day preached on Revelation 2: 10, the
passage in which St John reveals that the faithful will have tribulation
on earth, but a crown in heaven. Though Vaughan does not allude to
Charles's coronation in the Ascension poems, it is extremely doubtful that

he was ignorant of the widespread Royalist view that Charles's coronation robes were prophetic of the king's martyrdom in January 1649.[40]

After setting its meditative scene as the departure of Christ from Mount Olivet, 'Ascension-day' is structured by a series of time slips which push the speaker's mind forward and back from the meridian point of Christ's Ascension to the beginning and end of time. The poem's vision of first and last things is relayed with a rare blend of poetic élan and ingenuous wonder by Vaughan's speaker, whose mental journeying is propelled, so to speak, by a repeated vision of folds of white cloth: first the angels' and the saints' robes (ll. 25–32), then the fresh robes of Eden (ll. 39–48), then those of the two men in white who prophecy Christ's return after the Ascension (ll. 58–9), and finally the white robes of two mysterious witnesses in Revelation.

Vaughan's inspiration for taking the Ascension as his apocalyptic locus at the start of *Silex* (1655) may have been the Prayer Book, which reflects a long tradition of liturgical association.[41] Its epistle for Ascension Day, Acts 1: 1–11, culminates in the prophecy of two men in white that Christ 'shall so come, even as ye have sene him goe into heaven' (*BCP*, 127), while the Collect for the same day takes faith in Christ's Ascension for hope in our own: 'that like as we doe beleve thy onely-begotten sonne our lorde to have ascended into the heavens; so we may also in heart and mind thither ascende, and with him continually dwell' (*BCP*, 127). From 1 Peter 4, the epistle for the following Sunday, Vaughan chose the epigraph to *Silex*'s first apocalyptic poem, 'Day of Judgement': 'The ende of all thinges is at hand; be ye therfore sobre, and watch unto praier' (*BCP*, 129).

The white-robed angels of Vaughan's Ascension vision melt into the similarly clad 'Saints and Angels' (l. 26) who will feature in the apocalyptic procession:

> They pass as at the last great day, and run
> In their white robes to seek the risen Sun;
> I see them, hear them, mark their haste, and move
> Amongst them, with them, wing'd with faith and love.
>
> (ll. 29–32)

---

[40] Potter, *Secret Rites*, 77.

[41] Literary and dramatic tradition is less significant here. Rosemary Woolf notes that English play cycles were unusual in finishing with a play on the Last Judgement rather than the Ascension or Pentecost (*English Medieval Mystery Plays* (Oxford, 1970), 299).

Stevie Davies has appreciated the *trompe l'œil* used in this poem to 'trick us into the illusion of an eavesdropping Vaughan literally encompassed by misty, fast-moving presences', a comment which does justice to the way Vaughan thinks himself into the middle of things, but whose sense of *mistiness* is in danger of obscuring the scriptural costuming of Vaughan's scenes.[42] For not only are the Saints now winged like the angels (in Revelation 12, a woman, thought to represent the church, is given wings so that she can escape the assaults of the dragon of Satan[43]) but they are all kitted out in white robes, the promised reward of their faith: 'These are they which came out of great tribulation, and have washed their robes, and made them white with the blood of the lamb' (Revelation 7: 14). So transformed, the Saints are truly *gwyn*: whitened in their pure robes, but also holy, blessed and beautiful, according to the figurative senses of the Welsh word.[44]

Having seen the end of all things, Vaughan's narrator returns to the gospel era, slipping back before the Ascension to Christ's posthumous ministrations, his 'forty days more secret commerce here, | After thy death and Funeral' (ll. 33–4). He finds himself back in Bethany, from where Luke says Christ 'was parted from them, and carried up into heaven' (24: 51) and once more into the presence of the shining robes of Christ's angelic train. At the sight of their white garments, the poem's vision refreshes itself again, now showing the world's very first beginning:

> I walk the fields of *Bethani* which shine
> All now as fresh as *Eden*, and as fine.
> Such was the bright world, on the first seventh day,
> Before man brought forth sin, and sin decay;
> When like a Virgin clad in *Flowers* and *green*
> The pure earth sat, and the fair woods had seen
> No frost, but flourish'd in that youthful vest,
> With which their great Creator had them drest.
>
> (ll. 37–44)

The Ascension, the Apocalypse and now this first Sunday are all felt as spiritual springtimes, a conceit which recalls that 'new Spring' of the pilgrim's soul in 'Regeneration'. Like the *Meditations on the Six Days of*

---

[42] Davies, *Henry Vaughan*, 167.   [43] See Rev. 12: 14 and cf. Ps. 55: 6.

[44] *Geiriadur Prifysgol Cymru: A Dictionary of the Welsh Language*, 3 vols. (Cardiff, 1968–87) gwyn, 1.a. white, greyish-white, pale; light, shining bright; brilliant, white hot; c. holy, blessed, beatific, good, happy (sanctaidd, bendigaid, gwynfydedig).

Creation attributed to Traherne, Vaughan's picture of a 'pure earth' looks back to a largely medieval tradition of hexameral contemplation.[45] But where the author of the *Meditations* was drawn to the tremendous *usefulness* of the earth for all Adam's needs, its 'Beauty, Profit, and Pleasure' (a very Trahernian usage, which has misled scholars), Vaughan admires the unfallen world for sweetness and purity. His Eden is like the original of Thomas Carew's Spring, that time when 'now no more the frost | Candies the grasse' and 'The Vallies, hills, and woods, in rich araye | Welcome the comming of the long'd for May'.[46] Vaughan, too, dresses Eden metaphorically as a 'Virgin clad in *Flowers* and *green*', a 'youthful vest'; but of course the clothes he describes are God-given creations. They are also the key to Vaughan's meditations in 'Ascension-day'.

When Vaughan's speaker looks up from the vestments of Eden it is straight to heaven: 'Heav'n above them shin'd like molten glass, | While all the Planets did unclouded pass | And Springs, like dissolv'd Pearls their Streams did pour' (ll. 45–7). This vision of prelapsarian clarity in which man could gaze at heaven without meteorological impediment starts the meditating mind moving forward to the resumption of God's eternal spring at the Last Judgement. The crystalline heaven begins to blend into the New Jerusalem described in Revelation as 'like a jasper stone, clear as crystal' and 'pure gold, like unto clear glass' (Revelation 21: 11, 18) and the *Streams* of dissolved pearl recall Vaughan's vision of the last changes in 'L'Envoy', the final poem in *Silex Scintillans* (1655):

> Arise, arise!
> And like old cloaths fold up these skies,
> This long worn veyl: then shine and spread
> Thy own bright self over each head,
> And through thy creatures pierce and pass
> Till all becomes like cloudless glass,
> Transparent as the purest day

---

[45] *Meditations on the Six Days of Creation (1717)*, The Augustan Reprint Society No. 119, introd. George R. Guffey (Los Angeles, 1966). The *Meditations* were probably written by a member of Traherne's circle, such as Susannah Hopton. On the hexameral tradition see Guffey's introduction, p. vii, and Michael A. E. Fox, 'Augustinian Hexameral Exegesis in Anglo-Saxon England: Bede, Alcuin, Ælfric and Old English Biblical Verse', Ph.D. thesis (Cambridge, 1997). Later hexameral literature is discussed by R. A. Sayce, *The French Biblical Epic in the Seventeenth Century* (Oxford, 1955); Frank Egleston Robbins, *The Hexaemeral Literature* (Chicago, 1912).

[46] Traherne (attrib.), *Meditations*, 32; Thomas Carew, *Poems 1640 Together with Poems from the Wyburd Manuscript* (Menston, 1969), 3.

And without blemish or decay,
Fixt by thy spirit to a state
For evermore immaculate.

('L'Envoy', ll. 7–16)

While 'these fair thoughts' are leading 'Ascension-day' back to Bethany, their eschatological undercurrents guide the poem to the two men in white who appear after the Ascension to prophesy the Apocalypse. As Vaughan versifies from Acts 1: 10–11:

Having lost thee, behold two men in white!
Two and no more; *what two attest, is true,*
Was thine own answer to the stubborn Jew.
Come then thou faithful witness! come dear Lord
Upon the Clouds again to judge this world!

(ll. 58–62)

Biblical allusions come thick and fast in these difficult and powerful lines. Vaughan first vindicates the prophecy of the men in white by remembering what Jesus said when asked to prove his identity to the Pharisees: knowing that Jewish law demanded two witnesses to a truth, Jesus offered them the double proof of His word and that of His father—'though I bear record of my self, yet my record is true' (John 8: 14)—making him a unique but faithful witness. However, *faithful witness* is not Vaughan's coinage, but comes from Revelation 1: 5, where John calls Christ 'the faithful witness, and first begotten of the dead, and the prince of the kings of the earth' (a passage which Vaughan recalls elsewhere in 'Man in Darkness' (*V*, 188)). Other texts also impinge: in Revelation 3: 14 God is 'the Amen, the faithful and true witness', and it is likely that Vaughan also is thinking of 1 Timothy 6: 13, where Paul tells Timothy that 'Jesus Christ . . . before Pontius Pilate witnessed a good confession'. And in John 18: 37 Jesus tells Pilate that 'Thou sayest that I am a king. To this end was I born, and for this cause came I into the world, that I should bear witness unto the truth'.

Vaughan affirms the prophecy of the two men in white by conflating Luke's account in Acts with Christ's in John's gospel; this defence also introduces the idea of *witness*. To all who care to listen (and to stubborn Esaus who will not) Vaughan proposes the bible as an incontrovertible witness to the Second Coming of Christ, instancing most powerfully the 'true and faithful witness' of this fact: Christ himself. Jeremy Taylor's *An*

Apology for Authorized and Set Forms of Liturgy against the Pretence of the Spirit (1649) takes up a position close to Vaughan's here when it criticizes the fashion for *ex tempore* prayer over liturgical or other set forms:

We are sure that Christ and Christ's spirit taught us this prayer; they only gather by conjectures and opinions that in their *ex tempore* or 'conceived' forms the Spirit of Christ teacheth them. So much then as certainties are better than uncertainties and God's word better than man's, so much is this set form, besides the infinite advantages in the matter, better than their *ex tempore* or 'conceived' forms.[47]

In Vaughan's view as in Taylor's, the witness of the Word of God—both in the sense that the bible is the Word and that Christ is the Word made flesh—trumps the words of men. A Puritan belief in the Christian duty of witnessing one's faith in speech or writing lay behind the sharing of spiritual narratives of rebirth and regeneration in church meetings, and so also ultimately behind the growth of early modern life writing. But the mid-seventeenth century also threw up extreme strains of personal witness in the shape of radical apocalyptic preachers and prophets, men and women who professed their dreams and visions as divine messages. Vaughan bemoans this explosion of new witness at the expense of the old, the self-scripted in place of the scriptural, the unfaithful in place of the 'true and faithful' witness.[48]

'Ascension-day' identifies the men in white as anti-millennial witnesses because their vision includes the detail that Christ shall return 'as ye have seen him go into heaven'. According to Luke, this was through the clouds—'And a cloud received him out of their sight' (Acts 1: 9)—or, as Vaughan put it, Christ will come 'Upon the clouds again to judge this world!' (l. 62). Since Vaughan's poems so regularly envisage Christ as Morning Star or heavenly Sun, it makes poetic and anti-millennial sense to them that Christ should come shining through the clouds at whatever

---

[47] Taylor, *Works*, v. 288.

[48] Spiritual autobiography, the most common form of written witness, reflected the verbal testimony of the working of faith required for entry to the gathered churches. See L. Lerner, 'Puritanism and the Spiritual Autobiography', *Hibbert Journal,* 55 (1956–7), 373–86; Paul Delany, *British Autobiography in the Seventeenth Century* (1969), 81–104. Examples of verbal testimony can be easily found in *The Minutes of the First Independent Church (now Bunyan Meeting) at Bedford 1656–1766*, ed. by H. G. Tibbutt, Bedfordshire Historical Record Society vol. 55 (Bedford, 1976), e.g. 'John Wilson's desire of joyning with the congregation was mentioned, and it was agreed that he should give an account of the worke of grace in his soule, next meeting' (23); cf. William Erbery's collected writings, published posthumously as *The Testimony of William Erbery* (1658).

time the Last Day is to begin. Adding to the anti-millenarian argument of 'Ascension-day', the bible's best-known images of clouds are all from Revelation. Chapter 1, for instance, reveals 'Behold, he [Christ] cometh with clouds; and every eye shall see him, and they also which pierced him' and later on John sees an angelic Christ figure 'clothed with a cloud' (1: 7, 10: 1).

Of even greater significance to 'Ascension-day', as to *Silex Scintillans* as a whole, is the prophecy of Christ's riding on a cloud, a passage recalled at the end of 'Corruption' (in *Silex* Part 1) and 'The Seed growing secretly' (Part 2), both of which yearn for the reaping of Christ's spiritual harvest:

And I looked, and behold a white cloud, and upon the cloud one sat like unto the Son of man, having on his head a golden crown, and in his hand a sharp sickle. And another angel came . . . crying . . . Thrust in thy sickle, and reap: for the time is come for thee to reap; for the harvest of the earth is ripe. And he that sat on the cloud thrust in his sickle on the earth; and the earth was reaped. (Revelation 14: 14–16)[49]

Vaughan takes anti-millennial comfort from the scriptural provenance of the two men's prophecy that Christ 'shalt make the Clouds thy seate' ('Day of Judgement'), and he is almost certainly also thinking—in yet another allusion made by these astonishing fleet lines—of Christ's lesson to the disciples:

Moreover if thy brother shall trespass against thee, go and tell him his fault between thee and him alone: if he shall hear thee, thou hast gained thy brother. But if he will not hear thee, then take with thee one or two more, that in the mouth of two or three witnesses every word may be established. (Matthew 18: 15–16)

Two witnesses to Christ's cloudy return suffice to establish its truth, just as two Anglicans ('two or three gathered together', as the Prayer Book litany remembers[50]) could witness this truth against any number of their enemies, with the full authority of the Word.

Two final New Testament passages lend scriptural witness. First, Vaughan glances at the famous 'cloud of witnesses' passage of Hebrews (12: 1–2), which urges comfort to Christians in the remembrance of their fellow pilgrims. Second and more importantly for Vaughan's anti-millennial effort, 'Ascension-day' recalls the most mysterious of all

---

[49] Compare 'Corruption', ll. 39–40; 'The Seed growing secretly', 47–8.

[50] *BCP*, 367: 'Almightie god, which hast geven us grace at this time with one accorde to make oure common supplicacions unto thee, and doest promise that when two or three be gathered in thy name, thou wilt graunte their requestes'; cf. Matt. 18: 20.

persecuted witnesses, those two sackclothed figures in Revelation 11 whose ministry, death and ascension God reveals to John:

> I will give power unto my two witnesses, and they shall prophesy a thousand two hundred and threescore days, clothed in sackcloth . . . And when they shall have finished their testimony, the beast that ascendeth out of the bottomless pit shall make war against them, and shall overcome them, and kill them . . . And after three days and an half the Spirit of life from God entered into them, and they stood upon their feet; and great fear fell upon them which saw them. And they heard a great voice from heaven saying unto them, Come up hither. And they ascended up to heaven in a cloud; and their enemies beheld them. (Revelation 11: 3, 7, 11–12)

Since the Reformation, many had attempted to identify these two witnesses with actual historical figures and thereby to place the immediate present in the context of an unfolding apocalyptic drama. The more extreme of their number in Vaughan's day, notably Richard Farnham and John Bull in the 1640s and Lodowick Muggleton and John Reeve in the 1650s, revived a medieval tradition of declaring themselves to be the witnesses, often declaring the 1,260 days of their preaching (according to Revelation) to have begun.[51]

Vaughan's counter-claims adopt slightly different means in 'Ascension-Hymn', next in *Silex* Part 2. The white robes of Revelation reappear, now juxtaposed with allusions to Old Testament prophecies of Apocalypse, which act as a scriptural complement to the predominantly New Testament scripture uses of 'Ascension-day'. Malachi's prophecy of the Fuller is Vaughan's best text:

> But since he
> That brightness soil'd,
> His garments be
> All dark and spoil'd,
> And here are left as nothing worth,
> Till the Refiners fire breaks forth.
>
> Then comes he!
> Whose mighty light

---

[51] See Rodney L. Petersen, *Preaching in the Last Days: The Theme of the 'Two Witnesses' in the Sixteenth and Seventeenth Centuries* (New York, 1993), 3–27, 200–26; Capp, *Fifth Monarchy Men*, 43; and for Farnham and Bull, see Thomas, *Religion and the Decline of Magic*, 159–61; John Reeve, *A Transcendent Spiritual Treatise* (1652) and Lodowick Muggleton, *The Acts of the Witnesses of the Spirit* (1699).

> Made his cloathes be
> Like Heav'n, all bright;
> The Fuller, whose pure blood did flow
> To make stain'd man more white then snow.

(ll. 25–36)

The sullying of the Fall requires Christ's blood, a paradoxical whitening agent, to turn man's spiritual clothing into the white garments of the Saints.[52] Malachi's prophecy that God will come 'like a refiner's fire, and like fullers' soap: and he shall sit as a refiner and purifier of silver' (Malachi 3: 2–3) was so congenial to Christianity that the book of Malachi was placed last in the Old Testament, nearest to the gospel, by the early Christian councils.[53] Luther understood the application of its cleaning metaphor to Christ when he explained that fuller's soap is 'a sharp cleaning agent or soap that washes stains out of garments' and that He would use it to bleach man's soul; or, as an exegete of Vaughan's day, William Sclater, put it: 'he scoureth, and purgeth them [his servants] from their sins; no fire so purging as Christ; the fullers sope makes not so white, as the bloud of Christ'.[54]

The word *fuller* connects Malachi with Mark's account of Christ's transfiguration, since there the Fuller is himself bathed in divine light so that his raiments shone 'white as snow; so as no fuller on earth can white them' (Mark 9: 3). Vaughan clearly knew the tradition of medieval exegesis which figured Christ's Incarnation as a clothing with flesh,[55] remembering it in 'The Incarnation, and Passion' (*Silex* Part 1), which looks forward to the time when Christ will purify the flesh of the ancients through the power of his own sacrificed flesh:

> To put on Clouds instead of light,
> And cloath the morning-starre with dust,

[52] Also the subject of 'Easter Hymn', another calendrical poem (ll. 1–4).

[53] For contemporary commentary, see William Sclater, *A Brief, and Plain Commentary, with Notes: Not More Useful, Than Seasonable, upon the Whole Prophecie of Malachy* (1650), 124–36; George Hutcheson, *A Brief Exposition on the XII Small Prophets*, 3 vols. (1654–5), III, 274–9, 289–93; Edward Pococke, *A Commentary on the Prophecy of Malachi* (Oxford, 1677), 82–90; Hessayon, '"Gold tried in the fire"', ch. 2, details Theauraujohn Tany's intriguing appropriation of this text.

[54] *Lectures on the Minor Prophets*, ed. by Hilton C. Oswald, vol. xviii of *Luther's Works*, ed. by Jaroslav Pelikan and Helmut Lehmann (Saint Louis, Mo., 1975), 410 (Luther's lectures were first published in the Wittenberg edition, vols. iv and v (1552, 1554)); Sclater, *Commentary*, 134.

[55] This tradition is discussed by Douglas Gray, *Themes and Images in the Medieval English Religious Lyric* (1972), 106–9.

Was a translation of such height
As, but in thee, was ne'r exprest.

(ll. 5–8)

When the morning star reappears, bursting through the clouds to begin
the Last Day, it will be without clothes and untranslated, as man finally
sees God face to face and becomes dressed in light himself.

'Ascension-Hymn' ends with a reassurance of apocalyptic transformation at the Last Judgement inspired by the prophecy of Ezekiel:

Hee alone
And none else can
Bring bone to bone
And rebuild man,
And by his all subduing might
Make clay ascend more quick then light.

(ll. 37–42)

To Ezekiel, the dry bones which 'came together, bone to his bone . . . and
they lived, and stood up upon their feet, an exceeding great army' reveal
Israel united in the promised land (Ezekiel 37: 7, 10). Through the eyes of
the New Testament, they promise heavenly life, the joining of the bones
signifying not only the unifying of the Christian family, but the bodily
resurrection, an idea signalled by Vaughan's word *subdue*, which looks to
Philippians 3: 20–1: 'the Lord Jesus Christ who shall change our vile body,
that it may be fashioned like unto his glorious body, according to the
working whereby he is able even to subdue all things unto himself'.[56]
Vaughan's concern with the covenant by which God has promised that
He will 'ne'er betray man's trust' is a point of return for *Silex Scintillans*;
and it is clear from Vaughan's prose too that Ezekiel 37 spoke strongly to
him.[57] 'Man in Darkness' cites the prophecy as a comforting promise of
resurrection: 'These last words [Job 14: 12] were put in for our *comfort*,
and imply the *resurrection* or the time of restoring of all things. This was
manifested to *Ezekiel* in the vision of dry bones' (*V*, 175). This theme was
picked up neatly by Vaughan's admiring imitator Nathaniel Wanley, who

---

[56] The prophecy has also been thought to pertain both to the General Resurrection and
to the restoration of the Jewish Nation (see William Lowth, *A Commentary upon the
Prophet Ezekiel* (1723), 301–2).

[57] For instance 'To the pious memory of C.W.', published in *Thalia Rediviva* but written in 1653 to Vaughan's cousin Charles Walbeoffe: 'For the great Victour fought for us, and
Hee | Counts ev'ry dust, that is lay'd up of thee' (ll. 81–2).

asked 'Can death be faithfull or the grave be just | Or shall my tombe
restore my scattred dust?'[58]

Like 'Ascension-day', then, 'Ascension-Hymn' proposes the Last
Judgement as the Christian's true focus of apocalyptic hope. It celebrates
Christ's preparation for the Ascension of Man through his own Ascension, stressing that reward comes only at the very last, and draws a clear
distinction between earthly and heavenly life. This distinction prepares
for, as it underlies, the next poem in Part 2, and one of Vaughan's greatest
achievements, 'They are all gone into the world of light!'

> They are all gone into the world of light!
>   And I alone sit lingring here;
> Their very memory is fair and bright,
>   And my sad thoughts doth clear.
>
> .   .   .   .   .
>
> O Father of eternal life, and all
>   Created glories under thee!
> Resume thy spirit from this world of thrall
>   Into true liberty.
>
> Either disperse these mists, which blot and fill
>   My perspective (still) as they pass,
> Or else remove me hence unto that hill,
>   Where I shall need no glass.
>
> (ll. 1–4, 33–40)

It is hard not to respect and be moved by the distinction these elegiac lines
draw between this *world of thrall* and the heavenly *world of light*, not least
because the spirit of their author is sitting with such longing sadness and
desire on the threshold of grace. 'Vanity of Spirit', placed early in *Silex*
(1650), renounces as hubris the effort to peer into the heavens in order to
'Descry some part of his great light' (l. 8). Vaughan's humility leaves him
only the peepings of dreams and shadows of eternity and the knowledge
that when the Day-star smiles, he shall put on a new life and awareness as
if it were a white robe:

> Dear, beauteous death! the Jewel of the Just,
>   Shining nowhere, but in the dark;
> What mysteries do lie beyond thy dust;
>   Could man outlook that mark!
>
> (ll. 17–20)

[58] *Poems of Nathaniel Wanley*, 17.

THE PATIENCE OF THE SAINTS

Though it is possible that Vaughan scholars occasionally 'regard him as inevitably correct, by virtue of status and education',[59] Vaughan liked to advertise his own failures if he felt a lesson could be drawn from them. His persistent and principled opposition to the millennium is no exception. At the very point where 'White Sunday' seeks to embarrass false prophets with a series of millenarian parodies, for instance, Vaughan witnesses improperly zealous wishes of his own:

> Not, but that I have wishes too,
> And pray, *These last may be as first,*
> *Or better*; but thou long ago
> Hast said, *These last should be the worst.*

> (ll. 25–8)

As Vaughan turns inward the scripture light that has just exposed 'new lights' as false prophets, what had seemed a meditative satire on Puritan scripture reading becomes an admission whose frankness surprises and invigorates the poem's admonitions with the testimony of personal faith, and lifts 'White Sunday' above the worthy but one-dimensional anthems of Christopher Harvey and Jeremy Taylor.[60] By giving in to the demands of conscience, Vaughan's little admission allows further reference to the prophecy that '*These last should be the worst*' and attests once more to the powerful and saving *but* of scripture. Vaughan's double concession *not, but* is remarkable for being at once a guilty confession, and also something of a conscious display of apocalyptic fervour, showing in equal measure Vaughan's desire to celebrate the Apocalypse and to be innocent of doing it wrongly. It is the passionate caution of an anti-millennialist clearing a space for his yearning amidst the debris of British Christianity. And it suggests that there may be an apocalyptic side to that other great arena of Vaughan's scripture use: his meditations on the Patriarchs. Their days of close commerce with the divine are precisely the sort of purer time which the poet might have mistakenly hoped and prayed for, given the tone of poems like 'Religion', 'Corruption' and 'The Rain-bow'. As well as the '*bright days*' of Eden, the patriarchs' days of 'familiar' 'Conf'rence' are the first times which the last will not resemble for all man's wishes.[61]

---

[59] Smith, *Literature and Revolution*, 270.

[60] Christopher Harvey, *The Synagogue*, 3rd edn. (1657), 161; Jeremy Taylor, *The Golden Grove*, in *Works*, vii. 660–1.

[61] 'Corruption', l. 20, 'Religion', ll. 14, 20.

Enduring the last times without false or extraordinary hope was the great task to which *Silex Scintillans* (1655) is both a testimony and a help to others. In contrast to millenarians, who saw spiritual change all around them, Vaughan learned to take strength in the unchangingness of God and His covenants with man:

> But while time runs, and after it
> Eternity, which never ends,
> Quite through them both, still infinite
> Thy Covenant by *Christ* extends.
>
> ('The Agreement', ll. 49–52)

This strong joy in eternals is a bright counterpoint to *Silex*'s gloomy view of man's greater and greater corruption. Though sin increases, God and His promises remain the same.

> thou the great eternal Rock
> Whose height above all ages shines,
> Art still the same,
>
> .   .   .   .
>
> art the same this day
> And ever, as thou wert of old,
> And nothing doth thy love allay
> But our hearts dead and sinful cold.
>
> ('White Sunday', ll. 45–7, 49–52)[62]

Nothing changes until everything changes. The order and obedience of the stars that Vaughan praises in poems such as 'The Constellation' is itself an apocalyptic sign, since Christ prophesied that 'the stars shall fall from the heavens' before the Day of Judgement comes (Matthew 24: 29). For this star-gazing poet, the continued heavenly presence of the constellations revealed God's unchanging governance of the creation in time; and the same apocalyptic faith underlies 'The Timber', placed sixteenth in *Silex* Part 2, where Vaughan writes of the 'old and still enduring skies' (l. 7).[63]

Vaughan was suspicious of the shifts and changes of mutability. He

---

[62] For God as a rock, see Deut. 32: 4 (Moses' song), 2 Sam. 22: 47 ('the rock of my salvation'), Ps. 18: 2, and 1 Cor. 10: 4 ('the spiritual rock that followed them, and that rock was Christ').

[63] See 'The Constellation', 'Midnight', 'Joy of my life!' stanzas 2–4, and in Part 2, 'The Starre' and the comments of Fowler, *Times Purpled Masquers*, 63–4, 72–4. Fowler's account of 'stellification' might be fruitfully applied to the the elegies in *Silex Scintillans* Part 1.

despaired over man's rebellious 'state untir'd', and elegies published in
Olor Iscanus and *Thalia Rediviva* praise the loyalty and constancy of
dead friends as qualities lacking in the time's changelings.[64] The worst
of Vaughan's disgust in 'The Proffer' (which succeeds 'White Sunday')
is reserved for the proffering authority's idea that Vaughan too might be a
willing turncoat:

> And having born the burthen all the day
> Now cast at night my Crown away?
>
> (ll. 29–30)[65]

Though the 'night' of the last times has led many to weave '*Self-ends*, and
the *Publick* good' ('An Elegie on the death of Mr. *R. W.*', l. 47), the poet
will not give up his crown: not the 'crown of life' promised to 'the man
that endureth temptation' in the epistle of James, nor the 'crown of righteousness' from 2 Timothy 4: 8, nor indeed the 'crown' proffered in two
passages of Revelation: 'Fear none of those things which thou shalt suffer:
behold, the devil shall cast some of you into prison, that ye may be tried;
and ye shall have tribulation ten days: be thou faithful unto death, and I
will give thee a crown of life'; 'Behold, I come quickly: hold that fast
which thou hast, that no man take thy crown' (Revelation 3: 11; 2: 10).
Vaughan's hope to be crowned with eternal life is intimately connected
with his conviction that those who had overthrown the crown of England
were enemies of God as well as Charles. 'The Proffer' answers its crowning question—shall I 'cast at night my Crown away?'—with a prophetic
ejaculation reflecting Vaughan's loyalty to the Church of England and his
belief that it retained primitive holiness: 'Then keep the antient way!'
(l. 43). Even Vaughan's assiduous editors have missed the scripture uses of
this cry, which fuses the 'strait' and 'narrow' way which leads to life from
the Sermon on the Mount (Matthew 7: 14) with God's vow to Jeremiah
that He will lay waste the land as a punishment: 'Because my people hath

---

[64] See 'An Elegie on the death of Mr. R. W. slain in the unfortunate differences at
Routon Heath, neer *Chester*, 1645', ll. 39–50 and '*To the pious memory of* C. W. Esquire', ll.
23–34.

[65] On the autobiographical hints in 'The Proffer', see Rudrum, 'Resistance, Collaboration, and Silence', 110–12; *Life*, 125; Durr, *Mystical Poetry*, 101–11; Simmonds, *Masques of
God*, 105–7; Post, *Henry Vaughan*, 181–5; Davies, *Henry Vaughan*, 155–6. For another contemporary use of 'proffer' to reject Parliamentary advances, compare the defiant letter of
James Stanley, 7th Earl of Derby, to Ireton, July 1649: 'his late Majesty's service, from which
principles of loyalty I am not a whit departed. I scorn your proffer; I disdain your favour; I
abhor your treason.' (*The Oxford Book of Letters*, ed. by Frank Kermode and Anita
Kermode (Oxford, 1995), 35).

forgotten me, they have burned incense to vanity, and they have caused them to stumble in their ways from the ancient paths, to walk in paths, in a way not cast up' (Jeremiah 18: 15). Vaughan speaks like Jeremiah, a good man in evil times: the eighteenth chapter of Jeremiah's prophecy ends with a prayer to God to save him from his enemies who are plotting to kill him, and 'have digged a pit for my soul' (Jeremiah 18: 20).

From his translations of Boethius and early Christian poems like 'Affliction [I]' and 'The Mutinie' to the lamentations of 'Man in Darkness' and the translation of Nieremberg's 'Of Temperance and Patience' in *Flores Solitudinis*, Vaughan wrote extensively of the suffering of the just. The eschatological poems which open *Silex* (1655) emphasize patient suffering as the true way to earn a saint's white robes (witnessed in the Ascension poems) and a crown of life (grasped firmly in 'The Proffer'). Their anti-millennial images of the Apocalypse also resist the millenarian belief, current in the 1650s, that Christian suffering was at an end because of the impending millennium: this is another way of looking at the happy last age which Vaughan rejects in 'White Sunday'. As Michael Walzer's study of *The Revolution of the Saints* has noted, by overturning Calvin's view that the world and the Christian are in perpetual conflict, radical Christianity laid new ground for rebellion and revolution.[66]

Like the crown of life, palm trees held strong connotations for Royalists after one appeared on the frontispiece of the *Eikon Basilike* in 1649.[67] Flourishing more the more it was weighed down, the tree becomes an emblem of the patience and suffering of the Saints in Vaughan's 'The Palm-tree', which makes yet another swift venture into apocalyptic scripture, introducing a text which became Vaughan's most potent counter-millennial witness, Revelation 13: 10:

> Here Spirits that have run their race and fought
> And won the fight, and have not fear'd the frowns
> Nor lov'd the smiles of greatness, but have wrought
> Their masters will, meet to receive their Crowns.
>
> Here is the patience of the Saints: this Tree
> Is water'd by their tears, as flowers are fed
> With dew by night; but One you cannot see
> Sits here and numbers all the tears they shed.
>
> Here is their faith too.

(ll. 17–25)

[66] Walzer, *Revolution of the Saints*, 291.   [67] Wilcox, 'Language of Devotion', 79.

Like the life of a true Saint, this poem has no point of easy rest. Lines end in struggle, and turn only to begin new strife. One must fight (break) *and* win the fight; merely fighting is not enough (ll. 1–2). One must not fear the frowns of greatness (break) *but also* refrain from loving the smiles of the great. The second stanza breaks its pentameter couplets into five shorter lines of iambic tetrameter, as if Vaughan is hymning the Saints; yet this too breaks expectations, causing the verse to hover in ambiguity at the end of lines. So the first line of stanza two makes sense even before the line is turned ('This tree is the emblem of saintly patience') then the sense is renewed and changed ('This tree is watered by the tears of the saints') and so on.

The patience taught by Vaughan's syntax extracts the lessons of his chosen texts. Vaughan knows that 'patience' is not used in the Old Testament but exclusively in the New and to greatest effect in the epistles—one thinks in particular of the 'cloud of witnesses' passages he alludes to in line 17 above and in 'Ascension-day': 'let us run with patience the race set' (Hebrews 12: 1). The epistles provided Vaughan with many of his most unusual lessons and topics of meditation (like the animals waiting for the Apocalypse in 'And do they so?') and Romans, Hebrews and both Corinthians often provided the marrow of his theology. The patience of 'The Palm-tree' picks up the associations of Hebrews, but its pedigree is even more apt, since Vaughan is citing it from the heart of Revelation: 'He that leadeth into captivity shall go into captivity: he that killeth with the sword must be killed with the sword. Here is the patience and the faith of the saints' (Revelation 13: 10).[68] In stark contrast to the Parliament of Saints convened in 1653 and the empowered Welsh Propagators, Vaughan's saints are obscure, powerless and persecuted. The contrast is so obvious that there is an almost audible stress on the word 'Here' in line 21, as if to distinguish the *here* of powerless tears from the *there* of political triumph.

The long-suffering and patience of true Saints is the subject of the most important anti-millenarian moment in *Silex Scintillans*, 'The Men of War'. The poem is implicitly addressed to Vaughan's Breconshire antithesis, the Fifth Monarchist preacher Vavasor Powell (and beyond, to Thomas Harrison and the Barebones Parliament) and to Powell's

---

[68] The persecutory sense is also opened by Rev. 1: 9: 'I John, who am also your brother, and companion in tribulation, and in the kingdom and patience of Jesus Christ, was in the isle that is called Patmos, for the word of God, and for the testimony of Jesus Christ'; see also Rom. 5: 3, 'tribulation worketh patience' and James 1: 3, 'faith worketh patience'.

associate Jenkin Jones, appointed Propagator of the Gospel for Brecon. Since Vaughan was seldom out of Breconshire after 1648, the evangelizing of Powell, Jones and their associates around the Baptist churches of Brecon must have provided the Silurist with much of his impression of the demeanour of millenarian sanctity. Though Powell spent a large part of his career gathering congregations in north Wales, he also made several trips to Breconshire and kept in close contact with Jenkin Jones, who was based in Llanfaches, near Brecon; Vaughan would have known about Powell's Fifth Monarchist views and his success in gathering millenarian churches in the North.[69] Though there is no record of contact between poet and preacher, the two men were certainly aware of each other, having both gone up to Jesus College, Oxford, in 1638. Henry's two ejected clergymen friends Thomas Powell and Thomas Lewes wrote several times to Jones to complain of the shortage of preaching in the county, but their complaints fell on stony ground. Examples of Jones's extremely short way with similar petitions are displayed triumphantly in Alexander Griffith's rancorous account of his 1652 petition to Parliament *A True and Perfect Relation of the Whole Transaction Concerning the Petition of the Six Counties of South Wales, and the County of Monmouth* (1654).[70]

'The Men of War' begins with three different approaches to the biblical texts in whose presence the poem stands (to adapt a phrase of Geoffrey Hill's).[71] After the title, with a reference to its scriptural provenance, follows a paraphrase of words from the mouth of 'holy *John*'.

> The Men of War
>   S. Luke, chap. 23. ver. 11.
> *If any have an ear*
> Saith holy *John*, then let him hear.
> *He that into Captivity*
> *Leads others, shall a Captive be.*
> *Who with the sword doth others kill,*
> *A sword shall his blood likewise spill.*

[69] Powell gathered at least twenty new Independent churches, although it is uncertain how many of these were Fifth Monarchist (Capp, *Fifth Monarchy Men*, 76).

[70] *Life*, 37, 110–21. Two letters to Jenkin Jones co-authored by Thomas Lewis, Thomas Powell and Griffith Hatley are given in Griffith, *A True and Perfect Relation*, 50–2, along with one response. For an account of Thomas Powell's role in these communications, see Brown, ' "Learned friend and fellow prisoner" '; cf. F. Rees, 'Breconshire during the Civil War', *Brycheiniog*, 8 (1962), 1–9 (6–9) for other petitions and complaints.

[71] Geoffrey Hill, 'A Pharisee to Pharisees', 98.

> *Here is the patience of the Saints,*
> *And the true faith, which never faints.*

(ll. 1–8)

This is one of fourteen poems in *Silex* Part 2 which have biblical epigrams and one of eleven in which Vaughan leaves out the text itself, something he never did in the first volume of *Silex*.[72] The reader is thus offered an additional opportunity to open the bible, in this case to Herod's mocking of Jesus before the crucifixion: 'And Herod with his men of war set him at nought, and mocked him, and arrayed him in a gorgeous robe, and sent him again to Pilate' (Luke 23: 11). This is the first of several passages from Luke's and John's gospel singled out by 'The Men of War' to instance Christian conduct in the face of persecution, mockery and defeat. By naming it below the title, Vaughan makes Luke's text shine through the succession of verses the poem proceeds to cite from Revelation, so superimposing Christ's patience in defeat onto His patience in victory, and revealing them to be one and the same.

The poem opens a second time, so to speak, by paraphrasing Revelation 13: 10, the verse which comforts the centre of 'The Palm-tree'. As Jonathan Post has noted, Vaughan now adds the preceding verse from Revelation to provide 'a lesson in hearing. "*If any have an ear*," Vaughan abruptly begins—implying of course that many do not.'[73] This little phrase or formula of St John was understood (by no less a millenarian than Thomas Brightman) as 'the acclamatory conclusion, common to all *the Epistles*, whereby he teacheth that all men of what kinde soever they are, ought to bend their mindes in hearkening to these admonitions of *the Spirit*'.[74] Vaughan's use is feigning: he seems for a moment to speak as a radical prophet in the manner of Abiezer Coppe, who imitated the language, gestures and identity of Ezekiel in his *A Second Fiery Flying Roule* (1649), or Lady Eleanor Douglas, who construed her maiden name Eleanor Audeley as 'reveale, O Daniel'.[75] Vaughan's feint is a brief one, though:

---

[72] 'The Timber', 'The Feast' and 'To the Holy Bible' give their texts, whereas 'Jesus Weeping' (I), 'The Daughter of Herodias', 'Jesus Weeping' (II), 'The Seed growing secretly', 'The Stone', 'The dwelling-place', 'The Men of War', 'The Ass', 'The hidden Treasure', 'The Night', and 'The Throne' do not.

[73] Post, *Henry Vaughan*, 131.

[74] Thomas Brightman, *The Revelation of Saint John, Illustrated with Analysis and Scholios, Together with a Most Comfortable Exposition of the Last and Most Difficult Part of the Prophecy of Daniel* (Amsterdam, 1644), 18.

[75] On Coppe's prophesying, see Smith, *Perfection Proclaimed*, 54–65; Lady Eleanor

> *If any have an ear*
> Saith holy *John*, then *let him hear.*

The prophetic voice heard here is not Vaughan's, but that of a scriptural prophet—and so, for Vaughan, a true one. (Such temporary misdirection enables Vaughan to trick his reader into a similar double-take elsewhere in *Silex*. His translation of Psalm 121 begins:

> Up to those bright, and gladsome hils
>   Whence flowes my weal, and mirth,
> I look, and sigh for him, who fils
>   (Unseen,) both heaven, and earth.

(ll. 1–4)

For a moment, 'Up' leaps with an imperative joy, as if suggesting that the hills are in easy climbing distance; only in the third line does Vaughan reveal that this is spiritual window-shopping, and that only his eyes can make the journey.)

Vaughan was not the first to think of Herod's soldiers as a scriptural type of Vavasor Powell and his colleagues. The preface to *Mercurius Cambro-Britannicus; or, News from Wales* (1652) makes use of the same phrase in a list of reasons for the British public to thank the pamphlet's vehemently anti-Propagation author, Alexander Griffith:

2. The Army is beholding to him for discovering those that swallow up that *Treasure* which should either be employed for the *end* to which it was *designed* by Parliament, or else for the payment of their Arrears: Those *men* of *war* that now receive it, having scarce lost one drop of bloud in the late quarrels, nor had any greater enemy to contest withall then *Black-coats*, and the bridge of *Rosse*.[76]

An irascible and relentless opponent of Powell, Griffith vociferously attacked the Propagation Committee's dispersal of Wales's £20,000 of tithe money in this pamphlet and his *Strena Vavasoriensis, a New-Year-Gift for the Welch Itinerants, or a Hue and Cry after Mr. Vavasor Powell, Metropolitan of the Itinerants* (1654), which also details Powell's preaching in Breconshire and the other Welsh counties. The basis of Griffith's appellation, as of Vaughan's, was Powell's very real association with the army in the 1640s when, with Morgan Llwyd and Walter Cradock, he had preached to Parliamentary troops as their chaplain. Though Powell was

Douglas, *The Restitution of Prophecy; That Buried Talent to be Revived* (1651; repr. Exeter, 1978), Prefatory note, p. [i].

[76] Griffith, *Mercurius Cambro-Britannicus*, sigs. *2^r–v.

wounded during General Mytton's attack on Beaumaris in September
1648, injuries and losses were not great among the Welsh Saints, a fact perhaps remembered by Griffith's scornful remark about their 'one drop of
bloud'.[77]

How easily one might become a 'man of war' is the subject taken up by
Vaughan's own words after the paraphrase of Revelation 13. A pun on
enact aims these words at the Propagators with a deadly specificity, since
only Parliament's men had the force of an *Act* behind their superficial *act*
(in Vaughan's eyes) of piety:

> Were not thy word (dear Lord!) my light,
> How would I run to endless night,
> And persecuting thee and thine,
> Enact for *Saints* my self and mine.
>
> (ll. 9–12)

Repeating the rhetorical turn used in 'White Sunday', Vaughan's admission of weakness enables further praise of the Word's corrective power; it
also implies, of course, that his present understanding reflects the wisdom
of scripture. Vaughan lends scriptural support in the next two lines,
which like the opening couplet defers authority from themselves to the
bible: 'For in this bright, instructing verse | Thy Saints are not the Con-
querers' (ll. 17–18). The chapter in question is 2 Timothy 3, Paul's warning
quoted in 'White Sunday' that the times before the Apocalypse will be the
worst of all. Verse 16, to which Vaughan's 'instructing' alludes, was a
favourite text of the Reformation, and particularly popular with Puritans
since it offered strong support to the idea of *sola scriptura*:

from a child thou hast known the holy scriptures, which are able to make thee
wise unto salvation through faith which is in Christ Jesus. All scripture is given by
inspiration of God, and is profitable for doctrine, for reproof, for correction, for
instruction in righteousness. (2 Timothy 3: 15–16)[78]

Paul's advice to the faithful in the last times never had a greater influence
on Vaughan than in this exhortation to use the scriptures for wisdom
against deceivers and as 'instruction in righteousness'. Vaughan acts on

---

[77] *Biographical Dictionary of British Radicals in the Seventeenth Century*, ed. Richard L.
Greaves and Robert Zaller, 3 vols. (Brighton, 1982–84), iii. 55. Cradock preached to the
Army, and to Royalist prisoners after Naseby; Morgan Llwyd travelled extensively around
England and Scotland as a stipendiary itinerant preacher, often with the Parliamentary
armies (ibid. i. 188; *DNB*).

[78] Examples of its usefulness are given by Green, *The Christian's ABC*, 21–3.

Paul's words, taking Revelation 13: 10 as his own 'bright, instructing verse'. To learn from it the passivity and contentedness of Christian patience, and then to allege *this* scripture (the deictic is important) against *those* that the millenarians could throw at it, is the achievement of 'The Men of War'.

Vaughan's instructive verse teaches him that Christ's patience before Herod is the same power which shall win the day in the Apocalypse:

> For in this bright, instructing verse
> Thy Saints are not the Conquerers;
> But patient, meek, and overcome
> Like thee, when set at naught and dumb.
> Armies thou hast in Heaven, which fight,
> And follow thee all cloath'd in white,
> But here on earth (though thou hast need)
> Thou wouldst no legions, but wouldst bleed.
> The sword wherewith thou dost command
> Is in thy mouth, not in thy hand,
> And all thy Saints do overcome
> By thy blood, and their Martyrdom.
>
> (ll. 17–28)

Making an absolute distinction between the heavenly and the earthly armies, these lines assault the popular millenarian identification of Parliament's conquering armies with those of Christ spoken of in Revelation, who sit 'upon white horses, clothed in fine linen, white and clean' (19: 14). Against every piece of scripture that can be alleged to support bloody fighting for Christ, Vaughan alleges ones which support bloodless resistance. Though Christ command by blood, it is not the blood of His supposed enemies, but His own blood, freely shed (ll. 24, 28); though He rule by a sword, it is not a soldier's blade, but the sword of the Word of God, an image which has the scripture backing of Revelation 19: 15 and Hebrews 4: 12, to which I will shortly come back. The modal verbs sound out God's choice, proof of his own will to suffer—'*wouldst* no legions, but *wouldst* bleed'—as Vaughan finds in God's decision a strong proof of the necessity of saintly suffering, which he urges in the face of earthly legions.[79]

---

[79] This theme is explored with delicacy in the two 'Jesus Weeping' poems, especially 'Jesus Weeping' (2), discussed in Chapter 5, above. Post lightly suggests that these poems 'prepare the way for a third, "The Men of War (Luke 23: 11)" by underscoring Christ's patient suffering and humanity' (*Henry Vaughan*, 131).

On 28 February 1650, Vavasor Powell preached a fast sermon to Parliament. Its expression of millenarian hope for the Propagation Act proved acceptable to the auditory and Powell's words became one of the last fast sermons to be published when they appeared in 1651 as *Christ Exalted above All Creatures by God His Father*.[80] There is every chance that Vaughan had read this state-approved work by the time he wrote 'The Men of War'; or, if not, that he had experienced its teachings at first hand when Powell was in Breconshire.[81] Even if the Silurist missed the most famous Propagator in person, he would certainly have encountered Powell's friend Jenkin Jones, who had become notorious among the Anglican community of south Wales for his millenarian activities.[82] *Christ Exalted* eloquently urges the millennial importance of Propagation and looks forward to the rule of the Saints, expressing its hopes in language which immediately recalls the passage from 'The Men of War' quoted above:

Is there not all the reason in the world they [the Saints] should [rule], seeing that the world is upheld for their sakes; also that they have been *sufferers* in times past, and are Conquerers of some parts of it at present, and doth not Christ promise, that he that *overcommeth, and keepeth his works until the end, to him will he give power over the Nations*, Rev. 2.26.[83]

Conquerors is perhaps the most striking resemblance, but it is Powell's use of *overcommeth* against Vaughan's *overcome* and *overcame* which reveals most powerfully the clash of scriptural interpretations that underlay Anglican and Puritan Apocalypses. Powell is quoting the word from John's letters to the seven churches of Asia in Revelation chapters 2 and 3, in this case the letter to the church of Thyatira, which tell of the rewards which will be given him 'that overcometh'.[84] *Silex Scintillans* often looks

[80] Powell was sponsored by his friend, Major-General Harrison. Two other preachers Harrison similarly sponsored to give fast sermons, John Simpson (preached 1651) and Christopher Feake (1652), were not well received (Capp, *Fifth Monarchy Men*, 61).

[81] Alexander Griffith notes that Vavasor Powell preached in Llandetti, Jenkin Jones's parish (*Strena Vavasoriensis*, 6). For Powell's life, see Nuttall, *The Welsh Saints*, ch. 3, 'Vavasor Powell and Morgan Llwyd: The Millenarian Impulse'; Jenkins, *Protestant Dissenters*, chs. 3–4; *DNB*; Wood, *Athenae Oxoniensis*, iii. 911 ff.; Capp, *Fifth Monarchy Men*, 54–5, 60–5, 259.

[82] *Life*, 37; see also 111, 116–20. Rees, 'Breconshire during the Civil War', 7–8 gives an account of Jones; on his role in the Scottish campaign of 1651 see Capp, *Fifth Monarchy Men*, 55. Contemporary hatred spills over in Griffith, *A True and Perfect Relation of the Whole Transaction*, 50–2 and the same author's *Mercurius Cambro-Britannicus*, 10–11.

[83] Powell, *Christ Exalted*, 57–8.

[84] Powell is citing the King James version, changing the pronouns since in Revelation this is God's promise.

to the same second chapter of Revelation, but always to the message for the Ephesian church, never to that for the Thyatiran.[85] Different rewards are promised to the two churches. God promises the Ephesians: 'To him that overcometh will I give to eat of the hidden manna, and will give him a white stone, and in the stone a new name written, which no man knoweth saving he that receiveth it' (Revelation 2: 17).[86] To the Thyatiran church, on the other hand, God promises more the rewards of power: 'And he [the faithful Saint] shall rule them with a rod of iron; as the vessels of a potter shall they be broken to shivers: even as I received of my Father. And I will give him the morning star' (Revelation 2: 26). Despite Vaughan's attraction to scriptural images of the Morning Star, he never alludes to or cites this passage, whose promises do not sort with his notion of saintly patience. To Powell, though, these words represented a scriptural foundation for the just rule of the Saints in the world's last age.[87] The selective quotation employed by both men reveals a profound disagreement over the meaning of Revelation and its application to the times, and illustrates powerfully the way scriptural interpretation in the 1640s and 1650s could lie at the very heart of political and literary actions.

Powell brought far more intelligence and sincerity to his ministry than *Strena Vavasoriensis* and *Mercurius Cambro-Britannicus* could admit. One sign of both is his awareness of the kinds of criticism levelled at the militant Saints, on account of which he included a diatribe (recalling James's epistle) at the heart of *Christ Exalted*, hoping to persuade objectors like Vaughan who might argue that 'Thy Saints are not the Conquerors | But patient, meek and overcome' ('The Men of War', ll. 18–19).

Object. But some will say, *The weapons of the Saints anciently were* faith, tears, prayers, and patience, *and they did then rather choose afflictions, and persecutions, then make resistance, and seek to reign over others.*

Answ. It's true, that faith, teares, prayers, &c. are the best weapons, and with these the Saints do chiefly warre. But yet it is as true, that the Saints may lawfully fight, for wee read that they are to [Psa. 149.6] have *a two-edged sword in their hands, as well as the high prayses of God in their mouthes,* and in another place we read,

---

[85] For other contemporary uses of the text, see Nathanael Culverwel, 'The white stone' in *An Elegant and Learned Discourse of the Light of Nature* (1652). The text is also popular in contemporary conversion narratives.

[86] 'H. Scriptures', 'In thee the hidden stone, the *Manna* lies' (l. 5).

[87] Of the gifts promised to the seven churches Brightman writes: 'The reward in every one of the Epistles is fitted to the times, and it is one and the same every where, *Jesus Christ alone*' (18).

that they that lead into captivity (meaning the Roman party) *should be led into captivity themselves.* But [Rev. 13.10] you will say by whom? Surely, by the Army of the Lamb, who are called, and chosen, and faithfull.[88]

So close is Powell's predicted objection to Vaughan's actual one that one must wonder whether they do not both partly recall debates on the meaning of Revelation in the 1650s. Though Powell ably counters the objections he raises, he was obviously aware that he needed to support his millenarian reading of Revelation 2: 26 from elsewhere in scripture, and so offers two texts as authorities: Psalm 149: 6 and Revelation 13: 10.

To uphold its millenarian message, Powell's sermon neatly trims Revelation 13: 10, the verse paraphrased at the start of 'The Men of War'. Jonathan Post has noted that both Powell and William Erbery tended to use only so much of a biblical quotation as suited their purposes, indiscriminately lopping off what was unwelcome to their cause.[89] Citing Revelation 13: 10, Powell writes '*that they that lead into captivity* (meaning the Roman party) *should be led into captivity themselves.* But [Rev. 13.10] you will say by whom?' To make his argument, Powell omits the second part of the verse which Vaughan versifies to make his: 'He that killeth with the sword must be killed with the sword.' Powell's careful editing suggests an admirable realization that to hand out swords with one scriptural injunction only to denounce their use with another might well have spoiled his speech. (It would surely have missed the press.) Privately, the Propagator may have believed that the omitted sentences could be explained without overturning the millenarian cause; but the occasion of his sermon and the desire to find justification for the Propagation Act demanded rather more enthusiasm and fervour than it did careful textual exegesis, despite Parliament's notorious appetite for lengthy sermonizing.[90]

Psalm 149, Powell's other text, gives thanks to God for giving the meek power of judgement and vengeance. Powell draws on its sixth verse:

---

[88] Powell, *Christ Exalted*, 58–9. The scripture references in square brackets were originally marginal.

[89] Post, *Henry Vaughan*, 131.

[90] Powell's later disputes are recorded in *Truths Conflict with Error* (1650), an account of the debates he held with Thomas Goodwin concerning Universal Redemption. A whole series of accounts and counter-accounts grew up surrounding his disputes with Dr George Griffith, an associate of Alexander Griffith. Beginning in *The Perfect Diurnall* of 2 Aug. 1651, their exchange continues in *A Welsh Narrative, Corrected* (23 July 1652) [Griffith's version of events] and *A Relation of a Disputation* (1 Feb. 1653) [Powell's version], where the two men deal with various contentious topics including kinds of prayer, but only after exhaustively clarifying the conditions and terms of debate.

Let the high praises of God be in their mouth, and a twoedged sword in their hand; To execute vengeance upon the heathen and punishments upon the people; To bind their kings with chains, and their nobles with fetters of iron; To execute upon them the judgment written: this honour have all his saints. (Psalm 149. 6–9)

This vision of the Saints wielding a sword of judgement agrees well with the 'power over the nations' promised in John's words to the Thyatirans. The idea that men might wield the 'sword of the Spirit' had played an increasingly important role for the seventeenth-century British Saints, who derived their military style from several scriptures, including Psalm 149, but particularly from Ephesians 6, which tells the Christian to take 'the shield of faith', 'the helmet of salvation' and 'the sword of the Spirit' ('the whole armour of God') in the fight against Satan. John R. Knott has written that 'the sword of the Spirit could be seen as a weapon wielded by the Christian soldier, as the power of religious truth understood more generally, or as the power wielded by God against his enemies.'[91] However, millenarians and Fifth Monarchists like Powell favoured a strong militant concoction of all three, seeing the sword promised to the Saints as a clear prophecy of the force needed to usher in the millennium. Arguing that theirs was the battle of good against evil, of Christ against Antichrist, Powell and the Saints urged action in the name of the imminent millennium in a way both novel and revolutionary. Before the Anabaptist and Puritan uprisings of the early modern period, Michael Walzer notes, only the Joachimites (in the thirteenth century) had succeeded in creating such a powerfully militant rhetoric in the name of the apocalyptic victory of the Lord.[92]

Vaughan, looking at the Last Days from the opposite end of the revolution, played down possible militaristic interpretations of God's sword, not by ignoring the Saints' rhetoric, but by finding further scriptural images of heavenly swords whose sharpness is only spiritually cutting. He found them in the New Testament, whose God (Jeremy Taylor noted) preferred the title '*God of peace*' to the Old Testament '*Lord of Hosts*'.[93] Vaughan's lines 'The sword wherewith thou dost command | Is in thy

---

[91] John R. Knott Jr, *The Sword of the Spirit: Puritan Responses to the Bible* (Chicago, 1980), 8. Knott quotes Milton's *Observations upon the Articles of Peace* (1649): 'the extirpation of "Popery and Prelacy", then of Heresy, Schism and prophaneness' promised in the Solemn League and Covenant 'can be no work of the Civil Sword, but of the Spirituall which is the word of God' (166).

[92] Walzer, *Revolution of the Saints*, 291–5.   [93] *Holy Living and Holy Dying*, 5.

mouth, not in thy hand' ('The Men of War', ll. 25–6) allude to Hebrews, where 'the word of God is quick, and powerful, and sharper than any twoedged sword' (4: 12) and also to Revelation, where John sees Christ in the last throes of the apocalyptic drama, leading a heavenly army of Saints: 'And out of his mouth goeth a sharp sword, that with it he should smite the nations: and he shall rule them with a rod of iron . . . And the remnant were slain with the sword of him that sat upon the horse, which sword proceeded out of his mouth: and all the fowls were filled with their flesh' (Revelation 19: 15, 21). This image of 'Christ militant' inspired millenarians in Parliament and the Army to use force to establish the rule of the Saints; Fifth Monarchists, too, believed in their own brand of armed resistance, organizing armed rebellions in 1657 (swiftly broken up by Parliamentary troops) and several times in the 1660s.[94] Powell denied these risings his support, but in the early 1650s he believed the Lamb's army to be one with the army which had liberated England and Wales from the shackles of antichristian religion and, like others, he identified the victories of the late 1640s with the battles described in Revelation.

Vaughan's interpretation of Christ's sword attempts to put out revolutionary sparks with a blanket of scripture. His connection of the Word and the sword recalls 'The Stone', a *Silex* Part 2 poem which paraphrases John's gospel on how the 'Scribe and Register' of nature records all sins so that no excuses will avail on the Last Day:

> If any (for he all invites)
> His easie yoke rejects or slights,
> The *Gospel* then (for 'tis his word
> And not himself * shall judge the world)
> Will by loose *Dust* that man arraign,
> As one then dust more vile and vain.
>   * St. John, *chap*. 12. *ver*. 47, 48.
>
>   (ll. 54–9)

In the passage Vaughan alludes to in conclusion, Christ teaches that 'the word I have spoken, the same shall judge him in the last day'. In 'The Men of War' as in 'The Stone', the Word of God is a rulebook in both senses: a guide to holy living, and the power by which offenders shall be judged. Superimposing the sword of Hebrews with Christ's sword from Revelation, Vaughan remembers 'The Stone' and removes the sting from the

---

[94] Knott, *Sword of the Spirit*, 8.

'sword' of the revolutionary Saints. He thus again postpones the victory of God's true Saints until the Last Day: only then will they be sharers in Christ's victory.

OVERCOMING THE WORLD

In November 1648, Cromwell sent a letter to Colonel Robert Hammond, Charles I's gaoler at Carisbrooke Castle and a man of some sympathy for the king. Its blend of caution and firmness signals Cromwell's awareness of Hammond's torn allegiances and a recognition of the lengths he would have to go to in order to justify direct action against his monarch:

My dear friend, let us look into providences; surely they mean somewhat. They hang so together; have been so constant, so clear and unclouded. Malice, sworn malice against God's people, now called Saints, to root out their name; and yet they, by providence, having arms, and therein blessed with defence and more. I desire, he that is for a principle of suffering would not too much slight this. I slight not him who is so minded: but let us beware lest fleshly reasoning see more safety in making use of this principle then in acting. Who acts, and resolves not through God to be willing to part with all? Our hearts are very deceitful, on the right and on the left.[95]

Although the elect have suffered, Cromwell argues, and must still be ready to face suffering in Christ's name (his 'principle of suffering'), they should not ignore the sword which Providence has put in their hands, but know themselves 'by providence, having arms, and therein blessed with defence' able to use God's gifts to defend against tyranny. Attempting to counter deeply rooted Christian ideas of patient fortitude, Cromwell paints Charles I as a worldly Caesar or Herod, a tyrant over men and a tormentor of the elect.[96] Only by standing firm to such a vision could Parliament defeat the old sense of righteous suffering, that 'worldly pessimism' fostered in Reformed religion by Calvin.[97]

For Vaughan, it was a false and unchristian vision resting on bad scripture using. 'The Men of War' makes its strongest challenge to the visions

---

[95] *The Writings and Speeches of Oliver Cromwell, with an Introduction and a Sketch of His Life*, ed. by Wilbur Cortez Abbott and Catherine D. Crane, 2 vols. (1937; reissued Oxford, 1988), i. 697–8.

[96] On the tone of this letter, see Worden, 'Providence and Politics', 95–6; cf. Milton's scriptural proofs that 'kingdom and magistracy [is] called "a human ordinance"' in *The Tenure of Kings and Magistrates* (1649).

[97] Walzer, *Revolution of the Saints*, 298.

of *Christ Exalted* when it engages Powell over meaning of the biblical verb *to overcome*, forms of which are vital to both works. *Christ Exalted* cites it from the letter to the Thyatirans in Revelation, where God reveals to John that: 'he that overcometh, and keepeth my works unto the end, to him will I give power over the nations'. Powell understood this to mean that those who actively overcome in the name of the Apocalypse will share the rule of Christ: those who 'are Conquerers of some parts . . . at present' will, by their further overcoming of God's enemies, lead to a quicker victory over the whole world for Christ and the Saints.[98]

Preferring a 'principle of suffering' over an unchristian victory in this world, Vaughan disagreed. In the 1650s, though, Powell's reading was clearly in the ascendant: millenarians looked eagerly to Revelation chapters 2 and 3 to see what the Saints could hope to enjoy on earth now they had overcome the forces of Satan. Thomas Brightman's writings taught that the rewards promised to the faithful were aspects of a single, ultimate reward, the enjoyment of Jesus Christ—'For what greater thing can he give to the Elect? Or what shall we want, if we enjoy him?'—and that St John's numerous formulations simply varied the promise 'according to the divers state of the times'.[99] Yet Brightman believed that the Apocalypse was unfolding on earth, and that rewards could be enjoyed by the Saints before the Last Day. For him, the epistle to the Thyatirans told of a 'promised power' for the Saints, 'a joynt partaking of the church in the victory against the *Papists*, which at this day all reformed Churches enjoy'.[100]

Powell expected a swift triumphal *overcoming* and the reward of 'power over the nations'. His sermon does not touch on the remaining six rewards John promises, whose emphasis on perseverance rather than on action could not have helped his expressions of chiliastic enthusiasm. The verses Powell omits are among the mental landmarks by which *Silex Scintillans* steers its path through the world, their rewards what Vaughan hoped for if he could *overcome*. To a reader more intimate with Vaughan's poems than with Revelation, chapters 2 and 3 of Revelation read like a storehouse of familiar phrases. To those who overcome, God reveals to John, 'will I give to eat of the tree of life' (2: 7); they 'shall not be hurt of the second death' (2: 11); to them 'will I give to eat of the hidden manna, and will give him a white stone, and in the stone a new name written,

---

[98]   Powell, *Christ Exalted*, 58.   [99]   Brightman, *Revelation*, 18.
[100]   Ibid., 28; see also 24–5.

which no man knoweth saving he that receiveth it' (2: 17); to them 'will I give power over the nations: and he shall rule them with a rod of iron; as the vessels of a potter shall they be broken to shivers: even as I received of my Father. And I will give him the morning star' (2: 26–8); 'the same shall be clothed in white raiment; and I will not blot out his name out of the book of life, but I will confess his name before my Father, and before his angels' (3: 5); to him 'will I make a pillar in the temple of my God, and he shall go no more out: and I will write upon him the name of my God, and the name of the city of my God, which is new Jerusalem, which cometh down out of heaven from my God: and I will write upon him my new name' (3: 12); to him 'will I grant to sit with me in my throne, even as I also overcame, and am set down with my Father in his throne' (3: 21); he 'shall inherit all things: and I will be his God, and he shall be my son' (21: 7).[101]

At the very heart of 'The Men of War' is Christ's promise in Revelation 3: 21 that the faithful soul will overcome in the same way *Christ* overcame: 'To him that overcometh will I grant to sit with me in my throne, even as I also overcame, and am set down with my Father in his throne'. When Vaughan pictured Christ's *overcoming*, it was not in a vision of the Lamb's apocalyptic victory over the Beast—'and the Lamb shall *overcome*' (Revelation 17: 14). This military defeat of Satan's troops, repeated in the account of Christ's victorious Army in Revelation 19 (where, however, there is no mention of overcoming) inspired and authorized the millenarian viewpoint of Vavasor Powell, but it was not Vaughan's vision. Rather, 'The Men of War' frowns at revolutionary interpretations of Revelation and recovers the favoured texts of chiliasts into its own fields of interpretation. When it thinks of the meaning of Christian *overcoming* it thinks biblically, and so subordinates the *overcoming* of the Lamb in Revelation to Christ's humbled and very untriumphant *overcoming* on the cross.[102] 'The Men of War', that is, uses Christ's sacrificial overcoming of the world through his death as a scriptural reply to Powell's military interpretation of overcoming; the poem synthesizes the bible's two contrasting

---

[101] Rev. 2: 17 appears in 'H. Scriptures', l. 5, 'Rules *and* Lessons', l. 28, 'The Evening-watch', l. 6; Rev. 3: 5 in 'Ascension-day', l. 30, 'The Proffer', l. 24, 'The Agreement', l. 15, 'The Seed growing secretly', l. 24, 'The Men of War', l. 22, 'L'Envoy', l. 4, 'The Evening-watch', l. 8; Rev. 3: 21 in 'Silence', l. 23. The tree of life, from 2: 7, appears in 'The Agreement', l. 21, by way of Gen. 22.

[102] There are only four uses of 'overcome' and its cognates in *Silex Scintillans*, 3 in 'The Men of War' and the other in 'To the Holy Bible', l. 24 ('Thou overcam'st my sinful strength').

images of Christ's victory through the word *overcome*, threatening to expose Powell's single quotation of Revelation 2: 26 as a forgery 'which impious wit | And power force on Holy Writ' ('The day of Judgement', ll. 34–5).

Vaughan's response to Powell assumes that his reader understands the import and source of the phrase 'to him that overcometh'. He could be fairly sure that it would be known to churchgoers, since the letters to the seven churches were often cited by preachers to warn Britons that they, like the Laodicean church of the epistle, were guilty of 'lukewarmness' (Revelation 3: 16).[103] (Thus the *overcometh* formula was probably as familiar to churchgoers as, say, the image of the candlestick from the same chapter of Revelation: 'and will remove thy candlestick out of his place, except thou repent' (Revelation 2: 5).[104]) Assuming some familiarity, 'The Men of War' establishes a relationship between Christ's apocalyptic *overcoming*, the way He *was overcome* on earth, and how his true followers will be persecuted before their ultimate reward. Forms of the crucial verb appear thirteen times in Revelation, by far the heaviest concentration in the New Testament, where it always translates the Greek νικάω (nikao), whose other biblical senses include victory in war, literal or spiritual, athletics and lawsuits.[105] Vaughan deploys the word in 'The Men of War' as a gloss on his versification of Luke 23: 11, the passage which gives the poem its title:

> For in this bright, instructing verse
> Thy Saints are not the Conquerers;
> But patient, meek and overcome
> Like thee, when set at naught, and dumb.
>
> (ll. 17–20)

'And Herod with his men of war set him at naught, and mocked him' (Luke 23: 11). Christ's perfect passivity is expressed through the mood of 'set at naught' and his strong silence by a further quotation of Luke 22: 19:

---

[103] For instance Sampson Price, *Londons Warning by Laodiceas Lukewarmnesse* (1613) and *Two Treatises the First . . . to the . . . Church of Laodicea* (1642).

[104] As used in the title of *Gemitus Ecclesiae Cambro-Britannicus: or, The Candlestick Removed, by the Ejectment of the Ministers of Wales, under the Power of the Late Act, for the Propagation of the Gospell There* (1654). The candlestick usually represents the word preached.

[105] Biblical uses in the appropriate sense are: John 16: 33; Rom. 12: 21; 1 John 2: 13–14; 4: 4; 5: 4–5; Rev. 2: 7, 11, 17, 26; 3: 5, 12, 21; 11: 7; 12: 11; 13: 7; 17: 14; 21: 7. The New Testament Greek νικαω (nikan) is discussed by John Sweet, *Revelation*, SCM Pelican Commentaries (1979), 82; Henry George Liddell and Robert Scott, *A Greek–English Lexicon*, rev. Sir Henry Stuart Jones with Roderick McKenzie (Oxford, 1996), 1176.

'Then he questioned with him in many words; but he answered him nothing'. The passive use of *overcome*, not present in Luke, hints to the biblically aware reader that the patient, meek suffering of Christ and his Saints should be connected with the triumphant overcoming in the Last Judgement, an overcoming which itself is not free from suffering. For it is only in Revelation that Christians are said to *be overcome*: first the two faithful witnesses are *overcome* and killed (11: 7) and then later the beast is given power to make war with the saints, and to *overcome* them (13: 7). Like the interrogated Jesus, Christians should prepare for the victory of the powerful, perhaps especially in the wicked times before the Last Day; but through Vaughan's use of passive and active senses of νικάω, 'to be overcome' is merely the preliminary to overcoming; one must be set at naught to be set on high.

Revelation continues to fuel the poem's scriptural defence of Christian passivity:

> Armies thou hast in Heaven, which fight,
> And follow thee all cloath'd in white,
> But here on earth (though thou hast need)
> Thou wouldst no legions, but wouldst bleed.

(ll. 21–4)

Here Vaughan places the martial victories of Revelation—those of Michael's army and the Army of the Lamb (Revelation 12, 19)—firmly outside time, denying that England's victorious armies can be one with the scriptural forces of good. Support comes in the next four lines, which point out that when God chose to intersect with time, He took on flesh and shed his blood rather than coming in glory with 'legions' of angels. His unique victory on the cross redefined for all time what it means to *overcome*:

> The sword wherewith thou dost command
> Is in thy mouth, not in thy hand,
> And all thy Saints do overcome
> By thy blood, and their Martyrdom.

(ll. 25–8)

The Saints overcome by Christ's blood and their own, not by spilling other people's, however much the opposite may seem to be true. Vaughan's lines have learnt another scriptural lesson from the Apocalypse, this time Revelation 12: 11, which teaches that the brethren of Christ 'overcame . . . by the blood of the Lamb, and by the word of their testimony; and they loved not their lives unto the death'. Sixteen hundred years on, Vaughan replaces 'testimony' with 'martyrdom', joining a history of persecutions to John's words, but otherwise deliberately expresses his argument in favour of scriptural commandment through the plainest of scriptural paraphrases.

'The Men of War' brings together gospel and Revelation to reveal the truth that Christ, his Saints, and by extension all Christians, *overcome* Satan by first *being overcome* themselves. Vaughan makes special use of John's gospel, where the word *overcome* features once, very prominently, when Christ is consoling the Apostles 'with doctrines with exhortations and with promises', and 'as a faithful friend, not willing to delude his disciples with false comforts . . . [tells] them what they were to meet with'.[106] He finishes his discourse of the sorrow to come, saying: 'These things I have spoken unto you, that in me ye might have peace. In the world ye shall have tribulation: but be of good cheer; I have overcome [νικάω] the world' (John 16: 33). This idea of *overcoming the world* is repeated in John's first epistle, where it is given a yet more unworldly spin: 'For whatsoever is born of God overcometh the world; and this is the victory that overcometh the world, even our faith. Who is he that overcometh the world, but he that believeth that Jesus is the Son of God?' (1 John 5: 4, 5); and the same word is used once earlier: 'Ye are of God, little children, and have overcome them [those with the spirit of Antichrist in them]: because greater is he that is in you, than he that is in the world' (1 John 4: 4).

As Christ *overcame* the world by rejecting its powers and so triumphing over death, the true Saints of God triumph in His blood and what Vaughan proleptically calls their 'martyrdom'. 'And they loved not their lives unto the death' concludes Revelation 12: 11, in the same mood of world-rejection of the Saints encountered in 1 John chapters 4 and 5. The consolatory value of this doctrine of overcoming by passivity is, of course, enormous. As the Edinburgh minister George Hutcheson noted in his commentary, 'Christs victory over the world is ground of encouragement to all his suffering people, against the power and policy of the world; considering, that however Christ will not exempt them from a battel and exercise, yet they are partakers of his victory by faith, 1 John 5: 4 and

---

[106] Augustine Marlorate, *A Catholike and Ecclesiasticall Exposition of the Holy Gospell after S. John* (1575), 518; George Hutcheson, *An Exposition of the Gospel of Jesus Christ According to John* (1657), 279.

(abiding in him) finde, in end, that they have to do with enemies already vanquished'.[107]

As it draws together its anti-millennial visions, 'The Men of War' continues to relate Revelation to a vision of Christian passivity derived from the gospels. Vaughan turns, ultimately, to the crucified Christ:[108]

> But seeing Soldiers long ago
> Did spit on thee, and smote thee too;
> Crown'd thee with thorns, and bow'd the knee,
> But in contempt, as still we see,
> I'le marvel not at ought they do,
> Because they us'd my Savior so;
> Since of my *Lord* they had their will,
> The servant must not take it ill.
>
>   (ll. 29–36)

Balanced as they are, these lines are surely close to losing their Christian patience in Vaughan's choice of a scriptural type for the Puritan mockery of Anglican bowing in church. It takes the words of Christ to control the poem's angry desire to witness for Him the contempt of the world. 'Marvel not' is a biblical injunction to be prepared for persecution, used by the preacher of Ecclesiastes 5: 8—'If thou seest the oppression of the poor . . . marvell not at the matter'—but in its most potent form by Christ, in John's first epistle: 'Marvel not, my brethren, if the world hate you' (1 John 3: 13). Accepting scorn in this spirit of prepared resignation, the Christian resembles his saviour and truly hears Christ's own commands. Vaughan's image of the servant sharing the lot of his master has a biblical origin, too; again it is Christ's 'comfortable doctrine'[109] given to the Apostles before he tells of his overcoming: 'If the world hate you, ye know that it hated me before it hated you . . . Remember the word that I said unto you [in John 13: 16], The servant is not greater than his lord. If they have persecuted me, they will also persecute you; if they have kept my saying, they will keep yours also' (John 15: 18–20). Playing beneath 'The Men of War', the music of these verses creates a new and surprising depth of harmony: it is the sound of Christ's promise of a 'Comforter' for the Apostles' afflictions

---

[107] Hutcheson, *Exposition of John*, 334; Marlorate wrote: 'they have overcome, who are as yet in the middest of the skyrmyshe . . . wee before wee encounter with the enemye, are conquerors: because our head Christ hath once overcome the whole worlde for us' (550).
[108] Noted by *R*, 624.   [109] Hutcheson, *Exposition of John*, 279.

(John 15: 26) becoming Vaughan's scriptural comfort and support in his own struggle to overcome.

Christ's ultimate overcoming, the defeat of Satan and the redemption of man, has been, will be, accomplished by strong patience, holy meekness and dumb silence; by the Word of God, which is the Sword of the Spirit, and not by the sword martial; by Christ's blood and the Saints' martyrdom, and not by martyring God's enemies and spilling their blood. Holding fast to this truth, 'The Men of War' welcomes affliction as Vaughan has so often in *Silex Scintillans*—as a 'sacred, needfull art'[110]—while it commends to the faithful a Christian duty of patience. Such great patience, ultimately exemplified in Christ, is the note on which this last exploration of Vaughan's scripture uses rests. It was the mark by which Vaughan recognized a true Christian in his day, and the keynote to many of the scripture uses that I have explored in *Silex Scintillans* and *The Mount of Olives*. To be patient with the hope and cheer that 'The Men of War' finds in Christ's comfort and promises was, in Vaughan's view, to be truly a Christian. To suffer without this 'bright grief' is not true overcoming but merely to 'νικάω, overcome, as those that in some diseases, cure without pain, or using Narcotick medicines do overcome the pain, *but Christian patience doth more.*'[111] How *much* more Vaughan's poetry overcomes through true patience, the scripture-using reader of *Silex Scintillans* alone can read.

---

[110] 'Affliction [I]', l. 38.

[111] Lancelot Andrewes, *The Pattern of Catechistical Doctrine* (1650), 177. Andrewes is deprecating the patience of the 'Circumcelliones', fourth-century bands of predatory peasants in North Africa (see *The Oxford Dictionary of the Christian Church*, 353).

Bibliography

Place of publication is London unless stated.

REFERENCE WORKS

ALLISON, A. F., *English Translations from the Spanish and Portuguese to the Year 1700: An Annotated Catalogue of the Extant Printed Versions (Excluding Dramatic Adaptations)* (1974).

BARDSLEY, CHARLES WAREING, *A Dictionary of English and Welsh Surnames: With Special American Instances* (1901).

BEAL, PETER, *Index of English Literary Manuscripts*, 2 parts: Part I [1450–1625], 2 vols. (1980); Part II [1625–1700], 2 vols. (1987–1993).

BLAYNEY, PETER W. M., *The Bookshops in Paul's Cross Churchyard* (1990).

BRIGHTMAN, F. E., *The English Rite: Being a Synopsis of the Sources and Revisions of the 'Book of Common Prayer'*, 2 vols. (1915).

CROSS, F. L. (ed.), *The Oxford Dictionary of the Christian Church*, 3rd edn. ed. E. A. Livingstone (Oxford, 1997).

FIRTH, C. H., and R. S. RAIT (eds.), *Acts and Ordinances of the Interregnum, 1642–1660*, 3 vols. (1911).

FORTESCUE, G. K. (ed.), *A Catalogue of the Pamphlets, Books, Newspapers, and Manuscripts Relating to the Civil War, the Commonwealth, and Restoration, Collected by George Thomason, 1640–1661*, 2 vols. (1908).

FRANK, JOSEPH, *Hobbled Pegasus: A Descriptive Bibliography of Minor English Poetry, 1641–1660* (Albuquerque, 1968).

Geiriadur Prifysgol Cymru: A Dictionary of the Welsh language, 3 vols. (Cardiff, 1968–87).

GREAVES, RICHARD L., and ROBERT ZALLER (eds.), *Biographical Dictionary of British Radicals in the Seventeenth Century*, 3 vols. (Brighton, 1982–4).

GREENSLADE, S. L. (ed.), *The Cambridge History of the Bible*, iii: *The West from the Reformation to the Present Day* (Cambridge, 1963).

GUFFEY, GEORGE R., *A Concordance to the English Poems of Andrew Marvell* (Chapel Hill, NC, 1974).

HANKS, PATRICK, and FLAVIA HODGES, *A Dictionary of Surnames* (Oxford, 1988).

HARFORD, GEORGE, and MORLEY STEVENSON (eds.), *The Prayer Book Dictionary*, rev. edn. (1925).

INGRAM, WILLIAM, and KATHLEEN SWAIM, *A Concordance to Milton's English Poetry* (Oxford, 1972).

KEEBLE, N. H., and G. F. NUTTALL (eds.), *Calendar of the Correspondence of Richard Baxter* (Oxford, 1991).

MARILLA, E. L., *A Comprehensive Bibliography of Henry Vaughan* (1948; repr. New York, 1972).

—— *Henry Vaughan: A Bibliographical Supplement 1946–60* (Tuscaloosa, Ala., 1963).

MORGAN, PAUL, *Oxford Libraries outside the Bodleian*, 2nd edn. (Oxford, 1980).

MORGAN, T. J., and PRYS MORGAN, *Welsh Surnames* (Cardiff, 1985).

MORRISON, PAUL G. (ed.), *Index of Printers, Publishers and Booksellers in Donald Wing's Short-Title Catalogue* (Charlottesville, Va., 1955).

NELSON, CAROLYN, and MATHEW SECCOMBE, *British Newspapers and Periodicals 1641–1700: A Short-Title Catalogue* (New York, 1987).

PIGLER, A., *Barockthemen: Eine Auswahl von Verzeichnissen zur Ikonographie des 17. und 18. Jahrhunderts*, 3 vols. (Budapest, 1974).

PLOMER, H. R. (ed.), *A Dictionary of Printers and Booksellers Who Were at Work in England, Scotland and Ireland from 1641 to 1667* (1907).

—— (transcr.), *A Transcript of the Registers of the Worshipful Company of Stationers from 1640–1708 A. D.*, 3 vols. (1913).

PREUSS, JULIUS, *Biblical and Talmudic Medicine*, trans. and ed. Fred Rosner (New York, 1978).

REES, WILLIAM, *An Historical Atlas of Wales from Early to Modern Times*, 2nd edn. (Cardiff, 1972).

A Short-Title Catalogue of Books Printed in England, Scotland and Ireland and of English Books Printed Abroad 1475–1640, first compiled by A. W. Pollard and G. R. Redgrave, 2nd edn. revised and enlarged, begun by W. A. Jackson and F. S. Ferguson, completed by Katharine F. Pantzer, 3 vols. (1976–91).

A Short-Title Catalogue of Books Printed in England, Scotland, Ireland, Wales and British North America and of English Books Printed in Other Countries 1641–1700, compiled by Donald Wing, 2nd edn. revised and enlarged by the Index Committee of the Modern Language Association of America, 3 vols.: i (New York; 1972; newly revised and enlarged 1994); ii (1982); iii (1988).

SIMPSON, J. A., and E. S. C. WEINER (eds.), *The Oxford English Dictionary*, 2nd edn., 17 vols. (Oxford, 1989).

STEPHENS, LESLIE, and SIDNEY LEE (eds.), *The Dictionary of National Biography*, 63 vols. (1885–1900).

TUTTLE, IMILDA, *Concordance to Vaughan's 'Silex Scintillans'* (University Park, Pa., 1969).

WOOD, ANTHONY, *Athenae Oxoniensis, an Exact History of All the Writers and Bishops Who Have Had Their Education in the University of Oxford*, 3rd edn. with additions, ed. Philip Bliss, 4 vols. (1820).

WRIGHT, CHRISTOPHER (comp.), *The World's Master Paintings: From the Early Renaissance to the Present Day* (1992).

PRIMARY WORKS

[Catalogue numbers from *STC* and *Wing* are added where applicable.]

AINSWORTH, HENRY, *Annotations upon the First Book of Moses, Called Genesis* (1621) [211].

ALLESTREE, RICHARD (attrib.), *The Practice of Christian Graces; or, The Whole Duty of Man Laid down in a Plain and Familiar Way for the Use of All, but Especially the Meanest Reader*, 2nd edn. (1659) [A 1170].

ALSTED, JOHANN HEINRICH, *The Beloved City; or, The Saints Reign on Earth a Thousand Years* (1643) [A 2924].

ANDREWES, LANCELOT, *XCVI Sermons*, ed. William Laud and John Buckeridge (1629) [606].

—— *A Manual of the Private Devotions and Meditations of the Right Revered Father in God, Lancelot Andrewes*, trans. R. Drake (1648) [A 3135].

—— *The Pattern of Catechistical Doctrine at Large; or, A Learned and Pious Exposition of the Ten Commandments* (1650) [A 3147].

—— *The Form of Consecration of a Church* (1659) [A 3126], in *The Minor Works of Lancelot Andrewes* (Oxford, 1846).

ASKEW, EGEON, *Brotherly Reconcilement: Preached in Oxford* (Oxford, 1605) [855].

AUBREY, JOHN, *Aubrey's Brief Lives*, ed. Oliver Lawson-Dick (1949; 1992).

AUGUSTINE, ST, *Lectures or Tractates on the Gospel According to Saint John*, trans. John Gibb, 2 vols. (Edinburgh, 1873–4).

—— *The City of God against the Pagans*, Loeb Classical Library, 7 vols. (New Haven, 1965).

AYLETT, ROBERT, *Divine and Moral Speculations in Metrical Numbers, upon Various Subjects* (1654) [A 4284].

BAILLIE, ROBERT, *A Dissuasive from the Errours of the Time* (1645) [B 456].

BAKER, SIR RICHARD, *Meditations and Motives for Prayer upon the Seven Dayes of the Weeke* (1642) [B 511].

BALCANQUALL, WALTER, *The Honour of Christian Churches; and the Necessitie of Frequenting of Divine Service and Publike Prayers in Them* (1633) [1237].

The Baronettage of England: Being an Historical and Genealogical Account of Baronets, from Their First Inception in the Reign of King James I, 2 vols. (1720).

BARTON, WILLIAM, *A View of Many Errours and Som Gross Absurdities in the Old Translation of the Psalms in English Metre* (1650) [B 1007].

—— *Hallelujah; or, Certain Hymns, Composed out of Scripture, to Celebrate Some Special and Publick Occasions* (1651) [B 1002].

BATT, ANTONIE, *A Hidden Treasure of Holie Prayers and Divine Meditations Newly Found Out in Holie Scripture* (Paris, 1641) [B 1142].

BAYLY, LEWIS, *The Practice of Piety: Directing a Christian How to Walke That He May Please God* (1611; 1640) [1623].

BAXTER, RICHARD, *Reliquiae Baxterianae*, ed. and abr. J. M. Lloyd Thomas (1931).

BEAUMONT, JOSEPH, *Psyche; or, Loves Mysterie, in XX Canto's* (1648) [B 1625].

BENEDICT, ST, *The Rule of the Most Blissed Father Saint Benedict, Patriarke of all Munkes*, trans. A. Gray (Gant, 1632) [1860].

BENLOWES, EDWARD, *Theophila; or, Loves Sacrifice* (1652) [B 1879].

The Bible [Genevan] (1610) [2211].

BILLINGSLEY, NICHOLAS, *A Treasury of Divine Raptures, Consisting of Serious Observations, Pious Ejaculations, Select Epigrams* (1667) [B 2913].

BOETHIUS, ANICIUS MANLIUS SEVERINUS, *The Consolation of Philosophy*, trans. I. T. [1609], rev. H. F. Stewart, Loeb Classical Library (New Haven, 1918).

BOLTON, ROBERT, *Some Generall Directions for a Comfortable Walking with God* (1626) [3251].

—— *Mr. Boltons Last and Learned Worke of the Four Last Things, Death, Judgement, Hell and Heaven* (1632) [3242].

BRAGGE, FRANCIS, *Practical Discourses upon the Parables of Our Blessed Saviour*, 2nd edn., 2 vols. (1706).

BRIGHTMAN, THOMAS, *The Revelation of St John, Illustrated with Analysis and Scholios, Together with A Most Comfortable Exposition of the Last and Most Difficult Part of the Prophecy of Daniel* (Amsterdam, 1644) [B 4692].

BRUCE, ROBERT, *The Way to True Peace and Rest: Delivered at Edinburgh in XVI. Sermons on the Lords Supper, Hezekiahs Sicknesse and Other Select Scriptures* (1617) [3925].

BUCKLER, EDWARD, *Midnights Meditations of Death with Pious and Profitable Observations, and Consolations: Perused by Francis Quarles a Little before his Death* (1646) [B 5350].

BUNYAN, JOHN, *The Life and Death of Mr. Badman*, ed. James F. Forrest and Roger Sharrock (Oxford, 1988).

BUNNY, EDMUND, *A Booke of Christian Exercise, Appertaining to Resolution, That is, Shewing How That We Should Resolve Our Selves to Become Christians in Deed* (1584) [19355].

BUTLER, SAMUEL, *Hudibras*, ed. J. Wilders (Oxford, 1967).

C., T., *A Glasse or the Times, by Which According to the Scriptures, You May Clearly Behold the True Minister of Christ How Farre Differing from False Teachers* (1648) [C 132].

CALVIN, JEAN, *The Psalmes of David and Others, with M. John Calvins Commentaries*, trans. A. Golding (1571) [4395].

—— *A Commentary of John Calvine, upon the First Booke of Moses called Genesis*, trans. Thomas Tymme (1578) [4943].

—— *Thirteene Sermons, Entreating of the Free Election of God in Jacob, and of Reprobation in Esau*, trans. J. Field (1579) [4457].

CALVIN, JEAN, *A Commentary upon the Prophecie of Isaiah by Mr. John Calvin*, trans. C. C[otton] (1609) [4396].

—— *Commentary on the Gospel According to John*, trans. William Pringle (Edinburgh, 1847).

CAREW, THOMAS, *Poems 1640, Together with Poems from the Wyburd Manuscript* (Menston, 1969).

CARTWRIGHT, WILLIAM, *Comedies, Tragi-Comedies, with Other Poems* (1651) [C 709].

CHARLETON, WALTER, *The Immortality of the Human Soul, Demonstrated by the Light of Nature* (1657) [C 3675].

CLEVELAND, JOHN, *Poems* (1651) [C 4684].

COBBET, THOMAS, *A Practical Discourse of Prayer Wherein is Handled the Nature, the Duty, the Qualifications of Prayer; the Several Sorts of Prayer; viz. Ejaculatory, Publick, Private, and Secret Prayer* (1654) [C 4779].

COLERIDGE, S. T., *Samuel Taylor Coleridge*, ed. H. Jackson, Oxford Authors Series (Oxford, 1985).

—— *Coleridge on the Seventeenth Century*, ed. Robert Florence Brinkley (New York, 1968).

COSIN, JOHN, *A Collection of Private Devotions in the Practice of the Antient Church: Called the Houres of Prayer* [1627], ed. P. G. Stanwood (Oxford, 1967).

COWLEY, ABRAHAM, Preface to *Poems* (1655), repr. in *Critical Essays of the Seventeenth Century*, ed. J. E. Spingarn, 3 vols. (Oxford, 1908–9), ii. 77–90.

CRADOCK, WALTER, *The Saints Fulnesse of Joy* (1646) [C 6764].

—— *Gospel-Libertie* (1648) [C 6762].

—— *Gospel-Holinesse* (1651) [C 6760].

CRASHAW, RICHARD, *The Poems, English, Latin and Greek, of Richard Crashaw*, ed. L. C. Martin, 2nd edn. (Oxford, 1957).

CROLLIUS, OSWALDUS, *Bazilica Chymica, et Praxis Chymiatricae; or, Royal and Practical Chymistry in Three Treatises*, trans. John Hartman (1670) [C 7022].

CROMWELL, OLIVER, *The Writings and Speeches of Oliver Cromwell, with an Introduction and a Sketch of His Life*, ed. Wilbur Cortez Abbott and Catherine D. Crane, 2 vols. (1937; repr. Oxford, 1988).

CULVERWEL, NATHANAEL, *An Elegant and Learned Discourse of the Light of Nature* (1652) [C 7569].

DANIEL, GEORGE, *The Poems of George Daniel*, ed. Alexander B. Grosart (Edinburgh, 1878).

DAVENANT, WILLIAM, *Gondibert: An Heroick Poem* (1651) [D 324].

DENT, ARTHUR, *The Plaine Mans Path-Way to Heaven* (1601) [6626].

DIODATI, JOHN, *Pious Annotations upon the Holy Bible Expounding the Difficult Places Thereof Learnedly and Plainly*, 3rd edn. (1651) [D 1507].

DONNE, JOHN, *Poems, by J. D. with Elegies on the Authors Death* (1633) [7045].

—— *The Poems of John Donne*, ed. Herbert J. C. Grierson, 2 vols. (Oxford, 1912).

—— *The Sermons of John Donne*, ed. George R. Potter and Evelyn M. Simpson, 10 vols. (Berkeley and Los Angeles, 1953–62).

—— *John Donne and the Theology of Language*, ed. P. G. Stanwood and Heather Ross Asals (Columbia, NY, 1988).

DOUGLAS, ROBERT, *The Forme and Order of the Coronation of Charles the Second, As It Was Acted and Done at Scone* (Aberdeen, 1651) [D 2026].

DREXELIUS, HIEREMIAS, *The Angel-Guardian's Clock Translated out of Latin into English* (1630) [7234].

—— *The Considerations of Drexelius upon Eternitie*, trans. Ralph Winterton (1632) [7235].

DRYDEN, JOHN, *John Dryden*, ed. Keith Walker, Oxford Authors Series (Oxford, 1987).

DUCKET, CHARLES, *Sparks from the Golden Altar; or, Occasional Meditations, Ejaculations, Observations, and Experiences* (1660) [D 2430A].

DYKE, JEREMIAH, *A Sermon Dedicatory, Preached at the Consecration of the Chappell of Epping in Essex, October 28, 1622* (1623) [7423].

EDWARDS, THOMAS, *Gangraena; or, A Catalogue and Discovery of Many of the Errours, Heresies, Blasphemies and Pernicious Practices of the Sectaries of the Time, Vented and Acted in England in These Four Last Years*, 2nd edn. (1646) [E 229].

ERASMUS, DESIDERIUS, *The Collected Works of Erasmus*, ed. R. J. Schoek, B. M. Corrigan and others, 86 vols. (Toronto, 1974–93).

ERBERY, WILLIAM, *The Bishop of London, the Welsh Curate, and Common Prayers, with Apocrypha in the End* (1652) [E 3223].

—— *The Testimony of William Erbery* (1658) [E 3239].

EVANS, ARISE, *A Voice from Heaven* (1651) [E 3468].

—— *An Eccho to the Voice from Heaven* (1652) [E 3457].

EVELYN, JOHN, *The Diary of John Evelyn*, ed. E. S. de Beer, 6 vols. (Oxford, 1955).

FELLTHAM, OWEN, *Resolves: A Duple Century*, 3rd edn. (1628–9) [10758].

—— 'An Anglican Family Worship Service of the Interregnum: A Cancelled Early Text and a New Edition of Owen Felltham's "A Form of Prayer"', ed. Ted-Larry Pebworth, *English Literary Renaissance*, 16 (1986), 206–33.

FERRAR, NICHOLAS, *The Ferrar Papers*, ed. B. Blackstone (Cambridge, 1938).

FILMER, SIR ROBERT, *Patriarcha and Other Writings*, ed. Johann P. Sommerville (Cambridge, 1991).

—— '*Patriarcha*' *and Other Political Works of Sir Robert Filmer*, ed. Peter Laslett (Oxford, 1949).

FITZGERALD, EDWARD, *The Letters of Edward Fitzgerald*, ed. Alfred McKinley Terhune and Annabelle Burdick Terhune, 4 vols. (Princeton, 1980).

FLETCHER, GILES, the Younger, *Christs Victorie in Heaven*, in *Giles and Phineas Fletcher: Poetical Works*, ed. F. S. Boas (Cambridge, 1908).

A Forme of Prayer Used in the King's Chappel upon Tuesdayes in These Times of Trouble and Distresse, 2nd edn. (The Hague, 1650) [C 4166].

FOX, GEORGE, *The Journal of George Fox*, ed. Norman Penney, 2 vols. (Cambridge, 1911).

FRANCIS OF SALES, ST, *An Introduction to the Devoute Life*, trans. J. Y. (Paris, 1637) [11322].

Gemitus Ecclesiae Cambro-Britannicus: or, The Candlestick Removed, by the Eject-ment of the Ministers of Wales, under the Power of the Late Act, for the Propaga-tion of the Gospell There (1654) [G 483].

GRIFFITH, ALEXANDER, *Strena Vavasoriensis, a New-Years-Gift for the Welch Itin-erants; or, A Hue and Cry after Mr Vavasor Powell* (1654) [G 1988].

—— *Mercurius Cambro-Britannicus; or, News from Wales* (1652) [G 1987].

—— *A True and Perfect Relation of the Whole Transaction Concerning the Petition of the Six Counties of South Wales and Monmouth, Formerly Presented to the Par-liament of the Common-Wealth of England, for a Supply of Godly Ministers, and an Account of Ecclesiastical Revenues Therein* (1654) [G 1989].

GRIFFITH, GEORGE, *A Relation of a Disputation between Dr. Griffith and Mr Vava-sor Powell and Since Some False Observations Made Thereon, by Dr Griffith (or One of His Symonicall Brethren) to Keep up the Crack'd Credit of Their Bad Call-ing and Cause* (1653) [G 1998].

HABINGTON, WILLIAM, *The Poems of William Habington*, ed. Kenneth Allott, Liverpool English Texts and Studies (Liverpool, 1948).

HALL, JOHN, *The Court of Virtue* [(1565); STC 12632], ed. Russell A. Fraser (1961).

HALL, JOSEPH, *A Sermon Preached at the Happily-Restored and Reedified Chappell of the Right Honorable the Earle of Exceter in his House of S. Johns* (1624) [12714].

—— *A Plaine and Familiar Explication of All the Hard Texts of the Whole Divine Scripture of the Old and New Testament* (1633) [12702].

—— *Cheirothesia; or, The Apostolique Institution* (1649) [H373].

—— *The Revelation Unrevealed* (1650) [H 410].

—— *Susurrium cum Deo, Together with the Souls Farewell* (1651) [H 419].

—— *The Holy Order; or, Fraternity of the Mourners in Sion* (1654) [H 354].

HARRIS, ROBERT, *Hezekiah's Recovery; or, A Sermon, Shewing What Use Hezekiah Did, and All Should Make of Their Deliverance from Sicknesse*, 2nd edn. (1626) [12837].

HARVEY, CHRISTOPHER, *The Synagogue; or, The Shadow of The Temple: Sacred Poems, and Private Ejaculations in Imitation of Mr George Herbert*, 3rd edn. (1657) [H 1046].

HAYTOR, RICHARD, *A Meaning to the Revelation* (1676) [H1225].

HERBERT, GEORGE, *The Temple: Sacred Poems and Private Ejaculations* (Cambridge, 1633) [13183].

—— *Herbert's Remains* (1652) [H 1515].

—— *The Works of George Herbert*, ed. F. E. Hutchinson (Oxford, 1941).

—— *The English Poems of George Herbert*, ed. C. A. Patrides (1974).

—— *George Herbert and Henry Vaughan*, ed. Louis Martz, Oxford Authors Series (Oxford, 1986).

Hermetica: The Greek Corpus Hermeticum and the Latin Asclepius in a New English Translation, with Notes and Introduction, ed. and trans. Brian P. Copenhaver (Cambridge, 1992).

HERRICK, ROBERT, *The Poetical Works of Robert Herrick,* ed. L. C. Martin (Oxford, 1956).

HIPPOCRATES, *The Aphorismes of Hippocrates, Prince of Physicians, with an Exact Table Showing the Substance of Every Aphorism, and a Short Comment on Each One, Taken out of Those Larger Notes of Galen, Heurnius, Fuschius, &c.* (1655) [H 2071].

HOOKER, RICHARD, *The Folger Library Edition of the Works of Richard Hooker,* gen. ed. W. Speed Hill, Medieval and Renaissance Texts and Studies, 6 vols. (Binghamton, NY, 1977–93).

HUME, ALEXANDER, *Poems 1557–1609,* edited from the text of Waldegrave by Alexander Lawson (Edinburgh, 1902).

HUTCHESON, GEORGE, *An Exposition of the Gospel of Jesus Christ According to John* (1657) [H 3826].

HYDE, EDWARD, *A Collection of Several Tracts of the Right Honorable Edward, Earl of Clarendon* (1727).

JAMES, THOMAS, *Catalogus Universalis Librorum in Bibliotheca Bodleiana Omnium Librorum,* 2nd edn. (Oxford, 1620) [14450].

JANSON, CORNELIUS, *Paraphrasis in Psalmos Omnes Davidicos* (Leiden, 1586).

JANSON, JACOB, *In Psalterium, et Cantica Quibus per Horas Canonicas Romana Utitur Ecclesia, Expositio* (Louvain, 1597).

JEFFS, ROBIN (ed.), *The English Revolution I: Fast Sermons to Parliament; Reproductions in Facsimile,* 34 vols. (1970–1).

JOHNSON, SAMUEL, *Samuel Johnson,* ed. Donald M. Greene, Oxford Authors Series (Oxford, 1984).

JONSON, BEN, *Ben Jonson,* ed. C. H. Herford, Percy and Evelyn Simpson, 11 vols. (Oxford, 1925–52).

—— *The Complete Masques,* ed. Stephen Orgel (New Haven, 1969).

JOSSELIN, RALPH, *The Diary of Ralph Josselin 1616–1683,* ed. Alan MacFarlane, Records of Social and Economic History, NS, 3 (1976).

KER, PATRICK, *An Elegy on the Deplorable, and Never Enough to be Lamented Death, of Charles II* (1685) [K 337].

KING, HENRY, *The Poems of Henry King,* ed. Margaret Crum (Oxford, 1965).

LITTLETON, ADAM, *Hezekiah's Return of Praise for His Recovery* (1668) [L 2562].

LLWYD, MORGAN, *Gweithiau Morgan Llwyd o Wynedd,* 3 vols: i: ed. Thomas E. Ellis (Bangor, 1899); ii: ed. John H. Davies (Bangor, 1908); iii: ed. J. Graham Jones and Goronwy Wyn Owen, with an Introduction by R. Tudor Jones (Cardiff, 1994).

—— *Llyfr y Tri Aderyn* (1653), trans. L. J. Parry in *Transactions of the New Eisteddfod of Wales* (1898), 192–275.

LODGE, THOMAS, *Prosopopeia: Containing the Teares of the Holy Marie* (1596) [16662a].

LONDON, WILLIAM, *A Catalogue of the Most Vendible Books in England*, 2nd edn. (1658) [L 2850].

LOVE, CHRISTOPHER, *Heavens Glory, Hells Terror; or, Two Treatises; the One Concerning the Glory of the Saints with Jesus Christ, as a Spur to Duty, the Other of the Torments of the Damned as a Preservative against Security* (1653) [L 3161].

LOWTH, WILLIAM, *A Commentary upon the Prophet Ezekiel* (1723).

LUTHER, MARTIN, *Lectures on the Minor Prophets*, ed. Hilton C. Oswald (Saint Louis, Mo., 1975), vol. xviii of *Luther's Works*, ed. Jaroslav Pelikan and Helmut Lehmann, 55 vols. (Saint Louis, Mo., 1958–9).

MANASSEH BEN ISRAEL, *The Hope of Israel* (1650) [M 375].

MARKHAM, GERVASE (attrib.), *Marie Magdalens Lamentations for the Losse of her Master Jesus* (1601) [17569].

MARLORATE, AUGUSTINE, *A Catholike and Ecclesiasticall Exposition of the Holy Gospell after S. John*, trans. T. Timme (1575) [17406].

MARVELL, ANDREW, *The Poems and Letters of Andrew Marvell*, ed. H. M. Margoliouth, 3rd edn. rev. Pierre Legouis with Elsie Duncan-Jones, 2 vols. (Oxford, 1971).

MATTHEWS, A. G., *Calamy Revised: Being a Revision of Edmund Calamy's Account of the Ministers Ejected and Silenced, 1660–2* (Oxford, 1934).

—— *Walker Revised: Being a Revision of John Walker's Sufferings of the Clergy During the Grand Rebellion 1642–60* (Oxford, 1948).

MEDE, JOSEPH, *The Key of the Revelation, Searched and Demonstrated out of the Naturall and Proper Characters of the Visions*, 2nd edn. (1650) [M 1601].

Metaphysical Lyrics and Poems of the Seventeenth Century: Donne to Butler, ed. Herbert J. C. Grierson (Oxford, 1921).

MILTON, JOHN, *Complete Prose Works of John Milton*, ed. Don M. Wolfe and others, 8 vols. (New Haven, 1953–82).

—— *Paradise Lost*, ed. Alastair Fowler, 2nd edn. (1998).

—— *Complete Shorter Poems of John Milton*, ed. John Carey, 2nd edn. (1997).

The Minutes of the First Independent Church (Now Bunyan Meeting) at Bedford 1656–1766, ed. H. G. Tibbutt, Bedfordshire Historical Record Society 55 (Bedford, 1976).

MUGGLETON, LODOWICK, *The Acts of the Witnesses of the Spirit* (1699) [M 3040].

NALSON, JOHN, *The Common Interest of King and People: Shewing the Original, Antiquity and Excellency of Monarchy, Compared with Aristocracy and Democracy and Particularly of our English Monarchy* (1677) [N 92].

NASHE, THOMAS, *Christs Tears over Jerusalem* (1593), in *The Works of Thomas Nashe*, ed. Ronald B. McKerrow, 5 vols. (Oxford, 1958), ii. 1–177.

OLDHAM, JOHN, *Some New Pieces Never Before Published* (1681) [O 248].

The Order of the Communion (1548) [16456.5].

OWEN, JOHN, *The Advantage of the Kingdome of Christ* (Oxford, 1651) [O 711].

P., J., *Oeconomica Sacra; or, A Paranaetical Discourse of Marriage: Together with Some Particular Remarks upon the Marriage of Isaac and Rebecca* (1685) [P 62].

PAGITT, EPHRAIM, *Heresiography*, 2nd edn. (1645) [P 175].

PANTER, P., *De Non Temerandis Ecclesiis: Whereof the Name and Sacrednesse of Churches, against Those, Who in Contempt Do Call Them Steeple-Houses, Proposed by Way of Conference* (1650) [D 639].

PAREUS, DAVID, *In Genesin Moisis Commentarius* (Geneva, 1614).

Parnassus Biceps; or, Several Choice Pieces of Poetry, Compiled by the Best Wits That Were in Both the Universities before their Dissolution, compiled by Abraham Wright (1656) [W 3686].

Patrologia Cursus Completus, ed. J.-P. Migne, 221 vols. (Paris, 1844–65).

PERERIUS, BENEDICTUS, *Commentariorum et Disputantionum in Genesin* (1589–98; Cologne, 1601).

The Perfect Diurnal, 138 (2 Aug. 1652) [No. 503.138A in Nelson and Seccombe, *British Newspapers and Periodicals 1641–1700*, above].

PERKINS, WILLIAM, *A Golden Chaine; or, The Description of Theologie, Containing the Order of the Causes of Salvation and Damnation, According to Gods Word*, 2nd edn. (Cambridge, 1592) [19661.5].

POCKOCKE, EDWARD, *A Commentary on the Prophecy of Malachi* (Oxford, 1677) [P 2661A].

PORDAGE, SAMUEL, *Mundorum Explicatio; Wherein are Couched the Mysteries of the External, Internal and Eternal Worlds* (1663) [P 2975].

POWELL, THOMAS, *Humane Industry; or, A History of Most Manual Arts, Deducing the Original, Progress, and Improvement of Them* (1611) [P 3072].

POWELL, VAVASOR, *Truths Conflict with Error; or, Universall Redemption Controverted in Three Publicke Disputations* (1650) [T 3167B].

—— *Christ Exalted above all His Creatures by God his Father* (1651) [P 3081].

—— *Spirituall Experiences of Sundry Beleevers* (1653) [P 3095].

PRICE, SAMPSON, *Londons Warning by Laodicea's Lukewarmnesse* (1613) [20333].

—— *Ephesus Warning before Her Woe; a Sermon Preached at Pauls Crosse* (1616) [20330].

—— *The Beauty of Holiness; or, The Consecration of a House of Prayer* (1618) [20328].

PRIDEAUX, JOHN, *Hezekiah's Sicknesse and Recovery, a Sermon Preached before the King's Majestie at Woodstocke* [20355], part of *Certaine Sermons Preached by John Prideaux* (Oxford, 1637) [20345].

—— *Ephesus Backsliding: Considered and Applied to These Times* (1614) [20352].

The Primer According to the Last Edition of the Roman Breviarie (1617) [16097].

Private Prayers Put Forth by Authority During the Reign of Queen Elizabeth, ed. W. K. Clay (Cambridge, 1851).

QUARLES, FRANCIS, *Divine Fancies Digested into Epigrammes, Meditations, and Observations* (1632) [20529].

—— *Francis Quarles: The Complete Works in Prose and Verse*, ed. Alexander B. Grosart, 3 vols. (Edinburgh [printed for private circulation], 1880–1; repr. Hildesheim, 1971).

QUARLES, JOHN, *Divine Meditations upon Several Subjects* (1679) [Q 125].

RANDOLPH, THOMAS, *The Poems and 'Amyntas' of Thomas Randolph*, ed. John Jay Parry (New Haven, 1917).

REEVE, JOHN, *A Transcendent Spiritual Treatise* (1652) [R 683].

RICHARDS, NATHANIEL, *Poems Sacred and Satyricall* (1641) [R 1372].

ROBARTS, FOULKE, *Gods Holy House and Service, According to the Primitive and Most Christian Forme Thereof* (1639) [21068].

ROBERTSON, BARTHOLEMEW, *The Crowne of Life* (1618) [21097].

ROGERS, THOMAS, *A Golden Chaine, Taken out of the Psalmes of King David* (1579) [21235].

ROSS, ALEXANDER, *Three Decads of Divine Meditations* (1630) [21331].

ROUS, J., *Catalogus Interpretum Sacrae Scripturae juxta Numerorum Ordinem, que Extant in Bibliotheca Bodleiana* (Oxford, 1620) [part of 14450].

SANDERSON, ROBERT, *A Liturgy in Times of Rebellion*, pp. 1–40 in *Fragmentary Illustrations of the History of the 'Book of Common Prayer'*, ed. W. K. Jacobson (1874).

—— *The Works of Robert Sanderson, D.D.*, 6 vols. (Oxford, 1844).

SANDYS, GEORGE, *A Paraphrase upon the Divine Poems* (1638) [21725].

SCLATER, WILLIAM, *A Brief, and Plain Commentary, with Notes: Not More Useful, Than Seasonable, upon the Whole Prophecie of Malachy* (1650) [S 913].

SEAGER, JOHN, *A Discoverie of the World to Come* (1650) [S2172].

SHELFORD, ROBERT, *Five Pious and Learned Discourses* (Cambridge, 1635) [22400].

SMART, CHRISTOPHER, *Christopher Smart: Selected Poems*, ed. Karina Williamson and Marcus Walsh (Harmondsworth, 1990).

SOUTH, ROBERT, *Forty-Eight Sermons and Discourses on Several Subjects and Occasions*, 4 vols. (1715).

SOUTHWELL, ROBERT, *Marie Magdalens Funerall Teares* (1609) [22953].

SPARKE, MICHAEL, *The Crums of Comfort with Godly Prayers, Corrected and Emended* (1627) [23015.7].

SPENCER, SIR EDWARD, *A Brief Epistle to the Learned Manasseh ben Israel in Answer to His* (1650) [S 4945A].

TAYLOR, JEREMY, *The Rule and Exercises of Holy Living* [1650] and *The Rule and Exercises of Holy Dying* [1651], ed. P. G. Stanwood, 2 vols. (Oxford, 1989).

—— *The Whole Works of the Right Reverend Jeremy Taylor, D.D. with a Life of the Author*, ed. Reginald Heber and Charles Page Eden, 10 vols. (1847–52).

TAYLOR, THOMAS, *Christ Revealed; or, The Old Testament Explained* (1635) [23821].

THOMPSON, WILLIAM, *Poems* (Oxford, 1757).

TITELMAN, FRANCIS, *Elucidatio in Omnes Psalmos* (Antwerp, 1531).

TRAPP, JOHN, *A Clavis to the Bible; or, A New Comment upon the Pentateuch* (1650) [T 2038].

A True Picture of Our Present Reformation; or, The Christians Prospective, to Take a Short View of the New Lights That Have Broke Forth Since Bishops Went Downe (1648) [T 2538].

Two Treatises the First . . . to the . . . Church of Laodicea (1642) [T 3541].

USSHER, JAMES, *Annales Veteris Testamenti* (1650) [U 147].

VAUGHAN, HENRY, *Poems, with the Tenth Satyre of Juvenal Englished, by Henry Vaughan, Gent.* (1646) [V 124].

—— *Silex Scintillans; or, Sacred Poems and Private Ejaculations; by Henry Vaughan Silurist* (1650) [V 125].

—— *Olor Iscanus. A Collection of Some Select Poems, and Translations, Formerly written by Mr. Henry Vaughan Silurist* (1651) [V 123].

—— *The Mount of Olives; or, Solitary Devotions. By Henry Vaughan Silurist* (1652) [V 122].

—— *Flores Solitudinis. Certaine Rare and Elegant Pieces . . . Collected in his Sicknesse and Retirement by Henry Vaughan, Silurist* (1654) [V 121].

—— *Hermetical Physick: or, The Right Way to Preserve, and to Restore Health. By That Famous and Faithfull Chymist, Henry Nollius. Englished by Henry Vaughan, Gent.* (1655) [N1222].

—— *Silex Scintillans: Sacred Poems and Private Ejaculations. The Second Edition, in Two Books; by Henry Vaughan, Silurist* (1655) [V 126].

—— *The Chymists Key: to Shut, and to Open: or, The True Doctrin of Corruption and Generation, in Ten Brief Aphorismes* (1657) [N1221].

—— *Thalia Rediviva: The Pass-Times and Diversions of a Countrey-Muse, In Choice Poems On Several Occasions. With Some Learned Remains of the Eminent Eugenius Philalethes. Never made Publick Till Now* (1678) [V 127].

—— *The Works of Henry Vaughan*, ed. L. C. Martin, 2nd edn. (Oxford, 1957).

—— *Henry Vaughan: The Complete Poems*, ed. Alan Rudrum, Penguin English Poets Series, 2nd rev. edn. (Harmondsworth, 1983).

—— *The Secular Poems of Henry Vaughan*, ed. E. L. Marilla, Essays and Studies on English Literature and Language 21 (Uppsala, 1958).

VAUGHAN, THOMAS, *The Works of Thomas Vaughan*, ed. Alan Rudrum with the assistance of Jennifer Drake-Brockman (Oxford, 1984).

—— *The Works of Thomas Vaughan*, ed. T. E. Waite, 2 vols. (1919).

VERNEUIL, JEAN, *A Nomenclature of Such Tracts and Sermons as Have Beene Printed or Translated into English upon any Place of Holy Scripture* (Oxford, 1637) [24674].

Vices and Virtues: Being a Soul's Confession of its Sins with Reason's Description of the Virtues; a Middle-English Dialogue of about 1200 A. D., ed. Ferdinand Holthausen (1886).

WANLEY, NATHANIEL, *The Poems of Nathaniel Wanley*, ed. L. C. Martin (Oxford, 1928).

WANLEY, NATHANIEL, *Peace and Rest for the Upright* (1678) [W707].

—— *Vox Dei; or, The Great Duty of Self-Reflection upon a Man's Own Wayes* (1658) [W 708].

WATKYNS, ROWLAND, *Flamma sine Fumo; or, Poems without Fictions* [1662], ed. P. C. Davies (Cardiff, 1968).

WATTS, ISAAC, *The Works of Isaac Watts, Containing, besides His Sermons, and Essays on Miscellaneous Subjects, Several Additional Pieces*, 6 vols. (1810).

A Welsh Narrative, Corrected, and Taught to Speak True English, and Some Latine; or, Animadversions on an Imperfect Relation in the Perfect Diurnall, Numb. 138, Aug.2. 1652. Containing a Narration of the Disputation between Dr Griffith and Mr Vavasor Powell, Near New-Chappell in Mountgomery-shire (1653) [W 1342].

WESLEY, SAMUEL, the Elder, *The History of the Old Testament in Verse: with One Hundred and Eight Sculptures*, 2 vols. (1715).

WESLEY, SAMUEL, the Younger, *Poems on Several Occasions*, 2nd edn. (Cambridge, 1743).

WHITE, GILBERT, *The Natural History of Selborne*, ed. Richard Maby (Harmondsworth, 1977).

WIED, HERMAN VON, *A Simple, and Religious Consultation*, 2nd edn. (1548) [13214].

WILLET, ANDREW, *Hexapla in Genesin; that is, A Sixfold Commentarie upon Genesis*, 3rd edn. (1632) [25684].

WILSON, ARTHUR, *The History of Great Britain, Being the Life and Reign of King James the First*, 2nd edn. (1653) [W 2888].

WILSON, JOHN, *The Treasury of Devotion, Containing Diverse Pious Prayers . . . Together with the Seaven Little Offices in Latin and English* (1622) [25773].

WITHER, GEORGE, *Britains Remembrancer, Containing a Narration of the Plague Lately Past* (1628) [25899].

—— *The Hymnes and Songs of the Church* (1623) [25908].

Witts Recreations: Selected from the Finest Fancies of Moderne Muses; a Facsimile Edition [of STC 25870] ed. Colin Gibson (Menston, 1990).

WOODFORD, SAMUEL: *A Paraphrase upon the Canticles, and Some Select Hymns of the New and Old Testament, with Other Occasional Compositions in English Verse* (1679) [B2632A].

YOUNG, PATRICK (after Nicetas), *Catena Graecorum Patrum in Beatum Job* (1637) [18527].

SECONDARY WORKS

ALLISON, ANTHONY F., *Four Metaphysical Poets: George Herbert, Richard Crashaw, Henry Vaughan, Andrew Marvell; A Bibliographical Catalogue of the Early Edi-*

tions of Their Poetry and Prose to the End of the Seventeenth Century (Folkestone, 1973).

ALVAREZ, A., *The School of Donne* (1961).

ANSELMENT, RAYMOND, *Loyalist Resolve: Patient Fortitude in the English Civil War* (1988).

ASALS, HEATHER, 'David's Successors: Forms of Joy and Art', *Proceedings of the PMR Conference: Annual Publication of the International Patristic, Medieval and Renaissance Conference*, 2 (1977), 23–37.

AUERBACH, ERICH, 'Figura', trans. R. Manheim in *Scenes from the Drama of European Literature* (New York, 1959).

—— *Mimesis: The Representation of Reality in Western Literature*, trans. Willard R. Trask (Princeton, 1953).

AYLMER, G. E., *The Interregnum: The Quest for Settlement, 1646–1660*, rev. edn. (1974).

—— *Rebellion or Revolution? England 1640–1660* (Oxford, 1986).

BAKER, J. N. L., *Jesus College, Oxford, 1571–1971* (Oxford, 1971).

BAROWAY, ISRAEL, 'The Bible as Poetry in the English Renaissance: An Introduction', *Journal of English and Germanic Philology*, 32 (1933), 447–80.

—— 'The Hebrew Hexameter: A Study in Renaissance Sources and Interpretation', *English Literary History*, 2 (1935), 66–91.

BAUCKHAM, RICHARD, *Tudor Apocalypse: Sixteenth-Century Apocalypticism, Millenarianism and the English Reformation* (Abingdon, 1978).

BAXANDALL, MICHAEL, *Patterns of Intention: The Historical Explanation of Pictures* (New Haven, 1985).

BELL, ILONA, 'Herbert and Harvey: In the Shadow of *The Temple*', 255–79 in Edmund Miller and Robert DiYanni (eds.), *Like Season'd Timber: New Essays on George Herbert*, Seventeenth-Century Texts and Studies (New York, 1987).

BENNETT, JOAN, *Five Metaphysical Poets: Donne, Herbert, Vaughan, Crashaw, Marvell* (Cambridge, 1966).

BETHELL, S. L., 'The Poetry of Henry Vaughan, Silurist', *Journal of the Historical Society of the Church in Wales*, 1 (1947), 112–40.

—— *The Cultural Revolution of the Seventeenth Century* (1951).

—— 'The Theology of Henry and Thomas Vaughan', *Theology*, 56 (1953), 137–43.

BICKNELL, E. J., *A Theological Introduction to the Thirty-Nine Articles of the Church of England*, 3rd edn., rev. H. J. Carpenter (1955).

BIRRELL, T. A., 'The Influence of Seventeenth-Century Publishers on the Presentation of English Literature', 163–73 in Mary-Jo Arn and Hanneke Wirtjes, with Hans Jansen (eds.), *Historical & Editorial Studies in Medieval & Early Modern English* (Groningen, 1985).

BISHOP, E., *Liturgica Historica* (Oxford, 1918).

BLENKINSOPP, JOSEPH, *A History of Prophecy in Israel: From the Settlement in the Land to the Hellenistic Period* (1984).

BLOCH, CHANA, *Spelling the Word: George Herbert and the Bible* (Berkeley, Calif., 1985).

BLUNDEN, EDMUND, *On the Poems of Henry Vaughan* (1927).

BOURDETTE, ROBERT E., 'Recent Studies in Henry Vaughan', *English Literary Renaissance*, 4 (1974), 279–310.

BOZEMAN, THEODORE DWIGHT, *To Live Ancient Lives: The Primitivist Dimension in Puritanism* (Chapel Hill, NC, 1988).

BRADSHAW, BRENDAN, and JOHN MORRILL (eds.), *The British Problem, c.1534–1707: State Formation on the Atlantic Archipelago*, Problems in Focus Series (Basingstoke, 1996).

BROCK, P., *Pacifism in Europe to 1914* (Princeton, 1972).

BROWN, ELUNED, '"Learned friend and fellow prisoner": Thomas Powell and Welsh Royalists', *National Library of Wales Journal*, 18 (1973–4), 374–82.

—— 'Henry Vaughan's Biblical Landscape', *Essays and Studies* 30 (1977), 50–60.

BURNS, MARTIN, 'Vaughan's "The World"', *TLS*, 3 Aug. 1933, 525.

BURNS, N. T., *Christian Mortalism from Tyndale to Milton* (Cambridge, Mass., 1972).

BUSH, DOUGLAS, *English Literature in the Earlier Seventeenth Century, 1600–1660*, Oxford History of English Literature, ed. F. P. Wilson and Bonamy Dobrée, 2nd rev. edn. (Oxford, 1945).

BUTTERWORTH, C. C., *The English Primers* (Oxford, 1918).

CALHOUN, THOMAS O., *Henry Vaughan: The Achievement of 'Silex Scintillans'* (Newark, NJ, 1981).

CAPP, BERNARD, *The Fifth Monarchy Men: A Study in Seventeenth-Century Millenarianism* (1972).

—— *Astrology and the Popular Press* (1979).

CAREY, JOHN, *John Donne: Life, Mind and Art* (1981).

CARLTON, CHARLES, *Going to the Wars: The Experience of the British Civil Wars, 1638–1651* (1992).

CARROLL, PETER N., *Puritanism and the Wilderness: The Intellectual Significance of the New England Frontier 1629–1700* (New York, 1969).

CARRUTHERS, MARY, *The Book of Memory: A Study of Memory in Medieval Culture* (Cambridge, 1990).

CARSCALLEN, JAMES, 'Editing Vaughan', *University of Toronto Quarterly*, 47 (1978), 267–73.

CHAMBERS, LELAND H., 'Henry Vaughan's Allusive Technique: Biblical Allusions in "The Night"', *Modern Language Quarterly*, 27 (1966), 371–87.

—— 'Vaughan's *The World*: The Limits of Extrinsic Criticism', *Studies in English Literature 1500–1900*, 8 (1968), 137–50.

CHARITY, A. C., *Events and Their Afterlife* (Cambridge, 1966).

CHEEK, PHILIP MACON, 'The Latin Element in Henry Vaughan', *Studies in Philology*, 44 (1947), 69–88.

CHRISTIANSON, PAUL, *Reformers and Babylon: English Apocalyptic Visions from the Reformation to the Eve of the Civil War* (Toronto, 1978).

CIPOLLA, CARLO, *Clocks and Culture 1300–1700* (1967).

CLARKE, ELIZABETH, *Theory and Theology in George Herbert's Poetry: 'Divinitie and Poesie, Met'*, Oxford Theological Monographs (Oxford, 1997).

—— 'The Ejaculatory Moment' (Paper given to the Northern Renaissance Seminar at Nottingham Trent, 1995).

CLEMENTS, ARTHUR L., *Poetry of Contemplation: John Donne, George Herbert, Henry Vaughan, and the Modern Period* (Albany, NY, 1987).

CLOUGH, WILSON O., 'Henry Vaughan and the Hermetic Philosophy', *Publications of the Modern Language Association of America*, 48 (1933), 1108–30.

CLYDE, WILLIAM, *The Struggle for Freedom of the Press* (Oxford, 1934).

COHN, NORMAN, *The Pursuit of the Millennium: Revolutionary and Mystical Anarchists of the Middle Ages*, 3rd edn. (1970).

COIRO, ANN BAYNES, 'Milton and Class Identity: The Publication of *Areopagitica* and the 1645 *Poems*', *Journal of Medieval and Renaissance Studies*, 22 (1992), 277–89.

COLIE, ROSALIE, *The Resources of Kind*, ed. Barbara K. Lewalski (Berkeley and Los Angeles, 1973).

COLLINSON, PATRICK, *The Elizabethan Puritan Movement* (1967).

—— *The Religion of Protestants* (Oxford, 1982).

—— *Godly People* (1983).

—— 'The Sense of Sacred Writ: Radical Politics and the Short-Lived Sovereignty of Scripture in England', *TLS*, 9 Apr. 1993, 3–4.

COOPER, JOHN W., *Body, Soul, and Life Everlasting: Biblical Anthropology and the Monism-Dualism Debate* (Grand Rapids, Mich., 1989).

CORNS, THOMAS N., *Uncloistered Virtue: English Political Literature 1640–1660* (Oxford, 1992).

CRANE, DAVID, 'The Poetry of Alchemy and the Alchemy of Poetry in the Work of Thomas and Henry Vaughan', *Scintilla*, 1 (1997), 115–22.

CRESSY, DAVID, *Literacy and the Social Order* (Cambridge, 1980).

—— *Bonfires and Bells: National Memory and the Protestant Calendar in Elizabethan and Stuart England* (1989).

—— *Birth, Marriage & Death: Ritual, Religion, and the Life-Cycle in Tudor and Stuart England* (Oxford, 1997).

CROSS, CLAIRE, *The Royal Supremacy in the Elizabethan Church* (1969).

CUMING, G. J., *A History of Anglican Liturgy* (1969).

DALY, PETER M., *Literature in the Light of the Emblem: Structural Parallels between the Emblem and Literature in the Sixteenth and Seventeenth Centuries* (Toronto, 1979).

DANIÉLOU, J., *From Shadows to Reality: Studies in the Biblical Typology of the Fathers*, trans. W. Hibberd (1960).

DAVIES, HORTON, *Worship and Theology in England, from Andrewes to Baxter and Fox, 1603–1690* (Princeton, 1975).

DAVIES, JULIAN, *The Caroline Captivity of the Church: Charles I and the Remoulding of Anglicanism 1625–1641* (Oxford, 1992).

DAVIES, P. C., 'Two Breconshire Contemporaries: Henry Vaughan and Rowland Warkyns', *Poetry Wales*, 11 (1975), 98–115.

DAVIES, STEVIE, *Henry Vaughan*, Borderline Series (Bridgend, 1995).

DAY, HILARY M., 'A Study of the Use of the Bible and the Book of Common Prayer in the Prose Works of Henry Vaughan', Ph.D. thesis (London, 1986).

—— 'Bayly's *The Practice of Piety*: A New Source for Henry Vaughan's *The Mount of Olives*', *Notes and Queries*, 233 (1988), 163–5.

DELANY, PAUL, *British Autobiography in the Seventeenth Century* (1969).

DICKSON, DONALD R., *The Fountain of Living Waters: The Typology of the Waters of Life in the Poetry of Herbert, Vaughan and Traherne* (Columbia, Mo., 1987).

DODD, A. H., *Studies in Stuart Wales* (Cardiff, 1952).

—— 'A Remonstrance from Wales', *Bulletin of Celtic Studies*, 17 (1958), 279–85.

DONAGAN, BARBARA, 'Understanding Providence: The Difficulties of Sir William and Lady Waller', *Journal of Ecclesiastical History*, 39 (1988), 433–44.

DONAHUE, C., 'Patristic Exegesis: Summation', *Critical Approaches to Medieval Literature*, ed. D. Bethurum (New York, 1960).

DURR, ROBERT ALAN, *On the Mystical Poetry of Henry Vaughan* (Cambridge, Mass., 1962).

ELIOT, T. S., 'The Metaphysical Poets', *TLS*, 20 Oct. 1921, 1–2.

—— 'The Silurist', *The Dial*, 83 (1927) 259–63.

ELLIS, STEVEN G., *Tudor Frontiers and Noble Power: The Making of the British State* (Oxford, 1995).

ELLRODT, ROBERT, *L'Inspiration personnelle et l'esprit du temps, chez les poètes métaphysiques anglais*, 3 vols. (Paris, 1960).

ELTON, GEOFFREY, *Reformation Europe, 1517–1559* (1963).

ELTON, WILLIAM R., *'King Lear' and the Gods* (San Marino, Calif., 1966).

EMPSON, WILLIAM, *The Structure of Complex Words* (1951).

—— *Seven Types of Ambiguity*, 2nd edn. (1953).

—— *Argufying: Essays on Literature and Culture*, ed. John Haffenden (1988).

EVANS, E. LEWIS, 'Morgan Llwyd and Jacob Boehme', *Jacob Boehme Society Quarterly*, 1 (1953), 11–16.

FINCHAM, KENNETH (ed.), *The Early Stuart Church*, Problems in Focus Series (Basingstoke, 1993).

FIRTH, C. H., *The Life of Thomas Harrison* (Worcester, Mass., 1893).

FIRTH, KATHERINE R., *The Apocalyptic Tradition in Reformation Britain, 1530–1645* (Oxford, 1979).

FISH, STANLEY, *Is There a Text in This Class? The Authority of Interpretive Communities* (Cambridge, Mass., 1980).

FITTER, CHRIS, 'Henry Vaughan's Landscapes of Military Occupation', *Essays in Criticism*, 42 (1992), 123–47.

FOREY, MADELEINE, 'Poetry as Apocalypse: Henry Vaughan's *Silex Scintillans*', *Seventeenth Century*, 10 (1996), 161–86.

—— 'Language and Revelation: Protestant Apocalyptic Literature 1500–1660', Ph.D. thesis (Oxford, 1994).

FOWLER, ALASTAIR, 'Robert Herrick', Warton Lecture on English poetry, *Proceedings of the British Academy*, 66 (1980), 243–64.

—— *Kinds of Literature: An Introduction to the Theory of Genres and Modes* (Oxford, 1982).

—— *A History of English Literature: Forms and Kinds from the Middle Ages to the Present* (Oxford, 1987).

—— 'The Civil War Canon', *Essays in Criticism*, 46 (1992), 52–60.

—— *Time's Purpled Masquers: Stars and the Afterlife in Renaissance English Literature* (Oxford, 1996).

—— *Triumphal Forms: Structural Patterns in Elizabethan Literature* (Cambridge, 1970).

FOX, MICHAEL A. E., 'Augustinian Hexameral Exegesis in Anglo-Saxon England: Bede, Alcuin, Ælfric and Old English Biblical Verse', Ph.D. thesis (Cambridge, 1997).

FRAISTAT, NEIL (ed.), *Poems in Their Place: The Intertextuality and Order of Poetic Collections* (Chapel Hill, NC, 1986).

FREEMAN, ROSEMARY, *English Emblem Books* (1948).

—— 'Parody as a Literary Form: George Herbert and Wilfred Owen', *Essays in Criticism*, 13 (1963), 307–22.

FREND, W. H. C., 'Paulinus of Nola and the Last Century of the Western Empire', *Journal of Roman Studies*, 59 (1969), 1–11.

FRIELING, RUDOLF, *Old Testament Studies: Essays: Trees Wells, and Stones in the Lives of the Patriarchs: From Sabbath to Sunday*, trans. Margaret and Rudolf Koehler (1963; Edinburgh, 1987).

From Persecution to Toleration: The Glorious Revolution and Religion in England, ed. Ole Peter Grell, Jonathan I. Israel and Nicholas Tyacke (Oxford, 1991).

GARDINER, S. R., *The History of the Great Civil War, 1642–1649*, 4 vols. (1886–91).

—— *History of the Commonwealth and Protectorate: 1649–1660*, 3 vols. (1894–1901).

GARDNER, HELEN, *The Limits of Literary Criticism, Reflections on the Interpreta-*

tion of Poetry and Scripture, Riddell Memorial Lectures 28th Series (Oxford, 1956).

GARDNER, N. H., *Gerard Manley Hopkins (1844–1889); A Study in Poetic Idiosyncracy in Relation to Poetic Tradition*, 2 vols. (1949).

GARNER, ROSS, *Henry Vaughan: Experience and the Tradition* (Chicago, 1959).

GEBER, PAT, *The Search for the Stone of Destiny* (Edinburgh, 1992).

GENTLES, IAN, *The New Model Army in England, Ireland and Scotland, 1645–1653* (Oxford, 1992).

George Herbert Journal: Special Issue on Henry Vaughan, 7 (1983–4), ed. Jonathan Post [Richard F. Kennedy, 'Henry Vaughan's Borrowings from Owen Felltham'; Suzanne Woods, 'Vaughan's Reflective Versification'; Cedric C. Brown, 'The Death of Righteous Men: Prophetic Gesture in Vaughan's "Daphnis" and Milton's "Lycidas"'; Jeff S. Johnson, 'Images of Christ in Vaughan's "The Night": An Argument for Unity'; Boyd M. Berry, 'Childhood and the Self in *Silex Scintillans*'; Janet E. Halley, 'Versions of the Self and the Politics of Privacy in *Silex Scintillans*'; Mary Doherty, '*Flores Solitudinis*: The "two ways" and Vaughan's Patristic Hagiography'].

GITTINGS, CLARE, *Death, Burial and the Individual in Early Modern England* (1984).

GRIFFITHS, ERIC, 'The Disappointment of Christina Rossetti', F. W. Bateson Memorial Lecture, *Essays in Criticism*, 47 (1997), 107–42.

GOODY, JACK, and E. P. THOMPSON, *Family and Inheritance: Rural Society in Western Europe, 1200–1800* (Cambridge, 1976).

GOULD, WARWICK, and MARJORIE REEVES, *Joachim of Fiore and the Myth of the Eternal Evangel in the Nineteenth Century* (Oxford, 1987).

GRAY, DOUGLAS, *Themes and Images in the Medieval English Religious Lyric* (1972).

GREEN, IAN, *The Christian's ABC: Catechisms and Catechizing in England c.1530–1740* (Oxford, 1996).

GREENWOOD, D. S., 'The Seventeenth-Century English Poetic Biblical Paraphrase: Practitioners, Texts and Contexts', Ph.D. thesis (Cambridge, 1985).

GUIBBORY, ACHSAH, *The Map of Time: Seventeenth-Century English Literature and Ideas of Pattern in History* (Urbana, Ill., 1986).

HALLER, WILLIAM, *The Rise of Puritanism; or, The Way to the New Jerusalem as Set Forth in Pulpit and Press from Thomas Cartwright to John Lilburne and John Milton, 1570–1643* (New York, 1957).

HAMMOND, GERALD, '"Poor dust should still lie low": George Herbert and Henry Vaughan', *English*, 35 (1986), 1–22.

HARDACRE, PAUL, *The Royalists during the English Revolution*, International Scholars Forum Series (The Hague, 1956).

HARRIS, VICTOR, 'Allegory to Analogy in the Interpretation of the Scriptures during the Middle Ages and the Renaissance', *Philological Quarterly*, 45 (1966), 1–23.

HEALY, THOMAS F., *Richard Crashaw*, Medieval and Renaissance Authors Series (Leiden, 1986).

—— and JONATHAN SAWDAY (eds.), *Literature and the English Civil War* (Cambridge, 1990).

HEATON, E. W., *The Old Testament Prophets*, 2nd edn. (Harmondsworth, 1961).

HESSAYON, ARIEL, ' "Gold tried in the fire": The Prophet Theauraujohn Tany and the Puritan Revolution', Ph.D. thesis (Cambridge, 1996).

HIGHAM, FLORENCE, *Catholic and Reformed: A Study of the Anglican Church 1559–1662* (London, 1962).

HILL, CHRISTOPHER, 'Propagating the Gospel', in H. E. Bell and R. L. Ollard (eds.), *Historical Essays 1600–1750 Presented to David Ogg* (1963).

—— *Antichrist in Seventeenth-Century England* (1971).

—— *The World Turned Upside-Down: Radical Ideas during the English Revolution* (1972).

—— *Milton and the English Revolution* (1977).

—— *The Experience of Defeat: Milton and Some Contemporaries* (1984).

—— 'Henry Vaughan', 207–25 in *The Collected Essays of Christopher Hill*, i: *Writing and Revolution in Seventeenth-Century England* (Brighton, 1985).

—— *Change and Continuity in Seventeenth-Century England*, rev. edn. (New Haven, 1991).

—— *The English Bible and the Seventeenth-Century Revolution* (1993).

HILL, GEOFFREY, 'A Pharisee to Pharisees: Reflections on Vaughan's "The Night" ', *English*, 38 (1989), 97–113.

HILTON, JAMES, 'The Coronation Stone at Westminster Abbey', *Archaeological Journal*, 54 (1897), 201–24.

HIRST, DEREK, 'The Politics of Literature in the English Republic', *Seventeenth Century*, 5 (1990), 133–55.

HOLMES, ELIZABETH, *Henry Vaughan and the Hermetic Philosophy* (Oxford, 1932).

HOWELL, A. C., 'Christopher Harvey's *The Synagogue* (1640)', *Studies in Philology*, 49 (1952), 229–47.

HUGHES, MERITT Y., 'The Theme of Pre-existence and Infancy in "The Retreat" ', *Philological Quarterly*, 20 (1941), 484–500.

HUNTER, C. F., 'Old Testament Sainthood', *Notes and Queries*, 209 (1964), 86–8.

HUTCHINSON, F. E., *Henry Vaughan: A Life and Interpretation*, corrected repr. (Oxford, 1971).

HUTTON, RONALD, *The Rise and Fall of Merry England: The Ritual Year 1400–1700* (Oxford, 1984).

—— *The Restoration: A Political and Religious History of England and Wales, 1658–1667* (Oxford, 1985).

—— *The Stations of the Sun: A History of the Ritual Year in Britain* (Oxford, 1996).

ISER, WOLFGANG, *The Act of Reading: A Theory of Aesthetic Response* (London, 1978).

JANELLE, PIERRE, *Robert Southwell the Writer: A Study in Religious Inspiration* (Mamaroneck, NY, 1971).

—— *The Catholic Reformation* (Milwaukee, 1949).

JENKINS, GERAINT H., *Literature, Religion and Society in Wales, 1660–1730*, Studies in Welsh History, 2 (Cardiff, 1978).

—— 'The Early Peace Testimony in Wales', *Llafur*, 4: 2 (1975), 10–19.

—— *The Foundations of Modern Wales, 1642–1780*, Oxford History of Wales (Oxford, 1987).

—— *Protestant Dissenters in Wales, 1639–1689*, Past in Perspective Series (Cardiff, 1992).

JENKINS, PHILIP, 'Welsh Anglicans and the Interregnum', *Journal of the Historical Society of the Church in Wales*, 27 (1990), 51–9.

JOHNSON, A. M., 'Wales During the Commonwealth and Protectorate', 233–56 in Pennington and Thomas (eds.), *Puritans and Revolutionaries* (below).

JONSON, OLIVER, 'Robert Bolton and Henry Vaughan's "Man in Darkness"', *Notes and Queries*, 229 (1984), 331–4.

KATZ, DAVID, *Philo-Semitism and the Readmission of the Jews to England 1603–1655* (Oxford, 1982).

KEEBLE, N. H., *The Literary Culture of Nonconformity in Later Seventeenth-Century England* (Leicester, 1987).

KENDALL, R. T., *Calvin and English Calvinism to 1649* (Oxford, 1979).

KENNEDY, GEORGE A., *Classical Rhetoric and its Christian and Secular Tradition from Ancient to Modern Times* (1980).

KERMODE, FRANK, 'The Private Imagery of Henry Vaughan', *Review of English Studies*, NS, 1 (1950), 206–25.

—— and ANITA KERMODE (eds.), *The Oxford Book of Letters* (Oxford, 1995).

KINNAMAN, NOEL, 'Notes on the Psalms in Herbert's *The Temple*', *George Herbert Journal*, 4 (1981), 10–29.

KLAUSE, JOHN L., 'Donne and the Wonderful', *English Literary Renaissance*, 17 (1987), 41–66.

KNOTT, JOHN R., Jr, *The Sword of the Spirit: Puritan Responses to the Bible* (Chicago, 1980).

KORSHIN, PAUL J., *Typology in England 1650–1820* (Princeton, 1982).

LAKE, PETER, *Moderate Puritans in the Elizabethan Church* (Cambridge, 1982).

—— *Anglicans and Puritans? Presbyterianism and English Conformist Thought from Whitgift to Hooker* (1988).

—— 'The Laudian Style: Order, Uniformity and the Pursuit of the Beauty of Holiness in the 1630s', 161–85 in Fincham (ed.), *The Early Stuart Church* (above).

LAMONT, WILLIAM, *Godly Rule: Politics and Religion, 1603–60* (1969).

LAMPE, G. W. H., and K. J. WOOLLCOMBE, *Essays on Typology* (1957).

LANDES, DAVID S., *Revolution in Time: Clocks and the Making of the Modern World* (Cambridge, 1983).

LASLETT, PETER, 'Sir Robert Filmer: The Man Versus the Whig Myth', *William and Mary Quarterly*, 5 (1948), 523–46.

—— 'The Gentry of Kent in 1640', *Cambridge Historical Journal*, 9 (1948), 148–64.

—— *The World We Have Lost*, 2nd edn. (1971).

LEARDI, MARGHERITA, *La Poesia di Henry Vaughan* (Florence, 1967).

LEGOUIS, PIERRE, *Andrew Marvell: Poet, Puritan, Patriot*, 2nd edn. (Oxford, 1968).

LEHMANN, RUTH PRESTON, 'Characteristic Imagery in the Poetry of Henry Vaughan', Ph.D. thesis (Wisconsin, 1942).

—— 'Henry Vaughan and Welsh Poetry: A Contrast', *Philological Quarterly*, 24 (1945), 329–42.

LERNER, L., 'Puritanism and the Spiritual Autobiography', *Hibbert Journal*, 55 (1956–7), 373–86.

LEUENBERGER, SAMUEL, *Archbishop Cranmer's Immortal Bequest: The Book of Common Prayer of the Church of England, an Evangelical Liturgy* (Grand Rapids, Mich., 1990).

LEWALSKI, BARBARA K., *Milton's Brief Epic: The Genre, Meaning and Art of 'Paradise Regained'* (Providence, RI, 1966).

—— '*Samson Agonistes* and the "Tragedy" of the Apocalypse', *Publications of the Modern Language Association of America*, 85 (1970), 1050–62.

—— 'Typology and Poetry: A Consideration of Herbert, Vaughan and Marvell', in Earl Miner (ed.) *Illustrious Evidence: Approaches to English Literature of the Early Seventeenth Century* (Berkeley and Los Angeles, CA, 1975).

—— 'Typological Symbolism and the "Progress of the Soul" in Seventeenth-Century Literature', 239–60 in Gary A. Stringer (ed.), *New Essays on Donne* (Salzburg, 1977).

—— 'Marvell as Religious Poet', ch. 12 of *Approaches to Marvell*, The York Tercentenary Lectures, ed. C. A. Patrides (1978).

—— *Protestant Poetics and the Seventeenth-Century Religious Lyric* (Princeton, 1979).

—— '*Paradise Lost' and the Rhetoric of Literary Forms* (Princeton, 1985).

—— (ed.), *Renaissance Genres: Essays on Theory, History and Interpretation* (Cambridge, Mass., 1986).

LEWIS, C. S., *Studies in Words* (Cambridge, 1960).

—— *Rehabilitations and Other Essays* (Oxford, 1939).

LILLY, GWENETH, 'The Welsh Influence in the Poetry of Gerard Manley Hopkins', *Modern Language Review*, 38 (1943), 192–205.

LINDEN, STANTON J., 'Alchemy and Eschatology in Seventeenth-Century Poetry', *Ambix*, 31 (1984), 102–11.

—— 'Walter Charleton and Henry Vaughan's "Cock-Crowing"', *Notes and Queries*, 234 (1989), 38–9.

LLASERA, MARGARET, 'Concepts of Light in the Poetry of Henry Vaughan', *Seventeenth Century*, 3 (1988), 47–61.

LLOYD, H. A., *The Gentry of South-West Wales, 1540–1640* (Cardiff, 1968).

LOBEL, MARY D., *The City of London from Prehistoric Times to c.1520* (Oxford, 1989).

LOW, ANTHONY, *Love's Architecture: Devotional Modes in Seventeenth-Century English Poetry* (New York, 1978).

—— *The Georgic Revolution* (Princeton, NJ, 1985).

LOWTHER, W. K., and CHARLES HARRIS (eds.), *Liturgy and Worship: A Companion to the Prayer Books of the Anglican Communion* (1932).

LOXLEY, JAMES, *Royalism and Poetry in the English Civil Wars: The Drawn Sword*, Early Modern Literature in History (Basingstoke, 1997).

LYONS, JOHN, *Semantics*, 2 vols. (Cambridge, 1977).

MACCABE, RICHARD A., *Joseph Hall: A Study in Satire and Meditation* (Oxford, 1982).

McEUEN, KATHRYN E., *Classical Influence upon the Tribe of Ben* (1939; repr. New York, 1968).

MACEY, SAMUEL L., *Clocks and the Cosmos: The Time in Western Life and Thought* (Hamden, Conn., 1980).

McGANN, J. J., 'The Monks and the Giants: Textual and Bibliographical Studies and the Interpretation of Literary Texts', 180–99 in J. J. McGann (ed.), *Textual Criticism and Literary Interpretation* (Chicago, 1985).

McGEE, J. SEARS, *The Godly Man in Stuart England: Anglicans, Puritans and the Two Tables, 1620–1670* (New Haven, 1976).

McGRATH, ALISTER E., *Reformation Theology: An Introduction*, 2nd edn. (Oxford, 1993).

McKENZIE, D. F., *Stationers' Apprentices 1605–40* (Charlottesville, Va., 1960).

—— 'The London Book Trade in the Later Seventeenth Century', The Sanders Lectures (Cambridge, 1976) [Cambridge University Library 850.b.188].

—— 'Typography and Meaning: The Case of William Cowper', in Giles Barber and Bernhard Fabian (eds.), *Buch und Buchhandel in Europa im achtzehnten Jahrhundert; The Book and the Book Trade in Eighteenth-Century Europe* (Hamburg, 1981).

MACQUEEN, JOHN, *Numerology: Theory and Outline History of a Literary Mode* (Edinburgh, 1985).

MADSEN, WILLIAM G., *From Shadowy Types to Truth: Studies in Milton's Symbolism* (New Haven, 1968).

MAHOOD, M. M., *Poetry and Humanism* (1950).

MALCOLMSON, CHRISTINA, 'George Herbert and Coterie Verse', *George Herbert Journal* 18 (1994), 159–84.

MALTBY, JUDITH, *Prayer Book and People in Elizabethan and Early Stuart England*, Cambridge Studies in Early Modern British History (Cambridge, 1998).

MARCUS, LEAH S., *Childhood and Cultural Despair: A Theme and Variations in Seventeenth-Century Literature* (Pittsburgh, 1978).

—— *The Politics of Mirth: Jonson, Herrick, Milton, Marvell, and the Defense of the Old Holiday Pastimes* (Chicago, 1986).

MARILLA, E. L, 'The Secular and Religious poetry of Henry Vaughan', *Modern Language Quarterly*, 9 (1948), 394–411.

—— ' "The Publisher to the Reader" of *Olor Iscanus*', *Review of English Studies*, 24 (1948), 36–41.

MAROTTI, ARTHUR F., *Manuscript, Print and the English Renaissance Lyric* (Ithaca, NY, 1995).

MARTIN, ANTHONY, 'George Herbert and Sacred "Parodie" ', *Studies in Philology*, 93 (1996), 443–70.

MARTIN, L. C., 'Henry Vaughan and the Theme of Infancy', 243–55 in John Purves (ed.), *Seventeenth-Century Studies Presented to Sir Herbert Grierson* (Oxford, 1938).

—— 'Henry Vaughan and Hermes Trismegistus', *Review of English Studies*, 18 (1942), 301–7.

—— 'Henry Vaughan and the Chymists Key', *TLS*, 11 Dec. 1953, 801.

MARTZ, LOUIS L., *The Paradise Within: Studies in Vaughan, Traherne, and Milton* (New Haven, 1964).

—— *The Poetry of Meditation: A Study of English Religious Literature of the Seventeenth Century*, rev. edn. (New Haven, 1962).

—— *From Renaissance to Baroque: Essays on Literature and Art* (Columbia, Mo., 1991).

MATHIAS, ROLAND, 'Poets of Breconshire', *Brycheiniog*, 19 (1980–81), 27–37.

—— 'In Search of the Silurist', 189–214 in Rudrum (ed.), *Essential Articles for the Study of Henry Vaughan* (below).

MAZZEO, JOSEPH ANTHONY, 'Light Metaphysics, Dante's *Convivio* and the Letter to Can Grande Della Scala', *Traditio*, 14 (1958), 191–229.

Meditations on the Six Days of Creation (1717), The Augustan Reprint Society No. 119, introd. George R. Guffey (Los Angeles, 1996).

MELBOURNE, JANE, 'Biblical Intertextuality in *Samson Agonistes*', *Studies in English Literature 1500–1900*, 36 (1996), 111–27.

MENDELSOHN, J. ANDREW, 'Alchemy and Politics in England 1649–1655', *Past and Present*, 135 (1992), 30–78.

MILLER, PERRY, *Errand into the Wilderness* (1956; New York, 1964).

MILTON, ANTHONY, *Catholic and Reformed: Roman and Protestant Churches in*

English Protestant Thought, 1600–40, Cambridge Sudies in Early Modern British History (Cambridge, 1995).

MILTON, ANTHONY, 'The Church of England, Rome, and the True Church: The Demise of a Jacobean Consensus', 187–210 in Fincham (ed.), *The Early Stuart Church* (above).

MINER, EARL, *The Metaphysical Mode from Donne to Cowley* (Princeton, 1969).

—— *Literary Uses of Typology from the Late Middle Ages to the Present* (Princeton, 1977).

MØLLER, JENS G., 'The Beginnings of Puritan Covenant Theology', *Journal of Ecclesiastical History*, 14 (1963), 46–67.

MONTROSE, LOUIS ADRIAN, '"The place of a brother" in *As You Like It*: Social Process and Comic Form', *Shakespeare Quarterly*, 32 (1981), 28–54.

MORE, PAUL E., 'Some Parallels in Henry Vaughan', *Nation*, 101 (1915), 516–17.

MORRILL, JOHN, 'The Church in England, 1642–49', 89–114 in John Morrill (ed.), *Reactions to the English Civil War, 1642–9*, Problems in Focus Series (New York, 1982).

—— *The Nature of the English Revolution* (1993).

MORTON, A. L., *The World of the Ranters: Religious Radicalism in the English Revolution* (1970).

MUNSTERBERG, MARGARET, 'The Swan of Usk, More Books', *Boston Public Library Bulletin*, 18, no. 7 (1943), 341.

NASH, RODERICK, *Wilderness and the American Mind*, 3rd edn. (New Haven, 1982).

NAUERT, CHARLES G., *Agrippa and the Crisis of Renaissance Thought* (Urbana, Ill., 1965).

NAUMAN, JONATHAN, 'A New Poem is New Evidence: Henry Vaughan and James Howell Reconsidered', *Notes and Queries*, 237 (1992), 460–2.

NICOLSON, MARJORIE HOPE, *Mountain Gloom and Mountain Glory: The Development of the Aesthetics of the Infinite* (New York, 1963).

NUTTALL, GEOFFREY F., *The Holy Spirit in Puritan Faith and Experience* (Oxford, 1946).

—— *Visible Saints: The Congregational Way, 1640–1660* (Oxford, 1957).

—— *The Welsh Saints, 1640–1660 (Water Cradock, Vavasor Powell, Morgan Llwyd)* (Cardiff, 1957).

ONIANS, JOHN, *Bearers of Meaning: The Classical Orders in Antiquity, the Middle Ages, and the Renaissance* (Princeton, 1988).

OSMOND, ROSALIE, *Mutual Accusation: Seventeenth-Century Body and Soul Dialogues in Their Literary and Theological Context* (Toronto, 1990).

OWEN, LEONARD, 'The Population of Wales in the Sixteenth and Seventeenth Centuries', *Transactions of the Honourable Society of Cymmrodorion* (1959), 99–113.

—— 'A Seventeenth-Century Commonplace Book', *Transactions of the Honourable Society of Cymmrodorion* (1962), 16–47.

PAGEL, WALTER, *Paracelsus: An Introduction to Philosophical Medicine in the Era of the Renaissance* (Basle and New York, 1958).

PANOFSKY, ERWIN, *Meaning in the Visual Arts: Papers in and on Art History* (Garden City, NY, 1955).

PARKER, WILLIAM RILEY, 'Henry Vaughan and his Publishers', *Library*, 4th series, 20 (1940), 401–11.

—— *Milton: A Biography*, 2nd edn., rev. and ed. Gordon Campbell, 2 vols. (Oxford, 1996).

PATRIDES, C. A., 'Renaissance Interpretations of Jacob's Ladder', *Theologische Zeitschrift*, 18 (1962), 411–18.

—— *The Grand Design of God: The Literary Form of the Christian View of History* (1972).

—— (ed.), *Aspects of Time* (Manchester, 1976).

—— (ed.), *George Herbert: The Critical Heritage* (1983).

—— and JOSEPH WITTREICH (eds.), *The Apocalypse in Renaissance Thought and Literature: Patterns, Antecedents and Repercussions* (Ithaca, NY, 1984).

PATTERSON, ANNABEL M., *Censorship and Interpretation: The Conditions of Writing and Reading in Early Modern England* (Madison, 1984).

PENNINGTON, DONALD and KEITH THOMAS (eds.), *Puritans and Revolutionaries: Essays in Seventeenth-Century History Presented to Christopher Hill* (Oxford, 1978).

PETERSEN, RODNEY L., *Preaching in the Last Days: The Theme of the 'Two Witnesses' in the Sixteenth and Seventeenth Centuries* (New York, 1993).

PETERSON, RAYMOND A., 'Jeremy Taylor's Theology of Worship', *Anglican Theological Review*, 46 (1964), 204–16.

PETTET, E. C., *Of Paradise and Light: A Study of Vaughan's 'Silex Scintillans'* (Cambridge, 1960).

Poetry Wales: A Henry Vaughan Number 11: 2 (Autumn 1975) [Roland Matthias, 'In Search of the Silurist'; Alan Rudrum, 'Some Remarks on Henry Vaughan's Secular Poems'; A. J. Smith, 'Appraising the Word'; Elured Crawshaw, 'The Relationship between the Work of Thomas and Henry Vaughan'; P. C. Davies, 'Two Breconshire Contemporaries: Henry Vaughan and Rowland Watkyns'; Peter Bement, 'Henry Vaughan's "Countrey Muse" '].

POOLEY, ROGER, *English Prose of the Seventeenth Century, 1590–1700* (1992).

POST, JONATHAN F. S., *Henry Vaughan: The Unfolding Vision* (Princeton, 1982).

—— 'Henry Vaughan', ch. 14 in Thomas N. Corns (ed.), *The Cambridge Companion to English Poetry: Donne to Marvell* (Cambridge, 1993).

—— *English Lyric Poetry: The Early Seventeenth Century* (London, 1999).

POTTER, LOIS, *Secret Rites and Secret Writing: Royalist Literature 1640–1660* (Cambridge, 1989).

POWELL, R. F. PETER, 'The Printed Road Maps of Breconshire 1675–1870', *Brycheiniog*, 18 (1978–9), 85–99.

PRESS, JOHN, *The Chequer'd Shade: Reflections on Obscurity in Poetry* (Oxford, 1958).

PRINEAS, MATTHEW, 'The Dream of the Book and the Poetry of Failure in Henry Vaughan's *Silex Scintillans*', *English Literary Renaissance*, 29 (1996), 333–55.

PRYNNE, J. H., 'English Poetry and Emphatical Language', Warton Lecture on English Poetry, *Proceedings of the British Academy*, 74 (1988), 135–69.

—— *Stars, Tigers and the Shape of Words*, The William Matthews Lectures 1992 (1993).

QUINT, DAVID, *Origin and Originality in Renaissance Literature: Versions of the Source* (New Haven, 1983).

QUISTORP, HEINRICH, *Calvin's Doctrine of the Last Things*, trans. Harold Knight (1955).

RADFORD, C. A. RALEGH, 'Tretower: The Castle and the Court', *Brycheiniog*, 6 (1960), 1–17.

RATCLIFF, EDWARD C., 'The Choir Offices', in *Liturgy and Worship*, ed. Lowther and Harris (above).

—— *The English Coronation Service* (1936).

RAY, ROBERT H., 'The Herbert Allusion Book: Allusions to George Herbert in the Seventeenth Century', *Studies in Philology*, 83 (1986), 1–82.

RAYMOND, JOAD, *The Invention of the Newspaper: English Newsbooks 1641–1649* (Oxford, 1996).

REED, JOHN CURTIS, 'Humphrey Moseley, Publisher', *Oxford Bibliographical Society Proceedings and Papers*, 2 (1930), 57–142.

REEDY, GERARD, *The Bible and Reason: Anglicans and Scripture in Late Seventeenth-Century England* (Philadelphia, 1985).

REES, SIR FREDERICK, 'Breconshire during the Civil War', *Brycheiniog*, 8 (1962), 1–9.

REEVES, MARJORIE, *The Influence of Prophecy in the Later Middle Ages: A Study in Joachimism* (Oxford, 1969).

RICHARDS, THOMAS, *A History of the Puritan Movement in Wales, 1639–1653* (Cardiff, 1920).

—— *Religious Developments in Wales, 1654–1662* (Cardiff, 1923).

RICKEY, ESTHER GILMAN, ' "Prophets and friends of God": Prophetic Discourse in Andrewes, Herbert and Vaughan', Ph.D. thesis (Los Angeles, 1990).

RICKEY, MARY ELLEN, 'Crashaw and Vaughan', *Notes and Queries*, 200 (1955), 232–3.

ROBBINS, FRANK EGLESTON, *The Hexaemeral Literature* (Chicago, 1912).

ROBINSON, H. WHEELER, *Inspiration and Revelation in the Old Testament* (Oxford, 1946).

ROSTON, MURRAY, *Biblical Drama in England from the Middle Ages to the Present Day* (Evanston, Ill., 1960).

RØSTVIG, MAREN-SOFIE, *The Happy Man: Studies in the Metamorphoses of a Classical Idea*, 2 vols. (Oslo, 1954).

—— 'Casimire Sarbiewski and the English Ode', *Studies in Philology*, 51 (1954), 443–60.

ROTHBERG, MICHAEL, 'An Emblematic Ideology: Images and Additions in Two Editions of Henry Vaughan's *Silex Scintillans*', *English Literary Renaissance*, 22 (1992), 80–94.

RUDRUM, ALAN, 'Henry Vaughan's "The Book": A Hermetic Poem', *Journal of the Australasian Universities Language and Literature Association* (1961), 161–6.

—— 'Vaughan's "The Night": Some Hermetic Notes', *Modern Language Review*, 64 (1969), 11–19.

—— 'The Influence of Alchemy in the Poems of Henry Vaughan', *Philological Quarterly*, 49 (1970), 469–80.

—— *Henry Vaughan* (Cardiff, 1981).

—— 'Henry Vaughan, the Liberation of the Creatures, and Seventeenth-Century English Calvinism', *Seventeenth Century*, 4 (1989), 33–54.

—— 'Resistance, Collaboration and Silence: Henry Vaughan and Breconshire Royalism', 102–18 in Summers and Pebworth (eds.), *The English Civil Wars* (below).

—— (ed.), *Essential Articles for the Study of Henry Vaughan*, Essential Articles Series (Hamden, Conn., 1987).

RUMMEL, ERICA, 'Quoting Poetry Instead of Scripture: Erasmus and Eucherius on *Contemptus Mundi*', *Bibliothèque d'Humanisme et Renaissance*, 45 (1983), 503–9.

RUSSELL, CONRAD, 'Arguments for Religious Unity in England, 1530–1630', *Journal of Ecclesiastical History*, 18 (1967), 201–26.

—— (ed.), *The Origins of the English Civil War* (1973).

RUTHVEN, K. K., 'The Poet as Etymologist', *Critical Quarterly*, 11 (1969), 9–37.

SALTER, ELIZABETH, 'Medieval Poetry and the Figural View of Reality', *Proceedings of the British Academy*, 54 (1968), 73–92.

SAYCE, R. A., *The French Biblical Epic in the Seventeenth Century* (Oxford, 1955).

SCATTERGOOD, JOHN, '*Pierce the Ploughmans Crede*: Lollardy and Texts', 77–94 in Margaret Aston and Colin Richmond (eds.), *Lollardy and the Gentry in the Late Middle Ages* (Stroud, 1997).

SCHOCHET, GORDON J., *Patriarchalism and Political Thought* (Oxford, 1975).

SCHOLZ, BERNARD F., '"Ownerless Legs or Arms Stretching from the Sky": Notes on an Emblematic Motif', 249–83 in Peter M. Daly (ed.), *Andrea Alciato and* the *Emblem Tradition: Essays in Honor of Virginia Woods Callahan*, AMS Studies in the Emblem (New York, 1989).

SELIG, SHARON CADMAN, *The Shadow of Eternity: Belief and Structure in Herbert, Vaughan and Traherne* (Levington, Ky., 1981).

SHARPE, KEVIN, *Criticism and Compliment: The Politics of Literature in the England of Charles I* (Cambridge, 1987).

—— *The Personal Rule of Charles I* (New Haven, 1992).

SHERMAN, STUART, *Telling Time: Clocks, Diaries, and English Diurnal Form, 1660–1785* (Chicago, 1996).

SHERRY, BEVERLEY, 'Speech in *Paradise Lost*', *Milton Studies*, 8 (1975), 247–66.

SHUGER, DEBORA K., *Sacred Rhetoric: The Christian Grand Style in the English Renaissance* (Princeton, 1988).

—— *The Reformation Bible: Scholarship, Sacrifice, and Subjectivity* (Berkeley, Calif., 1994).

SIMMONDS, JAMES D., 'The Publication of *Olor Iscanus*', *Modern Language Notes*, 76 (1961), 404–8.

—— 'Vaughan's Masterpiece and its Critics', *Studies in English Literature 1500–1900*, 2 (1962), 77–93.

—— 'Vaughan's Love Poetry', in Thomas Austin Kirby and William John Olive (eds.), *Essays in Honor of Esmond Linworth Marilla* (Baton Rouge, La., 1970).

—— *Masques of God: Form and Theme in the Poetry of Henry Vaughan* (Pittsburgh, 1972).

SIMPSON, C. H., *Thomas Harrison* (1905).

SMALLEY, BERYL, *The Study of the Bible in the Middle Ages*, 3rd edn. (Oxford, 1983).

SMITH, NIGEL, *Perfection Proclaimed: Language and Literature in English Radical Religion, 1640–1660* (Oxford, 1989).

—— *Literature and Revolution in England, 1640–1660* (New Haven, 1994).

SOMMERVILLE, JOHANN P., 'From Suarez to Filmer: A Reappraisal', *Historical Journal*, 25 (1982), 525–40.

—— *Politics and Ideology in England, 1603–1640* (1986).

SPUFFORD, MARGARET, 'The Importance of Religion in the Sixteenth and Seventeenth Centuries', 1–102 in Spufford (ed.), *The World of Rural Dissenters, 1520–1725* (Cambridge, 1995).

SPURR, JOHN, *The Restoration Church of England, 1646–1689* (New Haven, 1991).

STANWOOD, P. G., *The Sempiternal Season: Studies in Seventeenth-Century Devotional Writing* (New York, 1992).

STOCKER, MARGARITA, *Apocalyptic Marvell: The Second Coming in Seventeenth-Century Poetry* (Brighton, 1986).

STONE, LAWRENCE, 'The Educational Revolution in England 1560–1640', *Past and Present*, 42 (1969), 69–139.

STRANKS, C. J., *Anglican Devotion: Studies in the Spiritual Life of the Church of England between the Reformation and the Oxford Movement* (1961).

STRIER, RICHARD, *Love Known: Theology and Experience in George Herbert's Poetry* (Chicago, 1983).

SUMMERS, CLAUDE J., 'Herrick, Vaughan, and the Poetry of Anglican Survivalism', 46–74 in John R. Roberts (ed.), *New Perspectives on the Seventeenth-Century English Religious Lyric* (Columbia, Mo., 1994).

—— and TED-LARRY PEBWORTH, 'Vaughan's Temple in Nature and the Context of "Regeneration"', *Journal of English and Germanic Philology*, 74 (1975), 351–60.

—— (eds.), *'Bright shootes of everlastingnesse': The Seventeenth-Century Religious Lyric* (Columbia, Mo., 1987).

—— (eds.), *The English Civil Wars in the Literary Imagination* (Columbia, Mo., 1999).

SUMMERS, JOSEPH H., 'Some Apocalyptic Strains in Marvell's Poetry', *George Herbert Journal*, 16 (1992–3), 188–212.

SUTHERLAND, JAMES, *Restoration Literature, 1660–1700: Dryden, Bunyan and Pepys*, Oxford History of English Literature (1969; Oxford, 1990).

THIRSK, JOAN, 'Younger Sons in the Seventeenth Century', *History*, 54 (1969), 358–77.

THOMAS, HUGH, *A History of Wales, 1485–1660* (Cardiff, 1972).

THOMAS, KEITH, *Religion and the Decline of Magic: Studies in Popular Beliefs in Sixteenth- and Seventeenth-Century England* (1971).

THOMAS, NOEL KENNEDY, *Henry Vaughan: Prophet of Revelation* (Worthing, 1986).

THOMAS, P. W., 'The Poisoned Grove', *Scintilla*, 1 (1997), 27–44.

THORNTON, MARTIN, *English Spirituality: An Outline of Ascetical Theology According to the English Pastoral Tradition* (1963).

TOON, PETER (ed.), *Puritans, the Millennium, and the Future of Israel: Puritan Eschatology, 1600 to 1660* (Cambridge, 1970).

TREVOR-ROPER, HUGH, *Catholics, Anglicans and Puritans: Seventeenth-Century Essays* (1987).

TUDOR JONES, R., 'Religion in Post-Restoration Brecknockshire: 1660–1668', *Brycheiniog*, 8 (1962), 11–65.

—— 'The Older Dissent of Swansea and Brecon', 117–41 in Owain W. Jones and David Walker (eds.), *Links with the Past: Swansea and Brecon Historical Essays* (Llandybïe, 1974).

—— 'The Healing Herb and the Rose of Love: The Piety of Two Welsh Puritans', 154–79 in *Reformation, Conformity and Dissent: Essays in Honour of Geoffrey Nuttall*, ed. R. Buick Knox (1977).

TUVE, ROSEMOND, *Elizabethan and Metaphysical Imagery: Renaissance Poetry and Twentieth-Century Critics* (Chicago, 1947).

TYACKE, NICHOLAS, 'Puritanism, Arminianism and Counter-Revolution', in Russell (ed.), *The Origins of the English Civil War* (above).

—— 'Science and Religion at Oxford Before the Civil War', 73–93 in Pennington and Thomas (eds.), *Puritans and Revolutionaries* (above).

—— *Anti-Calvinists: The Rise of English Arminianism, c.1590–1640* (Oxford, 1987).

—— (ed.), *The History of Oxford*, iv: *Seventeenth-Century Oxford* (Oxford, 1997).

TYDEMAN, WILLIAM (ed.), *The Welsh Connection: Essays by Past and Present Members of the Department of English Language and Literature, University College of North Wales, Bangor* (Llandyssul, 1986).

UNDERHILL, EVELYN, *Mysticism* (1911).

—— *The Mystics of the Church* (1925).

VAUGHAN-POPPY, ITHIEL, 'The Homes of the Vaughans—Part I', *Brycheiniog*, 18 (1978–9), 103–9.

—— 'The Homes of the Vaughans—Part II', *Brycheiniog*, 19 (1980–1), 96–104.

VICKERS, BRIAN, 'Leisure and Idleness in the Renaissance: The Ambivalence of Otium', *Renaissance Studies*, 4 (1990), 1–37 and 107–54.

WALKER, D. P., *The Decline of Hell: Seventeenth-Century Discussions of Eternal Torment* (1964).

WALL, JOHN N., *Transformations of the Word: Spenser, Herbert, Vaughan* (Athens, Ga., 1988).

WALLEY, HAROLD R., 'The Strange Case of *Olor Iscanus*', *Review of English Studies*, 18 (1942), 27–37.

WALSHAM, ALEXANDRA, *Providence in Early Modern England* (Oxford, 1999).

WALTERS, R. H., 'Henry Vaughan and the Alchemists', *Review of English Studies*, 23 (1947), 107–22.

WALZER, MICHAEL, *The Revolution of the Saints: A Study in the Origins of Radical Politics* (1966).

WARREN, AUSTIN, *Richard Crashaw: A Study in Baroque Sensibility* (1939).

WATSON, GRAEME J., 'Political Change and Continuity of Vision in Henry Vaughan's "Daphnis: An Elegiac Eclogue"', *Studies in Philology*, 83 (1986), 159–81.

—— 'Two New Sources for Henry Vaughan's *The Mount of Olives*', *Notes and Queries*, 230 (1985), 168–70.

—— 'The Temple in "The Night": Henry Vaughan and the Collapse of the Established Church', *Modern Philology*, 84 (1986), 144–67.

WATT, TESSA, *Cheap Print and Popular Piety 1560–1640*, Cambridge Studies in Early Modern British History (Cambridge, 1991).

WEBSTER, CHARLES, *The Great Instauration: Science, Medicine and Reform 1626–1660* (1975).

WEIDHORN, MANFRED, *Dreams in Seventeenth-Century English Literature* (The Hague, 1970).

WELSBY, PAUL A., *Lancelot Andrewes 1555–1626* (1958).

WHITE, HELEN C., *English Devotional Literature [Prose], 1600–1640* (Madison, 1931).

—— *The Tudor Books of Private Devotion* (Madison, 1951).

WHITE, PETER, *Predestination, Policy and Polemic: Conflict and Consensus in the English Church from the Reformation to the Civil War* (Cambridge, 1992).

WHITELY, D. E. H., *The Theology of Saint Paul*, 2nd edn. (Oxford, 1974).

WILCHER, ROBERT, '"Daphnis: An Elegiac Eclogue", by Henry Vaughan', *Durham University Journal*, 67 (1974), 25–40.

—— '"Then keep the ancient way!": A Study of Vaughan's *Silex Scintillans*', *Durham University Journal*, 76 (1983), 11–24.

—— *Andrew Marvell*, British and Irish Authors Introductory Critical Studies (Cambridge, 1985).

—— '"The Present Times Are Not/To Snudge In': Henry Vaughan, *The Temple*, and the Pressure of History', 185–94 in Helen Wilcox and Richard Todd (eds.), *George Herbert: Sacred and Profane* (Amsterdam, 1995).

—— 'Henry Vaughan and the Church', *Scintilla* 2 (1998), 90–104.

WILCOX, HELEN, 'Something Understood: The Reputation and Influence of George Herbert to 1715', Ph.D. thesis (Oxford, 1974).

—— 'Exploring the Language of Devotion in the English Revolution', 75–88 in Healy and Sawday (eds.), *Literature and the English Civil War* (above).

WILDING, MICHAEL, *Dragon's Teeth: Literature in the English Revolution* (Oxford, 1987).

WILLIAMS, A. R., 'Welsh Names', *Folk-Lore: Transactions of the Folk-Lore Society*, 60 (1949), 392–3.

WILLIAMS, ARNOLD, *The Common Expositor: An Account of the Commentaries on Genesis 1527–1633* (Chapel Hill, NC, 1948).

WILLIAMS, D., *A History of Modern Wales*, 2nd edn. (1950).

WILLIAMS, GLANMOR, *Renewal and Reformation: Wales c.1415–1642*, Oxford History of Wales (Oxford, 1993).

—— (ed.), *The Welsh and Their Religion: Historical Essays* (Cardiff, 1991).

WILLIAMSON, HUGH ROSS, *The Gunpowder Plot* (1951).

WITTREICH, JOSEPH A., *Visionary Poetics: Milton's Tradition & its Legacy* (San Marino, Calif., 1979).

WOLF, EDWIN II, 'Some Books of Early English Provenance in the Library Company of Philadelphia', *Book Collector*, 9 (1960), 275–84.

WOOLF, ROSEMARY, *The English Religious Lyric in the Middle Ages* (Oxford, 1968).

—— *English Medieval Mystery Plays* (Oxford, 1970).

WORDEN, BLAIR, *The Rump Parliament 1648–1653* (Cambridge, 1974).

—— 'Providence and Politics in Cromwellian England', *Past and Present*, 109 (1985), 55–99.

WORDEN, BLAIR, 'Oliver Cromwell and the Sin of Achan', 125–45 in D. Beales and G. Best (eds.), *History, Society and the Churches: Essays in Honour of Owen Chadwick* (Cambridge, 1985).

WORDSWORTH, CHRISTOPHER, and HENRY LITTLEHALES, *The Old Service Books of the English Church* (1904).

WRIGHT, HERBERT G., 'The Theme of Solitude and Retirement in Seventeenth-Century Literature', *Études anglaises*, 7 (1954), 22–35.

WRIGHT, LOUIS B., 'The Reading of Plays during the Puritan Revolution', *Huntington Library Bulletin*, 7 (1934), 73–108.

YATES, NIGEL, *Buildings, Faith and Worship: The Liturgical Arrangement of Anglican Churches 1600–1900* (Oxford, 1991).

ZIMMERLI, WALTER, *The Law and the Prophets* (Oxford, 1965).

Index of Vaughan's Works

Scripture Index

Chapter numbers are given in bold

General Index